Schriftenreihe des Europäischen Zentrums für Föderalismus-Forschung Tübingen (EZFF)

Herausgegeben vom Vorstand des EZFF:

Prof. Dr. Gabriele Abels (Sprecherin des Vorstands)
Prof. Dr. Jochen von Bernstorff, LL.M.
Prof. em. Dr. Dr. h.c. Horst Förster
Dr. Martin Große Hüttmann (Geschäftsführendes Vorstandsmitglied)
Prof. em. Dr. Rudolf Hrbek
Prof. Dr. Sebastian Kinder
Prof. Dr. Martin Nettesheim
Prof. Dr. Barbara Remmert (Stellv. Sprecherin des Vorstands)
Prof. Dr. Oliver Schlumberger
Prof. Dr. Josef Schmid
Prof. Dr. Gunter Schubert
Prof. Dr. Christian Seiler
Prof. Dr. Hans-Georg Wehling
In Gemeinschaft mit Prof. Dr. Roland Sturm

Band 51

Rolf Frankenberger | Elena Chernenkova [eds.]

Local Governance and Public Wellbeing

Comparing Russian and German Examples

Nomos

This volume was funded by the German Academic Exchange Service DAAD.

The Deutsche Nationalbibliothek lists this publication in the Deutsche Nationalbibliografie; detailed bibliographic data are available on the Internet at http://dnb.d-nb.de

ISBN 978-3-8487-6532-4 (Print)
978-3-7489-0618-6 (ePDF)

British Library Cataloguing-in-Publication Data
A catalogue record for this book is available from the British Library.

ISBN 978-3-8487-6532-4 (Print)
978-3-7489-0618-6 (ePDF)

Library of Congress Cataloging-in-Publication Data
Frankenberger, Rolf / Chernenkova, Elena
Local Governance and Public Wellbeing
Comparing Russian and German Examples
Rolf Frankenberger / Elena Chernenkova (eds.)
250 pp.
Includes bibliographic references.

ISBN 978-3-8487-6532-4 (Print)
978-3-7489-0618-6 (ePDF)

Onlineversion
Nomos eLibrary

1st Edition 2020

Preface

Since 2014, there is a vital exchange and cooperation between scientists, civil society and administration representatives from Petrozavodsk, Republic of Karelia, and Tübingen, Baden-Württemberg. This cooperation builds un the now more than 30 years of sister city relations that were established in 1989. In 2016, an expert workshop on local politics was funded by the German Academic Exchange Service (DAAD) and held in Petrozavodsk. Social scientists and practitioners from politics and civil society analysed different aspects of local politics, participation and civil society. As follow-ups we were able to publish an edited volume on local politics in a comparative perspective, to present results of our work in conferences at St. Petersburg, Tübingen, Petrozavodsk and elsewhere. These activities were supported by Petrozavodsk State University and Eberhard Karls University Tübingen. Lively cooperation continued and resulted in a second application for conducting a workshop, the focus of which now was on wellbeing, participation and governance. We were grateful that the DAAD granted us funding for bringing together scientists, students, and civil society representatives in a seven-day workshop in Tübingen. The participants presented and discussed their research and practical experience on questions of fostering local development and enhancing wellbeing. In an intensive review, these first papers were developed into the contributions to this volume. As editors we would like to thank all authors for contributing to the volume and for being up to deal with the reviews they received on their papers. New projects are already under preparation, including a summer school on city-university relations, teacher exchange and joint research projects.

Some people deserve special acknowledgement for making this project a success. Stewart Gold served as a facilitator and project assistant. He took care of all issues and of all participants. Matthew McCormick did an excellent job in proof-reading and giving important valuable inputs in the review process of the articles. Olga Riedinger served as an interpreter and helped fostering mutual understanding. As always, Monika Przybysz at the DAAD had an open ear for administrative questions. Carmen Thamm at the European Center for Research on Federalism (ECRF) did an excellent job editing the volume. We are grateful to the DAAD for funding this volume. We also thank Stephan Klingebiel, Christopher Blum and Daniela Harsch, Major for Social Affairs, Order and Culture at the City of Tübingen, for supporting the workshop, Markus Trämer for providing insight in the LebensPhasenHaus, Markus Holz for his introduction to the work of the AiS gGmbH Mössingen, and Lilia Künstle from the West-Ost Gesellschaft Tübingen.

Petrozavodsk and Tübingen, April 2020

Rolf Frankenberger and *Elena Chernenkova*

Contents

Welfare, Wellbeing, and Local Governance. An Introduction and Outline of the Book

Rolf Frankenberger and Elena Chernenkova

Abstract: In this article, we delineate and discuss different approaches to welfare, life satisfaction and wellbeing. In doing so, we address two core questions: How are the concepts of welfare and wellbeing related? And what is the role of local government and governance in increasing individual wellbeing? Following main findings in the literature, we argue that it is a specific combination of good government and welfare provision, civic engagement and a prospering civil society that generates favourable conditions for wellbeing. To conclude we briefly outline the different contributions to the volume and relate them to the theoretical framework.

Keywords: Welfare, Wellbeing, Local Governance, civil society, participation

"Communal wellbeing is central to human life"
Yusuf Islam[1]

Local communities are the places where people live, dream and hope. Each of them has needs to be fulfilled and dreams to come true. In modern societies, individuals are embedded in social relations and societal, pollical, economic and cultural environments. As a consequence, their pursuit of happiness depends on circumstances and factors they have not chosen and they can only influence gradually, such as the place of birth, the family background, or even the kind of economic, social and political system they live in. But the better they are integrated in mutual relations, a decent local environment and functioning local communities, the happier they might be, as these local communities not only provide contacts, social services and security, but also opportunities for individual growth and happiness. This is maybe what British Singer/Songwriter Cat Stevens, today better known as Yusuf Islam, refers to when he highlights the role of communal wellbeing for human life. It finds its academic counterpart in Responsive Communitarianism, where local communities are considered to have an important role for human development and wellbeing.[2] [3]

Even though, this strand of literature did not focus on local governments or local governance arrangements, but rather on local voluntary communities, the former play important roles when it comes to wellbeing. We argue that local governance is especially important for individual and collective wellbeing. Governance can be defined as a set of structures and processes linking governmental and nongovernmental actors for purposes of decision making and implementation. According to Große Hüttmann, the

1 *Islam, Y.* 2001: Faith and the Future. In: The Guardian Online 18.09.2001. https://www.theguardian.com/world/2001/sep/18/september11.schools (31/03/2020).

2 See, e.g. https://communitariannetwork.org/ (24/03/2020).

3 *Etzioni, A.* 1996: The New Golden Rule. Community and Morality in a Democratic Society, New York.

"opening towards nonstate actors and representatives of civil society follows the logic of political inclusion. This increases acceptance and legitimacy of decisions and can minimize problems of the implementation, as those levels affected by the decisions are integrated very early in the policy process"[4]

It is these sometimes institutionalised, but often unique combinations of state and non-state actors that provide important places, services and goods fostering wellbeing.

In the following sections we delineate and discuss different approaches to welfare, life satisfaction and wellbeing. In doing so, we address two core questions: How are the concepts of welfare and wellbeing related? And what is the role of local government and governance in increasing individual wellbeing? Following main findings in the literature, we argue that it is a specific combination of good government and welfare provision, civic engagement and a prospering civil society that generates favourable conditions for wellbeing. To conclude we briefly outline the different contributions to the volume and relate them to the theoretical framework.

The Welfare State as a Safety Net in Industrialized Countries

Insecurity and risk in everyday life, e.g. physical or material insecurity or the risk of losing jobs, are heavy burdens on the shoulders of individuals. If they do not know how to fulfil basic needs in the next month, week or even day, they will hardly thrive and prosper. This is even true for individuals in rather wealthy, modern, highly industrialized and individualized countries: Albeit the levels of living standards are substantially higher than in developing and less developed countries, they still might face substantial and very specific risks like the loss of jobs, illness, or old age. To protect their members from such risks, many states have developed different levels of social security nets that link the individual and the collective to dispense the risks on more shoulders and to provide a system of welfare. In economics, welfare traditionally has been measured in terms of money, be it individual or collective income like the gross domestic product. The underlying assumption is that the more value is produced in a society, the better off the individual members of this society are. But the individual welfare effect of economic prosperity and growth strongly depend on how income, and wealth, are distributed among the members of the respective group. So, for example the Gini index of income and the ratio of persons below the poverty line are also crucial indicators for welfare.[5] As the distribution of the benefits derived from economic growth tends to be uneven, unequal and in favour of the already better off, as for example Piketty (2014)[6] shows, the provision welfare is usually regulated by the state and sometimes even provided by the state. Thus, a welfare state is the "government-protected minimum standards of income, nutrition, housing and education, assured to every citizen as a political right"[7]. It is understood as a state-centered, redistributive means to reduce inequality. For Richard Tit-

4 *Große Hüttmann, M.* 2017: Understanding Multi-level Governance. The Example of Migration Polics and Integration Management in Germany. In: *Frankenberger, R./Chernenkova, E. (eds.)*: Local Politics in a Comparative Perspective. The Cases of Petrozavodsk and Tübingen, Baden-Baden, pp. 35–42 (37).

5 *Greve, B.* 2008: What is welfare? In: Central European Journal of Public Policy Vol. 2,1, pp. 50–73 (53).

6 *Piketty, T.* 2014: Capital in the Twenty-First Century, Cambridge.

7 *Wilensky, H. L.* 1975: The welfare state and equality: structural and ideological roots of public expenditure, Berkeley, p. 1.

muss, welfare and the welfare state include social welfare, fiscal welfare, and occupational welfare. This includes all publicly provided and subsidized services, statutory, occupational and fiscal.[8] His concept of welfare is broader than a purely economic definition, but it strongly focuses on the economic sphere and state activity in social policy. But it does, for example, not include civil society.[9] Claus Offe argues that "the services of the welfare state are not major social accomplishments, as some commentators would have it, but, rather, are meagre compensations for the price of industrial development"[10]. Welfare in this sense is a compensation for the inequalities caused by the different individual opportunities to participate in modern industrial production regimes, and especially in the labour markets. According to Offe, "the welfare state tries to compensate for the new problems, which are the by-products of industrial growth in a private economy"[11]. These are dependence on labour, health and care, old age, education, training and skills, housing and the follow-up problems of individualization with the erosion of traditional family models and private social security. Welfare in this broader sense can be measured in terms of social expenditure in percent of the GDP. According to Eurostat[12], social expenditure contains social benefits (transfers in cash or in kind for households and individuals to relieve them of the burden of a defined set of risks or needs), administrative expenditures for holding up the provision of benefits; and other expenditures like rents for offices and so on.

As early as in 1950, T.H. Marshall[13] pointed out that welfare is more than redistribution to compensate for inequality in capitalist societies, but also a necessary condition for individual growth and the realisation of individual rights. He analyses the relationship between political equality as a core principle of democracy on the one hand, and economic and social inequality on the other. Thus, a howsoever defined minimum of welfare in terms of economic and social participation has to be provided by the state, because he argues that the exercise of individual political rights and civil liberties is only possible under conditions of equal share in the economy and in social life. This very early account anticipates a discourse on the expansion of the welfare concept that gained speed in the 1980ies and 90ies. There has been a shift in the discussion from objective concepts and measures of welfare towards an inclusion of more subjective and individual aspect of wellbeing.

---

8 *Titmuss, R. M.* 1960: The social division of welfare, Liverpool; *Titmuss, R. M.* 1968: Welfare state and welfare society. In: Nursing Mirror and Midwives Journal 126, 10, pp. 25–29.

9 *Greve* 2008 (fn. 5), p. 54.

10 *Offe* 1972: Advanced capitalism and the welfare state. In: Politics and Society 2, 4, pp. 479–488 (483).

11 Ibidem, p. 481.

12 *Eurostat* 2018: Expenditure on social protection data. https://ec.europa.eu/eurostat/tgm/table.do?tab=table&init=1&language=en&pcode=tps00098&plugin=1 (06/04/2020).

13 *Marshall, T. H.* 1950: Citizenship and Social Class. And Other Essays, Cambridge.

Wellbeing as Expanded and Comprehensive Concept for a Humane Life

C. Ryff[14], in his work happiness, developed a first systematic attempt to broaden the understanding of welfare towards an integration of individual assessments of their life satisfaction, or wellbeing. For him, wellbeing consists of autonomy, environmental mastery, positive relationships with others, purpose in life, the realisation of potential and self-acceptance. Quite similarly, Diener and Suh argue that subjective wellbeing consists of three interrelated components: "life satisfaction, pleasant affect, and unpleasant affect. Affect refers to pleasant and unpleasant moods and emotions, whereas life satisfaction refers to a cognitive sense of satisfaction with life. Both affect and reported satisfaction judgments represent people's evaluations of their lives and circumstances"[15].

The shift "away from social indicators designed to monitor the state of society as a collective whole, towards an emphasis on measuring individual wellbeing"[16] lead to a broader discussion on how wellbeing can be measured and what its relationship towards welfare is. Following Austin[17], concepts of wellbeing can be classified either as subjective-instrumentalist-monist or as objective-constitutive-pluralist.

The subjective-instrumentalist concepts follow the tradition of Bentham who defines utility as "that property in any object, whereby it tends to produce benefit, advantage, pleasure, good, or happiness"[18]. This led to a measurement of economic outcome in terms of GDP as the main indicator for wellbeing and happiness. Studies in subjective wellbeing share basic assumptions of this utilitarian approach as they highlight both individual and social good. As a result, measurements of subjective wellbeing, happiness and life satisfaction have become increasingly important and a variety of quantitative tools have been developed to analyze subjective wellbeing.[19] Dalziel et al. argue that this perspective still is driven by the idea that "wellbeing is enhanced when individuals can satisfy more of their personal preferences"[20], that people therefore should be free to make choices to satisfy their preferences, and economic growth should have priority for policy makers. This neoliberal and utilitarian

14 *Ryff, C.* 1989: Happiness is everything, or is it – Explorations on the meaning of pyschological well-being. In: Journal of Personality and Social Psychology, 57(6), pp. 1069–1081.

15 *Diener, E./Suh, E.* 1997. Measuring quality of life: Economic, social, and subjective indicators. In: Social indicators research, 40(1–2), pp. 189–216 (200).

16 *Austin, A.* 2016: On Well-Being and Public Policy. Are We Capable of Questioning the Hegemony of Happiness? In: Social Indicators Research 127 (1), pp. 123–138 (124).

17 Ibidem.

18 *Bentham, J.* 1982 [orig. 1789]: An introduction to the principles of morals and legislation, London.

19 *Diener, E./Diener, M./Diener, C.* 1995. Factors predicting the subjectuve well-being of nations. In: Journal of Personality and Social Psychology, 69(5), pp. 851–864; *Diener, E./Lucas, R./Oishi, S.* 2009: Subjective well-being: The science of happiness and life satisfaction. In: *Lopez, S./Snyder, C. (eds.)*: The handbook of positive pyschology (2nd ed.), New York; *Easterlin, R.A.* 2001a: Income and Happiness: Towards a unified theory. In: Economic Journal 111, 473, pp. 465–48; *Easterlin, R.A.* 2001b: Subjective well-being and economic analysis: A brief introduction. In: Journal of Economic Behavior and Organization, 45(3), pp. 225–226; *Clark, A./Frijters, P./Shields, M.* 2008: Relative income, happiness, and utility: An explanation for the Easterlin paradox and other puzzles. In: Journal of Economic Literature, 46(1), pp. 95–144.

20 *Dalziel, P./Saunders, C./Saunders, J.* 2018: Wellbeing Economics. The Capabilities Approach to Prosperity, Cham, p. 4.

perspective was taken into question by numerous scholars, as it is "not reasonable to presume that GDP growth, regardless of the nature of the growth, will increase wellbeing"[21].

As opposed to this approach, objective-constitutive approaches Objective-constitutive approaches define wellbeing "not as a particular psychological state, but as a way of living and being that can be evaluated objectively"[22]. This strand of literature argues that individuals need basic resources on order to pursue and achieve their life plans and thus can be happy. This includes "basic liberties and opportunities, including wealth and income, which provide individuals with the freedom and resources to pursue their life plans", as Austin[23] states with reference to John Rawls. The capabilities approach developed by Sen[24] is one of the most popular ones in this field Sen argues that persons need to have capabilities to "lead the kinds of lives they value – and have reason to value"[25]. If we want to improve individual wellbeing, we have to promote the development of individual skills ad liberties that enable people to make conscious and and reasonable judgements about their lives.

Latest with Walker[26] and Easterlin[27], the concept of welfare is systematically connected with the concept of wellbeing. Wellbeing as an individual experience is closely linked to welfare as a socially produced means. Easterlin[28] for example introduces individual happiness as a core element of collective welfare. Greve points out that in "this understanding welfare is a narrower concept than wellbeing which also includes more broader aspects such as satisfaction, the quality of work, health, belongingness".[29] [30] And Huppert[31] uses wellbeing in a very broad sense. It contains wellbeing as an objective state as well as a subjective experience. The first meaning includes objective facts of people's lifes that often are associated with the outputs of the welfare state, such as "education, health, employment, housing, security, and the environment". The latter meaning includes individuals' experiences and feelings about their lives. This broad definition combines classic welfare state definitions as the ones of Titmuss[32] or Wilensky[33] with newer concepts like happiness, mental health or

---

21 Ibidem, p. 8.

22 *Austin* 2016 (fn. 16), p. 132.

23 Ibidem, p. 132.

24 *Sen, A.* 1983: Development: Which Way Now? Presidential Address of the Development Studies Association. In: Economic Journal 93 (December), p. 745–762.

25 *Sen, A.* 1999: Development as Freedom, Oxford, p. 18.

26 *Walker, A.* 1997: "Whither welfare?" In: *Ballard, C./Gubbay, J./Middleton, C. (eds.)*: The Student's Companion to Sociology, Oxford.

27 *Easterlin* 2001a, 2001b (fn. 19).

28 *Easterlin* 2001a (fn. 19).

29 *Greve* 2008 (fn. 5), p. 55.

30 *Greve* proposes two dimensions of measuring welfare. On the macro level he argues that Gross National Product and total societal spending on welfare policies are good indicators of resources. In the micro level he offers subjective feeling of happiness and numbers living in poverty as indicators of wellbeing and avoiding of poverty. See *Greve* 2008 (fn. 5), p. 63. Using data from 18 European countries, he can show that there is a "clear connection between the degree of happiness and the economic wealth measured in terms of GDP per capita" (ibidem). He concludes that "the welfare state will thus not only have to ensure access to the classical benefits and services, but also be aware of how citizens can be happy" (ibidem, p. 69)

31 *Huppert, F. A.* 2014. The state of wellbeing science: Concepts, measures, interventions, and policies. In: *Huppert, F.A./Cooper, C.L. (eds.)*: Wellbeing: A complete reference guide, Hoboken, pp. 1–49 (2).

32 *Titmuss* 1968 (fn. 8).

33 *Wilensky* 1975 (fn. 7).

life satisfaction provided e.g. by Ryff[34] or Marks and Shah[35] and thus offers a more comprehensive combined approach to the different dimensions of wellbeing.

Wellbeing: Measures and Core Findings

The integration subjective and objective aspects guided more recent attempts to measure wellbeing. For example, Stieglitz et al.[36] proposed a combination of material living standards, personal activities, health, social connections and relationships, education, political voice and governance, environment and insecurity to assess conditions for wellbeing. The OECD's Better-Life Index is one operationalisation of this concept.[37]

The index offers an overall ranking as well as a dashboard for the eleven dimensions Housing, income, jobs, community, education, environment, civic engagement, health, life satisfaction, safety and work-life balance measured. Especially the dashboard enables more sophisticated comparisons. In 2019, the top ten are Norway, Australia, Iceland, Canada, Denmark, Switzerland, the Netherlands, Sweden, Finland and the US. The two cases under special consideration in this volume, Germany and the Russian Federation rank 15th (Germany) and 33rd (Russian Federation). A closer look reveals that Russia is particularly weak in safety, health, civic engagement and environment and above average in education and work-life-balance, whereas Germany is above average in all dimension, but, compared to its overall performance, rather weak in community, civic engagement, and safety health. Germany outperforms Russia in all dimensions, but it is striking that they are very similar terms of work-life balance (Russia: 8.3 out of 11 and Germany 8.4) and community (Russia 5.7 and Germany 6.2)[38].

Quite similarly, Huppert[39] adopts a multidimensional perspective and advocates for a measurement of wellbeing that goes beyond measures of life satisfaction like the one used by the World Value Survey on general life satisfaction[40], that often is used as a proxy for wellbeing. Based on an analysis of important studies in different disciplines, she highlights some drivers of wellbeing.[41] These in particular are:

- material living conditions and especially individual or household income are positively related with life satisfaction. Job insecurity, fear of crime and dept are negatively related with life satisfaction.
- employment and quality of work as well as work-life-balance and commuting time have positive influence on wellbeing.

---

34 *Ryff* 1989 (fn. 14).

35 *Marks, N./Shah, H.* 2004: A Wellbeing Manifesto for a Flourishing Society: The Power of Wellbeing, London.

36 *Stiglitz, J./Sen, A./Fitoussi, J.* 2009: Report by the Commission on the measurement of economic performance and social progress. www.stiglitz-sen-fitoussi.fr/ (06/04/2020).

37 *OECD* 2020: How's life? OECD Better Life Index Online. http://www.oecdbetterlifeindex.org/ (23/03/2020).

38 *OECD* 2020: How's life? OECD Better Life Index Online. Country data. http://www.oecdbetterlifeindex.org/countries/germany/; http://www.oecdbetterlifeindex.org/countries/russian-federation/ (23/03/2020).

39 *Huppert* 2014 (fn. 31).

40 The Item used by World Value Survey goes: "All things considered, how satisfied are you with your life as awhole these days?" see: *World Value Survey*. www.worldvaluesurvey.org (23/03/2020).

41 *Huppert* 2014 (fn. 31), pp. 17 ff; *Stoll, L./ Michelson, J./ Seaford, C.* 2012: Well-being evidence for policy: A review, London.

- both, poor subjective and objective health conditions have negative impact on wellbeing. Physical activity and sufficient sleep seem to have at last indirect positive effects.
- education and wellbeing seem to be linked indirectly and the relationship seems to be moderated by other factors like income or social mobility.
- Fifth, social relationships with partner and family are very important for wellbeing. Social trust is also linked positively with life satisfaction and happiness. In addition, "the number and strength of social connections are among the largest and most robust predictors of subjective wellbeing"[42]. Even more, volunteering and altruistic behaviour are as well as active participation linked positively with wellbeing. These findings highlight the importance of a vital civil society as a source of wellbeing.
- some political factors are also important for wellbeing. This is especially true for "the reported quality of public services, and trust in key public institutions such as government, the police and the legal system".[43] Also, discrimination is lowering subjective wellbeing, a problem that is especially experienced by immigrant communities.
- Last but not least, natural and physical environment seem to influence subjective wellbeing. For example, access to green space and natural landscapes for leisure activities seems to influence wellbeing positively. But also, the structure of urban space seems to be important: accessibility, walking distance to all core facilities, and street layout are also positive. Instead pollution and nous seem to have negative impact.

It should also be mentioned that personal characteristics like gender, age, personality and value orientations seem to influence the level of subjective wellbeing.[44] Women seem to be more satisfied than men, and age has a u-shaped influence: the mid-agers have the lowest rates of life satisfaction. Extraversion has positive and neuroticism has negative effects on subjective wellbeing. The same is true for postmaterialistic (positive) and materialistic (negative) values.

Wellbeing, Politics and Civil Society

As mentioned before, some political and social factors, such as the quality of public services or trust in political institutions, interpersonal trust and social capital influence wellbeing. Several studies have shown the impact of the political environment and the opportunities for being politically and socially active. For example, Pacek and Radcliff[45] show in their analysis of the EU member states that "citizens find life more rewarding as the generosity of the welfare state increases" and that the welfare state "is an agent of human wellbeing"[46]. Flavin

42 *Huppert* 2014 (fn. 31), p. 20.

43 *Huppert* 2014 (fn. 31), p. 21; *Helliwell, J. F./Putnam, R.* 2004: The social context of well-being. Philosophical Transactions of the Royal Society of London. In: Series B, Biological sciences 359, pp. 1435–1446.

44 *Huppert* 2014 (fn. 31), p. 22.

45 *Pacek, A./Radcliff, B.* 2008: Assessing the welfare state: The Politics of Happiness. In: Perspectives on Politics 6, 2, pp. 267–277 (267).

46 Ibidem, p. 273.

et al.[47] find that government intervention in the economy affects subjective life satisfaction. The more governments intervene in the economy, the higher is life satisfaction independently of individual income. They use government consumption as a share of GDP, total social welfare expenditures, welfare state generosity, and labour market regulation as indicators for government intervention and life satisfaction as dependent variable. All four variables have significant positive impact on life satisfaction. Most important are decommodification and labour market regulation, i.e. classical welfare state measures.

Altman et al.[48] analyse the influence of how democracy is institutionalised on life satisfaction in 21 OECD countries. They find that levels of satisfaction are higher in parliamentary that presidential, proportional representation electoral systems that in single member district systems. They argue that the quality and degree of representation, and responsiveness is higher in the former systems which leads to more satisfaction with governments. Unfortunately, there are no systematic studies on the impact of democratic versus authoritarian regimes on wellbeing. But in an analysis of wellbeing and good government, Helliwell and Huang[49] can show that quality of government is strongly correlated with quality of government[50], as well as GDP and quality of government are. The analysis shows that "honest and efficient government are of special salience for poorer countries, while voice, accountability and political stability are of greater relative importance for the richer countries"[51]. Looking at the core dimensions of good government as used here, one can argue that it can be closely associated with democratic government, as especially high voice and accountability, high rule of law and low levels of corruption are features of democracy. So, it is plausible to argue that democratic government has a positive effect on wellbeing.

Touchton et al.[52] analyse 5550 Brazilian Municipalities and provide evidence that participatory institutions, innovative social programs and a capable municipal state lead to lower infant mortality. Even more, the strongest influence on infant mortality has an ongoing interaction between these three components. They conclude that "political rights, including voting and direct participation, help citizens to claim social rights and monitor service delivery" and broadens citizens' capabilities.[53] It also points at the specific strengths of local governance arrangements that include civil society.

Dalziel et al. argue that "Persons can access enhanced capabilities for wellbeing by participating in institutions of civil society to collaborate with others in the pursuit of common interests and shared values"[54]. But strong inequality and a lack of interpersonal and institu-

47 *Flavin, P./Pacek, A.C./Radcliff, B.* 2011: State intervention and subjective well-being in advanced industrial democracies. In: Politics & Policy, 39(2), pp. 251–269.

48 *Altman, D./Flavin, P./Radcliff, B.* 2017: Democratic institutions and subjective well-being. In: Political Studies, 65(3), pp. 685–704.

49 *Helliwell, J. F./Huang, H.* 2008: How's your government? International evidence linking good government and well-being. In: British Journal of Political Science, 38(4), pp. 595–619.

50 Good government includes Voice and Accountability, Political Instability and Violence, Government effectiveness, regulatory burden, Rule of law, and graft (or corruption).

51 *Helliwell/Huang* 2008 (fn. 49), p. 601.

52 *Touchton, M./Sugiyama, N. B./Wampler, B.* 2017: Democracy at work: Moving beyond elections to improve well-being. In: American Political Science Review, 111(1), pp. 68–82.

53 Ibidem, p. 80.

54 *Dalziel et al.* 2008 (fn. 20), p. 69.

tional trust have negative impact on civil society cooperation. So, social capital and mutual trust are main resources for cooperation and the promotion of wellbeing.[55] But also, participation and civic engagement depend on rules, values and patterns of action learned in everyday life: "This stock of knowledge socialized in interaction between individuals thus is socially determined. It represents the reality that modifies our action, and that is modified through action"[56]. As a consequence, the creation of trust and especially bridging and linking social capital[57] strongly depends on an enabling political and social environment. Where political regimes take action to control, limit or even suppress civil society activities, the conditions for enhancing capabilities for wellbeing are restricted compared to open and encouraging political and social environments.

Wellbeing and Local Governance

Wellbeing is influenced by multiple factors, the most of which are under limited control of the people themselves. Even though individuals might do their best to get well-paid and satisfying jobs and comfortable housing, they strongly depend on the current situation on the labour and housing markets. Also, health issues are not always subject to change, e.g. in case of chronic diseases like diabetes or renal failure. Government and administrative quality can also be changed only indirectly and under conditions of democratic rule and accountability. In authoritarian regimes there is only limited, and sometimes dangerous, space for criticising governments and administrations. The same is true for environmental conditions. One might want to move out of highly industrialized and polluted areas but cannot afford it due to a lack of jobs elsewhere.

At the local level, at least, the chance to take the factors that influence subjective wellbeing, in one's own hands is higher than if we talk about macro factors like the economic conditions or the nature and quality of the political system as such. There are three main conclusions we can draw from the above discussed issues for local governance and the proliferation of wellbeing:

First, local governments and administrations are the main, and often legally obliged providers of services for the public such as securing livelihoods, public order, education, construction, traffic and public transport, provision and distribution of welfare benefits. They are subject to evaluation of outcomes and often are held responsible for negative situations and circumstances. These claims might be justified or not. As local administrations usually are much closer to the inhabitants, the latter can contact the former more easily and express their needs. Especially on the local level, participation of the citizens, if not the inhabitants, often is formalized and offers means of delegative, deliberative and direct participation, such as local elections, public hearings or public decision making. People thus have the possibility

---

55 *Woolcock, M.* 1998: Social Capital and Economic Development: Toward a Theoretical Synthesis and Policy Framework. In: Theory and Society 27 (2), pp. 151–208; *Putnam, R.D.* 1995: Bowling Alone: America's Declining Social Capital. In: Journal of Democracy 6 (1), pp. 65–78.

56 *Frankenberger, R./Buhr, D.* 2017: Lifeworld, Democracy and the Creation of Social Trust. In: *Frankenberger, R./Chernenkova, E. (eds.)*: Local Politics in a Comparative Perspective. The Cases of Petrozavodsk and Tübingen, Baden-Baden, pp. 43–57 (53).

57 *Woolcock* 1998 (fn. 55).

to influence administrative processes and decisions directly ls If local governments and administrations are responsive and can be called to account for their decisions, political participation is a powerful tool to influence the conditions of wellbeing.

Second, civil society can be a provider of welfare and wellbeing, too. Especially when it comes to social relations and opportunities for social contact, but also to changing the immediate environment, housing conditions, leisure and cultural activities, and even provision of basic welfare services, civil societies all over the world contribute substantially to the improvement of everyday life. From neighbourly help to organising cultural events, cleaning up parks to providing care for disabled or children, soup kitchen to renovating public schools, they organize a broad variety of activities to supplement public welfare beyond the mandatory provisions or even to fill in the blanks left by the public welfare system. Research clearly underlines the role of civil society for the enhancement of wellbeing, as Huppert states: "At a community or societal level, developing civic engagement, strong social networks, and identifying assets rather than deficits are all associated with increased wellbeing at both the individual and group level"[58].

Third, these two aspects can be combined in terms of local governance. Governance can be defined as a set of structures and processes linking governmental and nongovernmental actors for purposes of decision making and implementation. According to Große Hüttmann, the "opening towards nonstate actors and representatives of civil society follows the logic of political inclusion. This increases acceptance and legitimacy of decisions and can minimize problems of the implementation, as those levels affected by the decisions are integrated very early in the policy process"[59].

In terms of policy recommendations, fostering wellbeing then needs two things: First, Strengthening the economy and the welfare state will have sustainable impact on objective and subjective wellbeing. This also includes performance, transparency, accountability and responsiveness of the state as main provider of welfare – on the national, regional, and local levels. Second, another and often neglected dimension for enhancing wellbeing is to encourage civic engagement and to enable civil society activites. Also, participation leads to better outcomes both in terms of development and distribution of welfare. It contributes to the individual and collective formation of capabilities as well as it strengthens interpersonal, and maybe, institutional trust. It is especially the local level of governance as a laboratory for cooperation and co-creation, where this can be practiced easily and effectively

Examples from Baden-Württemberg and the Republic of Karelia the Contributions to this Volume

The articles in this volume all address the interrelatedness of civil society, local governance and wellbeing. The authors from Russia and Germany use cases and examples from the state of Baden-Württemberg, Germany and the Republic of Karelia, Russian Federation as to illustrate and highlight theoretical and empirical aspects of this complex relationship. They

58 *Huppert* 2014 (fn. 31), p. 32.
59 *Große Hüttmann* 2017 (fn. 4), p. 37.

all share the perspective of how to foster human wellbeing under very different conditions and circumstances. The chapters are organized in five sections, each of which focuses on another dimension of how to enhance wellbeing.

The first section addresses the question how *Wellbeing, Social Innovation and Participation* are interrelated. The articles provide theoretical foundations and practical examples on how social innovation and participation can lead to an increase of individual and societal wellbeing.

Daniel Buhr argues that wellbeing for as many citizens as possible should be at the heart of every welfare state policy. To achieve this, welfare states should widen their scope more towards future wellbeing than to stick with evaluations of current or past situations. A main goal of welfare policies then should aim at strengthening the innovation capabilities of a society: human capital, complexity capital, structural capital and relational capital. He argues that innovation and wellbeing are intertwined in two ways: on the one hand, innovation is a prerequisite for productivity, progress and growth, which can provide the means for a high level of wellbeing in the future; on the other hand, a high level of wellbeing in a society can provide a fruitful basis for innovation – on the supply as well as the demand side. Using Data for EU-Countries, Buhr shows that Scandinavian (social-democratic) welfare states are traditionally leading in both, wellbeing and innovation and discusses this finding.

Yuliya A. Petrovskaya analyses the role of public participation for implementing social innovation. Focusing on data from a study on the role of NGOs in the modernization of the Russian social service system and with a special focus on NGOs in the Republic of Karelia, she examines their activities in the field of social services, as well as the development of social entrepreneurship. She identifies main factors preventing the expansion of NGOs and the development of social entrepreneurs as providers of social services. The main obstacles proved to be administrative challenges and human factors involving interaction between administration, NGOs and the general population. The research concludes that in Russia it is still too early to talk about competition in the social services market between the state and non-state actors. NGOs and social entrepreneurs are not yet able to compete with state social service institutions and the general population remain unwilling to pay for social services from non-state providers.

Christopher Gohl argues that public dialogues are a core method to inquire into, evaluate, and provide for communal conditions for well-being. Starting with the idea of participative agency and provision in Aristotle's understanding of well-being, he offers an introduction into a contemporary variant of Aristotelian liberalism, the economist Amartya Sen's capability approach. Sen aims for substantive freedoms for everyone as precondition of realizing individual well-being on a mass scale. The argument concludes with a pragmatist model of public dialogue situated within an arena of "freedom politics" that allows for the practical adaptation of Sen's capability approach in political communities inquiring into their conflicting or desirable freedoms.

With their contribution on online-participation, *Anni Schlumberger* and *Elisa Söll* provide insights in foundations risks and promises of citizen participation in the production of wellbeing. They that citizen participation is vital for democracy, especially in times of perceived crises. If participation meets the criteria of transparency, information, offers a real choice and policy makers are committed to the process, participation and online participation can strengthen democracy and wellbeing. Using the example of Metzingen, Baden-Württemberg, they illustrate how risks of online participation like façade participation, low rates of people participating, lack of deliberation or high entry barriers can be overcome. Online participation can be an enabling and motivating as well as accessible and understandable tool for enhancing democratic participation

The five contributions to the second section on *Challenges for Wellbeing and Development* all identify migration as one factor closely linked with wellbeing. A lack of wellbeing and perspectives for a better future caused and still cause migration within countries and across boarder. This leads to different challenges for those countries who receive migrants and those who are losing people. Whereas integration in the social, political and cultural system is the challenge for the former, the latter often face a loss of creativity and manpower.

Migration and social policy have become fiercely contested issues in Europe and North America. In his contribution *Martin Seeleib-Kaiser* highlight how mobility and migration, on the one hand, and social policy, on the other hand, have historically been closely interwoven and shaped by power relations. He argues that European states actively assisted their poor to leave 'home' and settle in far-away places. He elaborates some of the tensions between freedom of movement and the role of social policy in the North German Confederation (Norddeutscher Bund; NDB) and the British Empire. Finally, he argues that many of the current challenges and issues associated with migration and social policy in Europe are historically not unique.

Given that especially the Nordic regions of Russia, but also other regions especially in southern and eastern Europe are affected by a brain drain, it seems to be important to develop attractive environments for the people. *Denis Sachuk* argues that this is especially true for the middle class and the creative class. They expect a creative urban environment that offers opportunities and structures for a good life. An expert survey in Petrozavodsk reveals that the creative class in Russia remains too small to lead the development of creative urban spaces. Thus, the middle class becomes key actor in the self-organization of citizens and in promoting participation in projects dedicated to the development of a creative urban space that includes four features: acknowledgement and representation of local cultural heritage, the presence of creative industries, tools to attract and retain creative professionals, and decision making on behalf of city management.

Kirill Fitisov focuses on the innovative potential of Youth in the Republic of Karelia and its innovative potential for socio-economic development. He uses survey data from 2019 to analyse level of digital economic competences and the innovative potential among young people in the Republic of Karelia. There are differences between urban and rural areas and there is a strong influence of schools and higher education institutions. He concludes with examining the possibilities for using this innovative potential as a social and economic resource for the region.

Anna Simakova, *Maria Pitukhina* and *Irina Stepus* present a large scale project to educate young people and to make the Arctic and the Far North regions more attractive as places for work and living: the regional vocational guidance program for pupils between grades 8 and 10 in the Republic of Karelia "Live, learn, work in Karelia!". The goals of the vocational guidance lesson are to convince local youth to stay in the Russian Arctic and the Far East, to attract human resources and youth to the Russian Arctic and the Far East, and to develop a positive image of these regions in terms of youth well-being and professional opportunities. The Karelian lesson has served as the model for a larger project at the federal level entitled "Start Your Career in the Russian Arctic and the Far East." This federal vocational guidance lesson was enacted in 2019 and covered 25 Russian regions and almost 50 000 pupils from 755 schools. A diagnostic survey following this guidance lesson to gather feedback from participants has shown that pupils' interest towards Arctic and the Far Eastern labour market and their perspective occupations has significantly increased after receiving information within vocational guidance lesson. Incentivizing and nurturing a desire to work in the Arctic or the Far East is an important element in the system of human resource recruitment of these regions in terms of both current and projected labour needs. Graduates from donor regions who start their careers in the Artic or Far East are an enormous human resource to these regions.

Alisa Kruglova highlights the necessity of creating a positive image of a territory in order to make it attractive for investors and (future) residents. Among other criteria, a positive image influences the success of a territory, be it a region or municipality. She presents an analysis of the factors that shape the image of a territory and the features of this process using the Republic of Karelia as a case study. Special attention is paid to the existing images of the region and the specific images practices that elites choose to promote.

As wellbeing decidedly includes the subjective perspective, *Wellbeing and Public Opinion* are closely linked, as the contributions to the third section illustrate. Public opinion can serve as a seismograph for individual and collective evaluations of their life satisfaction, and more specifically, for the problems that are salient within the population.

The quality of living space is increasingly becoming a top criterion in the assessment of the today person's quality of life. Drawing on a theoretical model of urban space proposed by Russian sociologist T. Dridze, *Irina Miljukova* and *Polina Kopteva* address this issue by presenting the results of exploratory research among residents of Petrozavodsk assessing the quality of their living space. An open-ended interview method was used to study the general ideas of the population about urban space. The research also aimed to discover the subjective image of Petrozavodsk and the social factors that determine the Petrozavodsk residents' perceptions and images of the city. Furthermore, the research focus touches upon issues of social activity by Petrozavodsk residents regarding urban improvement and interactions between the population and municipal authorities.

Individual wellbeing is affected by the political system and the welfare state, but also by social status and people's political lifeworld. Political lifeworlds are individual normative maps of the political world. They are shaped by everyday experiences and guide political action. If people make different experiences, new social cleavages might emerge and translate in a disintegration of political lifeworlds, which in turn can have destabilising effects on the political system and society as a whole. Political polarization and the success of the right-wing populist party Alternative for Germany (AfD) rise the question, if we currently witness such a profound and destabilising change in Germany. *Rolf Frankenberger* and *Daniel Buhr* present results from a study including 109 qualitative interviews from the State of Baden-Württemberg, Germany, with a special focus on the electorate of the AfD. Findings reflect the emerging cleavage between progressive, universalist and pluralist positions on the one side, and authoritarian, particularistic-nationalist positions on the other. A more detailed analysis of the lifeworlds shows that those with greater knowledge on the functioning of the political system as a system of rules and regulation are more satisfied and participate more than those who have strongly output-oriented and elite-centred ideas. AfD voters are disappointed by the current political system. They express an aversive attitude towards representative democracy that is rooted in populist and right-wing motives, but hardly translates into political action. People from these aversive lifeworlds might also be those with overall low levels of subjective wellbeing, even though they not necessarily belong to the poor.

Going deeper into these lifeworlds and the political actors closely linked with them, *Isabell Sinner* analyses populist political communication of AfD-voters and AfD party officials. Populist political communication has primarily been analyzed from a top-down perspective of parties' public communication. Little research focuses on individual-level communication by voters with populist voting preferences. Analyzing public political speeches and interview data of voters with the method of qualitative content analysis, this paper compares the political communication of party officials and voters for the German right-wing populist party Alternative für Deutschland (AfD). The results of the analysis show striking similarities regarding salient political issues, the characterization of elites as enemies, and specific rhetorical as well as linguistic traits – supporting the argument that communicated populism is of relevance both in parties and in their electorate.

The fourth section on *Civil Society, Governance and the creation of Wellbeing* comprises four chapters that shed light on the role of civil society and especially NGOs in producing wellbeing. Initiatives, NGOs and individuals often make valuable contributions to local welfare production and subsequently foster individual wellbeing by improving living conditions, providing care and assistance, refurbishing public space or offering cultural events. Sometimes they cooperate with local, regional or national authorities and build up governance networks.

Elena Chernenkova analyses the role of NGOs in the development of urban social spaces. She argues that the focus of modern city development strategies is on creating a comfortable and creative urban environment through the development of social partnership and intersectoral interaction. The role of civic engagement in achieving a new quality of life for urban populations is manifested both in the European and Russian official agendas and occupies a significant place in public and research discourse of various countries. In general, the contours of municipal policy are determined by the construction of ergonomic infrastructure and the production of an innovative environment. Social projects of non-governmental organizations have an essential place in this process. These projects can transform into drivers of social innovation theory by consolidating the work of many actors toward the implementation of urban development strategies. Chernenkova presents results of project activities of socially oriented organization in Petrozavodsk urban district. It focuses on projects supported by the Presidential Grants Foundation in the Petrozavodsk urban district. The Presidential Grants Foundation provides the largest support, by scale and volume, for innovative social projects, which in turn foster the development of NGO activities

In her contribution *Kseniia Chumak* considers the conditions of the Republic of Karelia for the development of civil society and interaction between Karelian NGOs and governmental authorities at the regional and municipal levels. Using a case study of one Karelian NGO, this article examines the various forms of cooperation between NGOs and authorities. These forms of cooperation are analysed in an attempt to define what problems may exist, and how these can be best addressed.

Anatoly Tsygankov takes stock of the development of local initiatives in the rural areas if the Republic of Karelia. Local self government is a core principle implemented in Russian and Karelian law. But as local government bodies face multiple problems and budgetary limitations, they often are not able to solve these problems. Dissatisfaction rises and People start initiatives. In 2014 the Republic of Karelia implemented a local initiatives support program (LISP) based on the Ideas developed by the World Bank This article presents an overview and analysis of local initiatives in the Republic of Karelia with a special focus on rural areas. This includes initiatives of territorial public self-government (TPSG) as well projects on public budgeting, and Comfortable urban environment. Successful initiatives enhance responsibility, independence and mutual trust among citizens and thus contribute to wellbeing in the, often neglected, rural areas.

Trade unions are important actors in the German collective bargaining system and tariff autonomy. They are also representing workers' interests concerning working conditions and work life balance. In addition, they are welfare providers themselves and represent employees and workers from the welfare sector. *Stewart Gold* and *Carmen Thamm* conducted a survey in Germany with trade union members from different trade unions like IG Metall or Verdi. They asked volunteers and professional officials and members of these unions for their concepts and strategies for producing welfare and enhancing public wellbeing and for practical examples where they contribute to wellbeing. To complement the survey, they conducted expert interviews with local trade union representatives from the Tübingen area. Findings leave space for improving both knowledge and strategies for fostering wellbeing.

Last, but not least, the fifth section of the volume deals with *Sister City relations and Wellbeing*. Sister-city relations are one core instrument of public diplomacy and often include both, political-administrative and civil society exchange and cooperation. They contribute to mutual understanding and provide space and opportunity for individual exchange and learning.

Natalya Lavrushina and *Ekaterina Shlapeko* outline practical and theoretical aspects of public participation in sister-cities relations. The sister-city phenomenon appeared after World War II and is typically defined by the establishment of social, cultural, and political ties between municipalities in separate nation-states. Using experience from the history of Petrozavodsk sister-city relations they argue that the role of public participation in sister-cities relations has grown significantly over the past years. The increase of international projects initiated by third sector actors is one striking result of the analysis. The authors conclude that public participation in sister-cities relations has a positive effect on the development of good neighbourly relations and stimulates local communities for solving urban-related problems.

Ekaterina Shestakova focuses on the concept of creativity which can push a city to a qualitatively new level of development. She argues that sister city cooperation is an important instrument for improving Petrozavodsk's cultural resources and to create social innovation for urban development. Using international cooperation of Petrozavodsk and its Northern European sister-cities, she analyses joint project activities, interviews with local specialists responsible for cultural policy and international relations, and a resident questionnaire survey. She concludes that accumulated positive experience of international sociocultural partnership requires further intensification given the specifics of civic activism in Petrozavodsk. Although the potential of sister-city connections aiding development is not fully utilized at this time, the untapped potential of such connections is widely discussed and the activity of the local community including NGOs confirms the existing understanding that combinations of cultural and scientific, as well as standard and non-standard approaches to urban problem solving can be a driving force for territorial development.

Lessons Learned: A Conclusion

Discussing and analyzing cases from different social and political environments with different historical experiences and cultural backgrounds, such as Petrozavodsk and Tübingen, nevertheless opens up opportunities for multiple comparisons and mutual learning. The contributions to this volume and the lively discussions in the workshop showed the possibilities of such rather analytic inductive than experimental or rigid comparative designs in identifying conditions affecting the potential of participatory deliberative practices in local governance and the creation of sustainable urban development.

Wellbeing and sustainable development depend on a multitude of factors, such as natural environment, historical heritage and economic development. If local actors want to enhance public and individual wellbeing, they deal with these structural constraints. For example, the effectiveness of participatory democracy and public dialogues is primarily associated with the degree of openness and responsiveness of the political system, specific characteristics of political regimes and institutional readiness to deal with citizens' interests. Different from democratic systems, autocratic political systems and authoritarian rule are, by definition, less responsive to and open for participation and public dialogues based on the principles of freedom of expression, association, or organization. The Russian version of interacting with the public is often interpreted as an imitation or façade of participatory politics. Numerous studies for example link the Russian specifics with the desire of the state and/or the political regime to preserve the monistic tradition of authoritarian rule or even enhance a power vertical. Non-state and civil society actors seem to have limited possibilities in shaping political agendas ad civil dialogues. But still, there can be options to influence future development, and wellbeing. First, sustainable development then depends on the quality and nature of management, opportunities and effects of the activities of local authorities related with the construction of public space. Second, the level and degree of involvement of civil society impacts local development, depending on the culture and the innovative potential of participation. Much then relies on the readiness of local authorities and institutions to incorporate innovations provided by civil society actors into everyday practice. And third, the nature and quality of dialogues depend on characteristics and skills of actors, on their role, position and status within the system, their capability of articulating and communicating their interests and their ability to interact with others. Even though we have to consider the special circumstances under which civil society actors operate in both, democratic and non-democratic regimes, the examples from Petrozavodsk and the Republic of Karelia provide encouraging examples, how issues, propositions for problem solving and the implementation of low scale solutions can be put on the political agenda.

The core principle for ensuring the sustainability of joint efforts of authorities and civil society to enhance local urban environments and wellbeing then is co-creation and co-determination of local development on the basis of principles of local self-government as well as formalized direct democratic and informal deliberative procedures of citizen participation. They are incorporated in various forms in legal frameworks and official agendas worldwide, and especially in the European Union and the Russian Federation. To be powerful tools of developing public space they need accountability, responsivity, and commitment of all actors involved. And often, it is a question of power. There is broad research addressing questions of local governance, development and welfare production. The volume at hand contributes to this body of literature by choosing a comparative perspective on the experiences of the two municipalities Petrozavodsk and Tübingen in their regional and national environments. Being aware of different historical traditions, different political systems and cultures, we provide insight regarding theoretical and methodological provisions on principles, variables, causes and outcomes of local governance, civic engagement, participatory democracy and public dialogues. One focus is on factors enabling a productive co-creation of welfare and wellbeing in urban spaces, the most important of which is a symmetry and equality of communication between all actors involved.

PART 1: WELLBEING, SOCIAL INNOVATION AND PARTICIPATION

Innovative Societies and Wellbeing

Daniel Buhr

Abstract: A good life could be defined as one with a high level (and duration) of wellbeing. It should be the aim of any welfare state to provide this to as many citizens as possible. Most of our welfare state policies and most of our measures to evaluate wellbeing, however, look at the past or the current situation of the people. If welfare states widen their scope more towards future wellbeing, it makes sense to strengthen the innovation capabilities of a society: human capital, complexity capital, structural capital and relational capital. Innovation and wellbeing are intertwined in two ways: on the one hand, innovation is a prerequisite for productivity, progress and growth, which can provide the means for a high level of wellbeing in the future; on the other hand, a high level of wellbeing in a society can provide a fruitful basis for innovation – on the supply as well as the demand side. By ranking EU countries according to their innovation capability, we can see that Scandinavian (social-democratic) welfare states are traditionally leading. It is the same welfare states that are also leading rankings like OECD's "How is life? 2020: Measuring Well-being" or the "World Happiness Report 2020". This article looks a little closer to this interesting relationship.

Keywords: Wellbeing; innovation; capabilities; welfare state; digitisation

1 Introduction

What is the ultimate normative goal of policy making? I would say: Better lives for as many people as possible. But what is a "good life"? It is one of these putative simple questions with many answers. First of all, it is highly subjective. And second – really hard to measure. It is even rather tricky to define. Having said this, a good life could be defined as one with a high level (and duration) of wellbeing. According to Naci/Ioannidis wellbeing

> "refers to diverse and interconnected dimensions of physical, mental, and social well-being that extend beyond the traditional definition of health. It includes choices and activities aimed at achieving physical vitality, mental alacrity, social satisfaction, a sense of accomplishment, and personal fulfillment."[1]

Traditionally, wellbeing has been measured by economists on the level of whole, national economies or societies in order to allow for international comparison. The easiest way of doing this was to look at the growth of gross domestic product (GDP), i.e. the value of all goods and services produced in a country within a year. For growth, it is argued by liberal economists like August von Hayek or Milton Friedman, raises the standard of living of the population, creates jobs, can help resolve social conflicts more effectively, facilitates structural change and ultimately also makes it possible to invest more money in tasks such as environmental protection and development aid.

---

1 *Naci, H./Ioannidis, J. P. A.* 2015: Evaluation of Wellness Determinants and Interventions by Citizen Scientists. In: JAMA. 314 (2), pp. 121–122 (121 f).

The theoretical connection for economic growth is the consequences of the increase in productivity. As soon as labour productivity rises faster than GDP, unemployment increases (if working hours remain the same). Growth thus serves to close this gap again and again. However, the side effects of this economic growth are enormous. The real problem is not growth per se, but the consumption of resources that has been associated with it up to now – in terms of raw materials, the environment and nature, as well as the effects on people. This has led to the demand for qualitative growth: According to this, growth should first and foremost be environmentally compatible and resource-saving. Technical progress, such as digitalisation, for example, should ensure that the value of goods and services increases through higher quality – and not through the use of more material or more bad jobs. In sum, these developments obviously affect the wellbeing of the people a lot.

This chapter is focussing on the the question, how wellbeing is related to the innovative capability within a welfare state. First, it is reflecting on the right measurement of wellbeing, especially when it comes to future wellbeing. This is followed by a section on comparative welfare state analysis, in order to see how innovative capabilities could be influenced by the specific type of welfare state. These welfare states provide the setting for social and technological innovation – on the demand (i.e. what kind of services and products are needed by whom?) and the supply side (i.e. "human capital") – which are important for the level of future wellbeing. How can this be fostered?

2 How to Measure Wellbeing

Measuring wellbeing is a rather complex task. Therefore, social scientists have been using various concepts such as wealth, education, status and resource distribution to judge quality of life: Higher income, more education, better social contacts are considered indicators of wellbeing. To obtain a balanced view of wellbeing, we need to find comprehensive measures. According to the OECD we need to look at various indicators[2] to answer the question: "How's life?" The OECD Well-being Framework includes 11 dimensions, in order to cover outcomes at the individual, household or community level, and relating to: *material conditions* that shape people's economic options (Income and Wealth, Housing, Work and Job Quality); *quality-of-life factors* that encompass how well people are (and how well they feel they are), what they know and can do, and how healthy and safe their places of living are (Health, Knowledge and Skills, Environmental Quality, Subjective Well-being, Safety); *how connected and engaged people are*, and how and with whom they spend their time (Work-Life Balance, Social Connections, Civic Engagement).

Ultimately, this OECD study also ties in with numerous distributional analyses that work out the connection between distributional structures in national economies and economic growth. One criterion is the distribution measure of the Gini coefficient, whose development is considered in a longitudinal section. On the other hand, the intra-societal distribution structures, in particular wage developments and the redistributive function of the tax and benefit system, are examined. This is then related to real economic development in order to draw

2 *OECD* 2020: How's Life? 2020: Measuring Well-being, Paris.

conclusions about how much more favourable economic growth would be if a socially equitable distribution could be achieved. Thus, distributional analysis becomes practical in that it identifies concrete criteria for wellbeing, seeks to anchor these empirically and follows their development. Social distribution issues and their expression in poverty or wealth and all their transitional stages are consequently political-economic. This means that they reflect both economic development and its significance for individual and social coexistence and wellbeing.[3]

Figure 1: The OECD Wellbeing Framework

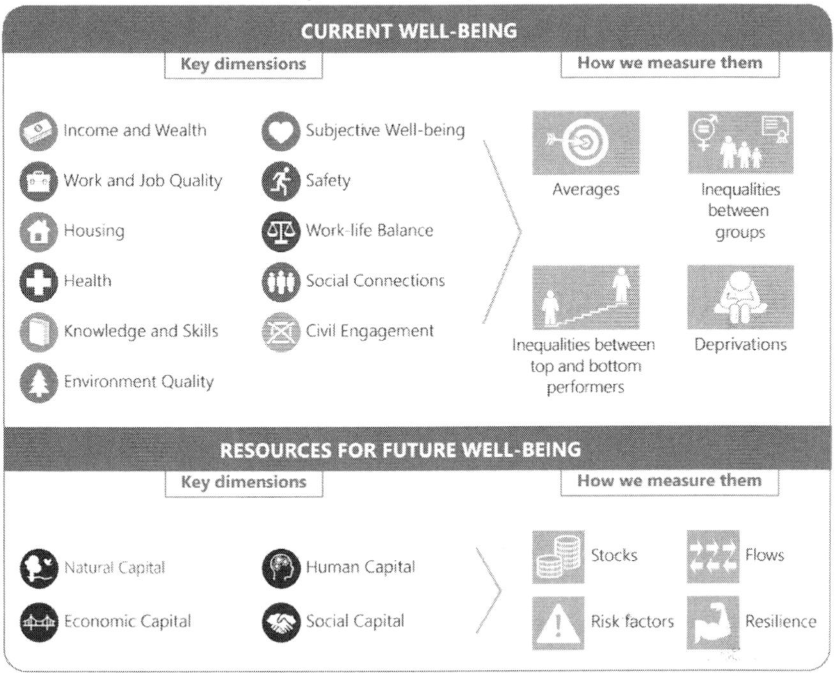

Source: *OECD* 2020.

These indicators encompass measures covering the current wellbeing. But what about the future wellbeing? According to the OECD wellbeing-framework, the resources that underpin future wellbeing are grouped into four types of capital (OECD 2020):

- Economic Capital, which includes both man-made and financial assets
- Natural Capital, encompassing natural assets (e.g. stocks of natural resources, land cover, species biodiversity) as well as ecosystems and their services (e.g. oceans, forests, soil and the atmosphere)
- Human Capital, which refers to the skills and future health of individuals
- Social Capital, addressing the social norms, shared values and institutional arrangements that foster co-operation

3 *Best, N./Boeckh, J./Huster, E.-U.* 2018: Armutsforschung: Entwicklungen, Ansätze, Erkenntnisgewinne. In: *Huster, E.-U./Boeckh, J./Mogge-Grotjahn, H. (eds)*: Handbuch Armut und soziale Ausgrenzung, Wiesbaden, pp. 27–57 (51).

In contrast to measures of current wellbeing, above mentioned capitals refer to the broad systems that sustain wellbeing over time. They often relate to public goods, rather than outcomes for individuals. The provision of these public goods, however, is very much determined by the welfare state. By definition, it is a form of government in which the state protects and promotes the economic and social wellbeing of the citizens, based upon the principles of equal opportunity, equitable distribution of wealth, and public responsibility for citizens unable to avail themselves of the minimal provisions for a “good life”. Today’s welfare states extent their activities to the provision of both cash welfare benefits (such as old-age pensions or unemployment benefits) and in-kind welfare services (such as health or childcare services). Through these provisions and their specific institutional settings, welfare states can affect the distribution of wellbeing and personal autonomy among their citizens, as well as influencing how their citizens consume and how they spend their time. If we look at the list of dimensions, it is easy to see how much they are formed by the surrounding institutions and by concrete policies that try to shape societies towards this overall goal of an increase of wellbeing for as many people (or citizens?) as possible.

3 Welfare States and their Comparison

These welfare states, however, differ. In comparative welfare state research, different types of welfare states are distinguished. They reflect the relevant experiences of the respective national political and social history as well as the political power relations.[4] The proposal of the Danish sociologist Gøsta Esping-Andersen[5], which met with a broad response and is still of great importance today, deserves special mentioning. His three worlds of welfare capitalism divide states into liberal, conservative and social democratic welfare states. Each of these welfare state types follows a historically based development path and thus has its own logic of the organization of social policy, the patterns of social stratification and inequality (especially in the employment system) and the forms of social integration or exclusion[6], that should have an influence on the wellbeing of the people as well as the innovation capability of a society. Esping-Andersen[7] defines three dimensions that have different effects on different types of welfare: Decommodification, stratification and residualism.

Decommodification refers to the relative independence of the social security of the individual from the constraints and risks of capitalist markets. In other words, the higher the level of decommodification, the lower the dependence on the sale of the commodity labour to ensure one's own survival. This is achieved through the type and level of social security benefits.

Stratification refers to the economic and social stratification of a society. It is thus a matter of describing social equality and inequality in terms of income and social status. By providing social security systems and services, the welfare state is an instrument of redistri-

4 *Schmid, J.* 2010: Wohlfahrtsstaaten im Vergleich. Soziale Sicherung in Europa: Organisation, Finanzierung, Leistungen und Probleme, 3rd updated and expanded edition, Wiesbaden, p. 99.

5 *Esping-Andersen, G.* 1990: The three worlds of welfare capitalism, Cambridge.

6 *Schmid* 2010 (fn. 4), p. 100.

7 *Esping-Andersen* 1990 (fn. 5).

bution "to influence and, if necessary, correct the structure of social inequality"[8]. At the same time, different types of welfare states themselves generate a specific form of stratification.

Residualism refers to the specific interaction between market, state and family with regard to the social security of the individual and thus the way in which the state intervenes in this mixed relationship between private and public provision.

Esping-Andersen developed three ideal types from the specific configuration of the above-mentioned dimensions, which will be discussed below: liberal, conservative and social-democratic welfare states. [9]

The *liberal* (or Anglo-Saxon) welfare state model emphasizes a restrained state social policy focused on the most needy, supports the welfare production functions of the market and leaves other welfare production to private provision and the family. The overall decommodification effect is low, social entitlement rights are low and linked to individual means testing, the reference to which is stigmatised.[10] One country example of this type is the United Kingdom of Great Britain, others are Canada, the USA or Australia.

The *conservative* (or continental European) welfare states are based on a socio-politically strong state that emphasises the preservation of the status of the insured, characterised by the social security model based on the Bismarck model, while the socio-political role of the market is generally low, but that of the family is highly valued in accordance with the principle of subsidiarity.[11] Linked to the principle of subsidiarity is the influential role of the churches, which are also formative for the obligation to preserve traditional family forms.[12] In contrast to the liberal model, the decommodification effect is more pronounced and the state intervenes more strongly. Social rights are tied to class and status, which leads to the preservation of status and group differences.[13] Archetypes of this welfare type are countries such as Germany, France and Austria.

Social democratic (or Scandinavian) welfare states are based on a social policy characterised by universalism, strong decommodification, ambitious ideas of equality and full employment, which seeks to minimise dependence on the market and the family.[14] The decommodification effects are most pronounced here. Examples of this type are the Scandinavian countries Sweden, Norway, Denmark and Finland.

Figure 2[15] summarises the main features of the three worlds of the welfare state in a systematic and comparative spatial triangle, which clearly shows the ideal-typical categorisation of Esping-Andersen and points to the hybrid forms that actually exist.

---

8 *Esping-Andersen, G.* 1998: Die drei Welten des Wohlfahrtskapitalismus. In: *Lessenich, S./Ostner, E. (eds.)*: Welten des Wohlfahrtskapitalismus. Der Sozialstaat in vergleichender Perspektive, Frankfurt a.M., pp. 19–58 (39).

9 Ibidem 1990 (fn. 5).

10 *Schmid* 2010 (fn. 4), p. 101.

11 *Schmidt* 2004: Wörterbuch zur Politik, Stuttgart, p. 807.

12 *Esping-Andersen* 1998 (fn. 8), p. 44.

13 *Schmid* 2010 (fn. 4), p. 101.

14 *Schmidt* 2004 (fn. 11), p. 807.

15 *Buhr, D./Christ, C./Frankenberger, R./Fregin, M.-C./Schmid, J./Trämer, M.* 2016: On the Way to Welfare 4.0? Digitalisation of the Welfare State in Labour Market, Health Care and Innovation Policy: A European Comparison, FES: Berlin; *Schmid* 2010 (fn. 4).

Figure 2: Three Worlds of Welfare States

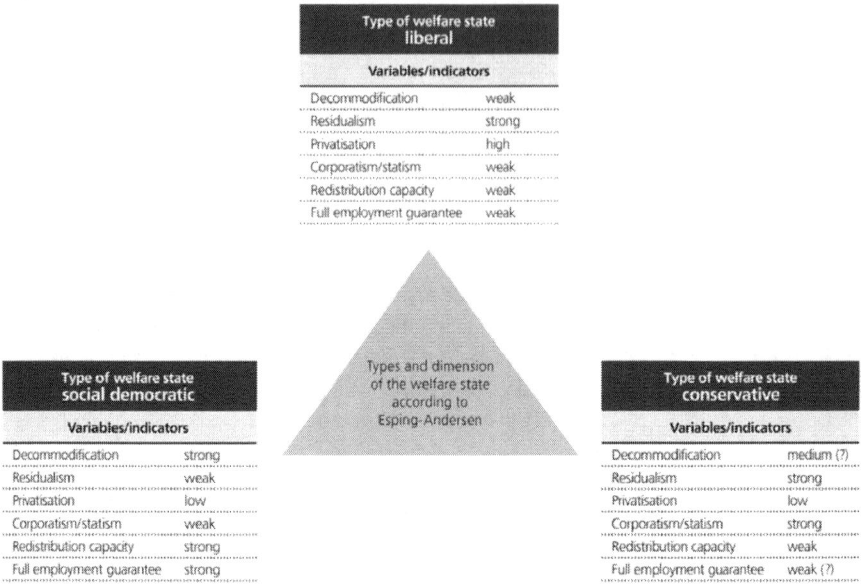

Source: *Buhr et al.* 2016.

In the meantime, Esping-Andersen's approach has been extended to include two further welfare state types: firstly, the type of the rudimentary or Mediterranean welfare state, which explicitly covers the countries of Southern Europe (Spain, Portugal, Greece, and to some extent Italy), and secondly, the type of the post-socialist welfare state, which can be found in the transformative political systems of Eastern Europe.

The Mediterranean welfare state can be characterized by a stronger role of the family and a lower level of social benefits. Moreover, this group of countries is characterised by the fact that social security systems are only partially developed and the right to welfare is not legally anchored. In this context, it should also be taken into account that this group of countries is made up of less industrialized, structurally weak and poor countries, i.e. only relatively low incomes are earned on the market. A specific characteristic of this type is the high level of employment protection.[16]

The collapse of the Soviet Union and the transformation of the former member states has added another welfare model: the post-socialist welfare state. It can be described as an authoritarian transformation of the social democratic welfare type.[17] The transformation towards a welfare system based on the Western European model is described as gradual and exhibits both old and new characteristics. According to Götting the post-socialist states are a hybrid: "The post-communist welfare states are currently institutional hybrids."[18]

16 *Schmid* 2010 (fn. 4).

17 See *Götting, U.* 1998: Transformation der Wohlfahrtsstaaten in Mittel- und Osteuropa, Opladen.

18 Ibidem, p. 274.

In sum, we can distinguish clusters or types of welfare states. While some of them heavily trust in the functioning of (private) markets, individual responsibility and not so much public intervention – i.e. liberal welfare states – do others provide publicly financed and organised welfare services following the concept of universalism and social justice (i.e. Social-democratic welfare states). Are these also the ones with the highest level of wellbeing?

4 Innovation and Wellbeing

If we, again, argue normatively, that the purpose of a welfare state is to provide the means for allowing as many people as possible to live a life with a high level of wellbeing, it might be not enough to look at decommodification, stratification and residualism only. We should rather also look how these welfare states prepare their citizens for the future, both, as a form of risk prevention as well as a way to foster autonomy and self-efficacy. If the aim is to achieve a high amount of people with a high level of wellbeing, and we also know that if labour productivity rises faster than GDP, unemployment increases, societies have to be innovative in the future, too. Innovation and wellbeing are intertwined in two ways: on the one hand, innovation is a prerequisite for productivity, progress and growth, which can provide the means for a high level of wellbeing in highly developped societies; on the other hand, a high level of wellbeing in a society can provide a fruitful basis for innovation – on the supply as well as the demand side.

Innovations are often referred to as the path to economic growth. They are made possible by visionary entrepreneurs, creative employees and smart users as well as promising, groundbreaking and revolutionary technologies, products and services. But innovation is more than just technologies that enable new products to be sold in emerging markets – markets that are often created by these innovations. Innovations in telecommunications (telegraph, telephone, radio, television, Internet), means of transport (trains, cars, aircraft) and health (penicillin, X-rays, vaccination) have not only created new product markets, but have often helped to solve societal problems and to rise the level of wellbeing in a society. At the same time, however, innovations are always ambivalent.[19] Because of their revolutionary nature, they can also have adverse effects. Structural change brought about by productivity gains can have negative effects on employment and industrial relations, and in some cases on the social cohesion. It is probably no coincidence that a single engine (the steam engine) is the symbol of the entire industrial revolution and the emergence of a new system of social relations.

Many experts compare the current technological process of digitalisation with the revolutionary effects of steam power. In their opinion, the so-called "second machine age"[20] will have similar consequences for labour and social relations as the first. As a result of the innovations of recent decades, the societies of the 21st century will experience a phase of in-

19 *Bader, V./Buhr, D.* 2020: Die Ambivalenz des Neuen. Sozialer Fortschritt durch Plattformen, Blockchain und KI? Bonn: Friedrich-Ebert-Stiftung. http://library.fes.de/pdf-files/wiso/15998.pdf (29/02/2020).

20 *Brynjolfsson, E./McAfee, A.* 2014: The Second Machine Age: Work, Progress, and Prosperity in a Time of Brilliant Technologies, New York.

tensive transformation.[21] Not just in Germany, the debate on the predicted digitisation of industry (Industrie 4.0) is being labelled "megatrend", which has the potential to fundamentally change both production processes and industrial relations in the coming years.

In addition to the changes in industrial production and social relations due to digitisation, societies at the beginning of the 21st century are already facing several other "major challenges": demographic ageing, climate change and increasing inequality, to name but a few. Innovations can foster technological developments such as the digitisation of industry, households and governments, but they can also be used to address societal challenges. In this case, technical innovations become "social innovations". In an analysis of the status quo, development and consequences of industrial digitisation in Germany ("Industry 4.0"), Buhr[22] defines social innovations as innovations that, on the one hand, contribute to the dissemination and diffusion of technical developments at the societal level and, on the other hand, represent practices that are developed and used by affected individuals, groups and organisations and serve to address societal challenges. According to Howaldt and Kopp[23], a social innovation is a reconfiguration of social practices in specific fields of action or social contexts, which starts from specific actors or constellations of actors and is aimed at satisfying or solving needs or problems better than is possible on the basis of established practices. According to the Vienna Declaration[24], social innovation is an urgent alternative to technology-oriented innovations that cannot solve the major societall challenges of our time on their own.

However, the impact of technological innovations on society depends on how it deals with them. And this in turn inevitably depends on the political measures that are intended to steer the course of technological innovations within a welfare state. This is where social policies merge with innovation policies. Normative spoken, by focusing on societal needs, the state must become an active and central actor in the promotion, development and regulation of innovations. More importantly, the state has to promote innovations in areas where market actors fail, which, however, are important for the wellbeing of the people (i.e. digitalisation as a prerequiste for digital health and care solutions, education and qualification, participation etc.). In her study on the emergence and development of innovations in Western societies in the 20th and 21st centuries, Mazzucato writes:

> "[T]he state has not acted as an intruder in the private sector in the past, but as an important partner of this sector [...] Governments have stepped in with the necessary investments along the entire innovation chain [...], which the private sector has been afraid to make."[25]

Such a state is not only a motor for innovation, but ideally also in a position to understand possible challenges for society and to address them adequately. With regard to the societal challenges mentioned above, to political participation, to the interaction of citizens, and to

---

21 *Rifkin, J.* 2014: The zero marginal cost society. The internt of things, the collaborative commons, and the eclipse of capitalism, New York.

22 *Buhr, D.* 2015: Social Innovation Policy for Industry 4.0, Good Society – Social Democracy #2017plus, Friedrich-Ebert-Stiftung, Bonn. http://library.fes.de/pdf-files/wiso/11479.pdf (29/02/2020).

23 *Howaldt, J./Kopp, R.* 2012: Shaping social innovation by social research, Berlin, p. 47.

24 *Vienna Declaration* 2011: Vienna Declaration: The most needed social innovations and other research topics. http://www.sfs.tu-dortmund.de/cms/en/social_innovation/publications/Vienna_Declaration_version_02.pdf (06/04/2020).

25 *Mazzucato, M.* 2015: The Innovative State: Governments should make markets, not just fix them: In: Foreign Affairs Jan/Feb https://www. foreignaffairs.com/articles/americas/2014-12-15/innovative-state (29/02/2020).

the way in which the Internet and social media can have redistributive effects, Runciman argues that it is here, where policies independent of corporate political power can enable and guarantee the positive social effects of technological and social innovations.[26] In times when the digital economy is changing both economic and social life, a state oriented towards the common good cannot simply stand on the sidelines as a spectator, but must find ways to channel technological and social transformations to the benefit of the vast majority of a society[27]: improving wellbeing. As Brynjolfsson et al.[28] argue, increasing digitisation of the economy and society can both improve living conditions and reduce social inequality, but it also carries with it the high risk of exacerbating negative trends (such as increasing inequality and capital concentration), given the changes in the labour market for unskilled and low-skilled workers. According to the authors, a social innovation policy must focus on an active role of the state in securing and regulating investments in areas such as education and basic research in order to ensure a positive development of the "second machine age"[29].

5 Fostering Innovation Capabilities

Welfare states, however, are not only provider of welfare services, they also pay for and procure social and technological innovations. They shape, according to their specific architecture and institutional setting, the needs and demands for those as well as the conditions for innovation on the supply side (i.e. "human capital", R&D investments etc.). These conditions could be subsumed as "innovation capability" of a society. Innovation capability is a precondition of innovative performance and the distribution of knowledge. Just like a person's intelligence is a precondition for his or her intellectual output. In a more digitalized world, companies and their personnel have to strengthen their "interaction competence"[30], which refers to skills and abilities of an organisation to successfully implement processes of (open) innovation even more. Due to the fact that these processes, innovative products and services are increasingly marked by cross-sector technological integration, economy demands networked collaboration between differing skill sets and knowledge caches. With growing digitisation, the latter will likely become codified and easily passed on. From this stems the need to combine each party's own competencies with the complementary knowledge and conduct of the others'.[31]

---

26 *Runciman, D.* 2015: Digital Politics: Why Progressives Need to Shape Rather than Merely Exploit the Digital Economy. In: Social Europe Online 22(1).

27 Ibidem.

28 *Brynjolfsson et al.* 2014 (fn. 20).

29 *Alaja, A./Andersson, L. F./Buhr, D./Fink, P./Stöber, N.* 2016: Policies for innovation in times of digitalization: a comparative report on innovation policies in Finland, Sweden and Germany. Bonn: Friedrich-Ebert-Stiftung, Division of Economic and Social Policy. Good society - social democracy #2017 plus. http://library.fes.de/pdf-files/wiso/12512.pdf (29/02/2020).

30 *Howaldt, J./Beerheide, E.* 2010: Innovationsmanagement im Enterprise 2.0 – Auf dem Weg zu einem neuen Innovatinosparadigma? In: *Howaldt, J./ Jacobsen, H. (eds.)*: Soziale Innovation, Berlin, pp. 355–370 (358 et seq.).

31 Ibidem.

On the level of the firm, this innovation capability is determined by

a. the stock of knowledge available for this firm and
b. the firm's ability to combine useful knowledge

Based on this, the German Institute for Innovation and Technology (IIT) developed the "Innovation Capability Indicator". The iit Innovation Capability Indicator consists of the four sub-indicators human capital, complexity capital, structural capital and relational capital. Well-educated workforce is a key factor for innovation capability. The IIT takes into account human capital, i.e. the qualification levels of formal and informal education and training. Innovation needs different ideas and concepts. The diversity of knowledge that enables the production of complex products is called complexity capital. Structural capital refers to internal structures and processes bringing together the heterogeneous knowledge that is distributed within an organization. An organization's ability to acquire and combine knowledge is also affected by its external relations, i.e. its relationships to external partners. This is referred to as relational capital.

By ranking EU countries according to their innovation capability, we can see that Scandinavian (social-democratic) welfare states are traditionally leading the IIT indicator:

Position	2014	2018
1.	Finland	Sweden
2.	Sweden	Austria
3.	Denmark	Finland
4.	Germany	Germany
5.	Austria	Slovenia
6.	Slovenia	United Kingdom
7.	United Kingdom	Denmark
…	…	…
21.	Lithuania	Portugal
22.	Romania	Romania
23.	Latvia	Bulgaria
24.	Greece	Latvia
25.	Bulgaria	Greece

Source: *IIT* 2018.[32]

In contrast to arguments by (neo)liberal authors like Hayek and Smith, highly developed labour market regulations, strong institutions and rather generous and universalistic welfare states might not be a downside for innovation and economic growth. Radcliff[33] was able to show how important labor organization are for promoting human happiness. His empirical analyses suggest two fundamental conclusions: (1) individuals who belong to (or are represented by) labor unions have higher levels of life satisfaction that others of similar income, education, age, gender, marital status, physical health, and other similar factors, and, more importantly (2) that the aggregate level of labor organization – the "density" of organi-

32 *IIT Innovation Capability Indicator* 2018: https://www.iit-berlin.de/en/indicator (29/02/2020).

33 *Radcliff, B.* 2005: Class Organization and Subjective Well-Being. In: Social Forces, vol. 84(1), pp. 513–530.

zation, meaning the percentage of the work force organized – appears to increase subjective appraisal of life for everyone, whether members of unions or not. These effects, he stresses, are independent of the impact unions might have on life satisfaction through their traditional support for the welfare state. Following Radcliff[34], who – based on the analysis of time serial data across various democracies – argued that the universality and generosity of the welfare state (i.e. the extent of decommodification) is the single most important societal-level structural factor affecting the quality of human life, we could ask: Are social standards, as in socially responsible regulations, not a disadvantage for economic growth, but rather the foundation of innovative societies in which both producers and users benefit from innovation? Then, a high level of wellbeing, i.e. a good health, housing and social life, a high level of self-effectiveness, education and skills, good work as well as stable political ("good governance") and economic conditions, would be a prerequisite for not only social but also economic progress.

Kattel/Mazzucato[35] show, that more and more states react towards this finding. Innovation policies are transforming. This transformation matter because,

> "[…] established practices and institutions continue to operate with the chief aim of improving innovation capacities by 'getting the structures right,' thereby sidestepping the question 'getting the structures right to achieve what?'"[36]

And thus, it is not only innovation policy which is affected but increasingly also its spillovers into other areas that influence the wellbeing of the people. According to Kattel/Mazzucato[37], this "normative turn" is based on much more "distributed agency" that has been the case with previous iterations. Besides governments, academia, business sector and other welfare service providers also civil society, NGOs and social movements play an increaseingly important role in shaping the innovation capability of a society.[38]

This is also touching questions of social justice and economic inequalities. If citizen wellbeing and happiness are truly the goals of government, then taking seriously research on institutional and cultural determinants of citizen happiness is the first step in starting an evidence-based journey towards fulfilling that goal.[39] Economic theory discusses the relationship between inequality or poverty on the one hand and economic growth, prosperity and wellbeing on the other. In principle, two opposing positions can be identified:[40] Willingness to perform and efficiency are threatened by inequality and lead to a lower development of

34 *Radcliff, B.* 2013: The Political Economy of Human Happiness: How Voters' Choices Determine the Quality of Life, Cambridge.

35 *Kattel, R./Mazzucato, M.* 2018: Mission-oriented innovation policy and dynamic capabilities in the public sector. UCL Institute for Innovation and Public Purpose, Working Paper Series (IIPP WP 2018-5). http://www.ucl.ac.uk/bartlett/public-purpose/wp2018-05 (29/02/2020).

36 *Lindner, R./Daimer, S./Beckert, B./Heyen, N./Koehler, J./Teufel, B./Warnke, P./Wydra, S.* 2016: Addressing directionality: Orientation failure and the systems of innovation heuristic. Towards reflexive governance'. In: Fraunhofer ISI Discussion Papers Innovation Systems and Policy Analysis No. 52, p. 2.

37 *Kattel/Mazzucato* 2018 (fn. 35).

38 *Kuhlmann, S./Rip, A.* 2018: Next Generation Innovation Policy and Grand Challenges. In: Science and public policy, Vol. 45, Issue 4, August 2018, pp. 448–454. DOI: 10.1093/scipol/scy011.

39 *Helliwell, J./Layard, R./Sachs, J. D./De Neve, J.-E.* 2020: World Happiness Report 2020, New York: Sustainable Development Solutions Network. http://www.worldhappiness.report/ (29/03/2020).

40 See also *Eißel, D.* 2018: Ungleichheit und Armut als Movens von Wachstum und Wohlstand? In: *Huster, E.-U./Boeckh, J./Mogge-Grotjahn, H. (eds.)*: Handbuch Armut und soziale Ausgrenzung, Wiesbaden, pp. 77–96.

prosperity if, as a result of inequality, the functioning of the economic system is threatened by disturbance of social peace, according to one thesis (e.g. Plato, John Maynard Keynes, John Rawls, Amartya Sen). Here, growing inequality can also lead to a lack of purchasing power for the poor, while the rich increase their savings, which leads to a decline in demand and could impair economic growth.

The drive to achieve general prosperity is attributed to inequality, according to the opposing thesis (e.g. August von Hayek, Milton Friedman, John Stuart Mill, and in part Adam Smith). The poor would make efforts to emulate the living standards of the rich, thus contributing to the general development of prosperity in society; the rich invest profitably in jobs and create conditions for the (unintended) wellbeing of the poorer. Their position is generally about the withdrawal of the state from the economy and the maximum release of market forces or the renunciation of the social correction of market activity.

When it comes to wellbeing, current empirical analyses show how important the social environment is not only for current life satisfaction but also for the future development of a welfare state. The World Happiness Report[41] uses six factors as predictors of life evaluation (and measuring wellbeing): GDP per capita, social support, healthy life expectancy, freedom to make life choices, generosity, and corruption. Social-democratic welfare states like Finland, Sweden and Denmark rank high not only in life satisfaction, but also in social support, freedom to make life choices, and lack of corruption. In fact, the Nordic countries occupy the top positions across the world for social support, and are all in top ten for freedom.

> "The Nordic countries are characterized by a virtuous cycle in which various key institutional and cultural indicators of good society feed into each other including well-functioning democracy, generous and effective social welfare benefits, low levels of crime and corruption, and satisfied citizens who feel free and trust each other and governmental institutions" (Helliwell et al. 2020: 140).

Another interesting finding: due to the universalistic approach of their welfare states, there is less inequality and less inequality in happiness in the Nordic countries. In more equal societies, people trust each other more.[42] This increased trust contributes in the long term to a preference for a stronger and more universal welfare state.[43]

Helliwell et al. also show

> "that individuals with higher levels of interpersonal and institutional trust fare significantly better than others in several negative situations, including ill-health, unemployment, low incomes, discrimination, family breakdown, and fears about the safety of the streets. Living in a trusting social environment helps not only to support all individual lives directly, but also reduces the well-being costs of adversity. This provides the greatest gains to those in the most difficult circumstances, and thereby reduces well-being inequality. As our new evidence shows, to reduce well-being inequality also improves average life evaluations."[44]

And: yes, there is a high correlation between wellbeing and innovativeness. One could argue that social and technological innovation provide the basis for this, thus not only fostering future growth, but also wellbeing. Those groups with a high level of formal and informal

---

41 *Helliwell et al.* 2020 (fn. 39).

42 *Elgar, F. J./Aitken, N.* 2011: Income inequality, trust and homicide in 33 countries. In: European Journal of Public Health, 21(2), pp. 241–246; *Uslaner, E. M./Brown, M.* 2005: Inequality, trust, and civic engagement. In: American Politics Research, 33(6), pp. 868–894.

43 *Delhey, J./Dragolov, G.* 2016: Happier together. Social cohesion and subjective well-being in Europe. In: International Journal of Psychology, 51(3), pp. 163–176.

44 *Helliwell et al.* 2020 (fn. 39), p. 14 f.

education and training (human capital; complexity capital) and wellbeing are the ones that trust other people and institutions (social/relational as well as structural capital) the most, which is, of course, very important and beneficial for (open) innovation processes.

6 Conclusion

Regarding wellbeing and innovative capabilities, we can see the benefit of a functioning welfare state and the need for greater public intervention. Alaja et al.[45] argue that this is indispensable for innovation processes within a framework of common welfare and future orientation. The modernisation of societies should then mean promoting not only economic growth but also social progress. With regard to the current economic strategies of various welfare states or the EU's ambition to create a (digital) single market, it is clear that in this context the talk is mainly of economic and technological performance, but very rarely a link is made to the growing participation of citizens or workers – and certainly not very much to the fight against social inequality.

It is therefore important to intensify the debate at European level, since societies in the individual Member States are strongly linked by the internal market and are therefore also affected by social standards, opportunities and restrictions in other European welfare states. Interestingly enough, innovation leaders like Germany and Austria, but even more Sweden, Finland and Denmark do have a very well-equipped welfare-state. Obviously, high social standards and a high density of labour organization are not hindering economic growth but instead foster the innovative capability of a society by providing a high level of publicly financed education and research as well as health, social security and participation.

Especially the social-democratic welfare states fared also very well in the 2020 World Happiness Report.[46] Its central purpose is to review the science of measuring and understanding subjective well-being, and to use survey measures of life satisfaction to track the quality of lives as they are being lived in more than 150 countries. Finland (1.), Denmark (2.), Iceland (4.), Norway (5.), Sweden (7.) finished for the years 2017-2019 all within the top ten of the study, which examines countries' happiness by income, healthy life expectancy, social support, freedom, trust, generosity and absence of corruption. Other wealthy countries such as Germany (17.), the U.S. (18.), South Korea (61.) and Japan (62.), but also Russia (73.) and China (94.), scored much lower in the ranking. When we think of welfare states as instituionalized enablers of the current as well as the future wellbeing of their citizens by also fostering the innovation capabilites of a society, this above-mentioned ranking should make us think a lot.

45 *Alaja et al.* 2016 (fn. 29).
46 *Helliwell et al.* 2020 (fn. 39).

Social Innovation and Public Participation

Yuliya A. Petrovskaya

Abstract: This article analyzes the role of public participation in the process of social innovation implementation. The article examines in detail the activities of NGOs in the field of social services, as well as the development of social entrepreneurship. Both of these forms of public participation are considered mechanisms of the modernization of the Russian social sphere. Social innovations are analyzed in terms of the positive changes they bring about in society and using an institutional approach. The empirical basis for this article is the results of a two-part study which included an analysis of the role of NGOs in the modernization of the Russian social service system, and the study of social entrepreneurship as it relates to social services. The main purpose of the study was to analyze the capabilities and potential of these two factors in the modernization of the social sphere, and to identify the main obstacles in their development in Russia. The study was composed of several different types of survey methods. The results of this research identified the main factors and barriers preventing the expansion of NGOs and the development of social entrepreneurs as providers of social services. The main obstacles proved to be administrative challenges and human factors involving interaction between the aforementioned groups and the general population. The research concluded that in Russia it is still too early to talk about competition in the social services market between the state and non-state actors. NGOs and social entrepreneurs are not yet able to compete with state social service institutions and the general population remain unwilling to pay for social services from non-state providers.

Keywords: social innovation, social wellbeing, social services, subjects of social services, social entrepreneurship, NGOs.

Introduction

As in many countries, the state remains the main provider of social services in Russia. Despite this, the provision of social welfare in Russia is no simple matter. The system is made up of a number of departments and governmental agencies as well as an increasing number of public organizations and other civil actors forming a complex net of available social services. As civil society continues to develop in Russia, the non-governmental sector has come to occupy an increasingly important position in all spheres of life. Non-profit organizations often perform functions that the state and governmental institutions cannot always perform. Because of this, NGOs have become an increasingly prominent part of the everyday lives of citizens and society. NGOs act as carriers of new ideas in the social sphere and apply their human and financial resources in order to promote the use of innovative approaches for solving important social issues.

There are many scientific approaches to understanding social innovation presented in the scientific literature. Some approaches focus on the role that new technologies, business models, and innovations have in developing groundbreaking products. Others prefer to analyze the social impact of innovations. This latter approach contends that the goal of social innovation is to improve people's wellbeing, quality of life, and the social infrastructure including new and accessible social services for the population based on information technologies, new forms and methods of work with different groups of the population . Geoff Mulgan is one of many academics who ascribe to this school of thinking. Mulgan focuses on the institutional and organizational aspects of social innovation and argued that "Social innovation is innovative activity and services which are designed to meet social needs, and which are mainly developed and distributed through social organizations"[1]. From this point of view, social innovations can be an effective tool for improving social welfare. Among the social organizations that develop, implement and distribute innovations, there may be not only state institutions, but also public organizations. In today's world, under conditions of resource scarcity, public participation is of particular importance.

Public participation is a continuous process of interaction between the organization responsible for decision-making and citizens whose interests may be affected by direct or indirect consequences of these decisions, as well as state regulatory bodies of various levels. At a minimum this process of interaction includes:

- Measures to promote a full public understanding of the decision-making processes of the responsible agency or agencies, and mechanisms for investigating emerging environmental and social problems;
- full public awareness of the status and stage of development of projects and policies;
- opportunities to receive information, provide feedback, regarding projects and policies;
- the active collection of opinions from all interested citizens regarding their perception of the goals and objectives of the project, as well as their preferences regarding the use of resources, alternative development strategies, and any other information related to the decision.[2]

Research Methodology and Methods

When analyzing the role of public participation in the innovative development of the Russian social sphere, it is necessary to pay special attention to two main forms of public participation: the expansion of NGO activities in the field of social services and the development of social entrepreneurship as providers of social services. Currently, Russia is in dire need of organizations that can provide quality social services that cover the gaps in coverage left by

1 *Mulgan, G.* 2006: The process of social innovation. In: Innovations, 2006, pp. 145–162. See also: *Mulgan, G./ Tucker, S./Ali, R./Sanders B.* 2007. Social innovation: what it is, why it matters and how it can be accelerate, London.

2 *Canter, L.W.* 1996: Environmental Impact Assessment, 2nd edition, New York.

the state[3]. Using innovative services and technologies, NGOs and social entrepreneurs have great potential to cover these gaps.

Currently, the system of social services in the Russian Republic of Karelia includes a large number of institutions providing social services to various categories of citizens. In the Republic of Karelia, 47 organizations have the status of social service providers. Only 11 of these organizations are non-governmental: six non-profits, and five commercial enterprises.[4] Thus, the Karelian social service system includes:

- State and municipal institutions:
    - 4 boarding houses for elderly and disabled persons
    - 2 psycho-neurological boarding houses
    - 1 children's house-boarding school for mentally disabled children
    - 1 social and health center
    - 1 social rehabilitation center for children
    - 1 rehabilitation center for children and adolescents with disabilities
    - 18 centers of social service of the population
    - 9 centers for children without parental care
- Non-governmental (commercial and non-commercial) social service organizations with social service provider status:
    - 3 charitable foundations
    - 3 autonomous non-profit organizations
    - 5 commercial organizations
- Socially oriented NGOs without social service provider status

The first stage of our research was devoted to the analysis of the role of non-profit organizations in the modernization of the social service system. Our analysis was based on the results of:

- semi-structured interviews of seven representatives of non-profit organizations which provide social services in the Republic of Karelia[5];
- semi-structured interviews of seven representatives of municipal and state institutions of social services for the population of Petrozavodsk[6];
- surveys of 40 representatives of different socially oriented NGOs in Petrozavodsk[7];
- interviews with two experts: 1 representative of the Ministry of social protection of the Republic of Karelia and 1 representative of Municipal Administration.

3 The framework of legal regulations is set up in the Federal Law "On bases of social services of citizens in the Russian Federation". *Russian Federation* 2013: On bases of social service of citizens in the Russian Federation (2013). The Federal law of 28.12.2013, No. 442-FZ. Taken by State Duma 23 of December 2013, Approved by Federation Council 25 December 2013. http://www.consultant.ru/document/cons_doc_LAW_156558/ (31/03/2020).

4 *Register of social service providers*: Official website of the Ministry of social protection of the Republic of Karelia. http://minsoc.karelia.ru/serviceproviders/index (31/03/2020).

5 General population at the time of the study – seven organizations.

6 General population – five public institutions of social services located in Petrozavodsk.

7 General population – 1361 non-profit organizations registered in the Republic of Karelia (as of March 4, 2018). The sample was stratified by the location of the organization. In addition, political parties, professional unions, religious, sports, environmental organizations, as well as private and educational institutions were excluded from the General population.

The use of empirical methods allowed us to determine the role of NGOs in the social service system, to analyze the main forms of their interaction with state social service institutions, state and municipal authorities, as well as the main barriers to intersectoral interaction in the social service system of the population of Petrozavodsk. The information obtained as a result of the study is applied, based on the experience of the respondents' professional activities.

The second stage of the study was devoted to development of social entrepreneurship in the social service system. Our analysis was based on the results of:

- Five semi-structured interviews with social entrepreneurs. The general population is relatively small, and its exact characteristics are not known for sure. Sampling was carried out using the available array based on the information about the participants of the contest "Best entrepreneur" in the category "Social entrepreneurship" held by the Ministry of economic development and industry of Karelia, based on data from "Directory of social entrepreneurs", information from the Register of providers of social services in the Republic of Karelia, as well as information retrieval.
- Interview with a representative of the Ministry of social protection of the Republic of Karelia.

This study uses a qualitative approach in the analysis of social entrepreneurship due to the uniqueness of survey and interview data that cannot be quantified.

Results

The results of empirical research have shown that today the number of NGOs providing social services does not fully meet the population's need for affordable social services, especially in rural areas. In addition, all NGOs that have the official status of a social service provider are concentrated on the territory of Petrozavodsk. In other regions of the Republic of Karelia, there are none.[8] At the same time, because of the long distances between cities and villages, rural areas have particular difficulties in obtaining social services provided by state institutions.

NGOs have great innovative potential for solving social problems because, as a rule, non-governmental actors of social services work locally. Therefore, they focus on local mitigation of acute social problems, and the provision of absent social services. Interaction between social service providers is situational rather than systematic. Most often, the interaction is carried out in the framework of joint projects, one-time events, and client specific cases. As a result, most interactions between organizations and citizens occur out of necessity. Despite this relative independence, the existing model of interaction between social entrepreneurs, NGOs and the state in the sphere of social services is characterized by a high degree of state control. Organizations with the status of social service providers have the right to receive compensation from the state for the provision of specific services, but in order to do so they must inevitably report their activities to the state. We do not claim to justify the need to decentralize the social service system in favor of NGOs. The state is the main subject of social protection of the population in Russia. However, NGOs have a great potential to com-

8 *Register of social service providers* (fn. 4).

plement the state's efforts to improve the quality and accessibility of social services, to introduce innovative technologies and projects in this area, and attract additional resources, including human resources. These provisions are also argued by other researchers.[9]

In the first phase of the study, we identified the main obstacles to increasing the participation of NGOs in the social service system. These obstacles could be divided into two groups. The first group is administrative and bureaucratic barriers. These included the lack of legislative regulation of intersectoral interaction (the absence of a legislative document regulating intersectoral social partnership, the distribution of responsibilities, and well-developed financial mechanisms for providing social services in NGOs) in the social sphere, different conditions for the provision of social services by state institutions and NGOs, a narrow list of social services that qualified for state subsidies, and the actual inability of NGOs and social entrepreneurs to receive compensation from the state for the provision of urgent social services. These circumstances limit the innovative potentials of non-profit organizations because NGOs-social service providers must pursue and provide publicly funded services instead of pursuing innovative alternative services.

The second group of obstacles is human and social barriers. These include a lack of readiness by the population to introduce innovations in the social sphere, the lack of basic competencies in the innovative economy, distrust of NGOs, the prevailing belief that providing social services is the prerogative of the state, and the concentration of non-state providers of social services in the city of Petrozavodsk, while the most acute situation with the availability of social services is in rural areas; etc. Our study allowed us to formulate an assumption about the low level of innovation susceptibility of the population of Karelia. This assumption was tested in another empirical study conducted by us in Petrozavodsk in 2018–2019.

The purpose of the study is to identify the main factors that affect the innovative susceptibility of organizations of various forms of ownership (state and non-state, including commercial structures and NGOs). The two-stage sample consisted of 30 organizations (10 of each type) selected using the available array method. At the second stage, respondents were selected. The main method used was a semi-structured interview based, rather, on a qualitative approach. In connection with the specifics of activity and management in organizations, it is necessary to analyze state institutions, business representatives and the "third sector" separately. In the study of innovative receptivity objectives were to identify what is perceived by the institution as an innovation introduced into the organization, and what innovations are most often introduced; to identify the main factors that hinder the innovation process in organizations.

Among the main interview questions relevant to the research objectives were the following: have any innovations been implemented in the organization over the past three years? If implemented, which ones? What information technologies are used in the organization? What, in the opinion of respondents, prevents the introduction of innovations in their organizations? How is the manager's personality, and which of his traits affect the process of introducing or restraining innovation in the organization? Does the social climate in their organization affect the innovation process? At the end of the interview, we asked the respondents

9 *Chernenkova, E.* 2016: About state support of socially oriented NGOs in municipalities of the Republic of Karelia. In: Selfgovernment, 2016, No. 5, pp. 38–41.

to evaluate the level of scientific and technical potential of the Republic of Karelia from the standpoint of their personal and professional opinion.

The study included interviews with representatives of government agencies in various fields. Most respondents noted that their organization has introduced any innovations over the past 3 years. The most frequently cited innovations by respondents were the use of new information technologies and the introduction of new methods of working with clients. The least frequent innovations were the development and implementation of a new organizational structure for managing the organization and the development of new markets and promotion methods. Thus, among employees of state institutions, innovation is primarily associated with the development of information and Internet technologies. Taking into account that there were no people working in production among the respondents, it is logical that the innovations that were mentioned do not relate to new production technologies but are more often aimed at improving the work with the client.

According to respondents, the main obstacles to innovation in the organization are lack of resources, human factors, and high costs. Half of all respondents believe that the main factor that most affects the containment of innovation in the organization is "lack of motivation" to innovations. Equally, the following options were noted: lack of interest in self-development and self-realization among employees; lack of work experience among specialists; insufficient competence and qualification of employees. Our respondents were asked about the role of the manager in implementing innovations in the institution. In most cases, respondents think that many government agencies simply lack experience in implementing innovations. Respondents, in this regard, noted that the management is not ready for the risk associated with innovations. Today, many state institutions are undergoing a process of unification and reorganization, which leads to a change of leadership. The new manager is not always familiar enough with the problems of this organization, which provokes a slowdown in the development of the organization, while the manager needs to actively cooperate with the team and work together to develop innovative solutions, since the social climate in the organization has a great influence on the motivation and perception of innovations. At the same time, respondents – representatives of state structures noted that the innovative, scientific and technical potential of institutions in the districts of the Republic of Karelia are different. Public sector organizations themselves are limited in their ability to innovate because of the rigid and inflexible system in which they operate.

When studying the innovative susceptibility of NGOs, 10 organizations were selected that carry out their activities in educational activities, protection of children's rights, promotion of a healthy lifestyle, prevention of socially significant diseases, regulation of interethnic relations, and the social sphere. Interviews were conducted with the heads of organizations. This is due to the peculiarities of the NGO structure. Quite often, the staff of NGO is very small, and employees, including the head, combine a number of functions. Sometimes only the manager is officially registered in such organizations. Over the past three years, 7 out of 10 organizations have introduced innovations in their activities. Just as in the case of government agencies, most of these innovations were related to the introduction of new methods of working with the client and new information technologies. This can be explained by the fact that often NGOs, especially socially oriented ones, work in areas of activity that are related to the activities of state institutions. None of our respondents indicated such options as "developing new markets and ways to promote services", "using previously unused methods of labor motivation".

Summarizing the results of interviews conducted with representatives of the "third sector", we can note that all of them use and implement new information and Internet technologies, electronic document management, local networks. In NGOs, according to the study participants, the key obstacle to innovative development is the human factor. As for resources, NGOs often do not apply for state funding, so their financial and resource support depends solely on the activity of the head and members of the organization. An important factor in implementing innovations in organizations is the qualification and experience of the managers themselves. According to the respondents, these professional qualities are not enough for modern managers. After all, the sphere of innovative development is specific and requires special professional and personal competencies.

The business sector has a number of features in terms of the target orientation of organizations. Any innovations, one way or another, are aimed at improving economic efficiency, even if they do not directly entail an instant increase in profits. As part of the study, interviews were conducted with representatives of 10 business sector organizations, mainly in the sphere of tourism and sales, all representatives of small and medium-sized businesses, that is, business structures typical for the Republic of Karelia. The interview was attended by specialists and managers of organizations.

According to the respondents, all organizations participating in the study have introduced any innovations over the past 3 years. Due to the specifics of organizations' activities, the answer "developing new markets and ways to promote products and services" was popular. The other two most frequently heard responses: "applying new information technologies" and "introducing new methods of working with clients" completely coincide with the situation in state institutions and NGOs. Attention is still focused on innovations related to information and Internet technologies: electronic document management, the Internet, licensed programs, and local networks. When analyzing the factors that hinder the introduction of innovations, business representatives indicate such a specific factor as the high cost of borrowed funds for the introduction of innovations. This is due to the peculiarities of doing business. For the rest, representatives of commercial structures, as well as state institutions and NGOs, emphasize the lack of resources and the human factor. The human factor is most often understood as a lack of experience among specialists, as well as a lack of motivation to implement innovations. In contrast to representatives of NGOs, employees of commercial organizations do not indicate a lack of competence and qualification of employees, since, as a rule, when applying for employment in a business organization, there is a strict selection of personnel. The human factor also applies to the head of the organization. Most often, among his qualities that prevent the introduction of innovations in the organization from the business sphere, is a lack of preparedness for risk.

The results of the study from the standpoint of the sociological approach allow us to conclude that the organizations of Petrozavodsk are not sufficiently high in terms of innovation susceptibility, regardless of the form of ownership. Government agencies, non-profit organizations and representatives of business structures note different, specific for their activities, factors that hinder the introduction of innovations, but all respondents note the human factor as such an obstacle, which is primarily expressed in low motivation to implement innovations. There is an assumption that insufficient motivation is generated by the lack of a clear understanding of the positive long-term consequences of innovation, and in some cases, the lack of necessary innovative competencies.[10]

The scientists from the Institute of Economics of the Karelian scientific center of the Russian Academy of Sciences noted that the quality, diversity and availability of social services lag behind the existing needs in society in these services. The study was conducted on the territory of municipal settlements of Pryazhinsky, Suoyarvsky and Olonetsky districts of the Republic of Karelia. The target sample was formed covering the following categories of citizens: elderly people, handicapped people, large families in a crisis situation, other categories of citizens. The sociological research was focused on the solution three complex tasks:

- determine the level of provision of social services in remote areas of Karelia, the level of training of specialists in providing services;
- investigate the quality, availability and need of social services provided to certain categories of the population;
- create a model for more effective service delivery in remote areas, and a theoretical basis for training workers in the provision of social services.

"The disparity between the demand for social services and their supply in Karelia can actualize further development of social services and a search for hitherto unused or overlooked resources in supplying social services"[11]. One of these resources is social entrepreneurship.

Social entrepreneurship is a relatively new phenomenon in Russia, and it is just beginning to develop. It holds the potential to be a promising new direction for solving and mitigating acute social problems, involving the creation of social welfare not through pure charity, but through profitable or partially profitable activities.

Researchers have not yet developed a unified approach to understanding the essence of this socio-economic phenomenon. Despite this, social entrepreneurship is an important subject for current and future study given its potential impact on the social sphere. Particular interest should be paid to the local features which contribute to or hinder its formation and development Social entrepreneurs have the opportunity to develop and offer completely new social services to communities and to compete against existing providers of social services in existing service provision. In addition, they work at the local community level, so they are able to solve people's problems purposefully.

In our research, we studied the activities of social entrepreneurs as providers of social services in Petrozavodsk. Our research identified the motivations, main forms, goals, and scale of the activities of social entrepreneurs in the region. It also identified the existing opportunities and barriers in the market of social services as well as the regulatory frame-

---

10 *Petrovskaya, Yu.* 2019: Innovative receptivity of organizations: sociological approaches. In: Vestnik of Lobachevsky State University of Nizhniy Novgorod. Social Sciences, No. 3 (55), Nizhni Novgorod, S. 107–114.

11 *Morozova, T./Kozyreva, G./Belaya, R.* 2015: Problems of formation of modern models of social services (on the example of remote territories of the Republic of Karelia). In: Proceedings of the Karelian scientific center RAS, 3, pp. 103–116. https://cyberleninka.ru/article/n/problemy-formirovaniya-sovremennyh-modeley-sotsialnogo-obsluzhivaniya-na-primere-otdalennyh-territoriy-respubliki-kareliya (31/03/2020).

work in which social entrepreneurship operates in Petrozavodsk. The general population of social entrepreneurs is small. The samples used for our data set were identified using the available array based on the information about the participants of the contest "Best entrepreneur" in the category "Social entrepreneurship" held by the Ministry of economic development and industry of Karelia, based on data from "Directory of social entrepreneurs", information from the Register of providers of social services in the Republic of Karelia, as well as information retrieval. The participants sampled all took part in the best entrepreneur contest held by the Minister of Economic Development and Industry of Karelia in the category of social entrepreneurship. The sample consisted of five heads of socially oriented commercial organizations:

1) "Medservice Plus" provides services in transportation of disabled people in the territory of Petrozavodsk, Karelia and the neighboring regions.
2) The "Planic" project has been producing cards for alternative communication, communication books and teaching textbooks for children with autism spectrum disorders, cerebral palsy, down syndrome and other diseases.
3) "Harmony" – medical massage room, on the basis of which working places for people with visual impairment are created. The organization provides medical massage services for people with limited mobility, helps people recover from injuries, etc.
4) "Regional service center" is a private boarding house for temporary stay of disabled and elderly people. Social services are provided to citizens in stationary and semi-stationary forms.
5) "Development" is an educational center providing speech therapy services for children and adults.

All of the aforementioned organizations are officially registered either as limited liability companies or as individual entrepreneurs. Two of the five carry out a portion of their activeities on behalf of NGOs. One of the most interesting examples in this regard is a boarding house for the elderly people "Regional service center". This organization is commercial, i.e. it serves the population on individual terms of cooperation for a fee. It is the only private commercial organization included in the register of social service providers of the Republic of Karelia. At the same time on the basis of this organization the charitable Fund "My grandmother" is created, thanks to that the organization has an opportunity to attract additional grant funds and charitable donations. Other 4 respondents-participants of our research indicated that they did not seek direct financial support from the state because of the heavy bureaucratic burden they preferred to avoid.

The vast majority of social entrepreneurs run small businesses, so they are more likely to mitigate one of the social problems than to solve them totally. In our study, we found the main constraint limiting the development of social entrepreneurship in Karelia to be financial. Private organizations can only apply for public financial support if they are included in the regional register of social service providers and subsidies paid only for those services provided to the population that are included in the list of social services. However, activities of many social entrepreneurs are often not compatible with the approved list of traditional social services and are therefore ineligible for state subsidies. Thus, organizations cannot receive a state subsidy for providing innovative social services and can offer these services to the population only for money.

What are the motivations of social entrepreneurs? Researchers in the field of social entrepreneurship often note that social entrepreneurship is often an attempt to cope with personal difficulties.[12] The issue of motivation for the activities of social entrepreneurs is important. The head of the massage room says the following about the reasons for this activity: "the idea of creating a massage room where people with visual impairments would work appeared while working at school. Children begin to learn massage from the age of 14. To get the right to work in this profession, you need to be trained in a special educational institution. But, even after receiving such a profession, not everyone had the opportunity to find a job in Petrozavodsk in their specialty". The head of organization himself also has a visual impairment. The project manager for the production of cards for special children became involved in this area of activity, having a need to provide her own child with special needs in the development of such communication materials. The trauma experienced on his own experience prompted another respondent to organize a service for transporting people with limited mobility. Thus, people often begin to engage in social entrepreneurship, trying to cope with a personal difficult life situation. Also, all respondents noted that the motivation for doing this activity was the desire to change the social reality, to solve or mitigate a certain social problem, love for their work, interest in the process of creating a new one or providing a service.

Among the fundamental characteristics of social entrepreneurship, experts highlight the financial self-sufficiency of activities, as well as the solution of social problems at the expense of income from their own economic activities.[13] All respondents noted that at the current stage of their activities, financial self-sufficiency had been achieved. It is achieved in different ways: the search for start-up capital; attracting grant funds; cooperation with governmental and municipal institutions in order to find premises and reduce rental costs; revenues from the provision of services; participation in governmental programs.

On the issue of self-identification of social entrepreneurs, one out of our five respondents in our survey noted that before the interview identify his organization or its work as a social entrepreneurial project. While other respondents had previously identified themselves as social entrepreneurs, only one respondent expressed interest in establishing and participating in an association of social entrepreneurs to protect their interests and rights. Many of those surveyed feared that new laws regulating social entrepreneurship and governing formal associations would only increase bureaucratic barriers for entrepreneurs. Only one of the four heads of organizations surveyed expressed interest in joining the register of social providers as a mechanism for obtaining financial support from the state. The rest of the respondents expressed concerns about bureaucratic barriers and a lot of paperwork that is required for inclusion in the register and further interaction with the state.

---

12 *Kickul, J./Lyons T.* 2016: Understanding Social Entrepreneurship: The Relentless Pursuit of Mission in an Ever Changing World, 2nd edition, London.

13 *Kaneyskaya, M.V. (ed.)* 2015: Social entrepreneurship as a form of civil participation (based on the results of FOM surveys). http://corp.fom.ru/uploads/files/Socpredprinimatelstvo.pdf.

Conclusion

The non-state sector of social services in the Republic of Karelia is still relatively small and concentrated mainly in the city of Petrozavodsk. Despite the large number of officially registered socially oriented NGOs, there are no NGOs in other districts of the Republic of Karelia with the official status of social service providers. As a result, the non-state sector of social services cannot yet solve one of the most important problems – the problem of access to social services for the entire population. Because of this, it is too early to talk about competition in the market of social services and reducing the burden on public social services institutions.

The main factors hindering the development of social entrepreneurship NGOs activity in the social service sphere are administrative and bureaucratic barriers, and the lack of readiness of the population to welcome innovations in the social sphere. Existing NGOs and social entrepreneurs do not have the opportunity to receive state compensation for their activities due to strict legal restrictions regarding the provision of social services. The development of non-governmental sector of social services in the Republic of Karelia needs serious institutional support.

Leading for Wellbeing with Public Dialogues

Christopher Gohl

Abstract: Public dialogues are a core method to inquire into, evaluate, and provide for communal conditions for wellbeing. Starting with the idea of participative agency and provision in Aristotle's understanding of wellbeing, the article offers an introduction into a contemporary variant of Aristotelian liberalism, the economist Amartya Sen's capability approach. Sen aims for substantive freedoms for everyone as precondition of realizing individual wellbeing on a mass scale. The argument concludes with a pragmatist model of public dialogue situated within an arena of "freedom politics" that allows for the practical adaptation of Sen's capability approach in political communities inquiring into their conflicting or desirable freedoms.

Keywords: Leadership, Wellbeing, Public Dialogues, Participation, Amartya Sen

1 Introduction

What kind of leadership is required for the wellbeing of all? That is a timeless and fundamental question at the heart of civic community building in European history. It has a long tradition in practical and political philosophy, leading us straight back to the ideas of Socrates, Plato, and Aristotle on the communal conditions of a good life. In their quest for answers since, secular philosophers, political leaders, and social scientists have explored different sources of the legitimacy of political order, functions of government, needs of the governed, and the rights, responsibilities, and relationships of all involved. They have done so in critical or inspired correspondence with religious traditions. Prophets, religious leaders, and theologians have cultivated their own perspectives on the communal requirements of religiously observant lives and forms of salvation in this or the next world. Not the least part of wellbeing, however differently understood throughout history, is dependent on the conditions and consequences of economic life, of course. As shall be shown, certain strands of economic discourse may even enlighten our understanding of local democracy and strengthen practical commitments to dialogue.

This article aims to show how and why public dialogues are a central method to inquire into, evaluate, and provide for communal conditions for wellbeing. Starting with the idea of participative agency and provision in Aristotle's understanding of wellbeing (II.), it offers an introduction into a contemporary variant of Aristotelian liberalism, the economist Amartya Sen's capability approach (III.). Sen aims for substantive freedoms for everyone as precondition of realizing individual wellbeing on a mass scale. The argument concludes (IV.) with a pragmatist model of public dialogue situated within an arena of "freedom politics" that allows for the practical adaptation of Sen's capability approach in political communities inquiring into their conflicting or desirable freedoms.

2 Aristotle: No Flourishing without Participative Agency

The common good, of course, came in a variety of shapes. Yet for all their historical variety, conceptions of the common good often trace back to Aristotle. In Aristotle's teleological theory of life, human beings realize their final ends as free agents when they realize *eudaimonia*, a form of ordered wellbeing rather insufficiently translated as "happiness", and sometimes understood as "welfare" or "flourishing". In his Nicomachean Ethics, Aristotle understands _eudaimonia_ to be

> „an objective state of being, to be attained by rational activity [...]. Individuals are 'happy' (well-ordered), when they rationally harmonize their outer and inner world so as to live self-sufficiently [...]. Not fortune or fortunes, but a communal and virtuous lifestyle makes for happiness."[1]

As the philosopher Martha Nussbaum explains, that while he was far from being a liberal in the modern sense of the world, personal agency and choice were very important to Aristotle. He believed that having no say or part in achieving one's own satisfaction was unworthy of your dignity and potential for virtue.[2] At the same time, personal choice wasn't everything. As the son of a doctor, Aristotle knew of the vulnerability of human beings. They need (political) communities to address and overcome their vulnerability and achieve *eudaimonia*. For the wise, balanced and harmonious management of one's own affairs, individuals rely on the presence of exemplary persons who may be imitated, on education provided, on customs and mores to be learned from, and indeed on governments: „(T)he job of government is to make all citizens capable of leading a flourishing life in accordance with their choice"[3].

Promoting a Diversity of Goods

Aristotle did not commit to one single understanding of what was required to achieve *eudaimonia*. He did not believe that one single good needed to be provided nor one single goal realized for all. Neither pleasure nor the satisfaction of certain desires were reliable goods and goals to him. And while wealth certainly was a means to a good life, it could never be equated with welfare itself, which is why he cautioned against an excess of moneymaking (*chrematistike*). In line with the idea of a happy as a well-ordered life, he pleaded for responsible household management (*oikonomia*), where moral laws (*nomoi*) govern households (*oikoi*). As households were an essential political unit, that contributed to the achievement of wellbeing for each and every citizen.[4]

In short, Aristotle understood the incommensurability of diverse goods diverse people rely on in order to achieve their own ends. He conceived of political planning, then, in a democratic city where it could only be concerned with providing conditions for *eudaimonia* to be realized through choices made by people themselves. „Any decent political plan, then, would seek to promote a range of diverse and incommensurable goods, involving the unfolding and development of distinct human abilities. Moreover, it must seek to promote them

1 *Dierksmeier, C./Pirson, M.* 2009: Oikonomia versus chrematistike: Learning from Aristotle about the future orientation of business management. In: Journal of Business Ethics 88, 3, pp. 417–430 (420).

2 *Nussbaum, M.C.* 2011: Creating Capabilities. The Human Development Approach, Cambridge, p. 125.

3 Ibidem, p. 128.

4 *Dierksmeier/Pirson* 2009 (fn. 1), p. 422.

not just for some overall aggregate but for each and every citizen"[5]. Each and every citizen meant, of course, not every human being. Only the Stoics, and later Christian thinkers, extended Aristotle's concern for free adult nonimmigrant males to human beings who by virtue of being human, bore equal worth and dignity.[6]

The Legacy of Aristotle

Aristotle's basic categories and insights into participatory agency in providing a diversity of goods in the service of the common good have inspired philosophers for centuries to come. From Aristotle and Thomas Aquinas to Adam Smith and Amartya Sen today, an ethics concerned with the common good and its participatory provision guided and guides their expectations and conceptions of politics and economics; of their teleological organization towards promoting, their coordination in pursuing, and the balance of individual freedom and collective order in protecting the achievement of the common good.

3 Wellbeing in the Capability Approach of Amartya Sen

Modern Economics and the Common Good

To be sure, modern economics and political thought has often attempted to overcome teleological thinking in the tradition of Aristotle, overloaded as it eventually became with metaphysical, scholastic, and monarchic baggage. With the rise the natural sciences and their methodological rigor, economics and political science have been more concerned about empirical observation of material facts, historic analysis, and sociological theories then with normative explorations.[7] Smith had first proposed that „the common good is not an objective goal to be discerned and pursued but rather the aggregation of individual goods".[8] Casting itself an empirical science in the mold of the natural sciences, economics after Smith turned to find individual preferences (and the common good as merely deductable sum of these), through analysis rather than philosophy and ethics. Over time, it switched from a teleological paradigm to a mechanistic paradigm, adopting epistemological materialism and quantitative reductionism as philosophical and methodological assumptions, and essentially exiling more traditional forms of ethics and questions of the good life and of the common good from economics.[9]

---

5 *Nussbaum* 2011 (fn. 2), p. 127.

6 Ibidem, pp. 128 f.

7 *Marx, K.* 1867: Das Kapital, Hamburg; *Weber, M.* 1918: Der Sinn der "Wertfreiheit" der soziologischen und ökonomischen Wissenschaften, Logos 7. In (reprinted): *Winckelmann, J. (ed.)*: Weber, Max: Gesammelte Aufsätze zur Wissenschaftslehre, Tübingen, 1988; *Almond, G./Powell, G.B.* 1966: Comparative Politics: A developmental approach, Boston.

8 *Etzioni, A.* 2015: Common Good. In: *Gibbons, M.T. (ed.)*: The Encyclopedia of Political Thought, 1st edition, p. 1. DOI: 10.1002/9781118474396.wbept0178 (04/04/2020).

9 *Dierksmeier, C.* 2016: Reframing economic ethics. The philosophical foundations of humanistic management, Basingstoke.

More recently, though, the question of the common good has made a comeback in political and economic discourse. The basic consensus is that while the common good is a „contested concept“, it is precisely the indeterminacy of the concept that makes it an organizing principle of civic life.[10] While it is believed that „a single conception of the common good was inappropriate for a pluralist society and that the common good could not be known“[11], the open search to determine what is best for all through various forms of deliberation or bargaining[12] is upheld as a meaningful and integrative exercise. In recognizing the role of participatory agency in delivering a diversity of goods to realize the common good, this basic belief mirrors Aristotle's setup. A version of this basic belief also informs Amartya Sen's work at the crossroads of welfare and development economics – with consequences for public dialogues in a local democracy.

The Capability Approach of Amartya Sen

In the Capability Approach, his major contribution to welfare and development economics first launched with his lecture "Equality of What? The Tanner Lecture in Human Values"[13], the Indian economist Amartya Sen rejects prevalent utilitarian, libertarian, and Rawlsian attempts to define wellbeing as the common good in terms of personal utility (focusing on pleasures, happiness, or desire fulfilment), absolute or relative opulence (focusing on commodity bundles, real income, or real wealth), assessments of negative freedoms (focusing on procedural fulfilment of libertarian rights and rules of non-interference), comparisons of means of freedom (e.g. focusing on the holdings of 'primary goods', as in the Rawlsian theory of justice), and comparisons of resource holdings as a basis of just equality (e.g. as in Dworkin's criterion of 'equality of resources').[14]

All of these measures, Sen argues, cannot do justice to the diversity of states of wellbeing that individuals, socialized as they are in different cultures, actually value. However, all of them require substantive freedoms to achieve wellbeing – that is, real opportunities to choose and achieve a lifestyle they value. Sen calls these wellbeing freedoms "capabilities"[15]. His capability approach is an invitation both to inquire scientifically into the capability sets which individuals and communities actually and empirically value in their lives, and to devise practical policies that enhance these substantive freedoms. The capability approach – eventually developed in critical partnership with the philosopher Martha Nussbaum[16] – both spawned an ongoing scientific and philosophical discourse. Since 2004, this discourse flourishes in the petri dish of conferences and journals advanced by the Human Development and

10 *Mansbridge, J.* 2013: The Common Good. In: *LaFollette, H.*: The International Encyclopedia of Ethics, Oxford, pp. 913–926.; *Etzioni* 2015 (fn. 8); *Steiner, J.* 2016: The Common Good. In: *Mazzoleni, G.*: The International Encyclopedia of Political Communication, Oxford, pp. 159–163.

11 *Mansbridge* 2013 (fn. 10).

12 *Steiner* 2016 (fn. 10).

13 *Sen, A.* 1979: Equality of What? The Tanner Lecture in Human Values. Delivered at Stanford University, May 22, 1979. http://www.ophi.org.uk/wp-content/uploads/Sen-1979_Equality-of-What.pdf.

14 *Sen, A.* 1993: "Capability and Well-Being". In: *Nussbaum, M./Sen, A.*: The Quality of Life, Oxford, p. 30.

15 *Crocker, D./Robeyns, I.* 2010: Capability and Agency. In: *Morris, C.*: Amartya Sen, New York, p. 62.

16 *Nussbaum, M.* 1988: Nature, functioning and capability: Aristotle on political distribution. In: Oxford Studies in Ancient Philosophy, Supplementary Volume, p. 145–184; ibidem 2011 (fn. 2).

Capability Association (HDCA), all the while inspiring practical policies all over the world from communal politics to the Human Development Index of the United Nations.

Freedom as Purpose and Principle of Human Development

All development policies rely on a certain understanding of means and ends to achieve a unified direction. To Sen, "(f)reedoms are not only the primary ends of development, they are also among its principal means"[17]. Freedom thus conceived has both an intrinsic, and an instrumental value.[18] In what is called with some caution "developing countries", development may "(require) the removal of major sources of unfreedom" such as poverty, tyranny, poor economic opportunities and systematic social deprivation, neglect of public facilities and intolerance or overactivity of repressive states.[19] "Developed countries" are to remain concerned with an agenda of "expanding people's freedoms and capabilities, [...] treating people as agents, and [...] plural principles of assessment"[20].

Sen's understanding of the idea, conceptions, and practical achievements of freedom is correspondingly complex; it is not a freedom of the negative kind that merely postulates freedom from interference, though Sen argues for the value of such an understanding while simultaneously valuing positive freedoms.[21] But Sen goes beyond the popular distinction of negative and positive freedom: He conceives of freedom as an "inherently diverse concept", relating to a variety of activities and institutions.[22] At the same time, freedom is an inclusive idea which finds its unity in the "overarching concern" with the commitment to the process of enhancing the individual freedoms of all.[23] Freedom, as Sen understands it, is intimately interrelated with responsibility, and ultimately depends upon a cosmopolitan social commitment to cultivate conditions of free agency for everyone.[24] "In Sen's conceptualization, freedom is quite clearly a good through which the basic capabilities enabling it are transcended and integrated"[25]. We shall solve the mystery of what is meant by that, step by step.

Substantive Freedoms in Opportunities and Processes

More precisely and systematically, Sen's understanding of freedom is threefold: Freedom has an (1) opportunity aspect, a (2) process aspect, and it (3) culminates in the idea of substantive freedom. Sen explains:

First, more freedom gives us more *opportunity* to achieve those things that we value and have reason to value. This aspect of freedom is concerned primarily with our *ability to achieve*,

17 *Sen, A.* 1999: Development as Freedom, Oxford, p. 10.
18 *Sen* 1993 (fn. 14), p. 39.
19 *Sen* 1999 (fn. 17), p. 3.
20 *Alkire, S.* 2010: Development: "A Misconceived Theory Can Kill". In: *Morris, C. (ed.)*: Amartya Sen, Cambridge, p. 191–219 (198).
21 *Sen, A.* 2002: Rationality and Freedom, Cambridge, MA/London, p. 646.
22 *Sen* 1999 (fn. 17), p. 298.
23 Ibidem.
24 Ibidem, p. 282–298; *Alkire* 2010 (fn. 20), p. 197.
25 *Dierksmeier, C.* 2019: Qualitative freedom – autonomy in cosmopolitan responsibility, Cham, p. 264.

rather than with the process through which that achievement comes about. Second, the *process* through which things happen may also be of fundamental importance in assessing freedom.[26]

While "opportunity freedoms" denote the material aspect of freedoms to realize meaningful options and achieve valued outcomes, "process freedoms" are freedoms of individual and collective agency, pertaining to the "freedom of action and decisions"[27]. While the two types of freedom denote different aspects, they also overlap, as opportunities must be chosen and acted upon. Both types of freedoms may be considered at the personal level (in terms of autonomy, immunity, education, etc.), or at the systemic level (where they are sustained by human rights, equity, or protection from downside risks).[28]

Moreover, through processes of free agency, better opportunities may be attained. Besides the intrinsic value of free agency and choice – it's inherently preferable to be an agent acting rather than a patient suffering –, the possibility to improve conditions is the instrumental value of free agency for development. Originally individual preferences may, through social coordination with like-minded or in conflict with contrarian-minded others, influence the social, economic, or cultural conditions that frame and co-determine the opportunities we are then free to choose from. Individual and collective freedoms are thus interrelated[29], and "individual freedom is a social product"[30]. The fact that we enjoy meaningful opportunities – life-chances, as Ralf Dahrendorf called them[31] – thanks to those who shaped our conditions of life through social coordination and institutions justifies our own responsible commitment to participate in enhancing the freedom of others.

For Sen, both of these freedoms need balance. None is more important than the other. Rather, they qualify each other in the cultivation of conditions of responsible freedom. The multiple interrelated components of freedom – the aspects of individual agency or the effects coordinated public action, the rights and institutions, and the opportunities thus created – together constitute the fabric of "substantive freedom". In the sense that these different kinds of freedoms are instrumental in contributing, "directly or indirectly, to the overall freedom people have to live the way they would like to live", Sen understands them to be instrumental freedoms (akin to conceptions of freedoms realizing the idea of freedom). This fabric includes "(1) political freedoms, (2) economic facilities, (3) social opportunities, (4) transparency guarantees, and (5) protective security." These freedoms all reinforce each other.[32]

Capabilities: Substantive Wellbeing Freedoms

With these clarifications, we can turn back to Sen's basic challenge to measure, determine, and provide for the wellbeing of everyone, all while recognizing that the human family is so diverse that conceptions of the good life differ greatly amongst individuals and collectives.

---

26 *Sen* 2002 (fn. 21), p. 585.

27 *Sen* 1999 (fn. 17), p. 17.

28 *Alkire* 2010 (fn. 20), p. 198.

29 *Dierksmeier, C.* 2013: Ökonomische Freiheit und Verantwortung bei Amartya Sen. Inaugurational lecture at the Eberhard Karls University Tübingen, p. 18.

30 *Sen* 1999 (fn. 17), 31.

31 *Dahrendorf, R.* 1979: Life chances: Approaches to social and political theory, Chicago.

32 Ibidem, p. 38 ff.

His basic intention was to concentrate on the provision of substantive freedoms that allow for the achievement of individual wellbeing. In other words, Sen is concerned with our provision to each other of real opportunities and choice procedures so that everyone can achieve and lead a good life he or she has reason to value.

To measure one's station in life, Sen distinguishes between actual achievements of wellbeing on one hand, and freedoms to possibly achieve wellbeing beyond the actualized achievements on the other hand.[33] (Furthermore, he also distinguishes between agency achievements and agency freedoms, which need not concern us here). "Wellbeing Achievements" already realized are "functionings" in Sen's terminology. "Functionings represent parts of the state of a person – in particular the various things that he or she manages to do or be in leading a life"[34]. Elementary functionings include being adequately nourished or being in good health, while others are more complex, such as achieving self-respect or being socially integrated.[35] Like modules, we build a good life – a satisfying life we have reason to value – from a combination (or set) of such functionings whenever we achieve them.

In contrast, capabilities represent various combinations of functionings – of beings and doings – that the person can possibly achieve, and thus choose from. Beyond the actualized wellbeing achievements of functionings, capabilities are freedoms to achieve more and other functionings. Thus, "(t)he freedom to lead different types of life is reflected in the person's capability set".[36] As a person's capability set is determined by the conditions of substantive freedom (the meaningful opportunity and real process freedoms) present in her community, capability sets as sets of substantive freedoms available for possible achievement. In its classical definition, capabilities are "the substantive freedoms he or she enjoys leading the kind of life he or she has reason to value"[37].

4 Participatory Agency in Public Dialogues

What does the capability approach mean for a political community such as a village or a city? How can local leaders provide for the wellbeing of their community? For various reasons, Amartya Sen himself leaves these questions rather open. Taking a few cues from the previous discussion, I will attempt to propose a practice of freedom politics, and outline a basic procedure of inquiry to determine capability sets that is both consistent with Sen's focus on freedom, and practical and open enough for a variety of applications.

33 *Crocker/Robeyns* 2010 (fn. 15), p. 62.

34 *Sen* 1993 (fn. 14), p. 31.

35 Ibidem.

36 Ibidem, p. 33.

37 *Sen* 1999 (fn. 17), p. 87.

Sen's Silence on Practical Applications of his Approach

In principal contrast to Martha Nussbaum, who has proposed a list of ten Central Capabilities[38], Amartya Sen has refused to draft a list of recommended capabilities. Though many practitioners and researchers are curious, and to the dismay of Nussbaum, he has also resisted the temptation to propose procedures of selecting capabilities: "However, beyond stating in general terms that some democratic process and public reasoning should be involved, Sen has never explained in detail how such a selection could and should be done"[39].

Sen remains deliberately vague on questions of how to determine capabilities.[40] Robeyns[41] names two reasons: (1) He does not want to turn his (inclusive and open) "capability approach" into an (exclusive and specific) "capability theory" (2). Taking his idea of freedom seriously, he also realizes that any inquiry and focus on capability-sets have "to be related to the underlying concerns and values"[42], so he wants to invite administrative officials and politicians to come up with their own choice procedures on how to determine sets of capabilities fitting their specific communities' circumstances and preferences:

Sen stresses the role of agency, the process of choice and the freedom to reason in the selection of relevant capabilities. He argues that we must leave it to the democratic processes and social choice procedures to define the distributive policies. In other words, when the capability approach is used for policy work, it is the people who will be affected by the policies who should decide on what will count as valuable capabilities in this policy question.[43]

Attempts by Scholars to Conceive of Democratic Processes to Evaluate and Determine Capabilities

Several capability scholars have attempted to propose features of a democratic process to evaluate and determine specific capability sets.[44] If an evaluation of these approaches is to be more than a bluffer's guise, it takes another article to do justice to all of the attempts proposed. Not here and now, though. Suffice it to say that there are two types of attempts, one rather theoretical in terms of proposing criteria for determining and weighing the importance of certain capabilities[45], and another more convincing and practical one relying on ideas of deliberative democracy[46]. I will instead propose a pragmatist perspective on collab-

38 *Nussbaum* 2011 (fn. 2), p. 33 f.
39 *Crocker/Robeyns* 2010 (fn. 15), p. 72.
40 *Dierksmeier* 2019 (fn. 25), p. 264.
41 *Robeyns, I.* 2003: The Capability Approach: An interdisciplinary Introduction, Amsterdam, p. 36.
42 *Sen* 1993 (fn. 14), p. 32.
43 *Robeyns* 2003 (fn. 41), p. 36.
44 *Crocker/Robeyns* 2010 (fn. 15), p. 73.
45 *Alkire* 2002 (fn. 20); *Robeyns* 2003 (fn. 41).
46 *Gastil, J./Levine, P.* 2005: The deliberative democracy handbook: Strategies for effective civic engagement in the twenty-first century, San Francisco; *Crocker, D.A.* 2008: Ethics of global development: Agency, Capability, and deliberative democracy, Cambridge.

orative democracy with a focus on organized public dialogues as processes of inquiry[47], and situate that proposal within a sketch of "freedom politics" – starting with the latter.

The Practice of Freedom Politics

Throughout his work, Claus Dierksmeier has shown the kinship of Amartya Sen's ideas to the ideas of German idealist Karl Christian Friedrich Krause.[48] In the first decades of the 19th century, Krause developed a theory of "participative freedom". Like Sen more than 150 years later, Krause took freedom to be both the aim and the means of a liberal conversation of the citizenry on concrete conceptions of freedom, encouraged by philosophers who themselves abstained from dominating it with armchair postulates.[49] Building on Immanuel Kant ("reflexive freedom") and Karl Christian Friedrich Krause, Dierksmeier integrates John Kenneth Galbraith ("fair freedom") and Amartya Sen ("responsible freedom") into a framework of "qualitative freedom"[50]. This understanding of freedom views freedom as a foundational value; recognizes the conceptual diversity of particular freedoms while insisting that their goodness be judged against the universal regulative idea of responsible freedom for every human being as a person; and recognizes qualitative freedom in the responsible – dialogic, participative – exercise of freedom with and for each other.[51] In short, Dierksmeier integrates Sen's argument into a certain tradition of comprehensive liberal ideas.

A public conversation informed by these ideas would understand any political problem in terms of conflicting freedoms of stakeholders. Freedom politics would aim to inquire and evaluate which and whose freedoms were at stake in a given public problem. It would then aim to creatively and responsibly rearrange and balance new configurations of freedoms in terms of empowerment, entitlements, opportunities, and shaped by moral consciousness, conventions, rights, procedures, and institutions – again, fundamentally a process of evaluating each other's freedoms participatively. Freedom being not only the aim, but also the means, the whole of the problem resolution process would have to be an exercise of "freedom as method"[52]. In Sen's terms, such "social choice"-procedures arrive at workable results only when purposes are found or formed which are acceptable to all concerned.[53]

47 *Gohl, C.* 2014: Demokratische Regierbarkeit als Herausforderung. In: *D'Amato, G./Karolewski, I.P.* 2014: Bürgerschaft und demokratische Regierbarkeit in Deutschland und Europa. Festschrift für Heinz Kleger. German and European Studies of the Willy Brandt Center at the Wroclaw University, Baden-Baden, p. 140–183.

48 *Dierksmeier* 2013 (fn. 29); ibidem 2016 (fn. 9); ibidem 2019 (fn. 25).

49 Ibidem 2019 (fn. 25), p. 103–153.

50 Ibidem.

51 *Gohl, C.* 2018: Weltethos for Business: Building shared ground for a better world. In: Humanistic Management Journal 3.2, pp. 161–186.

52 *Dierksmeier* 2019 (fn. 25), p. 46.

53 *Sen* 1999 (fn. 17), p. 79.

Leading Participative Public Dialogues as Problem Resolution Procedures

American pragmatism in the tradition of John Dewey offers a model of social inquiry that can be adapted as basic participative procedure for freedom politics. Dewey describes the democratic process as cooperative problem resolution.[54] In the tradition of Dewey, de Souza Briggs aptly speaks of "Democracy as Problem Solving." His definition of "(d)emocracy (a)s a recipe for structuring the participation of stakeholders in solving problems that confront them collectively"[55] demonstrates the proximity of pragmatism to stakeholder theory.[56] Dewey's basic thesis is that democracy is a communal practice of cooperative, dialogical and experimental problem resolution, producing intelligent solutions for an interdependent world.

In a democratic polity as a problem resolving community, all politics begins where the consequences of an individual's action affect other individuals involuntary, thus prompting a need for self-regulation. Where interdependent problems cannot be resolved alone, a public and cooperative political action comes into being.[57] The reorganization of a problematic situation is a process where reflection and action on probation weave into each other.[58] The experimental and reflective problem resolution includes all steps from analysis to implementation. In his work "Logic: The Theory of Inquiry"[59], Dewey describes the different phases of that inquiry: the qualification of a situation as a problematic, the experimental and rational test of a hypothesis, the reflexive establishment of a relationship between conception and reality, and the construction of judgment.[60] Rost argues that the practice of such public inquiries would result in a "continuously planning society"[61]. Such a society could be understood as a learning society, continuously reconstructing the consequences of problematic situations and searching for solutions.

Essentially, such an inquiry is a public dialogue. Within the dynamics of freedom politics, a Deweyan public dialogue would start with the problem of different freedoms unattainable or in conflict. Stated in in pragmatic terms, people would experience that either the absence of certain freedoms (as opportunity or processes of free agency), or the use of certain other freedoms (either as opportunities realized, or processes consummated, or both) leads to undesirable consequences. This unsatisfactory experience would be addressed in an open and reciprocal participative public dialogue where adaptions, new designs, and re-configurations of freedoms would be tested, with a pragmatistically understood Senian aim to

---

54 *Jörke, D.* 2003: Demokratie als Erfahrung. John Dewey und die politische Philosophie der Gegenwart, Wiesbaden, p. 233.

55 *De Souza Briggs, X.* 2008: Democracy as problem solving: Civic capacity in communities across the globe, Boston, p. 312.

56 *Freeman, R.E./Harrison, J.S./Wicks, A.c./Parmar, B./de Colle, S.* 2010: Stakeholder Theory: The state of the art, Cambridge.

57 *Dewey, J.* 1991: The Public and its problems, Athens, pp. 12 ff.

58 *Jörke* 2003 (fn. 54), p. 213.

59 *Dewey, J.* 2002: Logic: the Theory of Inquiry, Carbondale.

60 *Dewey* 2002 (fn. 59); *Krüger, H.* 2000: Prozesse der öffentlichen Untersuchung. Zum Potential einer zweiten Modernisierung in John Deweys "Logic: The Theory of Inquiry". In: *Joas, H.*: Philosophie der Demokratie. Beiträge zum Werk von John Dewey, Frankfurt a.M., pp. 212–227; *Rost, S.* 2003: John Deweys Logik der Untersuchung für die Entdeckung des Politischen in modernen Gesellschaften, Münster.

61 *Rost* 2003 (fn. 60), p. 12.

enhance the possible experiences of (substantive) freedoms of all through our mutually responsible use of freedom.

In a pragmatist perspective, a process which evaluates achieved and possible sets of capabilities should always be situated in the realm of experiences of actions and their consequences. As it anchors the evaluation of actually achieved and possibly desirable freedoms to concrete social conditions and individual preferences within problematic situations, it circumscribes ruminations about potentially desirable freedoms that, for want of practical relevance, must for now remain but exploratory ideas of people of good will. To lead and organize such process of inquiry into the respective values of our real and substantive, achieved and possible freedoms as they are inscribed into our communal conditions and practices is worthwhile for any community. Wellbeing, in that conception, is best served when we understand the common good to be cherished and cultivated as the conditions for, and practices of, a reciprocal, interdependent and responsible use of freedom of everyone.

Online Citizen Participation: Opportunities and Constraints

Anni Schlumberger and Elisa Söll

Abstract: We argue that citizen participation is vital for democracy, especially in times of perceived crisis in established democracies. If participation meets the criteria of transparency, information, if it offers a real choice and if policy makers are committed to the process, participation and online participation can strengthen democracy. Using the example of Metzingen, Baden-Württemberg, they illustrate how risks of online participation like façade participation, low rates of people participating, lack of deliberation or high entry barriers can be overcome. Online participation must provide an enabling and motivating as well as accessible and understandable tool for enhancing democratic participation.

Keywords: Democracy, Participation, Online participation, Deliberation, Metzingen

1 Online Participation: Rationale and Practice

1.1 Core Concept and Starting Point: Democracy

Online citizen participation is a peculiar feature of a specific type of political regime, namely democracy. Thus, in order to assess chances and limits, constraints, and opportunities of online participation, the underlying concept of democracy and its current challenges need to be clear: Although "democracy is a highly contested concept in the academic realm and public space",[1] a scientific consensus is reached on at least some basic characteristics that need to be met to name a political system a "democracy". A common starting point of defining democracies is the highest ideal of "the power of the people"[2] or democracy's imperative of "let[ting] the people rule"[3]. It is thereby important to notice that "the rule of the people" is not the same as "the rule of the majority": the concept of a "homogenous demos" is considered antiquated now and pluralism not only as "constitutive to modern democracy"[4], but one of its definitional elements.[5] Therefore, in a democracy, decisions cannot be guided by a singular, monistic "volonté générale," some imagined consensual will of all citizens as de-

1 *Mudde, C./Kaltwasser, C.* 2017: Populism. A Very Short Introduction, Oxford, p. 80. With Mudde and Kaltwasser following here, of course, Gallie's (1956) notion of „essentially contested concepts". See *Gallie, W.B.* 1956: Essentially Contested Concepts In: Proceedings of the Aristotelian Society, 56(1), pp. 167–198.

2 *Mouffe, C.* 2018: please add title etc., p. 14.

3 *Müller, J.-W.* 2016: What is Populism?, Philadelphia, PA, p. 6.

4 *Mouffe, C.* 2005: Politics and the Political. In: *Mouffe, C.*: On the Political, New York, pp. 8–34 (14).

5 We adopt, for this contribution, *Dahl's* (1971: ch. 1) eight constitutional guarantees of polyarchy as a synonym for democracy or, for that matter, *Diamond, Linz and Lipset's* (1988: xvi) more parsimonious definition of democracy as a political regime that is characterized by (1) meaningful and extensive competition; (2)a 'highly inclusive' level of political participation; and (3) a guaranteed level of civil liberties and political rights sufficient to guarantee the integrity of (1) and (2). See *Dahl, R.* 1971: Polyarchy. Participation and Opposition, New Haven, CT; *Diamond, L./Linz, J./Lipset, S.* 1988: Democracy in the Developing World, Vol. II: Africa, Baltimore, MD.

scribed by Rousseau.[6][7] Thus, liberal features such as the rule of law, equality before the law, protection of minorities, basic civic and political rights, as well as the separation of powers are fundamental elements of modern democracies in order to prevent a "tyranny of the majority." It is important to note that these characteristics are not "nice-to-haves", but integral to modern democracies in order to enable the most basic principle of democracy: that through citizens' participation in the political decision making process, political decisions are legitimized and the rule of the people upheld.[8]

1.2 Democracy Under Pressure?

Although most modern democracies appear to meet the aforementioned criteria of the concept of "democracy", scholars are increasingly concerned with the erosion of its innate participatory process: citizens – democracy's main actors – have become increasingly passive.[9] Decreasing voter turnouts are a case in point. A historical review of voter turnout in elections to the German Bundestag demonstrates: While in 1998 82,2 percent of the German people went to the ballots, this number decreased to 71,5 percent in 2013.[10] Similar developments are observable at the European level: In 1994 56,7 percent of Europeans who were eligible to vote actually went to the polls. In 2014, this percentage dropped to an all-time low of 42,6 percent. Although, voter turnout at the European level rose in 2019 (to 50,6 percent), this number is still far lower than it was in the 1990s.[11] If a democratic system's main characteristic is the legitimation of political decisions through citizens' participation, such developments must be seen as a sign of erosion. Moreover, the increasing support for radical and populist parties is read as another indication of not only a rejection of "mainstream" politics[12] but of its decay and death.[13] This is by now established knowledge in political science.

Voting, however, is but one form of participation available to citizens in democracies to express their preferences and make their voices heard, and thereby influence and legitimize political decisions: Amongst others, they can run for political office themselves, become members of political parties or trade unions, or take to the streets to demonstrate. All of these channels of participation are, however, just like voting, on the decline. For instance, political par-

---

6 *Müller* 2016 (fn. 3), p. 77; *Muddle/Kaltwasser* 2017 (fn. 1), p. 16.

7 Such monism, by contrast, has been identified as one out of six „general characteristics of totalitarian rule“ by *Friedrich, C.-J./Brzezinski, Z.* 1956: The General Characteristics of Totalitarian Rule. In: Totalitarian Dictatorship and Autocracy, Cambridge MA, pp. 15–27.

8 Among many others, *Buchstein, H.* 2006: Einleitung: Die Postdemokratie-Debatte#. In: Forschungsjournal Neue Soziale Bewegungen, 19 (4), pp. 16–22 (17); *Muddle/Kaltwasser* 2017 (fn. 1), p. 80.

9 *Buchstein* 2006 (fn. 8), p. 17.

10 *Statista* 2019: Statistiken zur Wahlbeteiligung. https://de.statista.com/themen/175/wahlbeteiligung/ (08/02/2020).

11 *Statista* 2020: Wahlbeteiligung bei den Europawahlen von 1979 bis 2019. https://de.statista.com/statistik/daten/studie/12230/umfrage/wahlbeteiligung-bei-europawahlen-seit-1979/. (08/02/2020).

12 *Norris, P.* 2011: Democratic Deficit. Critical Citizens Revisited. New York, p. 3.

13 See also the recent wave of contributions on the erosion or even death of democracy by, i.a., *Levitsky, S./Ziblatt, D. 2018*: How Democracies Die. What History Reveals About our Future, New York; *Mounck, Y.* 2018: The People vs. Democracy: Why our Freedom is in Danger and How to Save It, Cambridge, MA; *Snyder, T.* 2018: The Road to Unfreedom. Russia, Europe, America, New York; and others more.

ties in Germany have lost about 40 percent of their members since 1990.[14] Crouch (2008a)[15] traces this increasing disenchantment with politics to three main developments: First, the erosion of social classes and an increasing individualization of citizens has lowered the incentive for citizens to find common ground and compromise politically.[16] Second, the increasing influence of financial capitalism in politics has eroded the range of possible actions for elected politicians and thereby worn away democratic procedures.[17] [18] And last but not least, a lack of civic representation within political parties as political elites are increasingly entangled and amalgamated with financial elites and no longer represent civil society.[19] According to Crouch, these developments lead to an apathy of the *demos* concerning political processes due to feelings of powerlessness, intensified by poor information through mass media.[20] These feelings, in turn, are seen as a consequence of a growing opaqueness concerning those who *de facto* influence political decision-making formally and – more importantly – informally.

Given the claim that democracies should be systems "ruled by the people", such developments are worrying. If we want to keep on living in democratic societies, there is an urgent need to find ways by which the backbone of democracy – the *demos* itself – can come back into play and reassert its proclaimed sovereignty. Although this may require some effort to achieve, according to Crouch and others, the idea of democracy does not yet need to be buried. However, urgent action is required to find new ways of mobilizing and motivating participation amongst citizen. Initiatives such as 'Occupy Wall Street', 'Stuttgart 21' and the 'Friday's for Future' movement demonstrate citizens still have a political will and can be mobilized as political participants. These provide visible evidence that citizens in democracies remain highly politicized and willing to participate politically – albeit currently not necessarily through traditional channels as these have lost a good deal of their former appeal.

2 Some Rules for "Good Participation" and the Potential of Online Participation

2.1 What Can Avenues of Democratic Participation Look Like Today?

The current "crisis of democracy" is no longer simply a subject of scientific debate. The crisis is now an urgent issue of public discourse and the subject of both local and national schemes designed to turnaround civic participation. In 2016, for instance, the Irish government started discussing potential amendments to the constitution directly Irish citizens using

---

14 *bpb* 2018: Bindung an Interessensgruppen und politische Parteien. https://www.bpb.de/nachschlagen/datenreport-2018/politische-und-gesellschaftliche-partizipation/278496/bindung-an-interessengruppen-und-politische-parteien (08/02/2020).

15 *Crouch, C.* 2008a: Postdemokratie. In: Neue Gesellschaft, Frankfurter Hefte, 55(4), pp. 4–7.

16 Ibidem, p. 7.

17 Ibidem.

18 There is now an increasing literature on a generally tensious – if not antagonistic – relationship of capitalism and basic civil and human rights as such. For one argument, see *Zuboff, S.* 2019: Surveillance Capitalism. The Fight for a Human Future at the New Frontier of Power, New York.

19 Ibidem.

20 *Crouch, C.* 2008b: Postdemokratie, Frankfurt a. M., p. 64.

a so-called "citizens' assembly" where two-thirds of the body were citizens one-third consisted of MPs. At the time of this writing, private companies in Germany were organizing a "democracy festival" at the Olympic Stadium in Berlin, financed through crowd founding. The festival aimed to gather as many people as possible at the same time to sign various petitions addressing different topics from climate change to global injustice.[21] Another example is the "pulse of Europe" youth movement which seeks to strengthen the "European idea" and campaigns for so-called "home parliaments" in order to discuss European politics and formulate concrete demands towards members of the European Parliament.[22] These are only a few examples of programs aimed at enhancing civic participation to support democratic legitimacy and thereby "boosting democracy again"[23]. However, what these programs fail to address an important question: Is all participation necessarily *good* participation in the sense that it will revitalize democracy?

The simple answer to this question is 'no'. Democracy is more than just the idea of "the people" in power. If civic participation is an integral and even defining part of "democracy", there are conditions for *good* civic participation that will enhance liberal democracy's core rather than abuse citizens' voices and there also exists *bad* civic participation which is only a façade of *good* civic participation.

One key condition for *good* civic participation is *transparency towards the public concerning the goal and the purpose* of the participation process. In other words: It must be clear for what purpose citizens are involved into the political process, and in what way the results of such a process will be handled, i.e. in what way citizens' preferences will be taken into account in the decision-making process. Second, *policymakers must commit to the participation process*. Without the commitment of those who have been elected into power to abide by the rule, the process runs the danger of being irrelevant – which would increase rather than decrease public frustration with democracy. Third, the civic *participants must have a* real *choice*: Civic participation must not be turned into a means for professional decision-makers to legitimate choices that have already been made behind closed doors. Finally, good civic participation enables civil society to make well-informed decisions. Therefore, *all relevant information about the subject in question and the participation process itself must be made public* – and it has to be made public in such a manner that the subject matter is understandable for ordinary citizens outside professional politics.

2.2 Benefits of Online Participation

As traditional avenues of democratic participation such as elections and membership in political parties attract fewer people today, new avenues of participation must be developed that better match people's lives today and facilitate their inclusion into political decision-making processes. One technical prospect for widening the fields and possibilities for civic participation – and thereby strengthening democracy – is to make avenues of civic partici-

---

21 *Startnext* 2020: 12/06/2020. https://www.startnext.com/12062020 (11/02/2020).

22 *Homeparliament* 2020: European home parliaments. https://homeparliaments.eu/ (11/02/2020).

23 *Johnson, C.* 2005: Local Civic Participation and Democratic Legitimacy: Evidence from England and Wales. In: Political Studies, 63(4), pp. 765–792 (769).

pation available online (e.g. 'e-participation', 'e-democracy'). As the above-mentioned traditional ways of democratic participation such through as elections and membership in political parties become less used attract fewer people today, new ways must need to be developed that better fit match better with into people's lives today and thereby enable facilitate their incorporation inclusion into political the political decision- making process. Citizens should thus not be looked upon by politicians as a potential threat that might disrupt the implementation of their own preferences, but an asset that has the potential to enhance the quality of political outcomes.

Examples such as the 2011 Arab uprisings that could not have happened without the technologies of new and social media have given rise to the idea of the internet as a liberation technology[24] and a driving force for mobilizing people.[25] But online participation is also hailed in established democracies. Examples of online participation abound from tools to report damages in public space[26], apps that enable citizens to vote on specific issues approved by elected decision-makers[27], to online petitions spread via social media on any imaginable topic. Thus, it is not surprising, that online participation is widely perceived as positive avenue for deepening democratic processes by rendering them more inclusive as it can help to overcome problems deeply entrenched in traditional offline political participation modes.

First, online participation *can lead to better and more far-sighted decisions* as it is easier online than offline to gather all relevant information in a well-arranged manner at one place, accessible to all. The basis on which decisions are made is thereby often broader, and people tend to be better informed. Second, and connected to the first advantage, online participation *increases transparency of decision-making processes* as the internet enables the spread of all relevant information about the subject matter and the process itself to anybody who has access to an end-user device. Consequently, higher levels of legitimacy can be gained by using online participation techniques. Third, online participation is a mean to *reach new target groups and increase the number of participants*. Almost everybody in highly industrialized societies is online today, and the internet itself as well as its various social platforms create an online public sphere – meeting places that have a demonstrated potential to reach new people and inform about the process.[28] Moreover, people are more likely to participate in processes that take place in their immediate environment (which can literally be their couch), as it is more convenient and, also more feasible for some. Younger generations in particular, who are used to live their life online, are probably keener to participate in online processes as this reflects their daily habit.[29] A fourth advantage of online participation is the anonymity that can be created through the internet and that serves for the *reduction of social differences and resulting inhibitions*. This anonymity encourages the expression of opinions for the "participation-shy" because they know that their contribution will be assessed regard-

24 *Diamond, L.* 2010: Liberation Technology. In: Journal of Democracy, 21(3), pp. 69–83.

25 *Kneuer, M.* 2013: Mehr Partizipation durch das Internet? Mainz: Landeszentrale für politische Bildung, p. 13.

26 *Mannheim* 2020: Mannheim Mängelmelder. https://mannheim.mängelmelder.de/#pageid=1 (15/02/2020).

27 *BürgerApp Tübingen* 2020: Bürgerapp. https://www.tuebingen.de/buergerapp (23/02/2020).

28 *Sachs, M. et al.* 2018: Elektronische Bürgerbeteiligung in der Praxis. In: *Leitner, M. (ed.)*: Digitale Bürgerbeteiligung, Wien, pp. 41–68 (62).

29 Ibidem.

ing its content and not its author[30]; in that regard, it enhances *equality in participation* in a world where inequality of power, resources and influence seems more and more determinant for the ability to produce and influence outcomes. Fifth, online participation, by operating in certain time windows, *expands the window of opportunity for participants*. As online participation is not limited to time nor space, people can usually engage multiple times and take time to reflect, re-think and possibly modify their own preferences and decisions.

Yet, there are important conditions that must be met for deepening democracy by benefitting from these advantages; online participation also carries risks and disadvantages for democracy. According to Kneuer[31], a "net realistic" perspective is needed as the internet is not *per se* democratic and cannot by itself generate democratic spaces or democratic processes. In other words: online participation *has the potential* to enhance democratic processes, but it also carries inherent risks that need to be considered and taken seriously. What such risks consist of and how they can be successfully overcome is discussed below with the help of a concrete example of online civic participation. Online participation is thus not an automatic savior of democracy, but it can significantly ameliorate existing problems of participation if applied carefully and follows our rules for "good participation".

3 Online Participation in Practice: Risks and How to Overcome Them

3.1 Online Participation at the Local Level: The Example of Metzingen[32]

In 2017, the town council and public administration department of Metzingen, a small South German town, consensually agreed on organizing a civic participation process in order to decide on the future of local bathing facilities. Responsibility and authority for the decision on the subject matter were passed on directly to the ca. 22,000 inhabitants. This process is a showcase example of civic participation that managed to successfully overcome the risks and problems[33] inherent to offline and online participation processes by careful planning in advance.

3.1.1 Risk # 1: Façade Participation as a Pretext for Ex-post Legitimization

"Civic participation" does not always amount to actual civic responsibility or decision-making authority. Maybe the greatest danger for successful participation processes, offline as well as online, is that it opens a possibility for decision-makers to abuse and exploit them for legitimating political decisions without actually paying attention to the citizens' input , or by organizing an asymmetric informational situation so that the outcome is pre-determined before the "participatory process" even starts. This is why referenda are so popular among autocrats and would-be or real dictators, from Turkey's Erdogan to Egypt's General Sisi. Yet, the temptation of abuse is real as well for decision-makers on all three, the com-

30 Ibidem.

31 *Keuner* 2013 (fn. 25), p. 14.

32 This section is based on our experience of organizing the case study presented here. Comprehensive documentation of the process and its outcomes is accessible at www.metzingerbaeder.de.

33 Retrieved from *Sachs et al.* 2018 (fn. 28), pp. 64 ff.

munal, regional and national levels in established democracies. If such abuse of participatory instruments happens, it almost certainly leads to disenchanted citizens who not only feel badly represented and not taken seriously, but also feel even more deprived of their democratic rights. Therefore, any civic participation process must invariably and deliberately leave its end-result open and, additionally, that outcome must be guaranteed in advance to be at least considered by those political actors who ultimately take decisions.[34]

Figure 1: The process' timeline

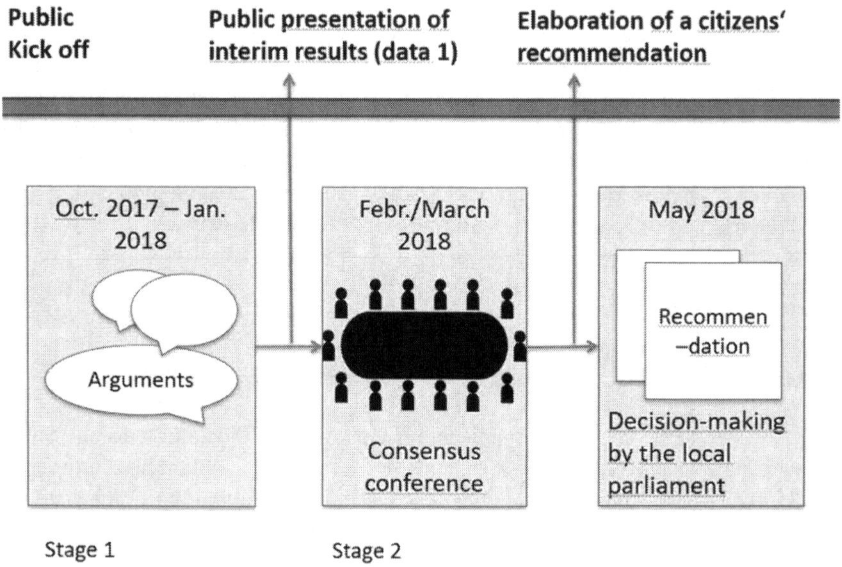

Source: own compilation.

In the Metzingen case, this risk was overcome by the community externalizing the entire organization and moderation of the process to two external advisors with no stakes in any of the possible outcomes. Needless to say: Such externalized organization and moderation must also be guaranteed to be free from any undue interference by the administration or political decision-makers as an integral part of the terms of reference to make and keep the process credible. By supervising the process, the external participation experts controlled and ensured that the outcome of the process was kept open and could not be geared in any direction by the city's officials. Second, these advisors structured the process in a way that allowed citizens to actually bring in their ideas and arguments and hold the local parliament responsible for justifying their decisions towards the citizenry: During the first stage of the process that was started with an open public assembly, arguments for possible future location(s) and for the interior of the future baths were collected both online and offline. Through generating a huge share of public awareness for the process by informing about the matter at local schools,

34 Ibidem, p. 66.

at the farmers' market, on facebook, as well as in the existing local public baths, the citizenry was enabled to constantly act as a supervisor throughout the decision-making process.

The second stage of the process consisted of a so-called "consensus conference" in which twenty random citizens were invited to work out a written recommendation for the future bathing facilities that considered all arguments brought in by the citizenry and collected on- and offline during the preceding first stage. Moreover, the citizen participants were provided with advice from legal, administrative, planning and architectural experts. Thereby, the final recommendation paper was not only based on citizens' arguments but had already taken into account a broad range of expert knowledge and comprised the "best" solution according to the citizenry of Metzingen.

In order to keep the process as transparent as possible, the paper was presented to the public and the municipal council at an offline public assembly in which 300 citizens took part and published online simultaneously. This second stage thus intensified the embeddedness of the citizenry into the overall process. Although the final decision on where to build what types of new public baths or how to renovate existing ones was left to the municipal council, the high level of civic inclusion into the process made it obligatory for the council to engage in detail with the citizens' recommendations. The recommendations also served as a reference document for everybody by the prior guarantee to disclose it to the citizenry. Therefore, it came as no surprise that the municipal council unanimously decided along the lines of what the recommendation had stipulated as the latter enjoyed broad-based approval among the local population – and therefore produced a highly legitimate decision on a previously extremely controversial issue.

3.2.2 Risk # 2: Low or "Feel Good" Participation

Connected to the above-mentioned risk of abusive online "participation" for the ex-post legitimization of pre-determined outcomes is the risk number two: The risk of civic participation failing to gain legitimacy despite politicians' actual will to consider their citizens' preferences, and despite an open-ended participatory process. This is the case if the percentage of citizens participating remains below a certain threshold, or if a critical mass does participate, but on the base of too low levels of information and knowledge on the subject matter (so-called "Feel-Good-Participation"). In that case, the gain in civic expert knowledge through the process is too low to make for an actual rise in legitimacy of the outcomes.[35]

In order to actually benefit politically from civic participation processes, it is indispensable to combine participation with encompassing information – otherwise citizens' demands are of little use as guidelines for political decisions, and the participation processes itself misses its purpose. The connex between risks one and two lies, of course, in the fact that decision-makers are usually in possession of exclusive information that can or cannot be made publicly available. A politician who wants to legitimize a certain outcome may thus be tempted to provide only partial or biased information to her citizens.

35 Ibidem, p. 63.

In Metzingen, citizens were therefore provided with information not only about the rules of the process itself but also about the technical, legal, hygienic and other details that public bathing facilities require in order to render *informed participation* possible, and, on that basis, to think also about possible alternatives.

Second, “Feel-Good-Participation” was avoided by refraining from offering a simple yes-or-no vote for only one pre-given alternative. Instead, citizens were asked for concrete arguments and the reasons of their arguments. Thus, for citizens to justify their preference against various possible alternatives, and to give reasons for their arguments it is inevitable to provide them with *access encompassing and understandable* information on all aspects of the subject matter. If one of the two (or even both) is compromised, the result will almost certainly be either bad decisions or a heightened danger of risk one discussed above, and the entire process will be flawed.

3.2.3 Risk # 3: Omitting Deliberative Democracy

Civic participation creates costs in terms of money, time and efforts. In addition, the more comprehensively a process is designed and the more exactly it is tailored to the needs of the relevant citizenry and the subject matter, the more expensive and time-consuming the process becomes. Therefore, participation processes are often reduced to one-size-fits-all-solutions – for instance by filling simple questionnaires that are easily adapted to any possible issue without much attention to mechanisms for ensuring high return rates.[36] However, such an approach only creates an illusion of cost-effectiveness: As stated above, if the goal of civic participation is, as its name states, to enhance participation and thereby increase democratic legitimation and public acceptance of political decisions, participation must not be reduced to simple public opinion polls. Rather, it has to raise public awareness, to *a priori* ensure high levels of information among the public on the subject matter and enable and facilitate transparent public discussion on the issue at stake. Although, this might be perceived as cumbersome or expensive by those who have to endorse it, the alternative of an only superficially conducted and truncated process of civic participation compromises not only the chances for public acceptance, broad-based legitimization of outcomes, and citizens’ expectations, but democracy as such. A thus flawed organizational set-up can be exploited too easily for legitimating great projects by asking for small-sized citizen actions, and by applying small measures with an initially broad publicity effect while actual decisions are taken on major issues without only a semblance of civil involvement.

By contrast, the process in Metzingen was designed to promote public engagement with the relevant topic: The way citizens could use to express their opinion was aimed not primarily on *what* they want but rather on arguments of *why* they want it. Thereby, the citizenry was forced to *engage with arguments for and against specific courses of action* and enabled to discuss diverging opinions. This was fostered not only in the respective online forum, but also during accompanying offline events to complement online participation in an integrated approach.

---

36 Ibidem, p. 66.

Moreover, while the collection of arguments was the main goal of stage (1) of the process, its second stage was dedicated solely to the discursive and deliberative character of democracy: During the consensus conference, participants were invited to engage with the whole range of arguments, independently of their own viewpoint. Thereby, understanding and respect for other opinions and decisions was successfully fostered.

3.2.4 Risk # 4: "Democratic Divide"

Online processes often claim to be open to every citizen as the internet allows for participation detached from temporal and spatial constraints. Yet, while it is correct that online participation can help to design participation processes more inclusively for citizens who cannot take part in offline events for whatever reason (inflexible working hours, disabilities of any nature, care responsibilities), the restriction of participation through online tools can also give an exclusionary character to the respective process since not every citizen is able or willing to use online tools. This effect is usually referred to as the "democratic divide".[37]

The risk of creating such a democratic divide can only be overcome by complementing every online process by offline elements that effectively enable all citizens to get offline access to the same level of information and the same chances for participation as online. During the Metzingen participation process, the external experts integrated offline and online tools on an equal level of importance and thereby created a holistic participation process that took place in both spheres. That means that the two main pillars of successful participation processes – empowerment of citizens through *information* and *participation* – were accessible both offline and online. Comprehensive *information* about the process itself, latest developments and all arguments put forth, was not only provided on the respective websites that was created for the participation process, but also offline through a series of public events that took place during and after each phase of the process. Moreover, every public assembly was recorded, and a report was put online to inform those who could not participate. Furthermore, participation in the process was not restricted to a form on the respective website, but also possible by post cards, phone calls, e-mails, as well as in person during the public events.

This inclusive and multi-channeled procedure ensured a process that benefitted from the advantages of combined on- and offline civic participation.

3.2.5 Risk # 5: Registration Requirements as Barriers for Participation

Potential barriers to participation are important factors that influence public acceptance - and hence should influence the choice of civic participation channels. Compulsory registration procedures, for one, may constitute a barrier that prevents people from participating. Yet, no

37 *Min, S. J.* 2010: From the Digital Divide to the Democratic Divide: Internet Skills, Political Interest, and the Second-Level Digital Divide in Political Internet Use. In: Journal of Information Technology and Politics, 7(1), pp. 22–35; *Sachs et al.* 2018 (fn. 28), p. 64; for a broader discussion: *Kersting, N.* 2016: Participatory Turn? Comparing Citizens' and Politicians' Perspectives on Online and Offline Local Political Participation. In: Lex Localis, 14(2), http://pub.lex-localis.info/index.php/LexLocalis/article/view/14.2.249263%282016%29 (28/02/2020).

registration at all increases the risk of low-quality contributions the possibility of identifying authors who post offensive material or do not respect the "netiquettes".[38]

In Metzingen, such registration disadvantages were balanced out by, first, establishing different possible participation channels, thereby giving citizens the choice to bring in their arguments through various channels of their choice, and, second, through a special high-maintenance online procedure: through unlocking postings only after actively having checked them no registration was needed. Users' mail addresses were required by the external moderators but remained anonymous to both the municipal administration and the public at large. They were thus used for requests for clarification by the moderators to the person posting an argument or for addressing the authors of offensive postings only.

4 Online Participation and Democracy: The Metzingen Lessons

After a quick recap of how liberal democracy is related to participation as a core definitional element of the former, this contribution has highlighted the potential of online participation in enhancing and deepening democracy in an age in which it has come under severe stress even in established democracies. The four abstract rules for good participatory processes deducted from our own professional experience as moderators and facilitators of civic participation processes include the following:

1) *Transparency concerning goal and purpose* of a participation process is an indispensable requirement of participation processes in order to prevent subsequent disenchantment and frustration among the citizenry
2) Participation processes need the *commitment of policy makers* in power to take effect.
3) Only by offering citizens the *possibility to* actually *take decisions*, participation processes can work as a proper mean to deepen democracy.
4) Citizens should only be asked for participation on the base of being provided with *all relevant information about the subject in question and the participation process itself.*

On the other hand, while the internet in general and new media in particular do offer new means of enhancing civic participation, they are by no means "liberation technologies" only. Instead, they inherently carry serious risks of abuse and malpractice which, if they remain unnoticed or unaccounted for, have the potential of not only compromising participation, but of weakening democracy as such. Five such dangers[39] – along with ways to overcome them – have been discussed with the help of relatively small and closely circumscribed, but comprehensive case of a successful online civic participation process in the Southern German city of Metzingen. These five risks are:

38 *Sachs et al.* 2018 (fn. 28), p. 63.

39 Retrieved from ibidem, p. 63–66.

1) Conducting façade participation to gain legitimacy for certain political decisions.[40]
2) Gaining no added value due to low numbers of participants or participation on the base of a low level of knowledge.[41]
3) Omitting the deliberative character of democracy by conducting civic participation without space for discussion and argumentation.[42]
4) Creating a "democratic divide" through building only on online tools and thereby excluding citizens who are not able or willing to participate via the internet.[43]
5) Achieving only low acceptance and adoption of online participation processes due to the creation of barriers for participation as registration requirements.[44]

As shown by the process in Metzingen, these risks can be overcome by carefully shaping the participation process not as a simple voting operation, but as a process enabling and motivating citizens to engage with the issue and thereafter form an opinion about it. Therefore, participation was put on the ground of comprehensive information accessible to all citizens – online as well as offline. Moreover, the procedure created space for an intensive examination of the issue in question and for the discussion of different perspectives. And finally, to avoid the portrayal of certain segments of society only, the process was designed in an inclusive manner by keeping in mind possible barriers for participation.

Finally, as the case study also demonstrated, online civic participation must not be seen as a substitute for offline efforts of fostering participation, but as a complement that bears the potential to enhance it. A naïve technological belief in the potential of online tools will not suffice to enhance participation in a democratic manner but can even do harm. Rather, it is an integrated approach that combines both on- and offline tools for civic participation what is needed if the core goals are to be reached. As the case study has shown, this integrated approach, in turn, has its own rules of how to successfully combine the broad range of instruments.

40 Ibidem, p. 66.
41 Ibidem, p. 63.
42 Ibidem, p. 66.
43 Ibidem, p. 64.
44 Ibidem.

PART 2: CHALLENGES FOR WELLBEING AND DEVELOPMENT

Migration, Social Policy, and Power in a Historical Perspective[1]

Martin Seeleib-Kaiser

Abstract: Migration and social policy have become fiercely contested issues in Europe and North America. In this paper I highlight how mobility and migration, on the one hand, and social policy, on the other hand, have historically been closely interwoven and shaped by power relations. It is argued that European states actively assisted their poor to leave 'home' and settle in far-away places. I will elaborate some of the tensions between freedom of movement and the role of social policy in the North German Confederation (*Norddeutscher Bund;* NDB) and the British Empire. Finally, it is argued that many of the current challenges and issues associated with migration and social policy in Europe are historically not unique.

Keywords: migration, assisted emigration, transnational social policy

Introduction

Migration has become a salient political issue in many European countries and North America during the past decade. In the social sciences it is discussed to what extent welfare states constitute welfare magnets[2] – populist politicians have used the derogatory terms of "benefit tourists", "asylum tourists" or "poverty migrants" to characterize current migrants. Much of the contemporary political debate is about closing borders or significantly restricting migration from poorer countries. In a 2016 referendum, the British electorate decided for the country to leave the European Union (EU) and 'take back control' of its borders to end 'uncontrolled' migration by EU migrant citizens. US President Donald Trump has promised to build a wall at the Mexican border, paid for by the Mexican people, to stop undocumented migration from Latin America. In 2018, the Italian Secretary of the Interior, Matteo Salvini, has denied ships with migrants rescued in the Mediterranean Sea access to Italian harbors. In an arrangement with the EU, Turkey has agreed to stop the migration into the EU and European institutions are trying to find arrangements with North-African countries to severely restrict migration. German local municipalities have called for restricting access to social rights by EU migrant citizens, as too many of them are said to have exploited or defrauded the welfare system […].

Although long-distance migration may seem a relatively new phenomenon to many contemporary citizens in affluent OECD countries, this is historically not the case. Long-distance migration has occurred during different times in history.[3] Between 1620 and the be-

1 Acknowledgement: This Article has first been published as *Seeleib-Kaiser, M.* 2019: Migration, social policy, and power in historical perspective. In: Global Social Policy, 19(3), pp. 266–274. https://doi.org/10.1177/1468018119832403 under the terms of the Creative Commons Attribution-NonCommercial 4.0 License. © 2019. Reprinted by permission of Sage Publications, Ltd.

2 *Borjas, G.J.* 1999: 'Immigration and Welfare Magnets'. In: Journal of Labor Economics, 17(4), pp. 607–637.

3 *Held et al.* (1999) differentiate four phases of global migration. Although the intensity of migration was relatively low in premodern times, the extensity of premodern migration was at times global, for instance the migration of nomadic Mongols. The early-modern times from 1500–1760 witnessed an increased intensity

ginning of the First World War, approximately 32 million people emigrated from Europe to North America, mostly for economic reasons. Between 1881 and 1915, each year approximately 900,000 people left Europe.[4] The current phase of migration[5] has, however, occurred against the backdrop of relatively low levels of immigration during much of European history since World War II.

In this paper, I highlight how mobility and migration, on the one hand, and social policy, on the other hand, have historically been closely interwoven and shaped by power relations. I will discuss examples of assisted emigration as a public social policy instrument in different European states during the 19th century, before discussing remittances in the 19th Century as an early form of 'private' transnational social policy; the link between freedom of movement and the role of social policy in the North German Confederation (*Norddeutscher Bund;* NDB) and the British Empire will also be discussed. In a final section, I will compare these historical developments with contemporary approaches to migration.

Mobility, Migration, and Social Policy in Historical Perspectives

Historically, in many European jurisdictions, landowners and (home) communities of residence were responsible to support the poor. Thus, poor people were regularly sent back to their 'home' community of residence.[6] This institutional arrangement also created the category of vagrants moving between municipalities. Increasing mobility and the need for workers in industrial urban centers required a reform of the system of poor support, hitherto based on promoting immobility. In England, the 1834 Poor Law Amendment Act created 647 Poor Law Unions responsible for the poor at a regional level, encouraging migration of able-bodied rural poor to manufacturing districts. At the same time, the New Poor Law also created the possibility of assisted emigration.[7] [8]

---

with transatlantic settlers and slave trade constituting new global flows. This phase was followed by migration in the modern era constituting largely of overland migrations by Russian colonists, transatlantic and Indian Ocean slave trades and by European colonizers to Africa and the Americas. The contemporary phase saw new migratory flows, including increasing numbers of tourists, travellers, and international exchange students and more recently the increase of refugees and migrants from low-income countries.

4 *O'Brien, P.* 1999: Philip's Atlas of World History, London; *Held, D./McGrew, A./Goldblatt, D./Perraton, J.* 1999: Global Transformations, Stanford, p. 290.

5 Globally, the number of migrants reached more than 250 million in 2017. Of those 250 million migrants approximately only half live in affluent Europe (78 million) and North America (58 million), while the other half lives in Asia (80 million), Africa (25 million) Latin America and the Caribbean (10 million), and Oceania (8 million). In 2016, the total number of refugees and asylum seekers in the world reached almost 26 million people; a minority of them have headed to Europe and North America. With 3.1 million refugees and asylum seekers Turkey hosted the largest number, followed by Jordan (2.9 million), the State of Palestine (2.2 million), Lebanon (1.6 million) and Pakistan (1.4 million). Despite Europe not being the primary destination of global migration, migration to Europe and intra-European mobility has increased significantly during the past decade, see *United Nations, Department of Economic and Social Affairs, Population Division* 2017: International Migration Report 2017: Highlights (ST/ESA/SER.A/404), New York. http://www.un.org/en/development/desa/population/migration/publications/migrationreport/docs/MigrationReport2017_Highlights.pdf.

6 *Hennock, E.P.* 2007: The Origin of the Welfare State in England and Germany, 1850–1914 – Social Policies Compared, Cambridge; *Tennstedt, F.* 1981: Sozialgeschichte der Sozialpolitik in Deutschland, Göttingen.

7 *Anderson, B.* 2013: Us and Them? The Dangerous Politics of Immigration Control, Oxford.

8 However, it needs to be highlighted that most emigrants were not assisted.

Emigration and Social Policy

Assisted emigration became an option for municipalities for "shoveling out paupers"[9] and for the poor to escape dire socio-economic conditions. It was justified as a measure to deal with surplus labor in rural regions of industrializing England, whilst at the same time constituting a measure to populate the empire.[10] However, promotors of assisted emigration as a form of social policy had to deal with the conflict resulting from emigration also being used as a form of punishment known in England as "transportation".[11] As the Law of Settlement remained in force, local parishes continued to be financially responsible for their poor in union workhouses. Thus, assisted emigration was one way for a parish to relieve itself of the future financial obligations of supporting its poor.[12]

The English counties with the highest number of assisted emigrants were areas with low wages and a depressed agricultural economy. Prior to the New Poor Law, parishes could also support poor agricultural workers; the new law, however, no longer provided the possibility of outdoor relief for able-bodied laborers, but only the 'option' of support in the union workhouse. Workhouses were feared and hated by the poor, which in some instances lead to riots and incendiarism. Under these circumstances, it would only seem rational for local parishes to support the emigration of their paupers. Howells[13] identified a positive statistical relationship between the cost for annual relief per head and the emigration rate among parishes in Norfolk. The overwhelming majority of those supported to leave the country were young families. Howells[14] wrote:

> "[...] [P]arish officers were assisting people who might produce more children in the future, but were not overly burdened with children at the present moment. By not being overburdened with children, emigrants also offered the emigrators a chance of saving money. The fewer children people had the cheaper they were to emigrate."

At the same time, stigma and the threat of the workhouse combined with stories of opportunities in far-away places are very likely to have had a positive impact on triggering also 'un-assisted' emigration of poor people.

Britain was not alone in 'exporting' its poor. For instance, in the 19th century, communities in Württemberg, a small state north of Switzerland, also assisted emigration of surplus laborers and paid for the passage of poor local families to North America. The emigration from Württemberg to North America in the 19th century took place in two waves subsequent to economic crises in 1817 and between 1846 and 1855. Assisted emigration was considered an effective social policy instrument, as it was perceived to be cheaper to assist the poor who

---

9 A phrase that was initially used by Charles Buller, a contemporary of John Stuart Mill, in his critique of assisted emigration; cf. *Howells, G.* 1996: Emigrants and Emigrators. A Study of Emigration and the New Poor Law with Special Reference to Bedfordshire, Northamptonshire and Norfolk, 1834–1860. Thesis submitted for the degree of Doctor of Philosophy at the University of Leicester, p. 18.

10 Although it has to be highlighted that the number of those assisted to emigrate was comparatively small. Over the 26-year period during which assisted emigration was employed, only twenty-six thousand people were assisted to leave, see *Howells* 1996 (fn 9), p. 54.

11 Ibidem.

12 This section mainly draws on the excellent doctoral dissertation on the topic by *Howells* 1996 (fn. 9).

13 Ibidem, p. 90.

14 *Howells* 1996 (fn. 9), p. 122.

'voluntarily' wanted to emigrate, than to support them for long periods in the municipality. Often 'agents' were used to arrange and facilitate the journey. Approximately eight percent of all emigrants from Württemberg to North America were poor emigrants assisted by local parishes as well as private and religious foundations. Although not on the same level as in England, the authorities of Württemberg also deported convicts to North America.[15] Assisted emigration was a coercive social policy instrument that simultaneously provided people from socio-economically disadvantaged backgrounds in Europe with the opportunity, and more often with the dream, of upward mobility in far-away lands. Its logic was rooted in asymmetrical power relations in the countries of origin, largely undemocratic class societies, and in the asymmetrical power relations in the territories of destination, which had to be populated and where the indigenous populations had been suppressed.

England and Württemberg are only two examples of European territorial entities that used assisted emigration as an instrument of coercive social policy within their poor relief arrangements in the 19th century. Ireland would be another example. How many other European jurisdictions made use of poor relief arrangements to 'export' their poor requires further systematic research. Nevertheless, what seems to be clear already from these two examples is that in times of economic crisis and surplus labor, European countries promoted and assisted emigration as part of their early social policy approaches.

However, emigration had an additional social policy dimension, namely in the form of remittances from the emigrants to their communities of origin. The 19th Century remittances by British emigrants were of utmost importance in supporting families and poor communities. Within the Empire remittances were handled by the Money Order Office (in 1904 formally becoming the Imperial Postal Order Service) of the Royal Mail.[16] Although at an aggregate level the amounts of money that were remitted back to Britain constituted less than 1 percent of GDP per annum in the late 19th Century[17], regionally remittances were of great importance for local communities. In this context the relationship between Cornish-born miners in South Africa and the communities of origin in Cornwall is particularly noteworthy. Magee and Thompson[18] report:

> "families who they [the Cornish miners; MSK] left behind anxiously awaited the arrival of a regular remittance in the South African mail. [...] Hence when the Cape mail arrived, people would flock into the towns from the surrounding villages to collect their money, and the business in local shops would boom. Conversely, when the 'home pay' did not arrive, the county's Board of Guardians were left to pick up the pieces – though they themselves were helped by the charitable work of several Cornish associations on the Rand, organizations that had played a key role in raising relief funds for the widows and orphans of the minors killed by accidents and lung disease. [...] With its constant flow of money orders back home, the colony was a lifeline for Cornwall until at least the 1920s."

It is very likely that emigrants from other parts of Europe, such as Württemberg, also sent remittances to support relatives and communities left behind. In other words, not only did local parishes benefit of a reduced caseload of paupers to support by assisted emigration, but also

15 *Krebber, J.* 2014: Württemberger in Nordamerika. Migration von der Schwäbischen Alb im 19. Jahrhundert, Stuttgart, p. 47.

16 *Magee, G.B./Thompson, A.S.* 2006: Lines of credit, debts of obligation: migrant remittances to Britain c. 1875–1913. In: The Economic History Review 59, 3, pp. 539–577 (543 f).

17 Ibidem, p. 554.

18 Ibidem, p. 557.

by emigrants' remittances to families that otherwise would have had to rely on poor relief paid by local authorities.

Immigration and Social Policy

Despite relatively high levels of emigration, European countries were also countries of destination for regional migrants, albeit at a much lower rate. Although poor relief and social protection was for a long time tied to the local parish or the nation state, we find historical examples of confederations of states where eligibility to poor relief and social protection was extended to include subjects and citizens of other Member States. The North German Federation (*Norddeutscher Bund; NDB*), established in 1867, was such a case. One of the first legislative acts of the NDB was to establish *freedom of movement* among the subjects and citizens of the Member States of the Confederation, which was considered a vital catalyst for industrialization. Pre-existing poor relief regulations of the Member States, however, remained in force, leading to significant variation of poor relief arrangements. Differing residency requirements in Member States could even lead to complete disentitlement and destitution of mobile people. Otto von Bismarck, Governor of Prussia and Chancellor of the NDB, understood that the fragmented system of poor relief was incompatible with the principle of freedom of movement among Member States of the NDB and, in 1869, introduced the "Bill to Support Residents" (*Unterstützungswohnsitzgesetz*). The bill stipulated that every 'Northern German' should be treated as a 'native' with regard to poor relief in every Member State. Bismarck's proposal was highly contentious politically. For instance, the State of Saxony highlighted that it received significantly more migrants than other States within the confederation[19], whilst smaller states argued that the proposed legislation would constitute an 'unbearable burden' for them.[20] Again, other states objected to the proposal as it would infringe on their sovereignty.[21] Despite the opposition by a significant number of Member States, Bismarck was successful in garnering a legislative majority for the law, providing access to poor relief to mobile Northern Germans irrespective of the duration of residence in a Member State.[22]

The British Empire can also be understood as a form of confederation. As the sun was already slowly setting on the Empire, the British Nationality Act of 1948 was enacted by Parliament with the aim to maintain the formal indivisibility of British subjecthood within the Empire. The Nationality Act defined in statute who was considered a British subject: citizens of the United Kingdom and Colonies, citizens of independent Commonwealth coun-

19 *N.N.* 1869: "Bericht des außerordentlichen Ausschusses an den Bundesrat." 1869 März 15. In: *N.N.* 2000, pp. 105–114 (108, 113).

20 *von Perglas, P./Joseph, M.* 1870: "Immediatbericht des Gesandten an den bayerischen König Ludwig II". In: *N.N.* 2000: Quellensammlung zur Geschichte der deutschen Sozialpolitik 1867 bis 1914. I. Abteilung. Von der Reichsgründungszeit bis zur kaiserlichen Sozialbotschaft (1867–1881), 7th vol., Armengesetzgebung und Freizügigkeit, 1st sub-volume, edited by *Sachße, C./Tennstedt, F./Roeder, E.*, Darmstadt, p. 152.

21 *N.N.* 1870: "Protokoll der ersten Sitzung der V. Kommission des Reichtags des Norddeutschen Bundes." 1870 März 3. In: *N.N.* 2000, pp. 178–186 (186).

22 *Bruzelius, C./Seeleib-Kaiser, M.* 2018: Freedom of movement and social assistance in (con)federations and the European Union, Unpublished paper Eberhard Karls University Tübingen.

tries, and a residual group of British subjects without citizenship. These three groups had the freedom to move to Great Britain and *new residents from the Empire had unconditional access to the newly established British welfare state.*[23] [24]

The examples provided in this section demonstrate how mobility, emigration and immigration have been closely linked with social policy. Assisted emigration from England and Württemberg was a social policy instrument used to export surplus laborers while providing those that were assisted the opportunity of a better life in the territory of destination. The examples of the NDB and the British Empire highlight that the issues and tensions associated with accessing social policies by intra-EU migrants today have not been unprecedented. Moreover, access to poor relief and social protection beyond citizens of the nation state within larger jurisdictions than the nation state was possible, if it was politically and economically perceived to be opportune or pertinent by the power elite.

Conclusion: 21st Century Migration and Social Policy in Historical Perspective

Although it is at times argued that welfare states constitute a major pull factor for today's migration to Europe,[25] there is no systematic evidence supporting this claim and the desire for a better life continues to be one of the main factors for migration,[26] very similar to the motivations of Europeans migrants in the 19th century. Although no systematic information seems to be available with regard to the degree and extent of formal state-assisted emigration as a *social policy* instrument in the main countries of origin of today's immigrants in Europe and North America, it would seem quite rational for local communities to support emigration in the hope to reduce the problem of surplus labor and for emigrants to support the community of origin through remittances in the future.[27] Moreover, the current debates relating to freedom of movement and access to social protection in the European Union is not unprecedented. However, contrary to today's untenable situation of blocking access to social assistance for newly arrived intra-EU migrants,[28] Bismarck understood that it is dysfunctional to create freedom of movement in a supra-national territory while simultaneously maintaining

23 *Anderson* 2013 (fn. 7), pp. 38–40; *Gosewinkel, D.* 2016: Schutz und Freiheit. Staatsbürgerschaft in Europa im 20. und 21. Jahrhundert, Frankfurt a. M., pp. 299–301.

24 As it turned out, migration was considerably higher than expected and restrictions were soon demanded and implemented. However, it should be noted that there are no statistical figures regarding the number of immigrants from Commonwealth countries available. Since 1968, the passport of a British subject was no longer sufficient to enter and settle in the UK; in addition to it, the person either needed to be born, or to have a parent or grandparent who had been born, in the United Kingdom.

25 *Borjas* 1999 (fn. 2).

26 *Castles, S.* 2013: "The Forces Driving Global Migration". In: Journal of Intercultural Studies, 34(2), pp. 122–140.

27 A number of Asian countries, e.g. the Philippines, formally support emigration. However, they do not seem to use their poor relief arrangements to 'export' poor families, but have a much more sophisticated system (cf. *Asis, M. M. B.* 2017: "The Philippines: Beyond Labor Migration, Toward Development and (Possibly) Return". In: Migration Information Source, The Online Journal of the Migration Policy Institute, July 2017. https://www.migrationpolicy.org/article/philippines-beyond-labor-migration-toward-development-and-possibly-return (29/10/2018).

28 *Bruzelius, C./Reinprecht, C./Seeleib-Kaiser, M.* 2017: "Stratified Social Rights Limiting EU Citizenship". In: Journal of Common Market Studies, 55(6), pp. 1239–1253.

a system of regionalized poor relief. After WWII, British politicians fathomed that, if they wanted to maintain the Empire, *all* its subjects living in Britain should be treated based on the principle of equality.

As has been shown, remittances have played an important role of transnational social policy in 19th century Europe. The role of remittances is quite similar in many low- and middle-income countries of today's world, albeit at a much higher level, contributing to the welfare and stability in many countries of emigration. In this context, Germano[29] speaks of "outsourcing welfare", whereby access to welfare services are not primarily provided by the state, but through the availability of remittances. International migrants sent an estimated 443 billion US Dollars to low-income countries in 2014, whereas the world richest countries donated only 135 billion USD in the form of aid and official development aid.[30] Remittances constitute a considerable proportion of GDP in many countries[31] and can function as a rudimentary safety net for families and assist them in acquiring basic goods and services, can have countercyclical effects, and reduce conflict.[32] Thus, remittances can contribute to socially and politically stabilizing countries of origin.[33]

Overall, mobility and migration have historically been in tension with social protection provisions. However, European states have explicitly used social policies to assist emigration of 'their' poor. In the context of current discussions of restricting 'undeserving' or 'unwanted' economic migrants from poorer countries coming to Europe and North America, it seems more than appropriate to remind the peoples of Europe and North America of these historical processes. The practices of the past and the rhetoric and practices of today are reflections of power relations. The difference of then and now is that the emigrants of the 19th century were the subjects and citizens of powerful colonial European countries and it is the same powerful countries or their democratic successors that today aim to close their borders or severely restrict migration from poorer countries.

---

29 *Germano, R.* 2018: Outsourcing Welfare. How the Money Immigrants Send Home Contributes to the Stability in Developing Countries, New York/Oxford.

30 Ibidem, p. 139.

31 In the Kyrgyz Republic, Moldova and the Gambia remittances are equivalent to more than 20 percent of GDP. In Algeria, Lebanon, and Jordan about 10 percent and in Nigeria, Mali and Senegal more than 20 percent of the population have reported receiving remittances (ibidem, p. 163). For the role of remittances played in the poorer countries of the EU see *Obrzut, R.* 2017: "Personal Remittances Statistics", Eurostat. http://ec.europa.eu/eurostat/ statistics-explained/pdfscache/39326.pdf.

32 The support by migrants of relatives and friends in countries of origin can go beyond sending money. In some cases, immigrants have set up innovative institutional arrangements to provide social services for communities in the country of origin. One such example is the partnering of Congolese immigrants in Belgium with Belgian mutual insurance funds to set-up special schemes that provide diaspora members in Belgium the opportunity to purchase health insurance for their relatives in Congo, see *Lafleur, J.-M./Lizin, O.* 2017: "Transnational Health Insurances as Social Remittances: The Case of Congolese Immigrants in Belgium". In: *Nowicka, M./ Šerbedzija, V. (eds.)*: Migration and Social Remittances in a Global Europe, London, pp. 211–234 (217).

33 *Germano* (2018, fn. 29) also acknowledges that remittances may also contribute to supporting unresponsive and authoritarian regimes.

The Role of the Middle Class in the Development of Creative Urban Space

Denis I. Sachuk

Abstract: The purpose of this article is to identify the specific features of the development of creative urban spaces in Russia. The author insists that creative urban space is a set of factors and conditions which are considered by native citizens as normal for this territory and influencing comfort of living in the city and plays a big role in economic, political and cultural life of modern city. In doing so, the article details the theory of creative city and creative class and details the process by which social structure transformation occurs and defines what creative urban space looks like in the modern Russian cities. This was done by surveying local experts. The conclusion was that the creative class in Russia remains too small to lead the development of creative urban spaces because of increasing of the precariat and therefore the middle class become key leaders in the self-organization of citizen and in promoting participation in projects which can develop the creative urban space. In addition, the experts surveyed concluded that creative urban space or a creative city required four features: acknowledgement and representation of local cultural heritage, the presence of creative industries, tools to attract and retain creative professionals, and decision making on behalf of city management that was unique to the city in question.

Keywords: Middle layers, middle class, creative urban space, creative class, transformation of modern Russian society.

Introduction

The definition "urban space" became popular in the field of urban sociology in the middle of the 20th Century. There are a lot of definitions of urban space. We can mention the opinion that modern cities have emerged as a strategic site for a whole range of new types of operations, some pertaining to the global economy.[1] On the other side, there are a lot of socio-cultural definitions of urban space which are connected with institutional arrangements and social nets which are necessary for modern efficient social order.[2] All these positions are united by one basic thought: urban space became a dynamic aspect of urbanization. In this article, urban space shall be defined as "a set of factors and conditions which are considered by native citizens as *normal* for this territory and influencing *comfort of living* in the city"[3].

Nowadays the development of urban space is closely connected to the theory of creative city that suggests that cities have to be attractive first in order to appeal to high-skilled and creative professionals who will give the economic system of the city its much needed im-

1 *Abrahamson, M.* 2004: Global Cities, New York.

2 *Graham, S.* 2001: Information Technologies and Reconfigurations of Urban Space. In: International Journal of Urban and Regional Research, 25, pp. 405–410.

3 *Lobodanova, D.L.* 2013: Comfort of environment as a factor of innovational development of city, Moscow.

provement.[4] The theory of creative class inspired by Richard Florida is one of the directions to develop the urban space of modern city, so we can say about *creative* urban space which has such advantages as liveliness, diversity, identification, attraction, economic value and partnership.[5] The development of creative urban space is set to become one of the most relevant fields of research in the field of urban management. As modern cities continue to grow and compete for resources from the surrounding territories, the most valuable resource will be that of human capital.

However, there is a strong discussion between Russian sociologists on the possibility of applying the concept of *creative class* in specific realities of modern Russian society.[6] R. Florida defines the creative class as "set of people producing economic values in the process of creative activity"[7]. So, middle class which is related with creative class and can be defined as

> "social group, united by the implementation of functions that are significant for Russian society: the development of the economic system, the development of institutions of consolidated democracy and civil society, the establishment of a high standard and lifestyle, as well as a stable, above average, level of material security"[8]

can become an organizer of creative urban space. The main topic of interest in this paper is the role of the Russian middle class in development of creative urban space in Russian city.

Theoretical foundations

It is important to understand the relationship between the concept of "creative class" and the development of creative urban space in modern, developed, post-industrial society. Because of this, the creative class is comprised of a variety of professions such as super-creative core and a creative environment (on the basis of the criteria for the ratio of creative and non-creative activities in the duties of a particular employee and a representative of a particular profession). The following professions belong to the *supercreative core*: programmers and mathematicians, architects and engineers, specialists in the field of natural and social sciences, specialists in the field of education, training, as well as librarianship; professionals from art, design, media, entertainment, etc. In turn, the *creative environment* is made up of representatives of the following professions: range of management professions; professions in business and finance, professions in the field of law, occupations in the field of healthcare (also technical specialists employed in this field), leading professions related to sales management.

In our research, we identified two key roles members of the creative class have in the development of creative urban space. Firstly, their specific labor contributions are a precondition for the economic development of a postindustrial society and allows for comprehensive economic development. The core idea of this development is pretty close to the concept of creative economy which is therefore a variant of the larger concept of digital economy,

4 *Nathan, M.* 2007: Wrong in the right way? Creative class theory and city economic performance in the UK. In: *Lovink, G./Rossiter, N. (eds.)*: My Creativity Reader: A Critique of Creative Industries, Amsterdam.

5 *Kalantari, B./Yary-gholi, V./Rahmati, A.* 2012: Public space and creative city. In: Manzar, 19, pp. 74–80.

6 *Kacherauskas, T.* 2017: Creativity and the concept of a creative society in sociology. In: Sociological studies, 10, pp. 26–35.

7 *Florida, R.* 2011: The rise of the creative class, Moscow.

8 *Sachuk, D.* 2018: Theoretical understanding of the political potential of the middle strata. In: Theories and problems of political research, 8, 1a, pp. 50–58.

which is seen as the result of vast transformative processes in modern life and work, brought about by information and communication technologies.[9] The creative economy is a variety of the knowledge economy in which the loosely defined creative industries play a central part. The core task of the creative industries is to develop and exploit intellectual property, which will ultimately generate prosperity and create jobs.[10] The obvious economic functional of the regional creative class, capable of mutual development which includes several arguments. Firstly, representatives of the creative class, being an organic and significant part of the labor market, are constantly working to ensure the stability of the economic development of society, forming the economic basis of a post-industrial society. Then, the creative class forms a consumer model of behavior, which gives an incentive to the development of the whole economic system. Also, the importance of the development of the layer of small and medium-sized businesses, which forms the components of the creative class, as well as creating new jobs for employees which is totally important for the market economy. Finally, the innovativeness of the economy, that is so desirable at the present stage of development of the economic system, is real due to the development of the creative class.[11]

Second key role of members of the creative class is developing of the *stable society* at the territory the live in. Definition of *stable society* implies the institutionalization of the uncertainty of certain roles and areas of political life, but at the same time, citizens gain confidence that the struggle for public office and / or influence will be fair and will not go beyond the predictable set of options. Modern, representative, political democracy rests on such a “bounded uncertainty” and conditional consent of actors to accept the results generated by it.[12] In turn, an *unstable society* could be characterized by the lack of institutional structure with which politicians could agree and which citizens are ready to support (that is important to develop any interaction about developing urban space). So, the main goal of a modern city is to attract members of the super creative core and creative professionals to the city. According to Richard Florida to do these cities need to possess:

- a dense labor market,
- an intense lifestyle,
- various opportunities for communication,
- diversity,
- an authentic and unique identity.[13]

When measured against the theoretical conditions necessary and supportive of the development of creative urban space, the realities in Russia are discouraging. The end of the twentieth century in Russia was marked by large-scale social transformations. Fundamental transformations in the economic and political spheres of life in Russian society, such as the tran-

9 *OECD* 2015: Addressing the tax challenges of the digital economy. https://www.oecd-ilibrary.org/docserver/9789264241046-en.pdf?expires=1586076078&id=id&accname=guest&checksum=91119E2934325EE1D2F6897E5D126F70 (04/04/2020).

10 *Peters, M.* 2010: Three forms of the knowledge economy: learning, creativity, and openness. In: British Journal of Educational Studies, 58 (1), pp. 67–88.

11 *Volkov, U.G.* 2013: Creativeness: creativity versus imitation, Moscow.

12 *Smitter, F.* 1996: Reflections on Civil society and consolidation of democracy. https://www.civisbook.ru/files/File/Shmitter_1996_5.pdf.

13 *Florida* 2011 (fn. 7).

sition to a market economy, an orientation toward democratic values, have radically changed the stratification system of Russian society and reduced the standard of living and quality of life. More than that, the territory in Russia is highly differentiated. Medium and small cities, such as Petrozavodsk, also combined with economic and industrial losses due to the transformation of a market economy and crisis phenomena in the economy, have much less resources to large economic centers such as Moscow and St. Petersburg. The reality is that many Russian territories lack the basic conditions necessary to sustain such development, and as a result there is little to no development of creative urban space. According to the experts interviewed there were several key factors missing.

First of all, in order for a creative class to exist there must be elite and mobile social groups. In Russia, these groups are very small and not well developed outside of the urban cores of Moscow and St. Petersburg.[14]

Besides the lack of an elite group, the Russian labor market suffers from a growing precariat class. British sociologist G. Standing introduced the concept of precariat into the study of the sociology of inequality. He defined precariat as set of features. These include the lack of job security and jobs; specific place in the distribution structure; deficit of civil, social, political, cultural, economic rights. The key sign is a feeling of insecurity, insecurity in the future, a feeling of social dysfunction.[15] The precariat sits in opposition to the salariat which is defined as "upper middle class with stable full-time employment and salary (mainly senior employees)"[16].

In other words, the precariat can be regarded as any group of persons which occupy an unstable position in the labor market. Representatives of the precariat occupy a large niche in the secondary labor market. The dual literature on employment in the secondary market has concentrated on four hypotheses. There actually is a secondary market that pays lower wages than a primary market. Then, its wage determination process differs from that in the primary market, especially by ignoring the major differences in human capital among workers. Third, as a consequence of institutional barriers on the demand side, there is little mobility between the two sectors. Fourth, underemployment is a pervasive characteristic of the secondary market.[17] Because of their unprotected position in the labor market, representatives of the precariat are forced to seek a guarantee of security for themselves, since the labor market is unable to provide them with this guarantee. Because the labor market cannot provide security for the precariat, it is logical that they seek security from the state and social services instead. Members of the precariat become dependent on the state both economically and politically. Dependence of members of the precariat on the state is initially seen in labor and socio-economic aspects. However, in the future, such dependence will logically grow into political dependence that contributes to the creation of an *unstable society*.

---

14 *Komarovsky, V.S.* 2017: Poverty and inequality as challenges of national-state identity to the formation of the civil nation of Russia. In: Power, 25, 1, pp. 5–11.

15 *Standing, G.* 2011: The Precariat. The New Dangerous Class, London.

16 Ibidem.

17 *Wachter, M.* 1974: Primary and Secondary Labor Markets: A Critique of the Dual Approach. In: Brookings Papers on Economic Activity, 3, pp. 637–693.

An influence and size of the precariat is growing at the moment, 45 percent of the working-age population in Russia works in conditions that the government knows almost nothing about, and the labor market as a whole can be considered illegitimate.[18] We are forced to state that this trend makes the development of the Russian young creative class, as a phenomenon opposed to the precariat, unpromising. The conditions laid out in the theoretical model for the development of creative urban space cannot be met in most Russian peripheries.

But E. Glaeser claims that the ideal lifestyle for creative professionals is similar to the classic lifestyle of the middle class.[19] These concepts are rather similar, but the concept of middle class is much better studied in Russian sociology. More than that, in opposite to *creative class* there are a lot of researches which describes the size and functions of Russian middle-class. So, we can try to find a way to connect Russian middle class (not creative class) and the development of creative urban space in Russian cities, towns and villages.

Method

Basic field of our scientific interest is Russian middle class. The exact theme of the science work is "Russian middle class: features of formation, current state, prospects of development". In theoretical part of our survey we used secondary analysis of data of sociological studies of a number of sociological centers and scientific institutions of the country: All-Russian Center for the Study of Public Opinion (WCIOM), Public Opinion Foundation (POM), Institute for Social and Political Studies of the Russian Academy of Sciences, Institute of Sociology, Russian Academy of Sciences, Levada Center, etc. We also analyzed the most significant developments of foreign and domestic sociologists in the field of social stratification and the study of the middle class.

We also conducted an independent empirical study of the regional aspects of the development of the Russian middle class on the example of the Republic of Karelia as a depressed region of Russia. We chose method of expert survey for our research. In total, data were received from ten key experts in the Republic of Karelia. In order to get the most detailed and wide picture of the regional realities of the Republic of Karelia, five main groups of alleged experts were selected: representatives of the regional executive branch; business representatives, entrepreneurs; specialists in the field of finance; specialists in the field of political science; the scientific community of the Republic of Karelia.

Experts have been selected in the survey according to their formal status, as well as reputation analysis. Ten conversations were held, lasting from 25 to 45 minutes. We chose a semi-formalized interview method, which is most suitable for an expert survey. On the one hand, we had a clear conversation plan and the wording of the main issues, both programmatic and questionnaire. On the other hand, a semi-formalized interview implies a certain flexibility in the course of the conversation, which allows clarifying the expert's views, as well as obtaining additional information through the examples of the cites.

---

18 *Golodets, O.* 2013: 38 миллионов россиян занимаются непонятно чем. [38 million Russians do not know for what to go in for]. https://www.vesti.ru/doc.html? id=1071317 (04/04/2020).

19 *Glaeser, E.* n.s.: Review of Richard Florida's the rise of the creative class. http://www.creativeclass.com/rfcgdb/articles/GlaeserReview.pdf.

Table 1: Surveyed experts

Experts	Role/function	Gender
1	Head of the Budget Department of the Ministry of Finance of the Republic of Karelia	female
2	vice-president of the Union of Entrepreneurs of the Republic of Karelia	male
3	Chairman of the Non-Profit Fund "Innovation Project Support Fund" "New Dimension", associate professor of the Department of State and Municipal Administration of the Karelian Branch of the RANEPA	male
4	Chairman of the Association "Karelian Resource Center of Public Organizations",	male
5	Head of the Center for Support of Export-Oriented Small and Medium Enterprises of the Republic of Karelia	female
6	Associate Professor of the Department of Foreign History, Political Science and Inter-national Relations of Petrozavodsk State University, Head of the Department of Humanitarian and Socio-Economic Disciplines at the Northern Institute of the Russian State University of Justice of the Russian Law Academy of the Ministry of Justice of Russia, Candidate of Philosophy	male
7	Acting Head of the Department of Sociology and Social Work of Petrozavodsk State University, Associate Professor, Candidate of Sociology	female
8	Director of the Petrozavodsk Directorate for Business Development of Gazprombank	male
9	leading researcher at the Institute of Economics of the Karelian Scientific Center of the Russian Academy of Sciences, doctor of economic sciences	female
10	senior citizen, ex-director of the timber industry	male

Source: own compilation.

Experts have been selected in the survey according to their formal status, as well as reputation analysis. Ten conversations were held, lasting from 25 to 45 minutes. We chose a semi-formalized interview method, which is most suitable for an expert survey. On the one hand, we had a clear conversation plan and the wording of the main issues, both programmatic and questionnaire. On the other hand, a semi-formalized interview implies a certain flexibility in the course of the conversation, which allows clarifying the expert's views, as well as obtaining additional information through the examples he cites.

An empirical study formulated three key questions. The program questions concerned the specifics of the Republic of Karelia as a region, the expert's theoretical views on the basic concepts of stratification theory, as well as the expert's assessment of the current position of the middle class in the Republic of Karelia, the main problems and prospects for its development. And our last program question contained in itself questions about urban space in Petrozavodsk.

Results and Analysis

Estimating the size of the Russian middle class is difficult. For example, in the Russian Federation, the standard of living is much lower than in most developed countries. As a result, we can find some middle-class conditions in Russia but no true Russian middle class. If we adopt a relative set of criteria applied only to the Russian Federation, then we can produce a strictly Russian definition of middle class. The key difference between the strictly Russian middle class and a traditional middle class is in the functions each plays within society. In a strictly Russian middle class, the functions of the middle class are:

- the development of economic activity (development of labor market, increasing consumption, forming new economic nets etc.);
- engaging in political activity (taking part in elections, development of civil society etc.);
- increase in stability of city society (institutionalization of the uncertainty of certain roles and areas of political life, at the same time, citizens gain confidence that the struggle for public office and / or influence will be fair and will not go beyond the predictable set of options);
- the development of the living environment (by setting a lif,estyle and consumption standard and providing the methods to make them to reality)
- one of our decisions in the process of our science work was to have a glance at some regional features of the way of the Russian middle class. 4 main regional features of the development of russian middle class have been found:
- the level of economic development of the region. This item consists of the prevailing types of economic activity, the nature of labor, whether the region is scarce or the donor region, etc.;
- socio-demographic composition of the region. This block of characteristics should include the gender composition of the population, which may vary significantly depending on the region, also its age characteristics etc.;
- characteristics of management in the region. A huge role in the formation of the middle class is played by both the distribution of government structures' power in the region and the work of state and municipal government structures. Moreover, here we come to the global problem of territorial marketing;
- cultural and historical characteristics of the region.[20]

Based on this analysis we made two hypotheses. Firstly, the development of creative urban space is closely correlated to traditional measures of economic and social development. As one respondent put it: "We still can't form an advanced middle class [in the Republic of Karelia] especially here on the periphery [...] what kind of creative class is there?". Secondly, the middle class and not the creative class are the driving force of creative urban space development in Russian society in contrast to the theory of creative urban development posited by Richard Florida.

20 *Sachuk, D.* 2012: Regional aspects of the study of the Russian middle class. In: Bulletin of Moscow State University, Series 18, Sociology and Political Science, 3, pp. 273–284.

According to the experts surveyed, the middle class plays a key role in preventing creative professionals from leaving the region, especially if this region could be named as depressive:

"Although there are uptrends in the regions of the north-west, including in the northern regions, that is, in this sense Karelia, we use the concept of a depressed region, unfortunately"– expert No. 9.

But the local middle class is ready and willing to fight for a certain standard of living and comfort. This sentiment was clear from the response of the experts interviewed. Experts highlighted four key directions of the development of creative urban space using the example of Petrozavodsk.

- Using "cultural heritage of the place" means commercialization and making business about cultural heritage of Petrozavodsk. As was mentioned by experts, souvenirs sale, new touristic ways and any developments of infrastructure of Petrozavodsk (hotels, cafes and restaurants etc.) are the main opportunities in that areas. Experts mentioned that new directions are possible: "For example there are educational programs for locals from National museum and National library" – expert No. 4;
- developing creative industries of the city. Creative industries rendered some assistance.[21] Experts focused at new self-organizing groups of active and creative people who tries to make business or improve the cultural life at the territory. As for expert's opinion, members of local middle class are that persons who organize ore become main clients of that kinds of project. And mostly they have some support from local government: "[…] but the fact that, for example, the willingness of ministers to communicate with representatives of non-profit organizations is higher, that is, communicative barriers are much less." – expert No. 3;
- keeping from leaving creative professionals. Russian middle class is ready to fight for their rights and the level of comfort life. So, the main idea that was mentioned by the experts was participation of local middle class in the priority project: "Comfortable urban environment". This project is really useful in Petrozavodsk, but it requires a lot of activity and labor from participants. Experts noted a high degree of differentiation of the territory of Karelia, where the city of Petrozavodsk acts as a center not only administrative, but also economic:

  "For residents who live in regional centers, villages [...] Petrozavodsk is such a [...] Light that attracts […] They think that having moved to Petrozavodsk, their life will radically change for the better." – expert No. 5.

  Members of middle class believe that the participation of the middle class in projects designed to develop creative urban spaces is vital. According to the experts such projects required a great deal of involvement and labor from participants, but the majority of the citizens in the region are passive. Because of this, the more active middle-class members become key leaders in the self-organization of citizen and in promoting participation in projects. Additionally, middle class members have the financial ability to travel and experience different countries, such as neighboring Finland, thus exposing them to higher standards of living which they will then want to achieve at home;

21 *Chumak, K.A.* 2017: Joining creativity, Petrozavodsk.

- taking part in adoption and implementation of original decisions of city management. It is rather sensitive theme for Russian system of management because of the political situation and negative role of increasing precariat. According to expert No. 6,
- "at the same time, one more thing, probably, as they told us there, Karelia is as close as Siberia to its capitals to Russia. [...]. And what does this mean? When here are fugitive, when are convicts who then remain in the settlement [...]. Well, first of all, it is a motley population, yes, in terms of composition [...] ethnic, national, and, most importantly, educational. And this kind of code, yes, which persists, let it be forms are preserved in the memory of the contemporary".

  But still city management is a direction of quite free way for locals to try to change something in this field. One of opportunities that the experts offered was taking part in public discussions. It takes some knowledges and active way of thinking – that are some features of local middle-class behavior. As expert No. 7 said:

  "Public discussions in city administration are very good example of our opportunities. If we want to live a comfortable life, we should put pressure on city administration. Nobody but us can influence on our administration [...]."

  But other experts were very careful in discussing of that opportunity of this direction of acting for local middle class. It can be connected with the fact that this behavior is close to political functions of Russian middle class which are still not clear.

Conclusion

The development of urban space in post-industrial society is closely connected to the theory of creative city that suggests that cities have to be attractive first in order to appeal to high-skilled and creative professionals. We identified two key roles members of the creative class have in the development of creative urban space: their specific labor contributions are a pre-condition for the economic development of a postindustrial society and developing of the stable society at the territory.

In the reality of Russian typical city middle class is that social group which can help to develop creative urban space. We should be attentive to some regional features of the development of russian middle class: the level of economic development of the region, socio-demographic composition of the region, characteristics of management in the region, cultural and historical characteristics of the region to correct our expectations about the development of creative urban space in Petrozavodsk.

The experts surveyed concluded that creative urban space or a creative city required four features: acknowledgement and representation of local cultural heritage, the presence of creative industries, tools to attract and retain creative professionals, and decision making on behalf of city management that was unique to the city in question. According to the opinion of local experts, the difference between the theoretical development of creative urban space and the realities of such development in Russia comes down to the definition of development. Local middle class understands its wishes about quality of life. Finally, the more active middle-class members become key leaders in the self-organization of citizen and in promoting participation in projects which can develop the creative urban space in Russian cities.

Innovative Potential of Youth as a Resource of Social and Economic Development (on the Example of the Republic of Karelia)

Kirill Fitisov

Abstract: This paper analyzes research on the innovative potential of youth in the Republic of Karelia and the opportunities this innovative potential creates for socio-economic development in the region. The research data was collected in 2019 and measured the level of digital economic competencies among the young people of the republic. During the research, the innovative potential of youth was estimated; the differences in the level of the innovation potential of the young people of urban and rural areas were identified; and the influence of schools and higher education institutions on developing the innovative competencies among youth of Karelia was analyzed. The ultimate goal was to examine the possibilities for using the innovative potential of youth in Karelia as a social and economic resource for the region.

Keywords: youth, innovation, innovative potential, social development, economic development.

Innovative Potential of Young People

Innovation defined as "the implementation of a new or significantly improved product (good or service), or process, a new marketing method, or a new organizational method in business practices, workplace organization or external relations."[1] (OECD 2005), is one of the drivers of development. In order to foster development, innovation and the innovative potential as the ability to see the need for innovations and the ability to successfully implementing them in practice become core factors. Under the *innovative potential* of the individual in the context of an innovative society of the 21st century, I understand, first of all, a combination of cognitive, personal and intellectual hidden resources of the personality, which can manifest itself at the moment when innovative activity is required. It more meaningfully reflects the essence of the concept. I argue that especially the youth[2] are of core importance for the realization of a societies' innovative potential.

The innovation potential of youth in this paper means the readiness of youth to project and make positive changes in their own lives and the life of society. Innovation potential also comprises the ability and readiness to adapt easily to social changes that occur because of the digital economy. The qualities and the main competencies of the innovative personality in Russia are defined by "The Strategy of the Innovative Development of the Russian Federation for the Period up to the Year 2020". Among these qualities and competencies are

---

1 *Organization for Economic Cooperation and Development (OECD)* 2005: Oslo Manual. The measurement of scientific and technological activities. Proposed Guideline for Collecting and interpreting technological innovation data. http://www.oecd.org/science/inno/2367614.pdf.

2 Youth is defined here as the age group from 14–30 years. This is a large social group with specific socio-demographic characteristics, value orientations, motivation, focus on social mobility, features of inclusion in various social and stratification layers, the construction of life plans, which is determined both by the age characteristics of young people and the fact that socio-economic situation and the spiritual world are in a state of formation.

the following: ability to adapt easily to innovations, ingenuity, high I.Q.-level, ability to think critically, ability to use the innovation technologies, ability to be a team player, ability to create, IT skills, ability and readiness for reasonable risk, ability of foreign languages as an instrument of communication, aspiration to study continuously and acquire new knowledge and competencies, and the ability to take the responsibility for the teamwork results.[3] In our opinion, the competencies that are defined in the strategy are very specific and correct for the development of a person in an innovative society. Therefore, a person can be considered to have an innovative personality fit for the twenty-first century if they have all the above-mentioned attributes and are socially oriented to improve the lives of themselves or their society.

The innovative potential of youth in Russia provides an important resource for the successful socio-economic development of the country. In order to effectively harness the innovative potential of youth in society, it is necessary to adapt a state youth policy, which creates favorable conditions for development.

In order to transition to an innovative development path, the Russian Federation must develop and nurture innovative human capital. Young people have a special role to play in the development of this new human capital. A special carrier of human capital, on which its qualitative and quantitative characteristics depend, is youth, which is a social group that is most mobile and susceptible to the changes that are taking place. Youth possess important qualities which predisposes individuals toward innovation such as computer skills and creation innovations. These qualities and skills if properly utilized, will help drive state development.

The innovative potential of youth is one of the most important factors of socio-economic growth and is an underutilized resource in many states. By studying the innovative potential of youth, we can analyze how best to develop this resource and make more effective policy recommendations in pursuit of innovative projects and development.

The theoretical basis of the work was the theory of authors such as Joseph Schumpeter. His approach to the definition of innovation is considered classic.[4] According to Schumpeter, innovations are technologically new or improved technological processes or methods of production (transfer) of services used in practice. V.N. Shevchenko examined the innovative personality through the prism of a general sociological personality and highlighted several main features and tasks associated with its formation: the ability to work; the presence of a certain intellectual resource; social maturity as a willingness to innovate; ability and readiness for activity in the collective subject of innovative activity. Of all the listed qualities, social maturity can be especially distinguished as a willingness to innovate, because innovation is, above all, a risk and a person must understand and predict the consequences of his work.

It is worth paying attention to the fact that such scientists as V.I. Pantin and V.V. Lapkin, developed a method of historical cycles, which reflects an understanding and assessment of the prospects for the cyclical development of innovative technological civilization. This method comprehensively analyzes political, economic, technological, social and other cycles

---

3 *The Russian Government* 2008: Concept of long-term socio-economic development of the Russian Federation until 2020, approved by Government Directive of November 17, 2008. No. 1662-r. http://www.consultant.ru/document/cons_doc_LAW_82134/79d98ab0c15af433ffc39eee86f1c76b48dced89/ (31/05/2019) (in Russian).

4 *Schumpeter, J.A.* 2008 (first 1934): The Theory of Economic development: An Inquiry into Profits, Capital, Credit, Interest and the Business Cycle, translated from German by Redvers Opie. New Brunswick.

and rhythms. V.I. Pantin and V.V. Lapkin is proposed to consider the evolution of the world system on the basis of three main cycles, the duration of which differs in comparison with Kondratiev's cycles, in addition, given the acceleration of historical processes in the global economy and innovative development. Each of these cycles, in which the evolution of economic, social, technological and political systems fits, includes four phases: structural crisis; technological revolution; great shocks; world market revolution. Thus, they proposed a "theory of accelerating innovation".

According to the Federal Service of State Statistics (Rosstat), at the beginning of 2018, the number of young people aged 14 to 30 permanently residing in Russia Federation was nearly 31 million people, while of the total population of the Russia Federation was 146 million.[5] Thus, young people make up a little more than one fifth of the national population. According to the Federal Service of State Statistics for the Republic of Karelia (Kareliastat), in the year 2018, the number of young people aged 14 to 30 permanently residing in Karelia was almost 96,800 people from a total population of 622,000.[6] Thus, young people make up only about one sixth of the population of Karelia. Compared to the Russian Federation, the Republic of Karelia, suffers from a lack of young people. Based on the results of our study, such conclusions were obtained: one reason why young people tend to live in cities is because a greater possibility for self-realization in cities than in rural areas. Young people are the most active, mobile, and dynamic part of the population, and they adapt quickly to changes in society caused by scientific and technological progress. Russian society and its authorities focus on young people as the most promising age group for social and economic activity. [7]Given their high educational potential, authorities believe that young people will be able to help to solve many social (for example poverty and income inequality) problems by introducing innovative social technologies into practice. Innovative social technologies are a procedurally structured set of techniques and methods aimed at studying, updating and optimizing innovative activities, as a result of which innovations are created and materialized that cause qualitative changes in various spheres of life, focused on the rational use of material, economic and social resources.

In order to recover from the social crisis in Russian Federation, it is necessary to develop a clear social development[8] strategy with both short- and long-term programs for innovative action. Today people-centered development – political, economic, and social changes focused on the social and human potential – provides a strategic vision for sustainable and dynamic social and economic progress. The implementation of innovative social technologies (for example, a group of young people created a donor base on the Internet. People enter their data, blood type and rhesus) is one way to pursue harmonious and well-balanced human and social development. Innovative social technologies develop the social environment and

5 The distribution of the population by age group [Electronic resource]. http://gks.ru/ (03/08/2020) (in Russian).

6 *The Government of the Republic of Karelia* 2018: The strategy of socio-economic development of the Republic of Karelia for the period until 2030, approved by Decree of the Government of the Republic of Karelia on December 29, 2018. No. 899r-P. http://economy.karelia.ru/action/4868/ (31/05/2019) (in Russian).

7 Ibidem.

8 Social development has to be understood as one of the forms of the society development, directed on transition to higher level of material production and welfare of the people, promoting successful operation and development of human personality.

contribute to scientific, technical, and information innovations. These innovations in turn improve efficiency and accelerate the introduction of new technical equipment and technologies thus reducing expenses.[9]

The Republic of Karelia because of its favorable geopolitical position, unique natural resources, abundant recreational resources, and centuries long cultural and historical heritage is of particular interest in terms of the topic of this research. The unique features of Karelia provide both advantages and challenges for the region's economic development. Notable features of the Republic include: As the Petrozavodsk City Council outlines in its "Strategy".

1 Its Status as a Border Region

The Republic of Karelia is in every sense a border territory. On the one hand, Karelia has the longest state border with the European Union – with Finland. On the other hand, within the country Karelia is bordered by the Leningrad, Arkhangelsk, Murmansk, and Vologda regions. Undoubtedly, its border status with Finland and the EU provides a number of benefits for socio-economic development. In addition, economic systems divided by state borders tend to have different capacities in different spheres – labor, capital, natural resources, technological development, etc. The potential difference between the economies of two countries tends to foster cross-border flow and cooperation, especially where the potential difference is significant, in particular, at the border between Russia Federation and Finland. In addition, socio-economic development of border regions is subject to the following principle – the more peripheral the region is, the slower it develops, while the positive impact of the border status is not decisive. Two of the three regions of the Russian Federation that border Finland – the Republic of Karelia and the Murmansk region – have low population densities and are remote from economic centers, and thus are peripheral. Another risk for border regions with inequitable development is a "brain drain".[10]

2 Its Climate

The Karelian climate is quite harsh and variable due to the oceanic climate of the North Atlantic and Arctic Ocieans. The Karelian climate is characterized by the short daylight hours, little sunlight during the cold season, and temperature extremes. The proximity of the Baltic, White, and Barents Seas cause intense cyclonic activity, high relative humidity, significant precipitation, and changeable weather conditions in all seasons. Such natural and climatic conditions for a long time formed the working capacity, endurance and patience of the Karelian people. This people are distinguished by the ability to concentrate physical and spiritual forces at the right time and to make super-effort when it seems that all the resources of a person have been exhausted.

---

9 *Mises, L.* 1981: Socialism. An Economic and sociological Analysis, Indianapolis, pp. 600–605 (600).

10 *The Petrozavodsk City Council* 2015: The strategy of socio-economic development of the Petrozavodsk urban district for the period until 2025, approved by the decision of the Petrozavodsk City Council of February 18, 2015. No. 27, pp. 31–489. http://docs.cntd.ru/document/465407025 (31/05/2019) (in Russian).

3 Its Economic Environment

Karelia is a region with low investment activity. According to Kareliastat, in 2017 the fixed capital investment in the region decreased by 5.1 percent.[11] The same year in Karelia, 1106 new companies were registered, while 2449 were liquidated. In 2015, six of Karelia's [#] municipalities, plus the urban city district of Petrozavodsk made up 79 percent of the region's fixed capital investments with Petrozavodsk accounting for 30.6 percent of this total. The Republic of Karelia is a "subsidized region" that receives annual funding from the federal center. Since [year #], the annual budget of Karelia has operated with deficit. Economic problems have led to weak infrastructure development and the reorganization and "optimization" of educational and social institutions in both cities and rural areas.

In order to overcome these development challenges, it is essential to mobilize all available resources including internal capacity for social and economic development of the region. Youth are traditionally considered one of the most mobile groups of the population; they adapt easily and quickly to technological changes and are capable of innovative initiatives. The research objective of this paper is to analyze the innovative potential of youth in Karelia and determine its potential influence on the social and economic development of the region. This paper will use the mastery of key competences of innovation economy as the measurement of innovative potential.

The major competences necessary for innovation in a digital economy are articulated in "The Strategy of the Innovative Development of the Russian Federation for the Period up to the Year 2020" adopted in 2011. During the research for this paper, an online survey was conducted. The quota sample included young people aged 14 to 30 living in Karelia (1100 people). In addition, a poll of 15 experts was conducted. The research subject was the innovative potential of youth of the Republic of Karelia. During the study, a survey of youth was conducted in order to measure and study the innovative potential of youth. The data obtained allow us to draw the following conclusions. It was also held a questionnaire of professors of the university to determine the level of, the sixth wave of innovation (digital economy, NBIC-technologies)[12], as well as readiness and motivation to develop key competences of the digital economy.[13]

Methods of Data Collection and Analysis:

The primary data for this paper comes from interviews of experts, an online survey (questionnaire) of young people, and a questionnaire of professors of Petrozavodsk State University.

---

11 *Molodtsova, A.V./Silantyev, A.E.* 2017: Analysis of the balanced budget of the Republic of Karelia [Electronic resource], StudArctic forum. Issue 3 (7), http://saf.petrsu.ru/journal/article.php?id=2185. (02/10/2020) (in Russian).

12 NBIC convergence is the hypothetical core of the 6th technological structure, based on the combination and synergistic enhancement of the achievements of nano-, bio-, information and cognitive technologies.

13 *Polanyi, K.* 2001: The Great Transformation: The Political and Economic Origins of Our Time, New York, pp. 360–370 (360).

The electronic questionnaire for young people contained 27 questions including the following: The resulting data was processed via Excel and SPSS software. The results of the expert survey were analyzed using the discourse analysis method.

Justification of the sample: for the questionnaire, 1100 young people aged 14 to 30 were interviewed. The sample formation was conducted by means of the spontaneous selection method. The questionnaire was distributed on social networks. This profile was posted on the social network in "vk.com". The sample of experts was undertaken using the "snowball" method. Ten experts were interviewed. Among them there were representatives of youth organizations in Petrozavodsk, PetrSU units responsible for innovative development, student organizations, as well as cultural and leisure associations. These people have a long experience in leadership positions and experience in the field of project activities with young people. Finally, 100 Petrozavodsk State University professors, selected by the available array method, were interviewed.

Among the respondents, 75.5 percent are female, 24.5 percent are male. According to age groups, respondents were divided as follows: 18 percent aged 14–17 years, 42 percent – 18–21 years old, 25.5 percent of people – 22–25 years, 15.5 percent – 26–30 years. The majority of respondents 34.8 percent study at institutions of higher professional education, 25 percent work, 23 percent study at school, 12 percent study at secondary vocational education institutions, 3 percent are unemployed, 2 percent study at primary vocational education institutions; 0.1 percent (8 people) at the time of the survey are on maternity leave; 0.1 percent indicated other activities. The survey covered almost all regions of the Republic of Karelia. So, 88 percent live in urban areas, 12 percent – in rural areas. At the same time, 80 percent study or graduate from a city school, 20 percent from a rural school. The obvious plus is that among the respondents, the majority fixes the presence of most of the qualities inherent in an innovative personality. However, it is worth noting that such important qualities as ownership of innovations and a high level of intelligence are at a low level. At the same time, it is worth considering that these are only the results of self-esteem of young people. The vast majority of young people (95 percent) have an interest in learning something new. A little more than half (55 percent) of respondents are engaged in creativity. Among the obstacles to creative work most often sounded: lack of time, laziness, lack of creativity. Response options related to the lack of conditions for creative work in the village and lack of funds were also possible. Not all young people easily adapt to changes in their lives. 52 percent said that adaptation depends on the severity of the change. When performing any educational, work or creative tasks, respondents approximately equally share different forms of work. The most common foreign language that young people speak is English, but their average level of knowledge is rated by 3 points. However, almost 27 percent indicated that they did not speak any foreign languages. At the same time, 70 percent of young people would like to study throughout their lives, constantly improve their intellectual level. The desire to continuously learn is a very important quality of an innovative personality. According to the results of subjective self-esteem, only 18 percent of youth own a computer by 5 points. Most (49 percent) rated this competency as 4 points.

An active life position and helping other people is an important quality of an innovative personality, however, 52 percent of respondents do not participate in the activities of any public organizations, movements, volunteer groups, etc. According to the survey, the school is not an active subject in the awareness of students about innovations in society but allows you to implement their own innovative projects and ideas. The situation at the university is much better (only those who graduated or study at the university answered the question).

During the survey, respondents were asked to rate the quality of the formation of a number of competencies on a 5-point scale: 1 point – very low quality, 2 points – low quality, 3 points – satisfactory quality, 4 points – good quality, 5 points – excellent quality. Most of the respondents surveyed noted their willingness and ability to take reasonable risks, but rated the level of formation by 3 points; ability and readiness for continuing education, continuous improvement, retraining, self-education (3 points); ability to work independently (4 points). It was proposed to answer the same question to those studying or studying at a university. Respondents emphasized: the ability to work independently (5 points), the ability to work in a team (5 points), the ability and readiness for continuing education and the acquisition of new knowledge (4 points). However, 77 percent of respondents do not have their own innovative ideas or projects. Based on research data the following conclusions could be drawn about Karelian youth in the categories of health, employment rate, and educational level:

- Health: The health of youth in Karelia is deteriorating. This is due to the social and ecological factors as well as the quality of health services and disease prevention practices in the region;
- employment Rate: In the Republic, the unemployment rate is very high. As the unemployment rate in municipalities has grown, the average income of the population has fallen. Youth have been particularly affected by the rising unemployment. In 2013, youth unemployment in Karelia reached nearly 20 percent compared to 2015;
- educational Level: The percentage of the Karelian youth with a university degree is increasing. Meanwhile, empirical studies estimate that for young people education is often just a tool. As a result, education is depreciating as a means of achieving professional mobility.

Based on the self-assessment survey of young people, we can conclude that the innovative potential of Karelian youth is heterogeneous. That is, consisting of parts that are different in composition, properties, origin. It is significantly higher in the city, than in the rural areas. According to respondents, schools, especially rural schools, play a smaller role in developing innovative competences than higher education institutions.

The development of innovative competences among young people must be a priority if Russia Federation is to transition to an innovative development path.[14] Higher education institutions have a special role to play in this transition. Universities act as centers for innovation development and innovative activity in the region and help attract and train the best and the brightest.

14 This is a path based on that knowledge and scientific achievements, due to which Russia must change its raw material orientation in world trade by 2020, as indicated in the "Concept for the Long-Term Socio-Economic Development of the Russian Federation".

The rate of innovation and development in twenty-first century society has left Russia behind in many ways. As in the 1930s when Russia Federation experienced the engineering revolution of industrialization, modern Russia Federation society requires a technological "leap"[15] in order to catch up with other developed nation. However, the personality type required to bridge this gap is no longer the same personality type of that bygone industrial era. The innovative society of the 21st century requires an innovative personality as a special social type, the characteristics of which have not yet been studied within sociological science. If Russia Federation is to catch up to other nations and transition to an innovative development path, then the mass development of this innovative personality and presence of such people in all spheres of society's life is required. In modern civilization, technological development has driven innovative personality type. The global trends of the innovative development in the XXI century reflect the main trends of the cyclical development of the world economy and its innovative component. The global trend of innovation in the twenty-first century reflects the cyclical development of the world economy. That's why, analysis of the genesis and development of these cycles can be based on Kondratiev's supercycles theory[16], Schumpeter's theory of innovation[17], neoclassical theory of innovation, the system paradigm in economic theory, as well as on the accelerating innovation theory.[18]

An innovative personality be explored in a framework and within a specific stage of the society technological development. As the innovative waves change, these requirements change as well, and society needs new innovations competences. In this case, the approach based on focusing on the individual personality qualities is not promising for understanding the phenomenon of innovative personality. The innovative personality and its potential should be considered as one having innovative mindset and a whole set of competences of the digital economy. In addition, young people are most of all involved in the education system, which is one of the most influential subjects of developing personal and professional competences.

Results of the Empirical Research

Research tasks are:

- To analyze the innovative potential of young people in the context of the innovative development of the Russian Federation;
- to explore the opinions of experts on the innovative potential of young people in the Republic of Karelia through interviews;
- to obtain a self-assessment of the innovative potential of young people in the Republic of Karelia based on survey results;
- to learn about the readiness of university teachers to develop the innovative competence of young people based on survey results.

15 *United Nations*: Human Development Reports – United Nations Development Program. http://hdr.undp.org/en/humandev (10/08/2019) (in Russian).

16 Kondratiev's cycles (K-cycles or K-waves) are periodic cycles of successive ups and downs of the modern world economy lasting 40–60 years, described in the 1920s by *Nikolai Kondratiev*.

17 *Schumpeter, J.* 1942: Capitalism, socialism and Democracy, New York, p. 381.

18 *Hayek, F.* 1935: Collectivist Economic Planning, Amsterdam, p. 308.

Results of Youth Poll

Figure 1: Innovative Qualities – self-assessment (Multiple choice)

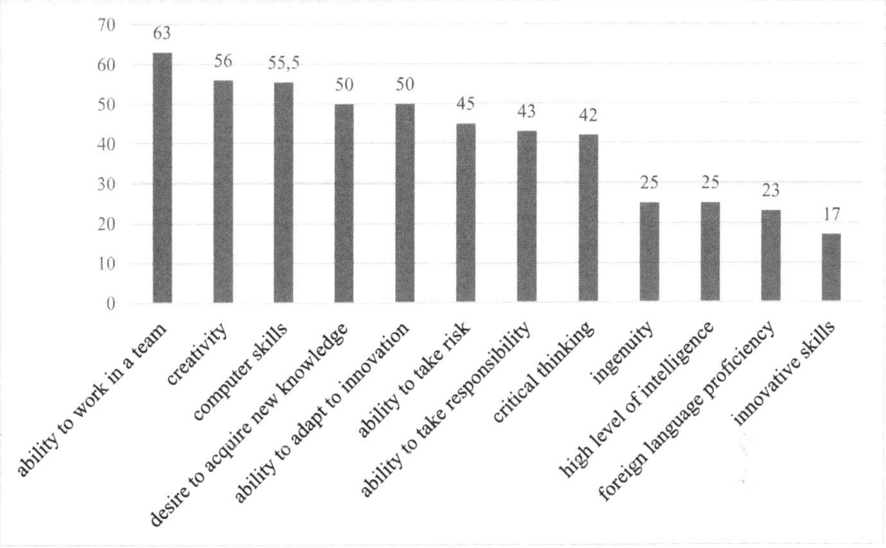

Source: own calculation.

However, young people were rather modest when asked to estimate their ability to handle innovations or their own intelligence. Still, self-assessments provide only a limited insight into the actual state of affairs.

The study attempted to analyze the innovative potential of young people based on their responses to the questionnaire as well as determining what role if any place of residence and level of education played in individuals' competencies. The analysis of innovative potential was determined by testing individuals' competencies in an innovation economy society.

In total 74 percent of respondents were female and 26 percent male. By age group, the respondents were as follows: 18 percent aged 14 to 17, 43 percent aged 18 to 21, 20.5 percent aged 22 to 25, and 18.5 percent aged 26 to 30. Of those 33 percent were enrolled in higher vocational education institutions, 31 percent were employed, 16.3 percent were enrolled in school, 14 percent were enrolled in secondary vocational education institutions, 3.5 percent were unemployed, and 2 percent are enrolled in primary vocational education institutions. A very small minority 0.1 percent (8 persons) were on parental leave at the time of the survey while a further 0.1 percent indicated they were involved in other activities. In terms of residence, 89 percent of respondents resided in urban areas compared to 11 percent in rural areas. This difference is due, inter alia, to the fact that young people move from rural to urban areas for further education. Seventy-nine percent study or have graduated from an urban school and 21 percent from a rural school. This information is important for further evaluation of the school's role in developing key innovative competencies.

Figure 2: Information about innovations in Society delivered by schools (absolute numbers)

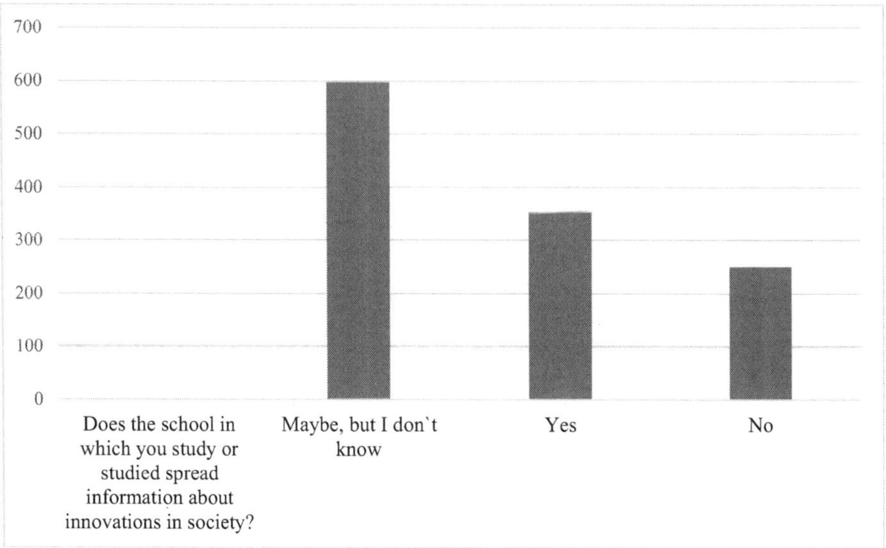

Source: own calculation.

Figure 2 shows that the school is not an active source of information about innovation for young people.

Figure 3: Opportunities to develop innovative projects and ideas at the university (absolute numbers)

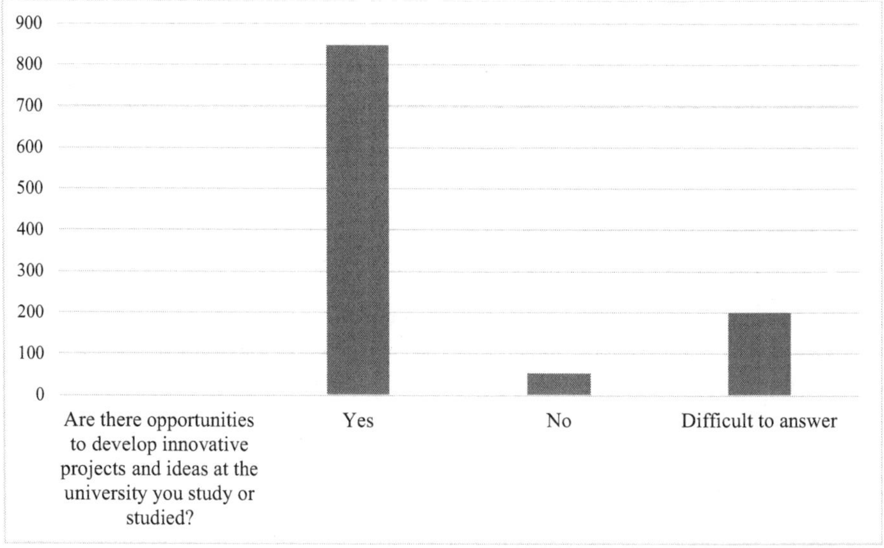

Source: own calculation.

The University distributes information about innovations and helps to implement collected innovative ideas and projects.

The Results of the Expert Survey

According to the experts surveyed, in order to successfully realize one's potential in a digital economy society, it is required to develop such competences as: interpersonal skills, networking skills, developed project thinking, creativity, learning ability, self-development and self-study skills, and the ability to work in a team. Experts identified project work [19]as one of the most effective ways for young people to develop and train these competences and increase their innovative potential. Successful development of these innovative competences among young people is possible if there is cooperation between the state, youth NGOs, and business. In addition, young people need to be more informed about possible events, contests, and competitions with educational or scientific specifics, thereby generating interest in development and self-development.

The third stage of the study was a survey of teachers asking them to compare the level of innovative competencies formation in students in the first and last year of university, as well as how prepared they were as teachers to teach students the necessary competences for forming innovative personalities. During the study, 100 teachers of Petrozavodsk State University were interviewed. The data obtained allow us to draw the following conclusions.

Figure 4: Students' innovative Competences (a teacher survey)

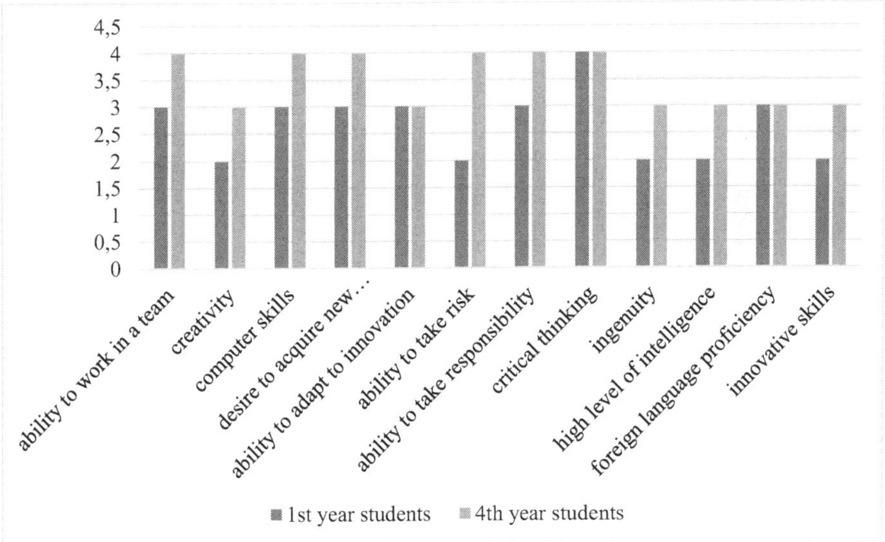

Source: own calculation.

19 The student's independent creative work carried out from the idea to its implementation with the help of teacher advice.

This graph shows professors' assessments of the innovative potential of first year and fourth year students in university.

Conclusion

Although the school develops some qualities of an innovative personality, but the quality is rather low. Therefore, there is a large gap between school graduates and university ones. The university is an active player in developing an innovative personality, according to the professors. Young people are the most economically active group of the population. Young people with high level of innovative potential accelerate the socio-economic development of the region and can be involved in solving socially significant problems. Therefore, the innovative potential of young people can and should be involved in the socio-economic development of the region.

Based on the results of the research, it is planned to develop a project to intensify the innovative potential of young people in the districts of the Republic of Karelia, where the respondents indicated the low level of developing the innovative qualities and competences. The research will be continued, as the phenomenon of innovative potential of young people requires further and deeper study. The level of innovation potential of young people is influenced by the several factors: the awareness of young people themselves of the innovations and the major trends in society, the socio-economic development of the state and the region, the informatization of society, the acceleration of the social progress pace, the level of professional information culture of an individual, and many others, which make the research subject complex and multidimensional.

Additional Reading

Government of the Republic of Karelia 2017: The state program of the Republic of Karelia "Formation of the modern urban environment for 2018-2020", approved by the Decree of the Government of the Republic of Karelia of August 31, 2017. No. 301-P, http://docs.cntd.ru/document/465414512 (31/05/2019) (in Russian).

Lange, O. 1936: On the Economic Theory of Socialism. In: The Review of Economic Studies 1936, no. 4 (2), pp. 123–142.

Vocational Guidance Lesson as an Innovative Tool for Youth Attraction to the Russian Arctic and the Far East including the Example of the Republic of Karelia[1]

Anna Simakova, Maria Pitukhina and Irina Stepus

Abstract: The article presents the regional vocational guidance program for pupils between grades 8 and 10 in the Republic of Karelia; "Live, learn, work in Karelia!". This vocational guidance program was developed by the authors and has been operating for three years already in the Republic of Karelia and the majority of Karelian schools participate at this event including remote rural schools. The goals of the vocational guidance lesson are: to convince local youth to stay in the Russian Arctic and the Far East, to attract human resources and youth to the Russian Arctic and the Far East, and to develop a positive image of these regions in terms of youth wellbeing and professional opportunities.

Vocational guidance lessons like this not only provide interactive vocational guidance resources but also advise pupils on perspective occupations both in forms of "professiongrams"[2] and "occupational barometers"[3]. This approach to vocational guidance allows pupils to form an understanding of their professional future, or to choose an appropriate major and even a potential employer.

The Karelian lesson has also served as the model for a larger project at the federal level entitled "Start Your Career in the Russian Arctic and the Far East." This federal vocational guidance lesson was enacted in 2019 and covered 25 Russian regions and almost 50,000 pupils from 755 schools.

A diagnostic survey following this guidance lesson to gather feedback from participants has showed that pupils' interest towards Arctic and the Far Eastern labor market and their perspective occupations has significantly increased after receiving information within vocational guidance lesson. Incentivizing and nurturing a desire to work in the Arctic or the Far East is an important element in the system of human resource recruitment of these regions in terms of both current and projected labor needs. Graduates from donor regions who start their careers in the Artic or Far East are an enormous human resource to these regions.

Keywords: vocational training, human resources, Karelia, pupils, survey

1 The article was prepared within the framework of 2 projects: "Start your career from the Arctic and the Far East" financed by the Presidential Foundation for civil society and RFFI grant "Live, Work or Leave! Youth – wellbeing and the viability of (post)extractive Arctic industrial cities in Finland and Russia".

2 Professiogram is an infographic on occupations presented in a concise and visualized manner. Professiograms contain a general description of occupation, a description of soft and hard skills, situation in a labor market (high/low demand, level of wages, list of employers' vacancies etc.).

3 Occupational barometer is an infographic on occupations presenting occupations which are in balance, proficit/deficit at municipal labor market.

Introduction

The idea for a vocational guidance lesson was born three years ago at Petrozavodsk State University in the Republic of Karelia. Brand new vocational guidance tools such as "occupational barometers" and "professiograms" were piloted on the web-portal http://mycareer.karelia.ru/.[4] In March 2019, the Republic of Karelia held the "Third Republican Vocational Guidance Lesson" as part of the federal lesson "Start Your Career in the Russian Arctic and the Far East." This third republican vocational guidance lesson was organized and conducted at 106 schools amounting to half of all schools located in Karelia. 7,558 of pupils, mainly from grades 8–10, took part in the third republican vocational guidance lesson from all Karelian municipalities.

In 2018, the idea of a vocational guidance program scaled up into a huge federal project entitled "Start your career in the Russian Arctic and the Far East". The project was supported financially by the Presidential Grants Foundation for Civil Society. In total, 50,000 pupils from the Arctic and Far East regions of Russia took part in this program using the web portal http://dv-arctic.labourmarket.ru.[5]

Federal Vocational Guidance Lesson as a Tool for Youth Attraction to the Russian Arctic and the Far East

The Russian Arctic zone and the Far East are two geostrategic territories of the Russian Federation in terms of both national security and economic development. The Russian government has declared the Far East to be "a national priority for the whole XXI century", and the Arctic – "the most important region of the future, determining both the power and capabilities of Russia for this and the next century."

So called "flagship zones"[6] in the Arctic region, and 'advanced socio-economic territories' in the Far East are currently sites of large-scale investment projects intended to spur socio-economic development in these regions.

It is intended that by 2025 the Far Eastern Federal District will include 18 territories of advanced socio-economic development and 5 free ports. A total of 1,375 projects and 3.8 trillion rubles for investment were announced with the intention of creating 134 000 new jobs in the region. As for the Russian Arctic zone, 145 large-scale investment projects amounting to 5 trillion rubles in investment are planned as well as the creation of 70,000 new jobs.

Both the Far East and the Russian Arctic face serious demographic challenges to their development. More than 20 percent of the population left the Far East during the post-Soviet period.[7] This outward migration continues to be a challenge today despite measures taken by the government. Most of those leaving are people of active working age with vocational

4 Live, study, work in Karelia. http://mycareer.karelia.ru/ (30/03/2020).
5 Start your career in the Russian Arctic and the Far East. http://dv-arctic.labourmarket.ru/ (30/03/2020).
6 Flagship zone is a territory of the Russian Arctic engaged in a large number of investment projects aimed at complex socio-economic development.
7 *Gurtov, V./Stepus, I./Shabaeva, S.* 2019: Vypuskniki vuzov na rynke truda Dal'nego Vostoka // Vysshee obrazovanie v Rossii. 2019. T. 28. No. 12, pp. 36–52. https://doi.org/10.31992/0869-3617-2019-28-12-36-52 (30/03/2020).

training[8]. This trend is especially troubling given this demographics' importance for the implementation of the aforementioned development projects.

Figure 1: Territories of the Russian Arctic zone and the Far East

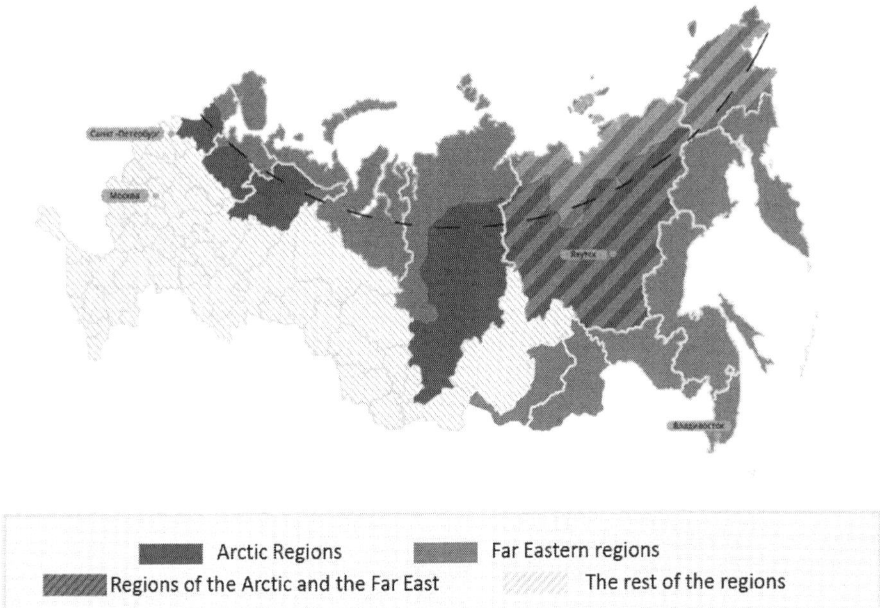

Source: own compilation. http://dv-arctic.labourmarket.ru/.

Thus, the question arises; who will develop the Arctic and the Far East? Nowadays the focus is on youth as the most mobile, creative, and ambitious social group ready to meet the challenge. Recruitment campaigns focus largely on middle school and high school pupils who are ready and willing to consider perspective occupation in the Arctic and Far East regions.

In order to attract youth from outside regions as well as retain local youth, the recruitment efforts highlight the specific occupations, salaries, living and working conditions, and social guarantees available in the regions. The use of professional self-determination services and programs are a key factor in making pupils aware of the potential career opportunities available in the region.

Because of these factors, the stakes for the federal vocational guidance program "Start Your Career in the Russian Arctic and the Far East" are extremely high. The principle goal of the program is build a more positive image of the regions by impressing on pupils between 8–10 grade the potentially prestigious career opportunities available in the Arctic and Far East. This in turn would bolster the potential of development in these geostrategic territories.

8 *Federal State Statistic Service of the Russian Federation* (GKS) 2019: Raspredelenie migrantov po vozrastnym gruppam (chislo vybyvshih 2010–2019) [jelektronnyj resurs] // Federal'naja sluzhba gosudarst vennoj statistiki. https://showdata.gks.ru/report/278986/ (30/03/2020).

Federal Vocational Guidance Lesson Toolkit

The federal vocational guidance programs cover 18 regions of the Russian Arctic and Far East as well as regions which have traditionally contributed youth to the Arctic and Eastern work forces. On December 17, 2019 a round table discussion called "Legislative mechanisms of youth attracting to the Arctic and the Far East" was organized by the State Duma to discuss the program.

The growing digitalization of society poses new challenges for the promotion of vocational training. The increased ubiquity of digital and mobile technology means that society is changing and the demands of consumers and youth for mobile and web services have grown. Youth in particular see digital resources as their primary source of information and such trends must be considered in attempts to engage them. In order to address this, Petrozavodsk State University (with the authors) developed a web-portal to promote the federal vocational guidance program at http://dv-artic.labourmarket.ru/. The portal acts as an interactive digital tool which allows pupils to explore perspective occupations in the Arctic and the Far East. The web-portal contains evaluations for pupils to explore their personal and professional preferences. For each of the 18 regions in the Arctic and the Far East regions, specific infographic passports were developed containing information about that region's employers, schools, and perspective occupations. The web-portal also provides information on state supportive measures for young people who would like to find a job and live in the Russian Arctic and the Far East.

In order to acquaint users with perspective occupations in the Arctic and the Far East, a new informative tool – "professiograms" – was developed detailing key characteristics of perspective occupations including: average wages, demanded skills, key regional employers etc.[9]

The web-portal "Start your career in the Russian Arctic and the Far East" is a completely new tool aimed at information dissemination. The web-portal contains another innovative tool, the occupational barometer. The occupational barometer provides information about occupations by categorizing them as in deficit, balance, or surplus in the region as seen in figure 2. The barometer covers both the two macro-regions (the Arctic and the Far East) as well as the 18 individual Arctic and Far Eastern regions.[10] Using this data, users can make informed decisions about types of training or retraining to pursue based on the available positions and their preferred regional destinations.

---

9 *Serova, L./Sigova, S./Mazaeva K./Fedorova E.* 2015: Citation: Professiogrammykak instrument povysheniya informirovannostinaseleniya o vostrebovannyhprofessiyah. ETAP: EkonomicheskayaTeoriya,Analiz, Praktika, 1, pp. 138–149.

10 *Sigova, S./Stepus, I./Mazaeva, K./Fedorova, E.* 2016: Citation: Barometrzanyatostikakotrazheniesituaciina regional'nomrynketruda. ETAP: EkonomicheskayaTeoriya, Analiz, Praktika, 2, pp. 99–113.

Figure 2: Occupational barometer of the Republic of Karelia

BALANCE	
Operator of ecological installations Archivist Librarian Geodesist Miner Journalist Dental Technician…	Plumbing installer Communications installer Machine and equipment adjuster Printing production operator Stove Food technologist Woodworker…
PROFICIT	
Bank employee Designer Breeder Storekeeper Controller Machinist boilers and steam turbines Manager…	Shoemaker Polisher Conductor Post officer Producer Product collector Machine operator woodworking machines
DEFICIT	
Web designer Aircraft Administrator Woodworking operator Fitter Aerodrome worker… Waiter	Further education teacher Baker Tiler Carpenter Cook Fireman Policemen

Source: own compilation. http://dv-arctic.labourmarket.ru/barometer/10.

The web-portal "Start your career in the Russian Arctic and the Far East" is the main information platform aimed at schoolteachers, pupils, career guidance specialists, and other independent users. The platform aims to encourage local youth stay in the Russian Arctic and the Far East, to attract human resources from other Russian regions to the Arctic and the Far East, and to develop a positive image of these regions in terms of wellbeing and professional opportunities.

Vocational Guidance Lesson Performance Indicators

Research on pupils' career path trajectory in the Russian Arctic and the Far East was conducted within the framework of the federal vocational guidance lesson "Start your career in the Russian Arctic and the Far East". This lesson aims to create a positive image of the Russian Arctic and Far Eastern regions development in terms of youth wellbeing and professional opportunities. The intended audience of the federal vocational guidance lesson are pupils in grades 8–10 from the 18 Arctic and Eastern regions and the 15 regions that have historically contributed youth to the Arctic and Far East workforces.

The federal vocational guidance lesson was introduced in 755 general educational organizations across the 18 regions of the Arctic and the Far East and 10 regions from which young human resources historically migrate to the region.

48,900 pupils between grades 8–10 took part in the federal vocational guidance lesson. An additional 1,800 pupils of other age categories also participated in the lesson. The total number of pupils participating at in the lesson exceeded 50,000[11].

Participation was dominated by pupils from the 8th and 9th grades, who accounted for 74,3 percent of all participants (see figure 3).

Figure 3: Pupils participation rate in federal vocational guidance lesson by macro-region and class year

Russian Arctic Zone	The Far East	Regions-donors
SCHOOLS		
431	247	77
PUPILS NUMBERS		

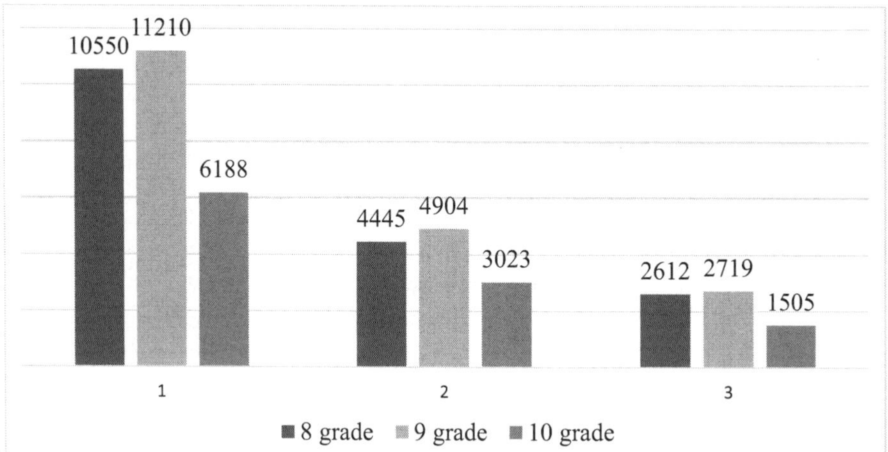

27 948	12 372	6 836

Source: own compilation.

Participation statistics can also be broken down to the regional and municipal level. For example, Krasnoyarsky region contains 61 municipalities but only 31 municipalities participated in the lesson (since only half of Krasnoyarsky region is the part of the Russian Arctic Zone). At the same time, the centers of participation were in Norilsk municipality, Lesosibirsk municipality and Taimyr Dolgan-Nenets municipal district where more than 1,000 pupils

11 Otchet o provedenii meroprijatij proekta "Nachni trudovuju biografiju s Arktiki i dal'nego Vostoka!" [jelektronnyj resurs] // Internet-portal „Nachni trudovuju biografiju s Arktiki i Dal'nego Vostoka!". http://dv-arctic.labourmarket.ru/docs/Отчет_Всероссийский%20профурок%202019.pdf (30/03/2020).

took part in the lesson. That is undoubtedly is the highest rate of participation based on the number of participating pupils coming from each municipality.

The lesson operates online at http://dv-arctic.labourmarket.ru/ with a youth professional inclinations evaluation, to catalogue the users career preferences, and then moves into a visual presentation about occupations in demand in the region. The lesson starts with a survey at the beginning of the lesson; at the end of the lesson pupils are surveyed for the second time. The aim of the first survey is to help youth identify potential professional interests and opportunities, and to identify what kinds of vocational training would be necessary for them. Pupils were also asked open questions. For example, "What do you think the occupation is?" or "How do you see your professional future?" The second survey (at the end of the lesson) help us to reveal which occupation is more attractive for the pupil, provides us the overall feedback of the lesson, was it useful etc.

Figure 4 – Pupils survey results before and after vocational guidance lesson in Karelia

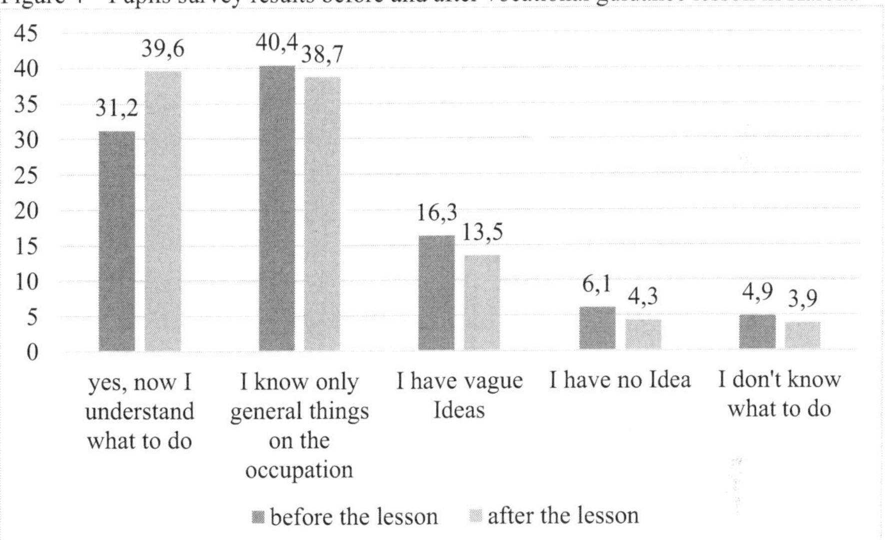

Source: own compilation.

This survey data was then analyzed using descriptive and content analysis methods. The total number of respondents' answers was distributed as follows: 51.8 percent – respondents from the Russian Arctic Zone, 26.7 percent – respondents from the Far East and 21.5 percent – respondents from regions-donors. The analyzing data was used from regions that completed the survey before and after the lesson. Thus, analyses of the completed questionnaires have showed that of the 12,179 students who took part at the first survey, only 8,876 completed the second survey at the end of the lesson. The results have shown that the lesson was generally successful – more than half of pupils (64.5 percent) chose their future occupation, 32.4 percent of pupils found out that information obtained during the lesson was "useful", and for 45.9 percent this information was "highly useful". Information on a career path development both in the Russian Arctic and the Far East was interesting for 41.2 percent of pupils coming from the donor regions.

Thus, the proportion of those pupils who either have vague ideas on the nature of their future occupation has decreased (a decrease by 2.8 percent) or do not have such ideas at all (a decrease by 1,8 percent). Also, the percentage of pupils who were not sure that they would go to work in accordance with their major has reduced by 1 percent.

Despite different total response rates within the regions, the distribution of respondents by grade level was relatively homogeneous across all regions with approximately 80 percent coming from the 8thand 9th grades and the remaining 20 percent from the 10thgrade. The actual responses to the survey did however show differences in opinion across regions.

Figure 5: Respondents' structural redistribution in terms of grades, macro-regions, in percent

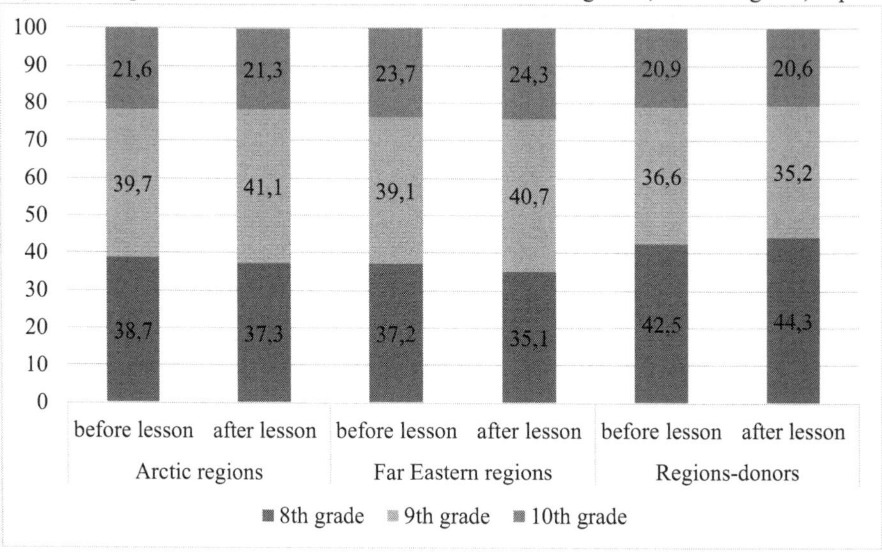

Source: own compilation.

According to the survey result, more than half of all participating pupils had already decided on their future occupation. It should be noted that not all pupils who had already made their career choice indicated a specific occupation on the survey. The ten most popular occupations were identical across all three regions. Statistics regarding the survey results, shares of the most popular careers, and participation are shown in table 1 below. At the beginning of the lesson pupils were asked the question "Have you decided on your future profession? If yes, please, indicate which occupation you have chosen". Thus, there were outlined the most popular occupations for all 3 types of macro-regions. Most of these occupations belong to a so called "mass occupations" type (universal), which is in demand in almost every Russian region.

The most popular occupations identified by pupils belong to the so-called "mass occupations" category. Mass occupations are occupations which are in high demand in almost every Russian region. A number of participants (115 out of 4 500) identified the ministries of emergency, internal affairs, and the federal security service as their preferred professional destinations however, they did not indicate any specific occupation available in these offices.

Table 1: Survey Results and Top Ten Careers by Region

Occupation title	Share of occupations in a general list of those indicated in the Russian Arctic zone, in %	Share of occupations in a general list of those indicated in the Far East, in %	Share of occupations in a general list of those indicated in donor regions, in %
Total number of answers	**2272**	**1338**	**949**
Total number of unique occupations	**368**	**270**	**238**
Doctor	6.7 %	5.9 %	7.9 %
Software developer	5.4 %	5.4 %	7.8 %
Lawyer	3.5 %	2.9 %	2.3 %
Dentist	3.0 %	2.2 %	1.9 %
Policeman	2.8 %	3.7 %	2.3 %
Military man	2.6 %	3.7 %	2.3 %
Psychologist	2.3 %	2.7 %	3.0 %
Engineer	2.2 %	2.2 %	3.5 %
Designer	1.5 %	1.6 %	2.3 %
Translator	1.3 %	1.9 %	1.2 %

Source: own calculation.

It shall be also noted that all occupations chosen by pupils require higher vocational education most of the time. At the same time demand for blue collar occupations with secondary vocational education prevails in a labor market of Arctic and Far Eastern regions.[12]

According to the first survey results around one in eight pupils would like to work in medicine – 13 percent; 12.9 percent of pupils prefer military service, police, security; culture and art – 10.1 percent; social sphere – 8.1 percent, IT – 8.3 percent; transport – 7.3 percent, pedagogy – 6.6 percent, 17.5 percent – other activities and 16.2 percent of pupils were not yet determined before the lesson start.

After the vocational lesson the pupils share who had no idea or only a vague idea of the occupation, they wished to pursue fell from 6,1 percent to 4,3 percent based on comparisons from the entry and exit surveys.

Pupils were also asked to evaluate the possibility of successful career opportunities in the Arctic and the Far East. Approximately one in every three pupils from the Arctic region (30.2 percent), the Far East (32.6 percent) and donor regions (35.3 percent) answered that it was certainly possible. One in every two said they were unsure but believed "this was more likely possible." An unequivocally negative opinion on the possibility for finding successful career opportunities in the Russian Arctic and the Far East was expressed by 6.1 percent of

12 *Pitukhin, E./Kekkonen, A./Shabaeva, S.* 2019: Citation: Ocenkapotencialasistemyprofessional'nogoobrazo vaniyaDal'negoVostokakakprioritetnojterritoriiRossii. Perspektivynaukiiobrazovaniya, 1, pp. 20–36.

pupils from Arctic regions, 61 percent from the Far Eastern regions and 7.4 percent from the donor regions.

Figure 6: "For which occupation you would like to have a vocational education?" (in terms of macro regions and percent)

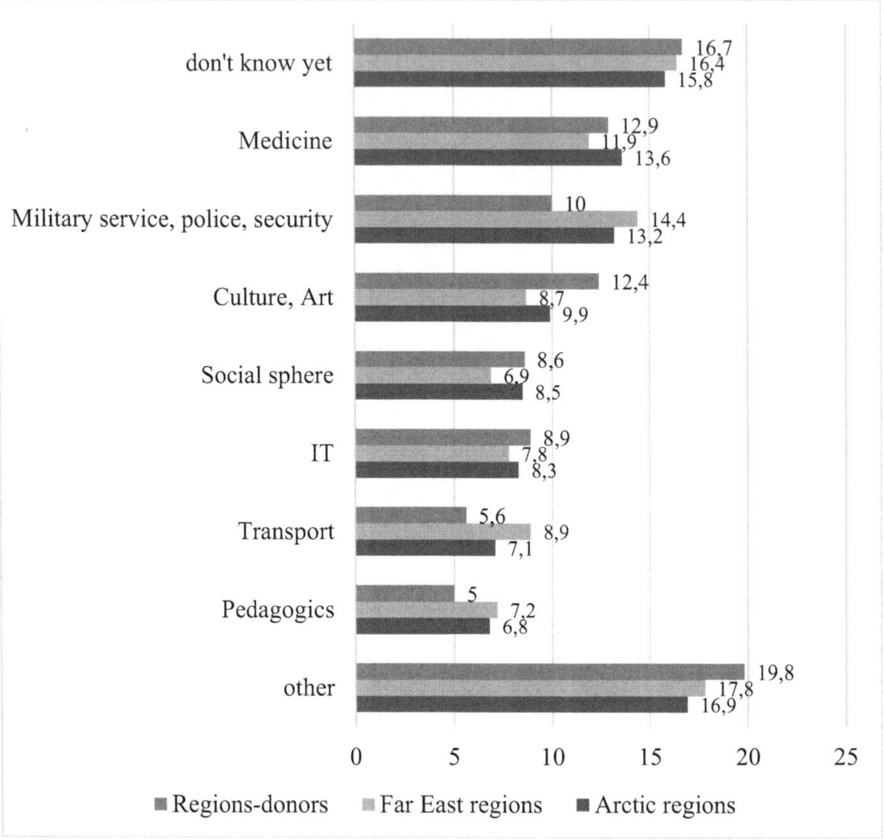

Source: own compilation.

In order to identify pupils' personal inclinations towards pursuing a career in the Russian Arctic or the Far East, pupils were asked: "Would you like to start your career in the Russian Arctic or the Far East?" The breakdown of their answers can be seen below in figure 7. Only 12.7 percent of surveyed pupils from Arctic regions and 23.7 percent from the Far East answered that they had definitely planned their career at companies located in the Russian Arctic and the Far East. 20 percent of pupils from the Arctic and Far Eastern regions as well as 13 percent of surveyed pupils from the donor regions said they started thinking of their future career in these regions after completing the program. Pupils who have expressed their direct and potential interest in future career in the Arctic and Far Eastern regions are the target audience in terms of providing additional information on regional labor market, career opportunities, living conditions and other social and economic effects.

Figure 7: "Would you like to start your career in the Russian Arctic or the Far East?" (in terms of macro regions and percent)

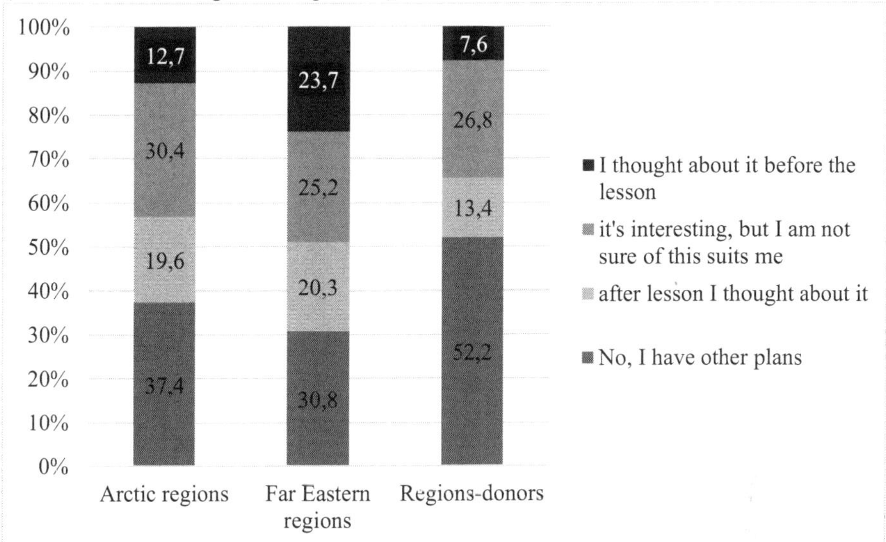

Source: own compilation.

Conclusion

Pupils' career trajectory development in the Arctic and the Far East is highly important for strategic recruitment needs in terms of both current and projected human resources shortage. One of the main sources for the recruitment needs is donor regions' graduates who traditionally start their career in the Arctic and Far Eastern enterprises. The federal vocational guidance lesson "Start your career from the Arctic and the Far East" proved to be highly attractive for pupils because it attempts to promote more motivated career development, to increase youth awareness on occupations in demand in the Arctic and the Far East, and to develop a positive image of the Arctic and Far East in the minds of Russian pupils.

It is hoped that the longer-term effect of the vocational guidance lesson will be increased rates of youth remaining and migrating to the Arctic and Far East regions including young specialists. The principal goal of the lesson is to change attitudes of all students to career development in the Russian Arctic and the Far East.

Overall, pupils held a positive view of their possibilities of career opportunities in the Arctic and Far East. For more than half of pupils (64.5 percent) the vocational guidance lesson clarified their occupation choice and future career path. For 32.4 percent of surveyed pupils, the information they obtained was "very useful". For 45.9 percent of surveyed pupils, the lesson was "quite useful". Even more encouraging was the fact that 41.2 percent of pupils from donor regions found the information on careers in the Russian Arctic and Far East to be interesting.

The Features of Territorial Image Formation (by the Example of the Republic of Karelia)

Alisa Kruglova

Abstract: The problems of creating a successful image of a territory are an urgent topic for research as they determine success in competing for resources, investments and new residents. These issues are especially relevant for the Russian Federation, which includes 85 territorial entities. This article presents an analysis of the factors that shape the image of a territory and the features of this process using the Republic of Karelia as a case study. Much attention is paid to the existing images of the region and the specific images practices that elites choose to promote.

Keywords: brand, image, territorial image, territorial marketing, Republic of Karelia.

Initially, the term "image" appeared in the field of aesthetics and art history. In the 1950s and 1960s, American economists addressed the problemata of image. In the 1970s, image began to be studied in the USSR. The long delay in studying image was in part due to the negative image held in the USSR around the topic. The concept of image was seen as a tool of bourgeois politics and media for manipulating the mass consciousness of the population. Over the next couple of decades, image became a very broad interdisciplinary concept. Today it is used in marketing, political science, psychology and among other fields.

The word "image" in Russian language has several meanings. There is a word "obraz" that can be translated as "image of impression" and a word "imidzh" that can be translated as "image of representation". There are two positions among scientists about these terms. Some scientists use these two terms as synonyms and define "image of representation" through "image of impression" in the texts.[1] The second group of experts divides the terms and emphasizes that "image of impression" changes spontaneously and exists continuously as a reflection of an object in the minds of people. "Image of representation" is a result of purposeful constructivist activity and it does not reflect reality so much as creates its own.[2] The second approach allows to see the artificial nature of image that can be studied from the political science perspective.

1 *Pankrukhin, A.P./ Ignatiev, A.Yu.* 2008: Image of the country: a paradigm shift. Views from Canada, Russia, the UK and Latvia. In: Corporate Image, 02 (03), pp. 8–15 (in Russian); *Vazhenina, I.S.* 2008: Image and brand of a region: essence and features of formation. In: Regional Economy, pp. 49–57 (in Russian).

2 *Shestopal, Ye.B.* 2008: Obraz and image in political perception. In: Images of states, nations and leaders, pp. 8–23 (in Russian); *Tatarinova, N.V.* 2009: On the concept of "image" and its difference from similar concepts of "image as impression", "reputation", "stereotype". In: Philological Sciences. Questions of theory and practice, No. 2, pp. 252–255 (in Russian); *Leontyev, D.A.* 2000: From "image as impression" to "image as representation": psychosemantic branding. In: Advertising and life, No. 1, pp. 19–22 (in Russian); *Greenberg, T.E.* 2009: The image as imression of the country or the image as representation of the state: the search for a constructive model. In: Press service, No. 2, pp. 74–82 (in Russian).

In the context of the constructivist approach, a territory is one of many possible objects of image formation. There are two types of factors that influence image forming: ***objective*** and *subjective*[3]. Objective factors include geographic location, environmental diversity and other natural resources which are not created by human activity. Subjective factors are those factors connected with human activity. They include the actions of authorities, the assessment of a territory by politicians, entrepreneurs, tourists and the characterization of a territory in the media. Besides objective and subjective factors, there are two additional features in the image formation process. The target group of a particular image and the image of constituent territories which may influence the image of the territory in question.

The image of a territory has important pragmatic functions. Building a strong image of a territory can be a determining factor in its development because an attractive and successful image creates valuable opportunities for recruiting investments and resources.

As mentioned previously, the image of a territory can be a result of the purposeful activity of authorities. In the process of developing an image strategy, authorities must choose the most suitable image. There are many options for the focus of a territory's image: cultural, sports, tourism, technological, environmental, historical, industrial, etc. Each requires a specific implementation program both within and outside a region in order to succeed. Igor Belskih adds that regions need to have multivariate images for successful promotion.[4]

At this time, very few territories in Russia are well positioned to promote their image. According to Irina Vazhenina, an expert in the study of territorial image problems, many regions of Russia are faceless and have "weakly expressed images"[5], which prevent not only foreigners, but also Russians from distinguishing one region from another for their unique qualities. Vazhenina emphasizes that need for regions to break free of centralization, both legally and in their identity, in order to promote and capitalize on their unique image.[6] Even so, actors must be aware of the context surrounding them as they pursue their own preference and goals. This is especially true of national regions because, in their role as components of a state, whose image should not conflict with the state's image.

To understand how the process of forming a territorial image works, we can consider the Republic of Karelia. Karelia is a republic in the North-West of Russia. On August 9, 1990, the Supreme Soviet of Karelia adopted a declaration on the state sovereignty of the Karelian SSR and highlighted their desire to establish a degree of autonomy from the federal center. Now there are no attempts to return to the discussion of the autonomy of the Republic of Karelia because of a strict vertical of power that controls any manifestations of separatist ideas in the regions.

A significant event of the 1990s was the adoption of regional symbols in the forms of: a flag, an emblem, and an anthem. This process was complicated and full of heated debates among the public. Some citizens wanted to return to the symbols of the Republic of Uhtua

3 *Chernaja, I.P.* 2002: Image marketing as a strategic direction of territorial marketing. In: Marketing in Russia and Abroad, No 4, pp. 15–21 (in Russian).

4 *Belskih, I.* 2014: The multivariate image of the territory in the internal and external markets of the global world. In: Regional Economics: theory and practice, (29), pp. 2–10 (in Russian).

5 *Vazhenina, I.* 2010: The image, brand and reputation as a competitive advantage in the region. In: Upravlenets [The manager], No. 5–6, pp. 4–9 (4) (in Russian).

6 Ibidem.

of 1920, while others favored the adoption of a new set of symbols for the new republic. The Republic of Uhtua was historically in the same place where The Republic of Karelia is located. An important actor of this process was the Karelian movement, defending the interests of Karelians and Finns, recognizing them as the original inhabitants of this territory and demanding the return of historical symbolism. Following a vote, on February 16, 1993, the Supreme Council of the Republic approved the official flag and emblem of the republic, both of which used symbols of the Republic of Uhtua.

Figure 1: The coat of arms of the Uhtua Republic

Source: Coat of arms of the Uhtua Republic.[7]

Figure 2: The coat of arms of the Republic of Karelia

Source: Coat of arms of the Republic of Karelia.[8]

By the late 1990s, the Constitution of the Republic of Karelia demanded changes because it was largely Soviet and did not comply with the Constitution of the Russian Federation. A new version of the Constitution was approved in 2001. The Constitution secured the distribution of powers between the republic and the federal center.

In general, the 1990s period was fundamental for the subsequent process of developing the image of Karelia. It was the time of registration of the official symbols of the region and changes in regional legislation. Karelia relied on the unique nature and culture of the region in strengthening its image, but the transmission of that image to the external market around the region was not conducted.

Taking into account that The Russian Federation consists of 85 subjects that has to compete for resources and markets, Karelia has begun developing image options to attract investors, tourists and new inhabitants. There were three key areas in which the image of the Republic of Karelia was shaped by authorities from the beginning of the 2000s to the present: tourism, investment and culture. The reason for these areas of focus were the objective factors (nature, history of the region and its culture) and the needs of consumers.

7 Coat of arms of the Uktha Republic. https://geraldika.ru/symbols/242 (04/04/2020). The colors of the flag are red (upper stripe) and green (lower stripe).

8 Coat of arms of the Republic Karelia. https://geraldika.ru/symbols/234 (04/04/2020) Colour of the frame is gold, the filling flag is red (upper), blue (middle) and green (lower stripe).

Tourist Image

Some of Karelia's most important objective traits are its nature and ecology and for many people it's the main associations with the region. The territory also benefits from its border position. As such, one of the images for Karelian authorities to bolster was the territory's tourist image.

In the early 2000s, the first serious attempts at promoting the tourist image of Karelia began. The year 2000 was declared as the "year of tourism" in Karelia and marked by the start of the project "Tourist Karelia"[9]. The project included a special exhibition with the participation of cities of the republic, museums, travel and transport companies and other representatives of the local tourism market. Within the framework of the project, the need was noted for the formation of event tourism programs and a long-term tourism development strategy in Karelia. In 2003, Karelia won the title "the best European region of the year". This helped to promote the tourist potential of the region to European markets outside of Russia.

As a result of these events the local authorities approved long-term tourism development programs for the region. Despite these developments, the rhetoric of regional and federal authorities showed discontent with the state of the region's image and its tourism potential. In 2011, Andrey Nelidov, the ex-head of the Republic of Karelia, declared "Karelia has a fantastic tourist potential, but, in my earnest conviction, it is not revealed yet. As Head of the republic I consider the results of the work of the travel industry unsatisfactory. Present results of the branch may not be compared to the republic's opportunities"[10]. In 2016, Nikolay Patrushev, Secretary of the Security Council of Russia, said "The Republic has significant tourism potential, which, unfortunately, is currently not fully implemented"[11].

It is important to note that the image of a territory is affected not only by the volume of its demonstrated advantages and the current level of infrastructure development, but also by its past. For example, the tourist image of Karelia was weakened due to the events of June 18, 2016, when 14 children died during a storm that caught a tour group on the lake Syamozero. "We promoted Karelia as a tourist paradise, but it turns out completely different"[12] said about the accident Alexander Khudilainen, who was the head of the region at that time. Tasks were set to restore the image of Karelia as a "beautiful republic" for safe tourism and recreation.

In 2017 the current head of the Republic of Karelia Artur Parfenchikov underscored an additional challenge to the tourist image of the republic. "Unfortunately, very few people know about Karelia in detail and specifically. We were convinced of this fact when communicating with travel companies that came to us as part of the TUI info-tour. For the 90 percent

---

9 The program "Promotion of the Republic of Karelia to the Russian and world market of cultural and tourist services". http://old.gov.karelia.ru/Power/Committee/Sport/Tourism/turizm3.html#01 (14/08/2019) (in Russian).

10 *The Government of the Republic of Karelia* 2011: Head of the republic: "Karelia has a fantastic tourist potential". http://old.gov.karelia.ru/News/2011/05/0523_02.html (14/08/2019) (in Russian).

11 *Interfax-Russia* 2016: Karelia needs to develop tourism potential. http://www.interfax-russia.ru/NorthWest/main.asp?id=787148&p=5 (14/08/2019) (in Russian).

12 *Tass* 2016: Head of Karelia urged officials to restore the image of the republic after an emergency at Syamozero. https://tass.ru/obschestvo/3390235 (14/08/2019) (in Russian).

of this audience this was the first time in Karelia. It suggests that we need to work for the future"[13]. Recognition and publicity are important for every image because without them image doesn't work and bring benefits for its regional community.

In order to achieve greater publicity, regional authorities worked with influential tour-companies in order to promote the region. In 2017, the republic entered into a partnership agreement with the tour operator TUI. Together with the tour operator the regional authorities create combined routes that include different types of tourism. Another area of cooperation is event tourism. With the help of TUI, the Ruskeala Symphony, an annual music festival in the marble canyon Ruskeala, became an international event and attended by more people from different countries.[14]

TUI is not the only tour operator developing tourist routes in conjunction with regional authorities. A tourist agency "Lukomorye" developed a new long tourist route "Karelia 555" last spring. The number 555 represents the following formula: 5 lakes + 5 waterfalls + 5 main attractions (including the cities of Petrozavodsk and Sortavala, the Kizhi Island and a couple of museums) = 555 kilometers of vivid impressions.[15] In this case, emphasis is placed on the nature of Karelia and its landscapes. Information about the route is actively broadcast by regional authorities through video advertising.

On June 1, 2019, the Ruskeala Express project was launched. This is a daily retro train connecting Sortavala and Ruskeala park. The launch of the train allowed to increase the number of visitors to the mountain park and rise the number of foreign tourists to 10–12 percent of the total number of visitors.[16]

It can be concluded that the tourist image of Karelia is still based on the idea of the region as "the land of lakes and forests". In order to be successful, regional authorities must promote the region as a year-round destination in order to provide the region with an even flow of tourists. It will help to attract more investments in the economy of the region, the hotels and recreation centers will be full of tourists and the local residents who are associated with the tourism sector will be provided with jobs. Therefore, it is necessary to expand the range of tourist activities.

Investment Image

Significant investments and business interest are required in order to realize the tourism potential of Karelia. Since the beginning of the 2000s, various programs have been implemented in Karelia to create an investment-friendly regime in the region and promote the economic development of the territory. Since 2013, the law "On State Support of Investment

---

13 *Atorus* 2017: TUI introduced to travel agents the tourism potential of Karelia. http://www.atorus.ru/ru/press-centre/new/41002.html (14/08/2019) (in Russian).

14 *TUI* 2018: Tour operator TUI becomes the general partner of the Ruskeala Symphony festival. Retrieved from https://www.tui.ru/news/ruskeala-symphony (15/03/2020) (in Russian).

15 *Agency Republic* 2019: A new tourist route will be opened in Karelia. http://rk.karelia.ru/ekonomika/novyj-turisticheskij-marshrut-otkroyut-v-karelii/ (15/03/2020) (in Russian).

16 *Agency Republic* 2019: Retro train transported more than 15 thousand tourists since the beginning of summer. http://rk.karelia.ru/social/bolee-15-tysyach-turistov-perevez-retropoezd-s-nachala-leta/ (15/03/2020) (in Russian).

Activities in the Republic of Karelia" has been in force. An investor can receive support from the local government for a project if it meets at least three criteria from the document. There are six possible criteria in the law: making investments in the form of capital investments; job growth; budget efficiency of an investment project; introduction of resource-saving technologies; social significance of an investment project; implementation of a project in one of the monotowns of Karelia[17]. A monotown is a city with an unstable economic and social situation. There are currently ten monotowns in Karelia which is higher in comparison to other regions. The criteria about the monotowns helps to intensify efforts to attract new investors to these territories, including small and medium-sized enterprises.[18]

Another investment program is centered around the preparation for the 100th anniversary of the Republic of Karelia. The program is made up of a large-scale package of measures designed to improve the standard of living of the population, increase economic productivity, and attract investments. Despite significant support for the program, there have been problems with the implementation of some projects due to delays in documentation and inadequate control by the executive authorities of the region.

Besides investing in its own future, Karelia has strengthened its image through participation in trade exhibitions and international cooperation. In particular, Karelia has cooperated extensively with the Chinese province of Fujian. As a result, Karelian products were showcased in the China International Trade and Investment Exhibition in September 2019 and attracted Chinese investors to projects in Karelia. Territories discuss the possibility of building wind farms in the north of Karelia, supplying granite to China and exchanging students between universities of China and the Republic of Karelia.[19]

In 2011, the Corporation for Development of the Republic of Karelia was established by the government. The corporation implements projects to unlock the investment potential of the territory. Among the ongoing projects is the product certification system "Made in Karelia". Locally manufactured goods which pass a laboratory quality test, are eligible for packaging with a "Made in Karelia" logo. The logo helps promote high quality goods to tourists and locals seeking to by Karelian products. Currently more than 20 manufacturers are eligible for "Made in Karelia" certification.[20]

---

17 Law of the Republic of Karelia of March, 5 2013 No. 1687-ZRK "On the State Support of Investment Activities in the Republic of Karelia".

18 *The Ministry of Economic Development and Industry of the Republic of Karelia* 2018: New investors come to the monotowns of Karelia. https://economy.karelia.ru/11650/news/22744.html (15/03/2020) (in Russian).

19 *The Government of the Republic of Karelia* 2019: Karelia and Fujian develop bilateral relations. http://gov.karelia.ru/news/26-03-2019-kareliya-i-provintsiya-futszyan-razvivayut-dvustoronnie-otnosheniya/ (15/03/2020) (in Russian).

20 The Corporation for Development of the Republic of Karelia: https://kr-rk.ru/.

Figure 3: The mark of voluntary certification "Made in Karelia"

Source: Development Corporation of the republic of Karelia.[21]

At the same time, the Corporation for Development of the Republic of Karelia does not have an investment strategy and indicators to evaluate the results of its work. The Corporation duplicates a number of tasks and functions of the Ministry of Economic Development.

In 2015, a ten-year investment strategy for the Republic was approved by the ex-head of the republic Alexander Khudilainen. The goal was to increase the volume of investments twofold from 2013, reduce threats to improving the investment climate of the republic, and to strengthen the image of Karelia as an investment-friendly region. However, from 2013 to 2016 annual investment rates declined. Despite positive growth in 2017, investment again fell slightly in 2018. The results of 2017 were largely achieved by the commissioning of a new paper machine at the Segezha Pulp and Paper Mill, a large enterprise located in the region. It attracted about 9 billion rubles. In 2018, high indicators were achieved due to the implementation of a larger number of investment projects, including in small business.[22] Despite these facts, Karelia is ranked second to last of all the regions in the Northwestern Federal District in terms of investment.[23]

Table 1: Investments in the fixed capital of the Republic of Karelia

Year	**2013**	**2014**	**2015**	**2016**	**2017**	**2018**
Investments	34204,0	33399,5	32373,1	34700,0	41567,8	41237,0

* In millions of rubles
Source: Federal State Statistic Service 2019.
http://old.gks.ru/wps/wcm/connect/rosstat_main/rosstat/ru/statistics/enterprise/investment/nonfinancial/.

At this stage, we can see positive trends in some investment areas, but overall investment has grown slowly. Structures such as the Development Corporation of the Republic of Karelia were created to increase the amount of investments but have had little impact.

21 About the mark of the system of voluntary certification of products "Made in Karelia". https://kr-rk.ru/sdelano-v-karelii (04/04/2020). Main colors are green, black (bear), and red (berries).

22 *The Ministry of Economic Development and Industry of the Republic of Karelia* 2019: The number of investment projects has increased in Karelia. https://economy.karelia.ru/11650/news/27167.html (15/03/2020) (in Russian).

23 *Federal State Statistic Service* 2019: http://gks.ru/.

Cultural Image

The cultural image of a given place is very difficult to change. For this reason, a clear strategy for working with existing material is important. The basis of the cultural image of the Republic of Karelia primarily includes indigenous peoples and their rich heritage: languages, cuisine, clothes, traditions. At the same time, there are a number of issues that relate to the basis of the cultural image and require effective actions by the authorities of the region.

The first problem is associated with a decrease in the number of people who identify themselves with the Finno-Ugric group.[24] The territory loses its natural basis that becomes more artificial. The second problem is related to the present state of cultural and historical monuments. According to the Head of the Monument Protection Department of the Republic of Karelia Yulia Alipova, more than half of the monuments of wooden architecture of Karelia do not even stand on cadastral registration.[25] No one is responsible for the safety of these objects.

Nevertheless, the national component of the culture and history of Karelia is actively replicated. Annually, festivals and exhibitions dedicated to the indigenous Karelian peoples are held in the republic. Musical ensembles, such as "Kantele" and "Toive", present the musical heritage of the peoples of Karelia outside the region. The participants of these ensembles play national instruments, sing songs of the indigenous Karelian peoples, wear traditional Karelian clothes and perform traditional dances.

On example of trying to maximize the cultural potential of Karelia is a project by the information agency "Republic". The agency created the book "100 Symbols of Karelia"[26] dedicated to the anniversary of the republic. The book is made up of ideas proposed by readers and selected by the agency's editors. Among the published symbols are elements of local nature (waterfalls, lakes, Karelian birches, forest), elements of Karelian culture (epic "Kalevala", kantele, Karelian dance, Kizhi Island), famous residents and historical events.

The creation of a cultural image is strengthened by new brands and the events held in the region. For 2020, Petrozavodsk will become the "Capital of Russian Design". The status implies a program of festivals, conferences and exhibitions with the participation of leading designers of Russia, creation of new art objects, audit of urban spaces and development of branding for the capital of Karelia. This status is important for the cultural image of the republic, because as part of the project, designers present works related to Karelian history, nature, indigenous peoples. It has to increase attractiveness and recognition of the territory and its capital for guests of the republic and for its inhabitants.

As a result, we can see that the basis of the cultural image of Karelia remains connected with indigenous Karelian peoples. We have opportunities to work with existing cultural material and don't invent an absolute new cultural story. There is a lack of funding to maintain

24 *The Government of the Republic of Karelia*: The Karelians: the current cultural and linguistic situation. http://old.gov.karelia.ru/gov/Power/Committee/National/karel_zaikov.html (15/03/2020) (in Russian).

25 *Hraniteli-nasledia* 2018: Julia Alipova: On the lack of funding for the maintenance of all cultural objects of Karelia. http://hraniteli-nasledia.com/articles/person/yuliya-alipova/yuliya-alipova-po-linii-kultury-vse-obekty-ne-potyanut/ (15/03/2020) (in Russian).

26 *Agency Republic* 2020: 100 symbols of Karelia. http://rk.karelia.ru/category/special-projects/100-simvolov - karelii/ (15/03/2020) (in Russian).

cultural and historical monuments in good condition that becomes a serious threat for the cultural image. The number of representatives of the indigenous Karelian peoples rapidly decreases from year to year. We already need to reproduce the culture of the indigenous peoples artificially.

Conclusion

The case of the Republic of Karelia approves that image is a complicated construction made up of many elements. In the case of a territory, the image is based on objective and subjective factors. The main actors who directs and controls the creation of an image are government authorities. Federal and local authorities decide what type of image and image strategies a territory should pursue given its objective factors, as well as relative advantages and disadvantages. An effective image is an important resource for a territory and can strengthen its competitiveness as the territory competes with other territories in the investment and tourism markets. In this way, an effective territorial image may help a territory receive more investments and thereby increase its possibilities for development. Therefore, territories should strongly consider hiring professional territorial marketing specialists to create and promote a strong image of a territory which highlights its uniqueness and opportunities to observers.

PART 3: WELLBEING AND PUBLIC OPINION

The Urban Environment through the Eyes of Residents of Petrozavodsk

Irina Miljukova and Polina Kopteva

Abstract: The quality of living space is increasingly becoming a top criterion in the assessment of the today person's quality of life. A federal project "Development of a Comfortable Urban Environment" has been implemented in Russia since the end of 2016. Its main goal is to create conditions for improving the quality and comfort of the urban environment throughout the country. The article presents the results of exploratory research among residents of Petrozavodsk assessing the quality of their living space. An open-ended interview method was used to study the general ideas of the population about urban space. The research also aimed to discover the subjective image of Petrozavodsk and the social factors that determine the Petrozavodsk residents' perceptions and images of the city. Furthermore, the research focus touches upon issues of social activity by Petrozavodsk residents regarding urban improvement and interactions between the population and municipal authorities. A theoretical model of urban space proposed by the Russian sociologist T. Dridze was used to systematize and analyze the data obtained. Following this model, four basic elements were distinguished in the structure of the urban space: natural, physical; informational and anthropocentric. The subjective perceptions of the city by its residents, their observations and assessments, are considered by the authors of this article as an important factor in the development of the urban space.

Keywords: urban space, social space, comfortable urban *environment, citizen participation.*

The global process of urbanization has transformed the world, and today more than half of the world's population lives in cities. Russia is no exception to that trend: according to official statistics, at the beginning of 2019, the urban population in Russia was at 74 percent.[1] Urban lifestyles and the increasing diversity of living conditions in the city have not only created new social and cultural rules, but also new forms of citizen participation and new indicators of the comfort. Urbanization represents both an opportunity and a new set of challenges for those concerned with protecting and promoting human wellbeing.

Today, the quality of the urban environment, both natural and social, is considered one of the important components affecting quality of life, alongside economic wellbeing and human capacity development.[2] The urban environment impacts many things, from people's mood to their health and future plans.

1 *Russian Federal State Statistics Service (Rosstat)* 2019: Demografiya [Demography]. http://www.gks.ru/wps/wcm/connect/rosstat_main/rosstat/ru/statistics/population/demography/# (23/08/2019).

2 *Gorina, E./Burdyak*, A. 2015: Vzglyad na kachestvo zhizni naseleniya skvoz prizmu gorodskoy sredy [The quality of life in big city through the urban environment perceptions]. In: Sotsiologiya Goroda [Sociology Of City], 2, pp. 11–31. http://vgasu.ru/attachments/sg_2-2015.pdf.

Currently, there are many ways to evaluate urban space. For example, the “Place Diagram”.[3] The diagram is based on four basic indicators shared by public spaces perceived as attractive (see figure 1).

Figure 1: Place Diagram

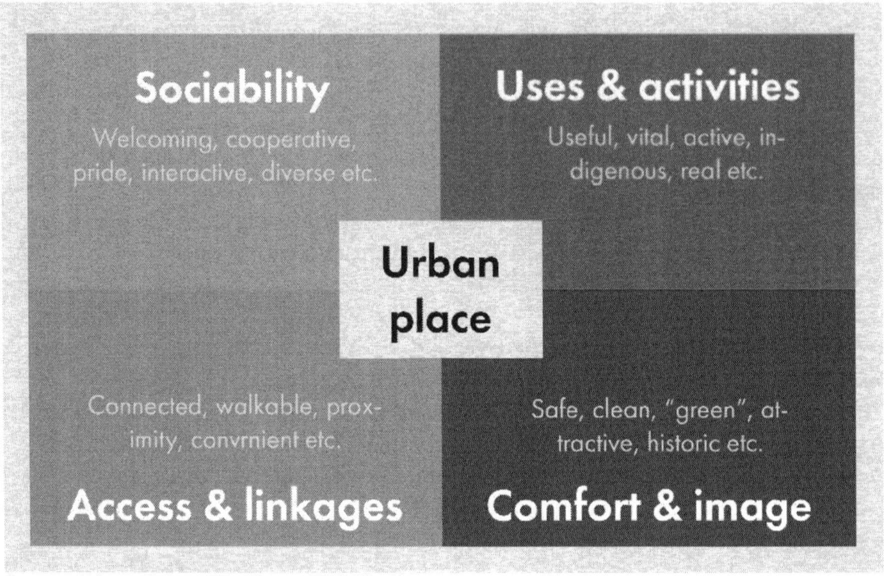

Source: *Ahlgren/Robson/Houthaeve* 2018 (fn. 3).

At the end of 2016, the Presidential Council for Strategic Development in Russia adopted a federal project “Development of a Comfortable Urban Environment” (2017–2022). Its main goal is to create conditions for improving the quality and comfort of the urban environment throughout the country. The potential impact of forming a comfortable urban environment affect the interests of more than 30 million residents of regional centers across Russia, and more than 13 million residents of mono cities (one-industry towns), and therefore increasing the satisfaction of citizens with the quality of their urban environments has become one of the priorities of the Russian President.

An Urban Environment Quality Index was developed in 2017 to assess the project’s implementation process. The Quality Index assesses how ready a city is for modern challenges and how well it meets the needs of its residents.[4] In 2019 the Quality Index is formed by Ministry of Construction, Housing and Utilities of the Russian Federation. The goal of the Urban Environment Quality Index is not only to rate the city, but to determine where improvements are necessary.

3 *Ahlgren, M./Robson, N./Houthaeve, R.* 2018: Urban space for people on the move – the living city. https://www.swecourbaninsight.com/urban-move/urban-space-for-people-on-the-move-the-living-city/ (04/04/2020).

4 *Golovkin, K.* 2017: Gde u goroda bolit, pokazhet “Indeks kachestva gorodskoy sredy” [‘The Quality Index of the Urban Environment’ will show where the city hurts]. http://strelka.com/ru/magazine/2017/07/17/russian-cities-index (23.08.2019).

In 2019, every city's final score was made on the basis of six clusters of indicators, each representing a certain type (field) of urban space: housing and adjacent spaces, street infrastructure, greening and water spaces, social and leisure infrastructure and adjacent spaces, public and business infrastructure and adjacent spaces, and citywide space. Each one was assessed on the base of six criteria (in 2017 was five criteria): security, comfort, ecological properties, identity and versatility, management efficiency, and how modern the environment is. In total, the Quality Index includes 36 indicators, for example, traffic congestion level, quantity and quality of green spaces, number of public transports stops etc. The data for every indicator is evaluated on a scale of one to ten.[5]

According to the 2017 index, Petrozavodsk scored 165 points out of 300 possible (55 percent). In 2019, Petrozavodsk scored 185 of 360 points (52 percent). According to the index scale, this only corresponds to a satisfactory urban environment. Petrozavodsk posted the third highest score of any settlement in the Republic of Karelia (see table 1).

Table 1: The Urban Environment Quality Index (Republic of Karelia, 2019)

Settlement	**Score**		**Population** (2018)
	points (max–360)	percent	
Pitkjaranta	197	55	10479
Sortavala	195	54	18801
Petrozavodsk	**185**	**52**	279190
Kondopoga	184	51	30299
Kostomuksha	172	48	29381
Pudozh	172	48	8897
Medvezhegorsk	168	47	14340
Belomorsk	163	45	9678
Kem'	147	41	11204
Segezha	140	39	26666
Olonets	138	38	8091
Lahdenpohja	128	35	7294
Suojrvy	116	32	8920

Source: *Federal Property Management Agency*. https://индекс-городов.рф/ (01/02/2020).

A breakdown of Petrozavodsk's score shows high marks public and business infrastructure and citywide space, and the lowest marks in the field of ecology and in the social and leisure sphere (see table 2).

5 For more details on the calculation method of the Index and descriptions of the data sources, please visit the project's official website: https://индекс-городов.рф/.

Table 2: Urban Environment Quality Index structure (Petrozavodsk, 2019)

Specific type (field) of urban space	**Score**	
	points (max–60)	percent
Citywide space	38	64
Public and business infrastructure	38	64
Housing	33	55
Street infrastructure	30	50
Social and leisure infrastructure	23	38
Greening and water spaces	23	38

Source: *Federal Property Management Agency*. https://индекс-городов.рф/ (01/02/2020).

As of today, more than 1100 cities in Russia have already been rated using the index. It should be noted that the findings are taken from official statistics, so we see the situation mostly from the top of the wave A common weakness of such projects and indices is excessive unification. Public perception and satisfaction are often not taken into account by municipal administrations when developing social programs. This leads to incorrect "targeting" and inefficient use of funds sometimes even causing discontent and mistrust among the population.[6] Therefore, it is vital to check the official scores against the opinion of residents.

It is clear that a more in-depth study and sociological analysis of the subjective assessments by the city's residents requires large-scale and representative public opinion polls, which in its turn require adequate funding.

The scientific potential of the research and the enthusiasm of sociology students of Petrozavodsk State University made it possible to successfully implement the exploratory study within the framework of a training course. The main research goal of this study was to discover the structure of a "comfortable and favourable urban environment" concept and to develop an initial hypothesis for a future representative descriptive survey.

The key research questions we hoped to answer were:

- What does the concept of 'comfortable urban environment' include according to average residents of Petrozavodsk?
- Which social factors influence the citizens opinions on concept of "comfortable urban environment"?
- How well does Petrozavodsk meet these conditions?
- How do respondents describe their own role in the creation and development of the urban environment?

Students conducted 15 citizen interviews using open-ended questions. The interview method allowed students to register the reactions of respondents and their emotions when answering questions. Both the development of research techniques and analysis of the data collected were carried out under the guidance of experienced professors of the sociology department of the university.

6 *Starikova, M.* 2018: Kachestvo gorodskoy sredyi s pozitsii zhilischnoy infrastrukturyi mikrorayonov [The quality of the urban environment from the position of the housing infrastructure of the microdistricts]. In: Sotsiologiya Goroda [Sociology Of City], 3, pp. 41–62. http://vgasu.ru/attachments/sg_11-18.pdf.

Table 3. Sample Description

N	**Gender**	**Age**	**Occupation**	**Duration of residence in Petrozavodsk** (years)	**Area of residence in Petrozavodsk**	**Children** yes/no
1	male	16	student	16	Klyuchevaya	-
2	male	19	student	19	Zareka	-
3	male	20	student	20	Zareka	-
4	male	21	student	2,5	Perevalka	-
5	female	21	student	3,5	Kukkovka	-
6	male	25	employed	25	Perevalka	-
7	male	31	employed	6	Drevlyanka	-
8	female	44	employed	3,5	Oktyabrskiy	-
9	female	47	employed	30	Oktyabrskiy	+
10	female	47	housekeeper	47	Center	+
11	male	50	employed	45	Center	+
12	male	51	employed	51	Oktyabrskiy	+
13	male	58	employed	40	Center	+
14	female	60	retired	60	Perevalka	+
15	female	69	retired	52	Kukkovka	+

Source: own compilation.

Figure 1: Map of Petrozavodsk with areas of residence

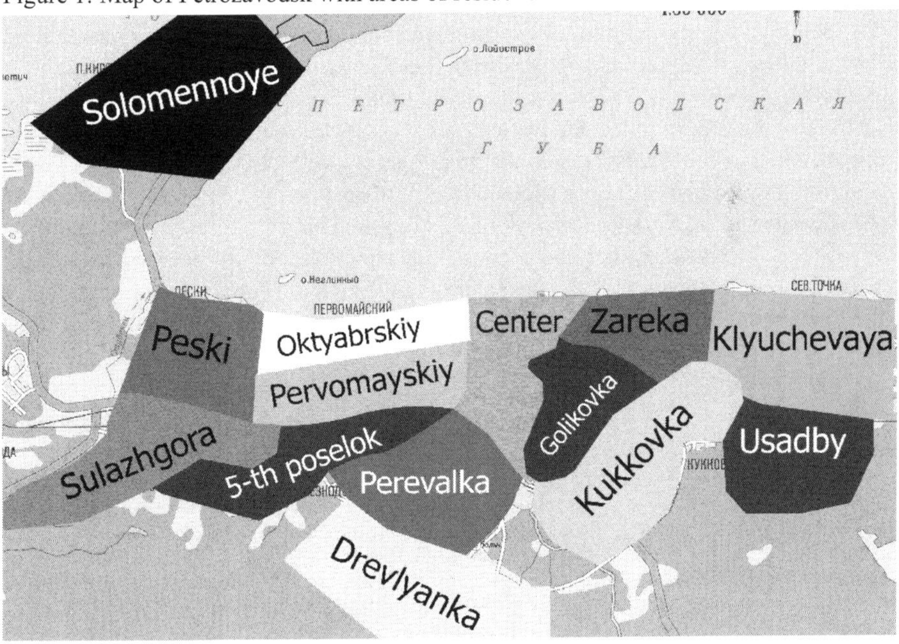

Source: own compilation.

To conduct the research was used volunteer sampling, a form of case selection which is purposive rather than based on the principles of random or probability sampling. It usually involves individuals who agree to participate in research. The sampling was organized in a way intended to cover people from a variety of socio-demographic groups, areas of residence, levels of education, and occupations. The age of the respondents ranged from 16 to 70, six of them were born in Petrozavodsk, and the duration of residency time in Petrozavodsk ranged from 3 to 60 years. Out of 12 main administrative districts of Petrozavodsk, residents of 8 districts participated in the study (see table 3 and figure 2). One of the factors was the ownership of the car, which depends the way a person moves around the city depends on it. At the same time, factors such as income level and type of housing were not taken into account.

Urban sociology and environment studies in Russia are usually based on a systematic approach and consider the impact of objective quantitative characteristics of the urban environment on the population. In contrast, an environmental approach shifts the focus to the residents themselves and their subjective perception, assessments, and opinions about the urban environment.[7] The latter serves as the theoretical and methodological basis for our study.

Urban public spaces are characterized by features that differ slightly from those typical of rural public spaces. These features depend on the meaning that such spaces have to their users. For residents it is essential that urban public spaces are usable, interactive, civic, political, axiological, symbolic and identifiable.[8] In contrast, rural areas often lack social facilities designed for leisure, recreational and sporting purposes. They are also deprived of representative areas with which local people could identify and where they could meet, organize events, etc.[9]

Residents' subjective perceptions of the urban environment play an important factor in the environment's formation. On the one hand, if city residents have an alienated and antagonistic relationship to their environment, it leads to a degradation of the urban space. On the other hand, if they form a cooperative and adaptive relationship to their environment, it brings about a positive development of the urban space.

Following well-known French sociologist P. Bourdieu, the authors of this article consider the physical and social city space as qualitatively different but closely interlinked. As Bourdieu posited "physical space is a social fabrication and projection of social space, a social structure in an objectified state,"[10]. The majority of social goods and services are distributed in the physical space, while the access of social agents to those services is determined not only by their status, but also by their geographical location in the city.

---

7 *Dridze, T./Akimkin, E. (eds.)* 2005: Sotsialno obosnovannoe gradoustroystvo v rezhime prognoznogo proektirovaniya [Socially sound urban planning in the predictive modelling mode], Moscow.

8 *Micek, M./Staszewska, S.* 2019: Urban and Rural Public Spaces: Development Issues and Qualitative Assessment. Bulletin of Geography. In: Socio-economic Series, 45(45), pp. 75–93. https://content.sciendo.com/configurable/contentpage/journals$002fbog$002f45$002f45$002farticle-p75.xml (04/04/2020).

9 Ibidem.

10 *Bourdieu, P.* 2018: Social space and the Genesis of Appropriated Physical Space. In: International Journal of Urban and Regional Research (2018), Vol. 42, No. 1, pp. 106–114 https://onlinelibrary.wiley.com/doi/full/10.1111/1468-2427.12534 (04/04/2020).

To analyze the data collected during the interviews, we found it useful to apply the theoretical model of urban space proposed by the well-known Russian sociologist Tamara Dridze.[11] According to this model, urban space consists of several basic elements:

- natural (air, flora, fauna, water resources);
- man-made or physical (constructions, equipment, technologies);
- informational or communications (transport infrastructure, social and leisure infrastructure, public and business infrastructure);
- anthropocentric (human values, lifestyle, cultural patterns).

To the question "What do you like / don't like in Petrozavodsk?", all the elements of the model above were reflected in the responses, but the frequency with which respondents referenced them differed substantially. For example, describing basic characteristics of the "comfortable urban environment" respondents mentioned greening spaces or street infrastructure much more than relations in the local community (see table 4).

Table 4: Data of the interviews systematized with model of urban space

Elements of model:	Number of respondents who mentioned	Frequency of mentions in the responses
Natural	15	35
Man-made or physical	13	24
Informational or communications	15	33
Anthropocentric	3	4

Source: own compilation.

When asked what a "comfortable and favorable city" included, most respondents answered that a comfortable city has to be clean above all else as well as green and safe. All 15 interviewees mentioned these criteria, some of them several times.

"For me it is important the availability of parks within walking distance, and safe playgrounds for children," (R10, female, 47). "I think the variety of safe and green places for walking with my friends is vital," (R6, male, 25).

In another study of another Russian city – Tolyatti (the second largest city in the Samara region of Russia, located in the middle reaches of the Volga River) – respondents noted the importance of "green areas" for recreation.[12]

According to respondents, other important characteristics of a comfortable urban environment included the quality of roads, a well-developed transport network, and an extensive social and leisure infrastructure designed for various social groups. Respondents also mentioned – though much more rarely – the historical appearance of the city, its architecture and planning as well as new workplaces, and the standard of living for citizens. Meanwhile, the importance of friendly relations with neighbors and other residents was mentioned only twice and both times by older female respondents.

11 *Dridze/Akimkin* 2005 (fn. 7).

12 *Lebedeva, L./Rostova, A./Urgalkin U.* 2014: Udovletvorennost' gorodskoy sredoy kak faktor innovatsionnogo razvitiya monogoroda [Satisfaction of the urban space as a factor in the innovative development of a single-industry town]. In: Vestnik Samarskogo munitsipal'nogo instituta upravleniya, 3, pp. 52–59. http://sagmu.ru/nauka/images/stories/vestnik/full_text/2014_3/lebedeva_rostova_urgalkin_52-59.pdf.

Does Petrozavodsk meet the requirements listed above, according to respondents? Based on our analysis the answer seems to be consistently, "yes- but […]". For instance, 10 of the 15 respondents said that the city had parks but complained that these were almost exclusively in center of the city and sometimes unsuited to recreation and sports. "There are some parks in the center of city, but I'm sure there should be much more, and in the suburbs also," (R7, male, 31).

Interestingly, one fact noted not only by respondents who were longtime residents, but also by young residents who had only been living in the city for three to four years was the abundance of cars in the city. Yes, Petrozavodsk is green and clean, especially compared to many other Russian cities, but it was cleaner and greener in the past. "In the past, Petrozavodsk was covered in greenery and had plenty of beautiful flowers, but today it is buried in cars and advertising," (R15, female, 69). The abundance of cars that 'occupy' the streets, courtyards, and squares, declining the level of comfort of pedestrian movement is considered by respondents, most of whom are pedestrians as a significant problem requiring immediate action. Petrozavodsk ranks first in the North-West region in the number of cars per capita, and third all of Russia. The situation continues to worsen each year.

"For the past 70 years, cities around the world have been designed from the car's perspective. To satisfy the needs of a car-dependent population, the form of the European city has transformed over time from the walkable, people-friendly traditional city into a place where the streets have become "spaces for cars" and public urban spaces "spaces for parking", ignoring their significance as spaces for interaction, diversity and exchange."[13]

Cars now dominate the green recreation areas, playgrounds, and sports grounds for teenagers. 6 out of 15 respondents highlighted this problem in their responses, and the alarm was not limited to one age group or social class.

"The cars regularly park on the lawn right under our windows, the engine makes a lot of noise, there are exhaust fumes everywhere […]. You know, I was doing everything to solve this problem, but still to no avail!" (R15, female, 69). "Instead of the yard, we are having a spontaneous parking place around my apartment building!" (R5, female, 21).

During the last five to seven years, an 'unspoken war' has been taking place in the city between the owners of cars and carless residents. Carless residents have used any available means, including home-made fences, car tires with planted trees and flowers inside, and even large stones to protect recreation zones from the intrusion of cars. Older residents, raised in the Soviet Union, try to give unsolicited advice to their neighbors about parking, as well as regularly call and send complaints to the city administration, police, and the Reception Office of the Head of the Republic. Nonetheless, the score in this 'war' is clearly not in favor of the fighters for the environment.

On the other hand, car owners and drivers have their own view on the issue. "The city is alarmingly short of parking places. Traffic lights are often unregulated," (R10, male, 50). The problem with parking lots is noted by residents in other Russian cities, for example, in Moscow.[14]

---

13 *Ahlgren/Robson/Houthaeve* 2018 (fn. 3).

14 *Notman, O./Bagirova A.* 2017: Dinamika gorodskoy infrastruktury v otsenkakh yekaterinburzhtsev [Dynamics of City Infrastructure in Estimates of the Population of Ekaterinburg]. In: IZVESTIA. Ural Federal University Journal. Series 3: Social and Political Sciences, 2, pp. 113–123. http://elar.urfu.ru/bitstream/10995/48944/1/iuro-2017-164-14.pdf.

The interviews also showed citizens' particularly skeptical attitudes towards the quality of the roads in Petrozavodsk and to the transport infrastructure in general. Potholes and traffic jams during the rush hour were among the most frequently mentioned issues by respondents who use a car in the city. Respondents who use municipal transport also had many complaints including: the ill-considered routes and schedule of the public transport, outdated trolleybuses, and high-ticket prices, as well as the lack of sidewalks and pedestrian crossings in some areas of the city.

9 out of 15 respondents considered Petrozavodsk a safe city. Although, one respondent, a young woman, reported that she always returns home by taxi because of the stray dogs and beggars in her district. Another respondent, a woman living in the city center, answered that she was afraid of letting her eight-year-old child play outside alone, because of the many cars and the lack of safe pedestrian crossings. Another respondent claimed he does not feel safe walking on the street due to a recent rise in cyclists as there are no separate biking paths. Furthermore, a retired respondent said that she generally avoids going out during winter at nighttime because "the ice is not cleaned up in the city and the lighting has become very bad," (R14, female, 60). In fact, nearly every respondent raised the issue of poor lighting in the city.

Several years ago, the city administration replaced the old lights with the energy-saving ones. Despite of their good intentions, streets became noticeably darker following the switch. In addition, some courtyards and parks have no lights at all: "It's really dark not only in the courtyard but even in the streets. Sometimes I feel uncomfortable," (R3, male, 20). The problem of poor lighting was shared by both men and women and crosscut age and social status as well.

The landscape of the city, its architectural design and urban planning, were also items of concern for most respondents. On the one hand, residents prefer not to observe any buildings in the center of Petrozavodsk that do not fit into the surrounding nature and architecture. They stated that any urban development plan or investment project should respect both the human and natural environments in which they take place, and that projects are more likely to be successful if they are linked with the cultural values and heritage of the region. One a more critical note, some esidents complained about the "poor-quality [of] redecoration," of apartment buildings, "falling plaster", and the density of apartments in the inner-city where "windows of apartments directly face the walls of neighboring buildings," (R11, male, 50).

In spite of their critiques, the interviewees all shared a positive perception of Petrozavodsk as a whole. They adore their city and sincerely admire its urban environment. "[Petrozavodsk is a] calm and quiet city. Residents do not need to rush anywhere and hurry," (R15, female, 69). The older generation prefers that it is "provincial and small, but cozy and calm," (R13, male, 58). Youth, on the contrary, enjoys the "hustle": "there are a lot of places to go out and have fun with friends," (R1, male, 16).

The historical city center is a favorite place for walking and relaxing among Petrozavodsk residents regardless of the respondent's age or their area of residence. It is clear from the interviews that the most loved part of the city is the Lake Onega promenade. "The lake is fantastic and chic! After a walk along the lake promenade, it is easier to breathe and to think," (R8, female, 44). It is important to note that people also enjoy walking here because of the interesting cultural objects placed on the promenade. All these monuments arrived at

Petrozavodsk as gifts from its' twin cities. In fact, the "Tübingen panel" given to Petrozavodsk in 1994 and placed on the lake promenade, is considered the most mysterious cultural object on the promenade and informally known as 'The Thinking Cane Reed' or 'A Set of Lock Picks' monument.

Some years ago, the sport exercise machines were set up on the Onego Lake promenade. Therefore, the opportunities to work out for free as well as to visit the amusement park nearby also attract people here.

At the same time, analysis of the data reveals new popular places for recreation and leisure in the city. For example, the shopping mall Lotos Plaza has become an attraction for many residents, including those from the Central district. It was built in the Drevlyanka suburb, and despite the fact that it is not easily accessible from the city center, people enjoy visiting Lotos Plaza because of the many entertainment options it offers. These include a Norway park (adventure playground[15]), an indoor skating rink, a zoo, slot machines, and a variety of restaurants and cafes. The well-maintained forest and duck pond nearby also offer alternatives for those who prefer to relax in quiet natural surroundings. Respondents agreed that Petrozavodsk possesses a high number of valuable cultural institutions far superior to institutions in other cities in north-west Russia. Petrozavodsk hosts a philharmonic orchestra, several theaters and concert halls, museums and exhibition halls, a conservatory, numerous libraries, and a state university. The presence of a state university allows to have a prestigious education, which attracts the youth of our region and from other regions of Russia.

5 respondents felt the cultural sites were insufficient, as most sites are concentrated in the city center and are not within walking distance of other districts. However, some respondents were dissatisfied with the programs and the quality of the performances, concerts, and exhibitions.

For residents, a 'comfortable urban environment' was directly linked to their everyday needs. When describing the characteristics of the city where the respondent would feel comfortable and good, he/she would first mention the things that were missing now.

Younger respondents closely connect the image a comfortable city to well-developed leisure infrastructure and possibilities to learn skills that are in high demand at the labor market. Middle-aged residents mentioned (more often than other groups) the development of business infrastructure and the creation of new jobs Older interviewees were more inclined to discuss the accessibility of health and care services as well as social infrastructure problems.

Respondents with children seemed to be more concentrated on the severe shortage of early-childhood education and care services or playgrounds than the other respondents.

> "There are a plenty of shops and supermarkets in the city. But where are schools, sports facilities, amusement parks?" (R11, male, 50). "Houses are being built [for families] but there are no schools and kindergartens nearby," (R9, female, 47).

Municipal statistics indicate that in August 2019 there were 7,086 families with pre-school children registered in Petrozavodsk but only 4,451 available kindergarten places for the new

15 An outdoor area that has fixed and movable structures (such as slides and rope ladders) on which children can climb and play and that often also has equipment and loose materials for building projects and modifying preexisting structures, see *Merriam-Webster.* (n.d.): Adventure playground. https://www.merriam-webster.com/dictionary/adventure%20playground (24/02/2020).

school year.[16] Despite efforts by the city's administration to deal with the shortage, the demand for childhood education is far outstripping the supply. Such a situation is completely at odds with a comfortable city according to the respondents. "New areas of residence are being built, but new schools and kindergartens are not being built. Only shopping centers are being built," (R6, female, 47).

Do Petrozavodsk residents participate in the development and improvement of their urban environment? The question is important in the context of the development of democracy and civil society in Russia. Because the involvement of city residents in the development of their urban environment is the most accessible form of direct citizen participation in local governance in Russia.

According to the survey, the most frequent and practically the only form of such participation was occasional participation in the so-called community clean-ups ('subbotniks') by citizens. Subbotniks are community-based activities which include cleaning and gardening of the area surrounding houses. In Soviet period, such activities were organised during the common day off (Saturday is 'subbota' in Russian, hence the name). "Yes, every year my family takes part in general cleaning up around the apartment's building," (R10, female, 47). Such events are usually initiated by the local administration and are organized by the buildings' management companies.

As a matter of fact, according to the results of a sociological poll in 2018, every third Russian (36 percent) participated in 'subbotniks' and environmental campaigns.[17] There is a curious tendency: the smaller the population of the settlement is the more people participate in its improvement.

A young girl, a student at Petrozavodsk State University, recalled another form of participation in the improvement of the city. She was talking about a so-called "popular vote" organized in the framework of the municipal program "Comfortable and well-developed environment." During one parliamentary election, residents of Petrozavodsk were given the opportunity to vote for the best projects for the development of the city's districts. The original goal of the initiative was increasing the turnout in the municipal elections, but the initiative led to ...[what?]. Despite the success, the initiative was a one-time only event. It is worth noting that some Russian cities hold, and consider the results of, online polls among their residents when choosing which development projects to finance from municipal budgets. Still, this kind of participation remains the exception and not the rule.

No other forms of direct citizen participation in urban development were included in the survey results besides these two. Although opportunities to participate constructively in urban development projects do exist, citizens seem to be either unable or unwilling to participate in these forums, as they currently exist.

5 out of 15 respondents were convinced that development of the city is a responsibility of the city administration. "The issues of developing the urban environment should be dealt with by the government. The ordinary person cannot do anything," (R15, female, 69). Others

---

16 *Informatsionnaya sistema "Doshkolnik" [IS "Preschooler"]* 2019. https://mdou.petrozavodsk-mo.ru/site/statistics (24/08/2019).

17 *Wciom.ru*. 2018: Dobrovolchestvo i volontyorstvo: kak myi pomogaem drug drugu? [Volunteering: How do we help each other?]. https://wciom.ru/index.php?id=236&uid=9380 (24/08/2019).

demanded greater support from civil society or local authorities, in order to participate. "We would have done more if we had been helped and supported," (R11, male, 31).

Nonetheless, 13 out of 15 respondents were convinced that any solution related to changes in the urban environment should involve both local authorities *and residents*, taking into account their views and assessments. Respondents believed that such a process would make residents more inclined to actively participate in the development programs of their city. "A decision-making process should be transparent and clear for people, then they themselves will want to participate," (R11, male, 31).

At the moment, the public opinion of Petrozavodsk residents is rarely taken into account by the local administration when planning the urban environment. Consequently, many decisions by the authorities do not meet the real needs of residents and are therefore not supported by them. That also means that the resource of citizen participation remains unexploited.

At the end of the interviews, we usually asked the respondents what they would change in the city if they suddenly became its mayor. Interestingly, at first, almost every respondent struggled to respond, and it was only after some time that they could provide an answer. Only one respondent – a young and energetic woman – said that she would start by researching.

> "It is crucial to ask the residents themselves what they need and what is still missing, what is required for Petrozavodsk to become even more comfortable and friendly for them. Such an approach would give residents the desire and opportunity to participate in the development of their environment," (R5, female, 21).

In the near future, this young woman is getting her degree in economics and management and is possibly applying for the city manager position.

A detailed and thorough analysis of the data collected allows us to draw some preliminary conclusions (that indeed need to be further tested in a representative survey).

1. Petrozavodsk residents associate the concept of a "comfortable urban space" primarily with a favorable natural environment and a safe physical space. Well-developed and benevolent social relations, including economic and cultural relations, fall by the wayside.
2. Petrozavodsk residents believe that, in general, the city meets the basic requirements for comfort and safety. Nonetheless, they criticize the development level of social and leisure infrastructure, as well as the roads condition and the traffic management. To the greatest extent, residents are satisfied with the city greening and the public and business infrastructure.
3. The degree of satisfaction by the quality of the urban environment is impacted the most by such social factors as the age of the respondents, the geography of their residence in the city, marital and economic statuses.
4. For the majority of respondents, the personal involvement in the improvement of the city environment goes as far as a willingness to manage only the area surrounding their building. The extent of residents' involvement in the municipal urban development programs is minimal. An important element in increasing the involvement of residents might become their inclusion in the design and implementation of the city development programs through NGOs and other civil society institutes.

To Participate or to Oppose: Political Lifeworlds between Affirmative and Aversive Critique of Representative Democracy[1]

Rolf Frankenberger and Daniel Buhr

Abstract: Individual wellbeing is affected by the political system and the welfare state, but also by social status and people's political lifeworld. Political lifeworlds are individual normative maps of the political world. They are shaped by everyday experiences and guide political action. If people make different experiences, new social cleavages might emerge and translate in a disintegration of political lifeworlds, which in turn can have destabilising effects on the political system and society as a whole. Political polarization and the success of the right-wing populist party Alternative for Germany (AfD) rise the question, if we currently witness such a profound and destabilising change. Following up to a study by Frankenberger et al.[2], we conducted 109 qualitative interviews in the State of Baden-Württemberg, Germany, with a special focus on the electorate of the AfD. Findings reflect the emerging cleavage between progressive, universalist and pluralist positions on the one side, and authoritarian, particularistic-nationalist positions on the other. A more detailed analysis of the lifeworlds shows: The more elaborate individual political lifeworlds are, the less likely is the tendency to vote AfD. Those with greater knowledge on the functioning of the political system as a system of rules and regulation are more satisfied and participate more than those who have strongly output-oriented and elite-centred ideas. AfD voters are disappointed by the current political system. They express an aversive attitude towards representative democracy that is rooted in populist and right-wing motives, but hardly translates into political action (except voting). Taking into account these findings, the overall model of lifeworlds is readjusted along the dimension aversive vs. affirmative criticism of the political system. Are these lifeworlds the ones with an overall low level of subjective wellbeing?

Keywords: lifeworld, democracy, cleavages, populism, Alternative for Germany (AfD), polarization.

When societies change, some people adapt to, or even profit from new developments. Others might fear, or witness, a loss of traditions and routines, social, cultural and economic security, and status. Or, to put it in other words, change has different impact on individual wellbeing. Wellbeing includes life satisfaction and happiness as well as "developing as a person,

---

1 This research was funded by Baden-Württemberg Foundation as a part of the joint research project "Demokratie-Monitoring Baden-Württemberg 2016/17". The article is a revised, updated and translated version of *Frankenberger, R./Gensheimer, T./Buhr, D.* 2019: Zwischen Mitmachen und Dagegen sein. Politische Lebenswelten in Baden-Württemberg. In: *Baden-Württemberg Stiftung (ed.)*: Demokratie-Monitoring Baden-Württemberg 2016/2017, pp. 149–172, Wiesbaden.

2 *Frankenberger, R./Buhr, D./Schmid, J.* 2015. Politische Lebenswelten. Eine qualitative Studie zu politischen Einstellungen und Beteiligungsorientierungen in ausgewählten Kommunen in Baden-Württemberg. In: *Baden-Württemberg Stiftung (ed.)*: Demokratie-Monitoring Baden-Württemberg 2013/2014, Wiesbaden, pp. 151–221; see also *Frankenberger, R./Buhr. D.* 2017: Political Lifeworlds in Baden-Württemberg. In: *Frankenberger/R./Chernenkova, E. (eds.)*: Local Politics in a Comparative Perspective – The Cases of Petrozavodsk and Tübingen, Baden-Baden, pp. 77–88.

being fulfilled, and making a contribution to the community"[3]. If people then make very different experiences under these conditions of change in terms of individual development, happiness, and the ability to contribute to the community, their levels of wellbeing change and leads to more inequality, disintegration, and political polarisation. State elections in Baden-Württemberg in 2016 and federal elections in Germany in 2017 provide evidence for such a political change, and even a polarisation of the political landscape. On the one hand, Bündnis 90/Die Grünen was able to defend the status as strongest political party in the State of Baden-Württemberg with 30,3 percent vote share. On the other hand, with the Alternative for Germany (AfD) a populist radical right party[4] was able to establish both on state level (15.1 percent) and federal level (12.6 percent). This development towards a pluralistic party system reflects the establishment of new socio-cultural cleavages. The starting point for this development is the 1970s, when the contrast between libertarian-universalist and authoritarian-communitarian, Eurosceptic positions condensed into a cleavage and increasingly spread throughout Europe.[5] At the latest with the successes of the AfD in state and federal elections, the ideological-programmatic polarisation of the party system, which had already progressed further in many other European countries, has also arrived in Germany.[6] Progressive universalist-pluralist positions are now opposed by authoritarian particularist-nationalist positions.[7]

The AfD electorate has been subject to several, mostly quantitative, studies. Berbuir et al.[8] show that AfD sympathisers are predominantly male (80 percent), well educated (almost 50 percent had a university degree), have a strong political interest and consider themselves to be predominantly middle class. In contrast, Hambauer and Mays[9] find that sympathizers are still predominantly male (75 percent), but tend to have medium or low educational qualifications, are far more likely to work full-time (64 percent) and to be blue-collar workers (27 percent) than the average. There are also regional differences between the East (more blue-collar workers, younger and, with 57 percent men, significantly more female) and the West (more white-collar workers, fewer women). They conclude that the AfD electorate is in-

3 *Shah, H./Marks, H.* 2004: A well-being manifesto for a flourishing society, London, p. 2.

4 *Lewandowsky, M./Giebler, H./Wagner, A.* 2016: Rechtspopulismus in Deutschland. Eine empirische Einordnung der Parteien zur Bundestagswahl 2013 unter besonderer Berücksichtigung der AfD. Politische Vierteljahresschrift 57, 2, pp. 247–275; *Decker, F.* 2017: Die Ankunft des neuen Rechtspopulismus im Parteiensystem der Bundesrepublik. In: *Bieber, C./Blätte, A./Korte, K.R./Switek, N. (eds.)*: Regieren in der Einwanderungsgesellschaft, Wiesbaden, pp. 55–61; *Schmitt-Beck, R./van Deth, J.W./Staudt, A.* 2017: Die AfD nach der rechtspopulistischen Wende. In: Zeitschrift für Politikwissenschaft 27, 3, pp. 273–303.

5 *Bornschier, S.* 2012: Why a right-wing populist party emerged in France but not in Germany: cleavages and actors in the formation of a new cultural divide. In: European Political Science Review 4,1, pp. 121–145 (123 f).

6 *Franzmann, S. T.* 2018. Von der EURO-Opposition zur Kosmopolitismus-Opposition. In: *Anders, L.H./ Scheller, H./Tuntschew, T. (eds.)*: Parteien und die Politisierung der Europäischen Union, Wiesbaden, pp. 365–402 (389 f).

7 *Schmitt-Beck, R.* 2018. Wähler und Parteien bei der Bundestagswahl 2017: Eine Analyse des Entscheidungsverhaltens auf Basis von Paneldaten der German Longitudinal Election Study. In: ZSE Zeitschrift für Staats- und Europawissenschaften / Journal for Comparative Government and European Policy 15, 4, pp. 627–656 (656).

8 *Berbuir, N./Lewandowsky, M./Siri, J.* 2015: The AfD and its sympathisers: finally a right-wing populist movement in Germany? In: German Politics 24, 2, pp. 154–178.

9 *Hambauer, V./Mays, A.* 2018: Wer wählt die AfD? Ein Vergleich der Sozialstruktur, politischen Einstellungen und Einstellungen zu Flüchtlingen zwischen AfD-WählerInnen und der WählerInnen der anderen Parteien. In: Zeitschrift für Vergleichende Politikwissenschaft 12, 1, pp. 133–154.

creasingly recruited from the lower classes, and especially from working class.[10] Thus, there seems to be at least a partial change in the electorate. Besides fears of the "refugee crisis" (80 percent), they strongly express fears of economic decline (41 percent) and job losses (33 percent), pronounced party scepticism (82 percent) and a strong political interest (58 percent). In a study on Baden-Württemberg, Schmitt-Beck et al. identify several core factors that determine voting for the AfD. In particular, negative assessments of the performance of the federal and state governments are the driving force for voting for the AfD.[11] In addition, gender, subjectively felt material disadvantage, distrust of other people, political interest[12] and right-wing ideology contribute to the choice of AfD.[13] AfD-sympathisers also show clear preferences for direct democratic procedures.[14] An analysis of voter behaviour in the 2017 federal elections confirms some of these assumptions, as Schmitt-Beck[15] shows: AfD voters are above average male, with a tendency to be less educated, and usually belong to the so-called old middle class (self-employed and farmers) or are blue-collar workers. They often obtain information via private media and especially online and social media, while they tend to reject public media, which points to an echo chamber effect. The driving themes are the rejection of immigration, general economic pessimism and dissatisfaction with the achievements of democracy.[16] There is thus clear evidence for the new cleavage mentioned above: the AfD profits from more backwarded and groups opposing change and being discontent with democracy, whereas Bündnis90/Die Grünen gain from progressive and content parts of the society.

This polarisation combined with a deep dissatisfaction of some parts of the people is a severe challenge for democracy. If basic values of democracy are rejected and their legitimacy is taken into question by growing shares of the population, this can have destabilising effects in the long run. If we want to evaluate these long-term effects, we need information not only on short term opinions and perceptions of current problems but also on underlying value orientations, biographical experiences and lifeworld references.

Starting from the idea that political culture is an intellectual map,[17] political culture research can capture fundamental ideas rather than superficial attitudes and judgments of legitimacy, as these would better reflect the political culture of a state.[18] It is therefore not only a matter of an analytical separation between the level of attitudes and the more fundamental level of notions of order,[19] but also of a more profound conceptualisation of political cultural research. The concept of lifeworld[20] takes up Rohe's critique and thus can reduce

10 Ibidem, p. 142.
11 *Schmitt-Beck et al.* 2017 (fn. 4), p. 296.
12 Ibidem, p. 292.
13 Ibidem, p. 295.
14 Ibidem.
15 *Schmitt-Beck* 2018 (fn. 7), p. 650 ff.
16 Ibidem, p. 654.
17 *Rohe, K.* 1994: Politische Kultur: Zum Verständnis eines theoretischen Konzepts. In: *Niedermeyer, O./von Beyme, K. (eds.)*: Politische Kultur in Ost- und Westdeutschland, Berlin, pp. 1–21 (1).
18 *Greiffenhagen, S.* 2009: Theorie(n) der Politischen Kultur. In: *Salzborn, S. (ed.)*: Politische Kultur, Frankfurt, pp. 31–44 (17 f).
19 *Rohe* 1994 (fn. 17), p. 3.
20 *Schütz, A./Luckmann, T.* 2003: Strukturen der Lebenswelt, Konstanz.

the existing gap. It becomes the central category of analysis in order to grasp the subjective dimension of political realities, because the everyday lifeworld, the "world within current reach"[21], is the space where people develop a specific horizon of experience with individual realities, meanings and specific stocks of knowledge.[22] They are the basis for cognition and interpretation of everyday political life and for the formation of interests. Thus, the lifeworld approach assumes that it is not primarily socio-demographic, socio-economic or socialisation variables, but rather the everyday experience that shape individual knowledge and action.[23] The assumption that 'one's own reality' determines everyday knowledge and everyday actions can logically be transferred to the political.[24] According to Rohe's understanding, political life worlds reveal a comprehensive cognitive and normative map of the political world.[25] Lifeworld research then strives to uncover new, unsuspected relationships and structures that determine political reality.[26]

In the following sections we build upon the study on political lifeworlds in Baden-Württemberg.[27] Using 109 qualitative interviews with AfD-sympathisers and non-sympathisers recruited by using facebook targeting, we will reassess the lifeworld typology and have a special focus on the lifeworlds of AfD- sympathisers. Given the somewhat contradictory findings with regards to their socio-demographics, we can assume that they might share political lifeworlds instead. Drawing upon the findings reported above, we hypothesize that:

- AfD voters predominantly have a direct understanding of democracy, but at the same time show a low level of participation. This combination condenses into a new political environment;
- AfD voters are frustrated by the current political system and this is condensed into an aversive attitude towards representative democracy.

First, we present the findings from the Democracy-Monitoring 2013/14. They serve as a frame of reference. In a second step, we map the 2017 political life worlds and describe them along the analytical dimensions *meaning of politics* and *meaning of democracy*. In the interviews we asked the interviewees to specify their individual understandings of these terms and used the answers to construct a classification along these two dimensions and the dimension of reported political and social participation. Based on the findings, we readjust our overall model of lifeworlds by including the dimension aversive vs. affirmative criticism of the political system. Finally, some findings on AfD voters are discussed separately.

21 Ibidem, pp. 71 f.

22 *Frankenberger et al.* 2015 (fn. 2), p. 154.

23 *Flaig, B.B./Meyer, T./Ueltzhöffer, J.* 1994: Alltagsästhetik und Politische Kultur. Zur ästhetischen Dimension politischer Bildung und politischer Kommunikation. 2. Aufl., Bonn, p. 9; *Frankenberger et al.* 2015 (fn. 2), p. 215.

24 *Flaig et al.* 1994 (fn. 23), p. 28.

25 *Frankenberger et al.* 2015 (fn. 2), p. 152.

26 *Müller-Rommel, F./Poguntke, T.* 1991: Lebensstile und Wahlverhalten. In: *Wehling, H.-G./Schultze, R.-O. (eds.)*: Wahlverhalten, Stuttgart, pp. 179–193 (185).

27 *Frankenberger et al.* 2015 (fn. 2).

1 Political Lifeworlds: Concept and Initial Findings in 2014

For building a typology of political lifeworlds we use the notions of democracy and politics as expressed in the interviews. Interviewees provide everyday definitions and descriptions of these core concepts. They constitute the spaces of experiences within which events are perceived as genuinely political and distinguish them from other spheres such as the social, cultural or private. Ultimately, the individual political lifeworld is created through a self-definition of the political. Political lifeworlds were first examined systematically in a qualitative study in 2013/14.[28] In episodic interviews, 275 people in fourteen municipalities in Baden-Württemberg were asked for their understandings of democracy and politics as well as their participatory behaviour, biographical and life-course political experiences. The interviews were analysed by using qualitative content analysis of basic and spontaneous associations the interviewees had when asked for meanings of politics and democracy. In addition, we analysed knowledge, perceptions and evaluations of the political system as well as reported political and social participation. The associations, concepts and ideas of politics as a dimension of everyday life and democracy as a political order in which individuals locate themselves, are fundamental for the formation of political lifeworlds. In the initial study, we were able to identify seven distinct political lifeworlds with an above-average frequency. We combined them in three larger groups of political life worlds that each share a common core of political orientations, experiences and horizons: politically distant, delegative, and participatory lifeworlds.[29]

Politically distant life worlds are characterized by a rudimentary understanding of democracy, which can also include a more or less elaborate understanding of the political, but generally comes with a distinct distance to politics. People from politically distant life worlds scarcely participate and if they do so, only punctually and rather in a social setting. Altogether, these specific life worlds made up 22,5 percent of the analysed sample and considering the sample structure the actual empirical percentage is most likely higher than that. They contain the apolitical und distant life worlds.[30] These lifeworlds can be characterised by the idea that politics is what politicians do. This goes along with the conviction that a single person does hardly make any difference and that even elections hardly change anything. The distant lifeworld is rather output-oriented and characterized by tendentious dissatisfaction. Therefore, dissatisfaction with policies, policy outcomes and politicians are often articulated. This lifeworld is rather male and can be found in all age groups. Members are usually part of a middle class that is far removed from politics.

Delegative life worlds include a strong orientation on norms, rules and institutions of politics. Representative or norm-orientated understandings of democracy are strongly connected to government, institutions and rule-based fixed terms of politics. These life worlds are the backbone of representative democracy and include both, voters and elected officials and representatives. These life worlds account for 44,4 percent of the sample and are hence the biggest group of respondents. Delegative life worlds can be differentiated into so called

28 *Frankenberger et al.* 2015 (fn. 2); *Frankenberger/Buhr* 2017 (fn. 2).

29 *Frankenberger et al.* 2015 (fn. 2), pp. 201 f.

30 *Frankenberger/Buhr* 2017 (fn. 2), p. 81.

"Carers", "Electorate", and "Doers".[31] People from these lifeworlds are either politically or socially active, in some cases both. The level of participation is predominantly low or medium and limited to individually relevant areas of life. *Carers* are strongly oriented towards those who govern and act in government, although there is a strong reference to norms such as freedom, equality or tolerance, which structure coexistence in a democracy. *Carers* are very satisfied with the political system and are strongly socially active. People of all age groups and educational levels can be found in this world. Often, however, they are women, people with middle incomes and rather lower formal educational qualifications. Electorals are the core of representative democracy. Elections are of highest value. Beyond elections, political participation tends to be below average, and if so, Electorals are most likely to aspire to office or to be active in a party or trade union environment. There is a high level of satisfaction with the political system in this environment, even if politicians are more responsive to citizens. In this lifeworld, people with medium incomes, high educational qualifications and men between 35–44 and 55–74 years of age are overrepresented. *Doers* also show a representative understanding of democracy. They make very strong references to places of politics, i.e. parliaments or local councils, and assume that even on a small scale something can be changed. It is striking that the level of their political commitment is essentially grouped around two poles: *Doers* are either highly active in the political sphere, or they are – at least temporarily – politically inactive. In this lifeworld, fundamental satisfaction with the political system is very pronounced, partly because people with this orientation often take on formative roles. Across all age groups, however, this orientation is found particularly frequently in middle and high educational qualifications and incomes, among employees and civil servants.

Participatory lifeworlds are mostly distinguished by a participatory understanding of democracy and emancipatory approaches to politics. People of these groups strongly believe that active influence and shaping is possible. Following that, people in these life worlds are politically and socially active and advocate for themes and persons. 33.1 percent of the sample can be assigned to this group. These are the "Co-creators" and "Co-deciders".[32] Both display a participatory understanding of democracy and emancipatory approaches to politics. Co-creators want to be "asked" and be involved in processes of finding solutions to social problems. In addition to elections, a wide range of participation opportunities are anticipated and often taken advantage of. They are socially and politically active in many ways and are highly satisfied with the political system. People over 45 with middle and high incomes and high formal educational qualifications are strongly overrepresented here. In contrast to "Co-creators", "Co-deciders" do not only want to be involved, but actually also want to have a say in decision-making. They see direct-democratic procedures as the highest degree of realisation of this co-determination, which means that although they regard democracy as valuable in principle, they clearly articulate a perceived lack of direct democracy. This lifeworld is socially and politically active, and there are often high incomes and formal educational qualifications, civil servants and employees with a good chance of a high level of well-

31 Ibidem, p. 81.
32 Ibidem.

being.[33] Figure 1 summarises the lifeworlds along the dimensions *meaning of democracy*, *level of participation* and *understanding of politics*.

Figure 1: Political Lifeworlds in Baden-Württemberg 2014

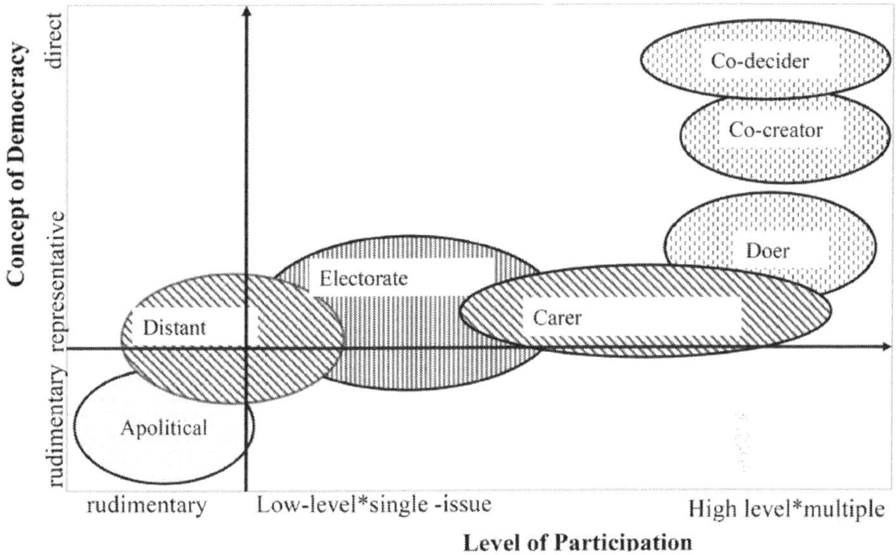

Legend:
Dashed vertical stripes: Social and political participation Diagonal stripes: Social participation.
Vertical stripes: Political participation.
Grey: No participation.
Source: *Frankenberger/Buhr* 2017 (fn. 2).

2 Political Lifeworlds in 2017

In order to review the 2013/14 model, we used the categories developed in this study as well as a systematic openness for new categories to analyse the 109 qualitative interviews conducted in 2017. We coded the respondents' spontaneous associations with politics and democracy. In doing so, we were able to test the initial category system and to adjust it by using inductively found new categories. In a second step, we used the categories to form new types of political lifeworlds. Here, too, the mixed deductive and inductive approach makes it possible to both review and expand the model.

33 *Helliwell, J./Layard, R./Sachs, J. D./De Neve, J.-E.* 2020: World Happiness Report 2020, New York: Sustainable Development Solutions Network. http://www.worldhappiness.report/ (29/03/2020).

2.1 *Meanings of Politics*[34]

The fine coding of meanings of politics yielded a total of 212 codes in 21 subcodes. These subcodes could be clustered and the categories then were consistent with the five categories developed in 2013/14.[35]

- The *emancipatory concept of politics* contains all passages whose content focuses on the ability to shape the political community: Participation and power to shape are the central aspects of content.
- The strong focus on state and government and the exercise of power characterizes the *governmental concept of politics*. This includes statements about government, parliament, politicians and parties as well as references to their activities of governing and ruling.
- The *institutional concept of politics* focuses more strongly on the polity dimension. It is not about processes of governing, but about places and levels where politics takes place: Federal, state, local or EU level.
- The *regulatory-systemic concept of politics*, in turn, summarizes statements that understand politics as a system of rules through which coexistence in a community is controlled. This includes laws, legal frameworks and regulations, although the "who and where" of regulation is not specified.
- A further category is the *universal concept of politics*, which is based on the idea that politics permeates the whole of life and that the private sphere is also political.

A total of 95 of 109 respondents (87.1 percent) actively produce their own meanings of politics. There are both pure and mixed types. Compared to the initial study, there are some shifts in the frequency of orientations.[36] With 38.5 percent, the most frequently expressed orientations including dominant mixed types are the regulatory concepts (2013/14: 10.5 percent), followed by the governmental with 27.5 percent (2013/14: 37.5 percent). There are also institutional (11 vs. 17.1 percent) and universal (6.4 vs. 2.5 percent) orientations. Emancipatory orientations are hardly found with only 3.7 percent of the respondents showing such orientations, whereas in 2013/14 they accounted for 24.1 percent of the sample. The shifts are most likely due to the sampling strategy, which recruited dissatisfied people in particular. Nevertheless, the shifts between regulatory, governmental and emancipatory orientations are particularly striking. While regulatory orientations are much more strongly represented, there are fewer governmental and hardly any emancipatory orientations.

---

34 In German, there is only one word for the different meanings of politics, policy, and polity. All of these are subsumed under the term *Politik.* In our study we asked for individual meanings of Politik. Depending on individual knowledge and experience the answers included different aspects of what would be separated into the three english terms.

35 *Frankenberger et al.* 2015 (fn. 2), pp. 191 f.

36 Ibidem, p. 194.

2.2 *Meanings of Democracy*

Asking for meanings of democracy aims at fundamental principles and concepts that people associate with democracy. Analogous to the procedure for political concepts, the spontaneous expressions were fine-coded along the categories developed in 2013/14.[37] Here, too, the category system could be reproduced and did not have to be expanded inductively. In the process, 215 text units were coded in 29 subcodes, which are distributed among the five following categories:

- The *norm-based meanings of democracy* include all codes that establish a direct reference to individual norms that are considered by the persons concerned to be sufficient in terms of definition.
- The category *rudimentary meanings of democracy* includes all those text units in which a reference to democracy is established but not further explained. As a rule, these are terms such as majority voting, popular government or co-determination.
- Whenever clear references to representative democracy were expressed, such as elections, or representation, or in cases where democracy is defined directly by the term elections, these fall into the category of *representative meanings of democracy.*
- A *deliberative meaning of democracy* is present if the respondents express clear associations with deliberative procedures and public hearings. It must be clear here that it is not the actual decision-making process that is involved, but rather involvement in the process of preparing the decision.
- Last but not least, units are assigned to the category *participatory direct democratic meaning of democracy,* if the respondents explicitly associate co-determination of decisions with the term democracy. At the same time, there must be linguistic indications that direct democratic procedures such as referenda are meant by this term. The mere mention of corresponding terms such as co-determination is not sufficient.

A total of 99 out of 109 people actively expressed ideas about what democracy means to them, 22 of whom expressed only rudimentary ideas about democracy as a form of government. This means that 70.6 percent of the respondents have a more or less sophisticated idea about what democracy is or at least associate democracy with individual norms and values. The individual meanings of democracy are again present in pure form or as dominant mixed types. With 23.8 percent, norm-based understandings of democracy are found almost as frequently as representative (22.9 percent) and rudimentary (20.2 percent) ones. Direct democratic (13.7 percent) and deliberative (10.1 percent) orientations make up a smaller proportion. In comparison to the 2013/14 study, there are also shifts in emphasis here: While rudimentary (20.2 vs. 22.2 percent in 2013/14) orientations are comparatively stable, representative (22.9 vs. 28.1 percent in 2013/14), deliberative (10.1 vs. 15.7 percent) and direct democratic (13.7 percent vs. 17.8 percent) orientations are clearly less represented. In contrast, norm-based understandings of democracy are much more common (23.8 vs. 15.6 percent in 2013/14).

37 Ibidem, pp. 195 f.

3 The Lifeworld Matrix 2017

If we combine meanings of democracy and concepts of politics in a crosstabulation, we obtain a matrix of political lifeworlds. Table 1 displays this matrix and also highlights those combinations which make more than 5 percent of the sample (bold and italic) that are statistically significant in terms of overrepresentation (dark grey background) – and underrepresentation (light grey background).

Table 1: Matrix of Political lifeworlds in the 2017 study

			Concepts of Politics						
			emancipatory	governmental	regulatory	institutional	universal	rudimentary	overall
Meanings of Democracy	rudimentary	n	0	***9***	***15***	2	2	2	30
		expected	1,4	***8,5***	***11,8***	3,6	2,5	2,2	30
	Norm-oriented	n	4	***11***	***10***	3	4	5	37
		expected	1,7	***10,5***	***14,6***	4,4	3,1	2,7	37
	representative	n	0	*5*	***8***	***6***	1	0	20
		expected	,9	*5,7*	***7,9***	***2,4***	1,7	1,5	20
	deliberative	n	1	2	***7***	1	0	0	11
		expected	,5	3,1	***4,3***	1,3	,9	,8	11
	direct	n	0	4	3	1	2	1	11
		expected	,5	3,1	4,3	1,3	,9	,8	11
overall		n	5	31	43	13	9	8	109
		expected	5	31	43	13	9	8	109

Source: Adapted from *Frankenberger et al. 2019* (fn.1), p. 161.

Apolitical lifeworlds with a rudimentary understanding of democracy account for 27.5 percent (n=30). The most frequent combination is the one with regulatory political understanding, which altogether makes up half of this lifeworld (rudimentary-regulatory). In addition, the combination with governmental concepts of politics (n=9) is particularly significant. Together they account for 80 percent of the distant. While the rudimentary governmental ones are largely uncommitted, those with a rudimentary regulatory orientation participate at least occasionally in political or social life.

A second focal point of the sample is the *norm-oriented types* with 33.9 percent (n=37). Here it is particularly the combination with norm-oriented meanings of democracy, which forms the strongest, and slightly overrepresented group (n=11). In addition, there are the regulative-norm oriented types with n=10. Together they represent 56.8 percent of this group. The norm oriented-emancipatory (n=4) and -rudimentary types are also strongly overrepresented, although together they represent only 16.2 percent.

The *electoral types* make up 18.3 percent (n=20) of the sample, although here the original core of the representative-governmental orientation comprises only 5 persons. More important here are the representative-regulatory (n=8) and representative-institutional (n=6) orientations, whereby the former in particular were represented much less frequently in the 2013/14 study.

Only partial elements of the *participatory lifeworlds* can be found. For both the deliberative (n=11) and the direct democratic (n=11) orientations, firstly, the overall share of 10.1 percent each is significantly lower than in 2013/14 and, secondly, both types lack the emancipatory momentum that characterised them initially. It can therefore be assumed that these are new, different types. What is interesting here, is the strongly regulatory orientation of the deliberative lifeworlds in particular.

Compared to the 2013/14 study, especially the shift towards non-political and delegative lifeworlds and a qualitative change in the types identified as participatory, which lack the emancipatory aspect, is striking. The findings on the 2017 lifeworlds and the comparison with the findings on the sample of the 2013/14 study suggest several conclusions: First, the category system is stable and exhaustive across both studies, which confirms the assumption of a high theoretical saturation already in the first study. Secondly, all lifeworlds can be found in the current study, which points at the validity of the concepts. Thirdly, however, it is apparent that – due to the composition of the sample and the recruitment strategy aimed at dissatisfied persons – there are different emphases with regard to the living worlds. These suggest a consideration of the new focal points as well as a reflection of the lifeworlds model against the background of both studies.

There is another striking difference. In the 2013/14 study, more than three-quarters of the respondents were satisfied with the political system and democracy in Germany and Baden-Württemberg. Criticism was directed either selectively at individual actors in the political system or at political processes. In this respect, a critical or aversive dimension in the lifeworld typology seemed largely obsolete, as even the distanced and non-political were predominantly satisfied. In the current sample, 54.1 percent of those surveyed are rather or very dissatisfied with democracy as it functions in Germany. Taking into account these figures and the recent developments mentioned above, namely the stronger polarisation of the political system, the emergence of a extreme-right populist party that is at least fundamentally critical of the system and the elites, and correspondingly oriented social movements, the following question does indeed arise: are there anti-systemic, democracy-averse and negative-system-critical life-worlds?

Lifeworlds with rudimentary meanings of democracy account for 27.5 percent of the sample and display very different concepts of politics. varying of elaboration with regard to concepts of politics. Most of them have combinations with regulatory (13.8 percent or governmental (8.3 percent) concepts of politics. Both groups can be characterised by a distance to politics and low levels of participation, but they differ gradually: People with rudimentary governmental orientations are not socially active and hardly participate in politics. In contrast, people with regulatory orientations are at least occasionally socially and politically active. When these lifeworlds participate, this is primarily online by posting in forums or submitting signatures to online petitions. Participation in organised civic participation is found only among those with a regulatory orientation. In both life worlds we rather find middle and higher incomes, almost all of these people classify themselves as middle class, are predominantly non-religious and male. While rudimentary-governmental people tend to have rather low or medium educational qualifications and are employed, rudimentary-governmental people often have higher educational qualifications and are civil servants or freelancers. In both groups, the level of distrust of democracy is slightly above the mean, but anti-establishment attitudes tend to be below average. Neither right-wing extremism nor right-wing populism are particularly emphasized, but, here too, there are slightly positive characteristics. A majority of the respondents regards migrants (n=17) as problem. There is also a rather diffuse perception of political problems, so that other aspects, including the mentioning of Islam, which might be expected in connection with migrants, are cited particularly frequently.

In the 2013/14 study, only 22.5 percent belonged to these two a-political lifeworlds. We assumed that their share could be significantly higher, but the apparent increase to about 25 percent is weak. This is especially interesting, as our recruiting strategy tended to attract dissatisfied groups. The findings can be interpreted as a transformation within established lifeworlds rather than an an anti-systemic politicisation of the non-political. Those with a rudimentary governmental orientation appear to be more receptive to AfD. No less than four out of nine indicated this as their electoral preference, whereas only four out of eleven of the rudimentary regulatory ones did so.

The *delegative lifeworlds* show strong orientations towards (individual) norms, rules and institutions of politics. With 52.3 percent (n=57) they make up the majority of the respondents. Representative (20; 18.3 percent) and norm-based (37; 33.9 percent) meanings of democracy go hand in hand with governmental (16; 14.7 percent), regulatory (18; 16.5 percent) and institutional (9; 8.3 percent) political concepts. In detail, the findings suggest that the delegative lifeworlds need to be differentiated again. There are several consistent groups with a relevant number of cases.

The *norm-oriented governmental* lifeworld is the largest subgroup with 10.1 percent (n=11). When members of this group participate, it is almost exclusively political and only occasionally. Forms of internet-based opinion articulation are in the foreground: writing comments and participating in online petitions are the most frequently mentioned activities. Migration and threats to freedom of opinion are particularly cited as problems. The majority of this lifeworld indicated to vote AfD. Here, there are mainly people with middle and higher incomes and educational qualifications who consider themselves to be middle class and are employed. They are predominantly male.

Although people with a *representative-governmental* orientation account for only 4.6 percent (n=5), they are strongly influenced by right-wing populism, similar to the norm-oriented governmental orientation. Here again, the majority votes AfD. Migration and the "lie press" are perceived as the main problems, and online participation in the form of commentary is the main form of political activity.

The *norm oriented-regulatory* lifeworld accounts for 9.2 percent (n=10). People from this lifeworld are comparatively strongly socially and politically engaged. They also participate primarily online in the form of commentaries and petitions, but also seek contact with politicians and take part in organised forms of civic participation. In contrast to people with a governmental orientation, they hardly see migration as a problem, but perceive increasing authoritarianism and right-wing populism as a threat. Consequently, there are hardly any AfD supporters in this lifeworld, although it is just as likely to be male as the norm-oriented-governmental lifeworld, and there are also many employees with medium and high incomes and educational qualifications.

Even if the *representative-regulatory* orientation (7.3 percent; n=8) regards migration and EU integration as core problems, shares for the AfD are significantly lower than in the governmental lifeworlds, but still above average. People from this lifeworld tend to be more active than others acive. They come from all income groups, the majority of them belong to the middle class and have higher educational qualifications.

The *representative-institutional* lifeworld comprises only 5.5 percent (n=6) of the interviewees, but its members are comparatively active and, similar to representative-regulatory, define migration and EU integration as core problems. They participate primarily online and make very active use of the commentary function. Predominantly male, members of this group vote slightly above average for AfD. Together with the representative governmental lifeworld, which has a much stronger affinity to AfD, these two environments form the electoral ones.

In the 2013/14 study, 44.4 percent (n=122) belonged to these delegative lifeworlds. In the current study, they account for 52.3 percent (n=57). Delegative lifeworlds are the backbone of representative democracies in terms of their basic orientation, and their somewhat greater importance today can be explained by selection effects of recruitment. Parts of them are particularly dissatisfied and felt particularly appealed by the study. Accordingly, the majority of AfD supporters are also to be found here in specific orientations. The level of participation in these life-worlds varies. About two thirds are either not socially or politically active, or only occasionally. However, about one third are also politically and socially active. Above all, the norm-oriented regulators should be mentioned here, who also have the highest level of trust in democracy. It is interesting to note that the majority of those currently engaged are people who were previously neither socially nor politically engaged. Apparently, there are clearly identifiable mobilisation effects due to current political issues in the delegative environments. While norm oriented-regulatory people have a comparatively low value of 2.6 for mistrust of democracy,, which is clearly below the arithmetic mean (3.55), the representative-regulatory people have a value of 2.9, which is close to the neutral value, while all others and especially the governmental people are clearly above the arithmetic mean (3.9). Here the mistrust in the government is thus relatively higher. This pattern is also evident in anti-establishment attitudes. While the norm-oriented-regulatory and the representative-regulatory and institutional attitudes have much lower values (2.1, 2.9 and 2.9 respectively), the normoriented-governmental (3.3) and representative-governmental (3.8) attitudes against the political "establishment" are much stronger. Accordingly, the latter two groups also have high values on the right-wing populism scale and on Nationalism, while the former have a positive attitude towards the EU.

Here we witness a split of the delegative lifeworlds that can be explained by the different concepts of politics. Those strongly oriented towards individual norms and at the same time towards the government and governmental action are more dissatisfied with democracy and the elites, are against the EU. At the same time, they have stronger populist attitudes and do rarely participate. People from lifeworlds with a strong focus on regulation, steering, and implementation of decisions instead are more satisfied, more active, less populist, and tend to be pro-European.

Participatory lifeworlds do have emancipatory approaches to politics and strongly link participation and co-decision with democracy. Compared to the 2013/14 study these lifeworlds are clearly underrepresented (33.1 vs. 20.1 percent). Also, and even more important, emancipatory approaches are barely relevant in the actual study. *Instead, half of these lifeworlds shared a regulatory understanding of democracy.*

At 20.1 percent (n=22) they are clearly underrepresented compared to the Democracy Monitoring 2013/14 (33.1 percent). In addition, emancipatory approaches are hardly relevant, whereas about half of them are characterised by a regulatory understanding of politics. Deliberative-regulatory (6.4 percent) are the strongest group, followed by direct governmental (3.6 percent) and direct regulators (2.7 percent). These lifeworlds are definitely socially and/or politically engaged, either socially or politically or both. Here, too, scepticism about the way democracy works is evident, but less so about the political elites. However, there is an above-average potential for populism as well as an increased dissatisfaction with democracy. Moreover, the four direct-governmental orientated people are those who have the highest mistrust of democracy and the highest values in questions of a perceived Islamic conspiracy and new right-wing attitudes. The decidedly emancipatory orientation found in 2013/14 cannot be not found here in any of the groups with a direct or deliberative democratic orientation. Deliberative-regulatory groups are at least EU-friendly and not right-wing, while the direct-democratic lifeworlds show high values for anti-establishment, mistrust of democracy and right-wing attitudes. These differences are also reflected in voting behaviour. While the majority of deliberative-regulatory orientated people do not vote for AfD and participate in various ways, the vast majority of direct-democratic orientated people vote for AfD and participate online, at best. Again, there are signs of a split in participatory lifeworlds, which stands in sharp contrast to the findings of 2013/14, but which should not be overemphasised due to the low case numbers. And once again, the regulatory elements seem to be moderating towards a systemic orientation, satisfaction and activity, while the direct democratic elements are non-moderated drivers of asystemic criticism.

3.1 Re-adjustment of the Lifeworld Model: Critical-affirmative vs. Critical-aversive

The split of the three broader lifeworlds runs along a dimension that has so far been considered at best implicitly in the lifeworld model: A division can be made along the question of whether one is critical and negative, satisfied, or critical and positively supportive of the political system. If one considers the voting preferences and problem perceptions of the individual persons, this runs parallel to the cleavage between progressive universalist-pluralistic positions and authoritarian particularistic-national positions. While some are decidedly dissatisfied, rejecting, critical and advocate for a change of the political system without being substantially involved, others are either satisfied or dissatisfied, but at least contribute and make claims for extending democracy beyond the already existing options. This split between critical-aversive and critical-affirmative attitudes drives the lifeworlds apart. This is new in this clarity, whereby more or less all different meanings of democracy are affected.

In addition to the attitudes and participatory behaviour of the interviewees, this differentiation can, above all, be found in the concepts of politics: The lifeworlds oriented towards individual norms and/or the government tend to be significantly more dissatisfied with democracy and the political elites than the others. In addition, there is an anti-EU attitude, that comes along with populist. At the same time, people from these lifeworlds are comparatively less committed and rely mainly on expressions of opinion in social networks and other online media. However, the critical-averse attitude towards the political system, its representatives and its achievements is, at least by now, not followed by political action beyond these activities, and voting. On the other hand, there are those whose life-worlds are more oriented towards aspects of regulation, control and the implementation of decisions for the benefit of the community. In general, people from these lifeworlds are more satisfied with democracy, have fewer or no populist tendencies and tend to be pro-European. In addition, they are actively involved in shaping the political community, even if they have points of critique.

Figure 2 shows the revised lifeworld model. It now includes the aversive vs. affirmative criticism dimension, which had not been included in the 2013/14 model. The proportions approximately reflect the frequencies of the respective lifeworlds (of the panel).

Figure 2: Lifeworlds in 2017

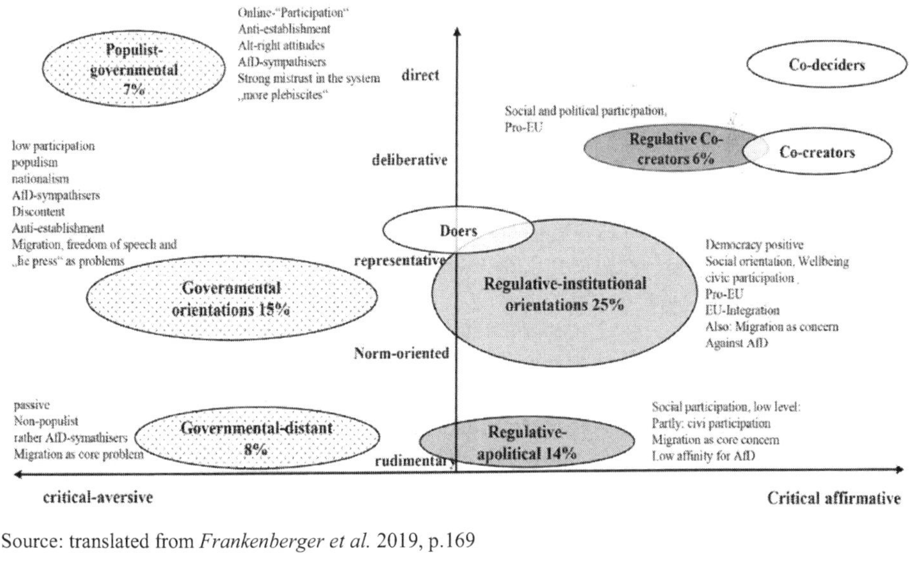

Source: translated from *Frankenberger et al.* 2019, p.169

3.2 *Political Lifeworlds, Discontent and AfD Sympathy*

Political lifeworlds reflect the cleavages between progressive universalist-pluralist positions and authoritarian particularistic-nationalist positions. It is especially the rudimentary and norm-oriented governmental lifeworlds that represent traditional, critical-aversive positions, identify numerous threats to Germany, take an Islam- and migration-hostile positions. They also express populist and alt-right views. Stronger regulatory and institutional orientations significantly reduce the tendency to choose AfD. Those who deal more intensively with the functioning of the political system as a regulatory system seem to take a more reflective approach to assessing the system, to be more satisfied and to participate more than those who have strongly output-oriented and elite-centred ideas of the political. The readjustment of the lifeworld model along the underlying line of conflict between critically aggressive and governmentally oriented as well as critically affirmative and regulatory orientations takes this differentiation of lifeworlds into account.

The assumption that AfD voters predominantly have a direct understanding of democracy, but at the same time show a low level of participation, and that this is the core characteristic of the new political lifeworld can only be confirmed in part. Although direct democratic orientations can also be found, most of them (31 percent or 13 people) are to be found in the norm-oriented life-worlds, especially in the norm-oriented governmental lifeworld. This strong fixation on individual norms is less surprising on closer inspection, since it is things such as freedom of opinion which are particularly highly valued here – admittedly, the own, supposedly restricted freedom of opinion of the “one will still be allowed to say that […]”. In this context, demands for direct democracy seem to be owed more to populist reflexes than to a deeper conviction. This seems to be confirmed by the fact that 69.1 percent (n=29) of AfD voters belong to the delegative worlds and have a governmental or regulatory understanding of democracy. They work hard on their representatives – critically and aversively, of course. The presumed low level of participation, however, can be confirmed. Actual political participation aimed at influencing political decisions is comparatively rare compared with mere expressions of displeasure, especially in social networks. Here, echo chambers and filter bubbles are more likely to be used or to express one's own disappointment. Often this is done with anti-elite, new-right and Islamophobic impulses.

The fact that AfD voters are disappointed in the current political system and that this is condensing into an aversive basic attitude towards representative democracy can be largely confirmed. It is interesting to note that representative democracy and its representatives nevertheless remain the central anchor point of the understanding of democracy. Although there are hardly any differences to non-AfD voters on the level of satisfaction with democracy as an idea, when it comes to assessing democracy as it functions in Germany and satisfaction with the political system in general, AfD supporters are much more dissatisfied. The aversive basic attitude is supported by populist and alt-right motives but is hardly translated into political activity. Most of the living environments covered here are those that do not participate but are exhausted in being against it. It would be interesting to extent future research on the question how these lifeworlds are exactly influenced by their objective (social, financial, participatory etc.) and subjective wellbeing.

Populist Political Communication: A Comparison of Party Officials and Voters of the Alternative für Deutschland

Isabel Sinner

Abstract: Populist political communication has primarily been analyzed from a top-down perspective of parties' public communication. Little research focuses on individual-level communication by voters with populist voting preferences. Analyzing public political speeches and interview data with the method of qualitative content analysis, this article compares the political communication of party officials and voters for the German right-wing populist party Alternative für Deutschland (AfD). The results of the analysis show striking similarities regarding salient political issues, the characterization of elites and specific groups of society as enemies, and rhetorical as well as linguistic traits – supporting the argument that populism, understood as a style of political communication[1] is of relevance both for parties *and* their voters.

Keywords: populism, political communication, voters, Alternative für Deutschland (AfD), Germany

1 Introduction[2]

Because if a democracy still exists in Germany, then we will be the ones that fulfill the democratic basic order. We are the ones that finally bring an alternative to the Bundestag and we are the ones that represent alternative politics. All the others are cartel or system parties and we do not want to have anything to do with them.
– AfD party official Alexander Gauland[3]

I have the slight impression that our democracy transitioned from the people, the will of the people, to the will of the parties.
– Voter of the AfD (Interview 006)[4]

The introductory quotations showcase a specific strand of political communication. They are examples of populist messaging to make political claims – the most essential being a negative portrayal of the political and democratic situation in Germany, where political parties are constructed in an antagonistic way towards the united German people or citizens, if any

1 *Jagers, J./Walgrave, S.* 2007: Populism as political communication style: An empirical study of political parties' discourse in Belgium. In: European Journal of Political Research, 46, pp. 319–345.

2 This article is based on the author's bachelor's thesis project supervised by Rolf Frankenberger. The author would like to thank Rolf Frankenberger who provided helpful guidance and support during the course of the research. See *Sinner, I.* 2019: Themen, Argumente und Sprache des Populismus: Eine vergleichende Analyse politischer Kommunikation von Parteifunktionär*innen und Wähler*innen der Alternative für Deutschland (Unpublished bachelor's thesis), Eberhard Karls University Tübingen, Tübingen, Germany.

3 *TransparentePolitik* (2016, October 04). Alexander Gauland am 09.09.2016 in Northeim. [Video file]. https://youtu.be/sQnU5z_1iDI (06/04/2020).

4 All German to English translations are the author's own. Some specific wordings and neologism are included in German when appropriate. Original quotations can be requested from the author.

represented by the Alternative für Deutschland (AfD). Considering that communication in the context of politics is never just a means of expression, but is connected to the implementation of specific world views and struggles for power,[5] this article takes a closer look at the political communication of the right-wing populist party AfD and its voters.

Since the foundation of the party in 2013 and its electoral successes at both the federal and state level in Germany, culminating a 12,6 percent share of votes in the 2017 federal elections[6], populist political communication has become omnipresent in political discourse in Germany and is therefore increasingly subject to controversial discussion in the political, public and medial arenas. By now, the AfD has moved away from the sheer Eurosceptic positions of its founding days and is commonly referred to as right-wing populist and at this point also classified accordingly within scientific research.[7] A similar change is reflected in voters of the AfD.[8]

The AfD's political communication has just recently been addressed as a potential factor for understanding its electoral successes. Qualitative and quantitative studies[9] find mixed results in respect to populist elements within the party's communication. Their findings point to an intra-party spectrum of populism that also varies at different points of time. Furthermore, they indicate effects of different communication types and channels.

The reproduction of populist communication on the individual level of voters is rarely included in existing analyses. AfD voters have so far mostly been analyzed in quantitative perspective and methodology, following the empirical puzzle of populist voting preferences by analyzing independent variables like socio-demographics or attitudes towards specific political issues.[10] Furthermore, voters of the AfD have been found to distinguish themselves

---

5 *Sarcinelli, U.* 2009: Politische Kommunikation in Deutschland: Zur Politikvermittlung im demokratischen System, 2nd edition, Wiesbaden, p. 17.

6 *Der Bundeswahlleiter* 2017: Bundestagswahl 2017: Ergebnisse Deutschland. https://www.bundeswahlleiter.de/bundestagswahlen/2017/ergebnisse/bund-99.html (06/04/2020).

7 *Dilling, M.* 2018: Two of the same kind? The rise of the AfD and its implications for the CDU/CSU. In: German Politics and Society, 36, pp. 84–104; *Lewandowsky, M./Giebler, H./Wagner, A.* 2016: Rechtspopulismus in Deutschland: Eine empirische Einordnung der Parteien zur Bundestagswahl 2013 unter besonderer Berücksichtigung der AfD. In: Politische Vierteljahresschrift, 57, pp. 247–275; *Rosenfelder, J.* 2017: Die Programmatik der AfD: Inwiefern hat sie sich von einer primär euroskeptischen zu einer rechtspopulistischen Partei entwickelt? In: Zeitschrift für Parlamentsfragen, pp. 123–140.

8 *Arzheimer, K./Berning, C. C.* 2019: How the Alternative for Germany (AfD) and their voters veered to the radical right, 2013–2017. In: Electoral Studies, 60; *Bieber, I./Roßteutscher, S./Scherer, P.* 2018: Die Metamorphosen der AfD-Wählerschaft: Von einer euroskeptischen Protestpartei zu einer (r)echten Alternative? In: Politische Vierteljahresschrift, 59, pp. 433–461.

9 See amongst others *Arzheimer, K.* 2015: The AfD: Finally, a successful right-wing populist Eurosceptic party for Germany? In: West European Politics, 38, pp. 535–556; *Franzmann, S. T.* 2016: Calling the ghost of populism: The AfD's strategic and tactical agendas until the EP election 2014. In: German Politics, 25, pp. 457–479; *Merkle, S.* 2016: Populistische Elemente in der Kommunikation der Alternative für Deutschland: Eine qualitative Analyse von Wahlwerbung und Pressemitteilungen im Europawahlkampf 2014. In: *Holtz-Bacha, C. (ed.)*: Europawahlkampf 2014: Internationale Studien zur Rolle der Medien, Wiesbaden, pp. 129–152.

10 *Goerres, A./Spies, D. C./Kumlin, S.* 2018: The electoral supporter base of the Alternative for Germany. In: Swiss Political Science Review, 24, pp. 246–269; *Hambauer, V./Mays, A.* 2018: Wer wählt die AfD? Ein Vergleich der Sozialstruktur, politischen Einstellungen und Einstellungen zu Flüchtlingen zwischen AfD-WählerInnen und der WählerInnen der anderen Parteien. In: Zeitschrift für Vergleichende Politikwissenschaft, 12, pp. 133–154; *Schmitt-Beck, R.* 2017: The 'Alternative für Deutschland in the electorate': Between single-issue and right-wing populist party. In: German Politics, 26, pp. 124–148.

from voters of other German parties by their persistent populist[11] and right-wing populist[12] political attitudes. The respective research fits into a broader picture where populist political communication is mainly analyzed from a top-down perspective with focus on parties, neglecting citizen's political communication and populism and leaving this nexus under-researched.[13]

This article aims at contributing a qualitative approach to understand how populism is produced and reproduced by researching not only party officials but also voters of the AfD. It therefore draws on an understanding of populism as a political communication style[14] [15] and seeks to address the following question:

> What are the main political issues, arguments and specific rhetorical and linguistic traits of the political communication of the right-wing populist party Alternative für Deutschland and to what extent are these also found in the voters of the party?

Qualitative content analysis is used to develop a code system for the AfD's political communication based on public speeches by party officials held on national and state level. It is then applied to qualitative interview data of AfD voters from the German state Baden-Württemberg. The interviews were conducted in a study analyzing the life worlds of AfD voters[16] and provide in-depth material for a tentative attempt to explore populist political communication beyond parties and to allow for a comparison of both groups' political communication.[17]

The relevance of this analysis of populist political communication for the subject of wellbeing lies in the connection of voters' political satisfaction to their subjective wellbeing. This is especially true, if we define wellbeing as including "basic liberties and opportunities, including wealth and income, which provide individuals with the freedom and resources to pursue their life plans"[18]. Then the political sphere becomes a main point of reference for wellbeing. Wellbeing is linked to the perception of the political system, the performance of

---

11 *Vehrkamp, R./Merkel, W.* 2018: Populismusbarometer 2018: Populistische Einstellungen bei Wählern und Nichtwählern in Deutschland 2018. https://www.bertelsmann-stiftung.de/fileadmin/files/BSt/Publikationen/GrauePublikationen/ZD__Studie_Populismusbarometer_2018.pdf; *Vehrkamp, R./Wratil, C.* 2017: Die Stunde der Populisten? Populistische Einstellungen bei Wählern und Nichtwählern vor der Bundestagswahl 2017. https://www.bertelsmann-stiftung.de/fileadmin/files/BSt/Publikationen/GrauePublikationen/ZD_Studie_Populismus_DE.pdf.

12 *Küpper, B./Berghan, W./Rees, J. H.* 2019: Aufputschen von Rechts: Rechtspopulismus und seine Normalisierung in der Mitte. In: *Schröter, F. (ed.)*: Verlorene Mitte – feindselige Zustände: Rechtsextreme Einstellungen in Deutschland 2018/19, Bonn, pp. 173–201.

13 *Reinemann, C./Matthes, J./Sheafer, T.* 2017: Citizens and populist political communication: Cross-national findings and perspectives. In: *Aalberg, T./Esser, F./Reinemann, C./Strömbäck, J./de Vreese, C.H. (eds.)*: Populist political communication in Europe, New York, pp. 381–394.

14 *Jagers/Walgrave* 2007 (fn. 1).

15 This definition has proved to be fruitful for the analysis of the AfD in previous research. See *Franzmann* 2016 (fn. 8); *Merkle* 2016 (fn. 8).

16 *Buhr, D./Frankenberger, R./Gensheimer, T.* 2019: Mehr Demokratie ertragen? Eine lebensweltliche Studie der AfD-Wählerinnen und -Wähler. In: *Baden-Württemberg Stiftung (ed.)*: Demokratie-Monitoring Baden-Württemberg 2016/2017, Wiesbaden, pp. 85–101.

17 When looking at the results of this analysis, it must be kept in mind that the data used is neither representative of the AfD nor of its voters in Baden-Württemberg or on the national level.

18 *Austin, A.* 2016: On Well-being and Public Policy. Are we capable of questioning the Hegemony of Happiness? In: Social Indicators Research 127, 1, pp. 123–138 (132).

the government and voters' own role in the political process. Populist political communication creates negative portrayals of the political sphere and its elites, shifts critique from specific policies towards the political system itself and its representatives and links diffuse negative perceptions with concrete enemy constructions and threat perceptions to 'the people', framed as a majoritarian entity. Political dissatisfaction of voters is fueled, limiting their wellbeing as participants of the political process in the long term.[19]

The results of the analysis point towards such a profound political dissatisfaction of voters. Both AfD party officials and voters discuss political issues with populistic claims of notions of 'the people'. Political and other elites and specific groups like refugees and migrants are characterized as enemies. Similarities between both groups are also found regarding the salience of issues like migration and integration as well as internal security, justice and police.

2 Populism as a Political Communication Style

There is no universal conceptualization of populism. Rather there are different strands of literature, defining populism as 1) an ideology; 2) a specific form of mobilization/organization and political strategy; or 3) a political communication style and form of discourse.[20]

This article makes use of the discursive understanding of populism, following Jagers and Walgrave who conceptualize populism as a specific political communication style that is not only limited to politicians but can also be used in different contexts by other actors to convey political messages.[21] In this logic, populism can become evident in "the oral, written and visual communication of individual politicians, parties, social movements, or any other actor that steps into the public sphere (including the media and citizens)"[22]. As previously mentioned, populist political communication on the individual voter level and the effects of it when used by party officials on the subsequent political communication of their target audiences remain under-researched.

Populist political communication can be distinguished by three inherent features that constitute either *thin* or *thick* populism: References to 'the people', anti-elitism, and the exclusion of specific groups of society.[23] Additionally, populist political communication draws on specific rhetorical and linguistic traits.

19 Cf. *Frankenberger, R./Chernenkova, E.* in this volume. They summarize some findings of the link between political factors and wellbeing, for example the influence of the institutional design, output and quality of government of a political system.

20 *Gidron, N./Bonikowski, B.* 2013: Varieties of populism: Literature review and research agenda (Weatherhead Center for International Affairs Working Paper Series No. 13-0004). https://scholar.harvard.edu/files/gidron_bonikowski_populismlitreview_2013.pdf; *Moffitt, B./Tormey, S.* 2014: Rethinking populism: Politics, mediatisation and political style. In: Political Studies, 62, pp. 381–397.

21 *Jagers/Walgrave* 2007 (fn. 1), p. 334.

22 *Aalberg, T./Esser, F./Reinemann, C./Strömbäck, J./de Vreese, C. H.* 2017: Populist political communication: Towards a model of its causes, forms, and effects. In: *Aalberg, T./Esser, F./Reinemann, C./Strömbäck, J./de Vreese, D.H. (eds.)*: Populist political communication in Europe, New Yok, pp. 12–25 (13).

23 *Jagers/Walgrave* 2007 (fn. 1), pp. 321–325.

Frequent References to 'the People'

'The people' as the dominant point of reference for political claims is the basic feature of what Jagers and Walgrave call *thin populism.*[24] Central within populist communication is "the communicative, discursive construction of an aggregate-level in-group or appeals and references to such a group"[25]. Within the respective political communication political actors attempt to generate a sense of belonging and social collective identity for citizens.[26] According to Cranmer these references can either be used by actors to position themselves as advocates of 'the common people', to emphasize accountability for the seemingly homogenous will of 'the people', or legitimize populist appeals.[27]

Anti-Elitism and the Exclusion of Specific Groups of Society

Anti-elitism and the exclusion of specific groups of society are additional features that can be combined with frequent references to 'the people', they then constitute *thick populism.*[28] Anti-elitism often takes the form of characterizing other political actors, the media, the state, members of economic or scientific communities, or any one else perceived to be part of the establishment as an enemy of the popular will.[29] Antagonisms are reinforced by the construction of specific groups of society as enemies, they are positioned against homogeneously displayed interests and values of 'the people'.[30] These excluded groups are characterized as being "responsible for the perceived threats and problems, or, in a lot of cases, serve as scapegoats"[31].

For voters, anti-establishment and exclusionist attitudes can be constructed through different antagonisms.[32] Chief among these antagonisms is the notion that the will of the majority of 'the common people' is being suppressed by politicians.[33] They can also take the form of the promotion of a self-understanding "working-class majority" against economic elites or by constructing 'the people' against intellectual elites.[34] Furthermore, constructions of a public of 'the people' against specific groups of society can be achieved with internal references to cultural, traditional or resource-distributional based arguments.[35]

24 Ibidem, p. 322.
25 *Aalberg et al.* 2017 (fn. 21), p. 16.
26 Ibidem, p. 19.
27 *Cranmer, M.* 2011: Populist communication and publicity: An empirical study of contextual differences in Switzerland. In: Swiss Political Science Review, 17, pp. 286–307 (292 f).
28 *Jagers/Walgrave* 2007 (fn. 1), p. 322.
29 Ibidem, p. 324.
30 Ibidem.
31 *Aalberg et al.* 2017 (fn. 21), p. 21.
32 *Hameleers, M.* 2018: A typology of populism: Toward a revised theoretical framework on the sender side and receiver side of communication. In: International Journal of Communication, 12, pp. 2171–2190 (2177 f).
33 Ibidem, p. 2177.
34 Ibidem.
35 Ibidem, pp. 2177 f.

Rhetorical and Linguistic Traits

Certain rhetorical and linguistic traits that accompany the expression of populist contents further distinguish populist political communication from other types of political discourse. These have been systematized within previous literature.[36] Examples include references to arguments displayed as common-sense, the construction of personalized enemies, or drawing on conspiracy theories to support populist political messages.[37]

3 Methodological Approach

Data

The corpus used for the analysis of this article consists of two parts: public political speeches of AfD party officials and qualitative interviews with AfD voters. Detailed descriptions of the material can be found in table 1.[38]

First, speeches delivered by well-known party officials and leading personnel of the AfD at the time of the analysis were analyzed to identify common issues and traits of their political communication. Most of the speeches specifically targeted public audiences and are accessible in video-format on the online platforms YouTube and Facebook. The selection was based on multiple dimensions of comparison, including different settings of speeches and various points of time. The corpus includes campaign speeches but also material of non-election contexts, like the AfD's federal party convention, a speech at a demonstration and an online New Year's address. Furthermore, party officials were selected from across the populistic spectrum within the AfD. In order to determine what if any similarities between party officials and the communication of party voters could be found, speeches from 2016, which predated the interview data, were used.

In the second step of the analysis, unique in-depth interview material of self-identified AfD voters from the German state of Baden-Württemberg was analyzed in comparison with the aforementioned speeches by party officials. The interview transcripts for this step of the analysis stem from the study "Mehr Demokratie ertragen?".[39] The study was conducted in 2017 as a sub-project of the "Demokratie-Monitoring Baden-Württemberg" edited by the Baden-Württemberg foundation and explored life worlds of AfD voters by employing a qualitative approach with semi-structured narrative interview methodology. The interviews

36 *Decker, F.* 2000: Parteien unter Druck: Der neue Rechtspopulismus in den westlichen Demokratien. Opladen, pp. 50–53; *Hirschmann, K.* 2017: Der Aufstieg des Nationalpopulismus: Wie westliche Gesellschaften polarisiert werden, Bonn, pp. 184–193; *Wodak, R.* 2016: Politik mit der Angst: Zur Wirkung rechtspopulistischer Diskurse, Wien/Hamburg, pp. 82 ff.

37 *Decker* 2000 (fn. 35), p. 51.

38 AfD party officials' speeches included speeches by Dr. Frauke Petry, Jörg Meuthen and Beatrix von Storch. Sources: Dr. Frauke Petry (2016, December 31). Neujahrsansprache Frauke Petry #AfD. [Video file]. https://www.facebook.com/Dr.Frauke.Petry/videos/1332160453503265/ (06/04/2020); *Phoenix* (2016, April 30). 5. AfD-Bundesparteitag: Rede von Jörg Meuthen am 30.04.2016. [Video file]. https://youtu.be/WcU2eLwVNsc (06/04/2020); *Radix* (2016, February 27). Beatrix von Storch, AfD, 25.02.2016, Backnang. [Video file]. https://youtu.be/6P-F-16ft5Q (06/04/2020).

39 *Buhr et al.* 2019 (fn. 15).

included questions on personal understandings of politics, polity and democracy, political trust, and participation and subjects had the chance to express and describe political issues salient to them in their own words[40], thus generating material of political communication fitted for the analysis of this article. Differences between strategic public political communication of professionalized party officials and spontaneous, unscripted life world narrations of voters nevertheless have to be kept in mind when interpreting the results.

Table 1: Comparative description of the material

	Speeches of AfD Party Officials	**Interviews with AfD Voters**
Sample	n=6 Non-representative sample of AfD party officials	n=42 Non-representative sample of Baden-Württemberg residents who voted for the AfD and/or one of its splinter parties (Allianz für Fortschritt und Aufbruch / Liberal-Konservative Reformer) in the 2016 state elections or had the intention to vote for one of them in the 2017 federal elections
Sampling	Explorative, non-randomized selection by the author; Accessibility and length of the speeches included for selection	Theoretical sampling; Self-recruitment of interview partners via Facebook adverts
Context	Face-to-face; Online-stream	Telephone interview
Time Period	02/2016 – 12/2016	01/2017 – 06/2017
Overall Length of Material [H:M:S-Ms]	02:41:16-2	32:58:21-208
Data Format	Online videos Clean verbatim transcription by the author of this article	Audio files Full verbatim transcription provided by transkripto.de

Source: Own compilation; *Buhr et al.* 2019 (fn. 16); *Gensheimer/Frankenberger* 2019 (fn. 45).

Method

A qualitative content analysis[41] with MAXQDA was used to assess textual contents and grasp characteristics of populist political communication. The code system for the political communication of the AfD was developed using an inductive approach and several rounds of coding to identify specific traits of the AfD's political communication. The final coding categories center around policies and political issues, common arguments, constructions and characterizations of enemies, descriptions of the AfD as well as categories grasping notice-

40 Ibidem, pp. 90 f.

41 *Kuckartz, U.* 2016: Qualitative Inhaltsanalyse: Methoden, Praxis, Computerunterstützung, 3rd edition, Weinheim/Basel.

able phrases, metaphors, and other rhetorical and linguistic traits. The entire coding process was undertaken by the author of this article. Overall, the corpus includes 9.678 coded segments in 204 categories. The coded segments cover single words up to whole paragraphs of the texts.

4 Results

In the following section, the empirical results of the analysis are presented, starting with a descriptive analysis of overall frequencies of policies and political issues mentioned to compare their salience for AfD party officials and voters (figure 1). After that, selected results of the analysis, pointing towards structural similarities or differences between party officials and voters are discussed in detail.

Figure 1: Policies and political issues of AfD party officials and voters[42]

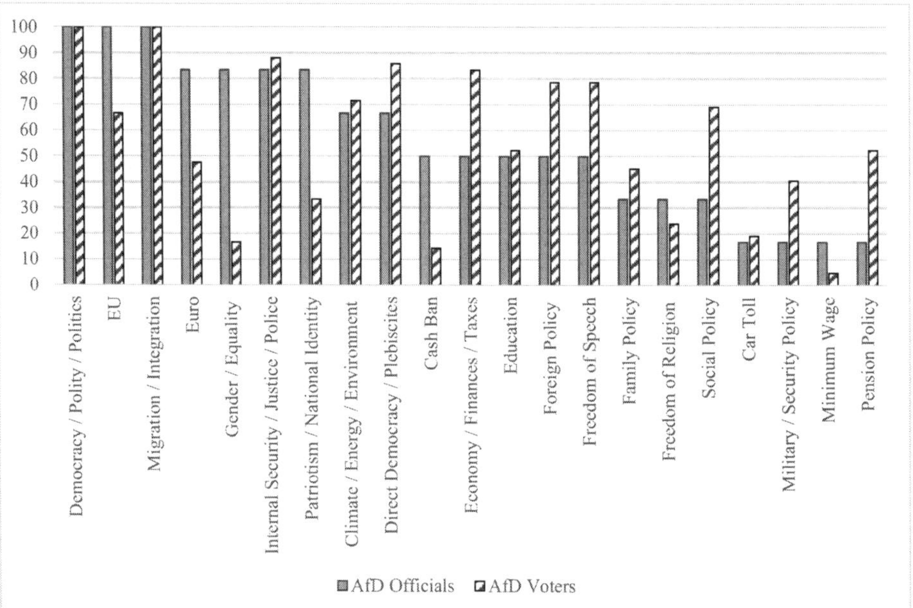

Source: own compilation.

42 The frequency (in percent of all speeches/interviews) with which specific policies and political issues were mentioned by AfD party officials and AfD voters in order of most to least frequently mentioned by party officials. It is possible for speeches and interviews to contain references to more than one issue or mention issues more than one time. Scores for each speech and interview only indicate the presence or absence of a theme and multiple references to a theme are not scored higher.

Besides democracy and polity/politics, both groups emphasized the importance of issues of migration/integration and internal security/justice/police.[43] On other policy areas there was less congruence between the communication of AfD party officials and voters. Whereas the party officials often mentioned issues of patriotism and national identity and took a negative view towards gender and equality issues, voters were far less likely to mention these topics in their interviews. Additionally, issues regarding the EU and the Euro were prominent in the political communication of the party, they seemed to be less salient for voters based on the interviews. In contrast, voters emphasized demands for direct democracy and plebiscites and concerns regarding the economy/finances/taxes. Additionally, issues like foreign policy, freedom of speech and concerns over the climate/energy/environment or social policy were mentioned frequently by voters.

Democracy/Polity/Politics

Both party officials and AfD voters tended to perceive or describe the current political situation negatively. A populist communication style characterized by antagonistic characterizations of different actors and enemy constructions was visible in all speeches and interviews with regard to political issues. Despite this shared trait, the targets of this antagonism varied between officials and voters. While AfD officials often attacked the German chancellor Angela Merkel and the political establishment in the form of other parties or specific politicians, voters articulated a more generalized critique of the political system and those in it. They addressed politics, politicians and parties in general as starting points for critique. Voters mentioned Angela Merkel less frequently than the party, but also seemed to view her negatively and often criticized her in connection with migration. Conspiracy theories and conspiracy rhetoric played a role in strengthening the negative perceptions of politicians:

> "What they dare to say at times, what is being done, where you ask yourself if Ms. Murxel[44] in reality is the helping hand of someone, yes, there are speculations about the high finance, the elites, they want to erase the German people in general" (Interview 099).

Both party officials and voters articulated similar arguments. One prominent argument was an alleged lack of responsiveness of 'mainstream' political parties to the electorate. Politicians were displayed as individuals who broke campaign promises, purposefully lied, acted egoistically, and were accused of being responsible for short- and long-term negative consequences for Germany and its citizens. The AfD was perceived as being less bureaucratized and less institutionalized by voters than other political parties. Both AfD officials and voters criticized these parties of being indistinguishable from one another politically or complained that the they would be dominated by individual party officials:

---

43 The interview guideline included a question asking the subjects about their trust in state institutions. Justice and courts were given as examples of such institutions by the interviewer, and participants responses made use of these examples more often than other possible institutions. My assumption is that this likely lead to an over-estimation of the importance of the issue of internal security/justice/police for the AfD voters.

44 The name "Ms. Murxel" is a reference to chancellor Angela Merkel using a wordplay including the German word "Murks", which can be translated as "botch".

"In the real, the really existing party democracy of the Federal Republic of Germany, an old-party-cartel [Altparteien-Kartell] has evolved, and it has become undistinguishable when it comes to the crucial issues. All of them, from the ones on the far left to the social-democratized Christian Democratic Union stand for energy-transition-madness, for EU-centralism, for Euro rescue programs, for gender mainstreaming and for multicultural madness" (Björn Höcke).[45]

"And there are no more differing opinions in the parliament. Right now, all we have is a kind of mishmash. Laws are passed without real consideration. There are no questions by the opposition. There is no opposition. Our democracy is devastated" (Interview 038).

The analyzed AfD officials often pointed to direct democracy as a solution, something that was also demanded by the voters for what they displayed as a negative political situation.

Migration/Integration and Internal Security/Justice/Police

Migration and integration were core political issues for both groups and were coded together in the analysis. They were mentioned in all analyzed documents[46] and most commonly invoked in the construction of an enemy construction associated with refugees and migrants. Analysis found this rhetoric in all party speeches and most interviews. The rhetoric of both groups also made mention of Muslims and radical Islamists as excluded groups of society and enemy characterizations, albeit less frequently.

Both AfD officials and voters used populist arguments in their political communication around migration and integration. Typical arguments included claiming a threatening displacement of national culture, religion and values or deeming integration impossible, partly because of a refusal of refugees or migrants themselves. In addition, they framed the number of arriving refugees and migrants as unmanageable and accused them of entering the country illegally, without a legal refugee status as economic migrants. Analysis of the data also showed that the issues of migration and integration and the respective constructions of enemies were often linked to discussions about democracy, politics or polity in general or to specific political issues and policies such as internal security/justice/police, freedom of speech, as well as social and retirement policy. The issues of migration and immigration seem to be a reference point for more general critiques of perceived negative developments within German politics and society and refugees and migrants serve as scapegoats.[47] The commonly made argument that refugees and migrants posed a threat to national and personal security followed this pattern. This can be seen in the following quotations from an AfD party official and a voter:

"[I] do not want to keep witnessing how the wheel of Enlightenment and freedom, the equality before the law are being dialed back by this religion and culture relativism that has become intolerable. And I am not just saying that as a German citizen, I am also telling you all this as a woman who is not ready to back away an arm's length from this tolerance of intolerance. From the kotow of our fun-loving society. From Merkel's

---

45 *AfD Bayern TV* (2016, April 29). Björn Höcke - Afd Demo Schweinfurt - AfD Bayern TV. [Video file]. Retrieved from https://youtu.be/AkERtdsZ1dA (06/04/2020).

46 For the interpretation it should be kept in mind that the importance of the issue can most definitely also be also ascribed to increased migration and the so called "refugee crisis" around the year 2015 and beyond which led to a politicization and made the issue highly salient within German political discourse.

47 *Gensheimer, T./Frankenberger, R.* 2019: Themen, Thesen, Argumente: Die Bedeutung von politischem System, Politikfeldern und Beteiligungsangeboten für AfD- und Nicht-AfD-Wähler im Vergleich. In: *Baden-Württemberg Stiftung (ed.)*: Demokratie-Monitoring Baden-Württemberg 2016/2017, Wiesbaden, pp. 103–128 (113).

welcome culture. Because people who trample on our legal and value order and do not give a damn about our legal order should forfeit their right to hospitality immediately" (Alice Weidel).[48]

"But when I saw the people in Budapest at the station, so violent and shouting 'Germany, Germany' that was a very bad moment for me. That was when I saw a lot of things coming that are becoming reality right now, the increased criminality and stuff; I have feared a lot of this" (Interview 018).

Patriotism/National Identity

This category was of fundamental importance within the AfD officials' political communication and illustrates the party's right-wing populist stand very clearly. Demands for more open patriotism were often based on the argument that such displays of national pride would be common in other countries and Germany should be no exception. AfD party officials often referenced German cultural heritage, values and norms as well as Germany's traditional Christian religious affiliation. This also attempts a self-positioning of the party in the conservative political spectrum. AfD voters also referenced Christian values frequently. Compared to party officials, the issues of patriotism and national identity were mentioned relatively infrequently by AfD voters. Rhetorically, voters seem to build their national identity more in opposition to certain groups of society like refugees and migrants rather than articulating an independent identity.

Freedom of Speech/Media

Freedom of Speech was displayed as very important, especially by AfD voters. Both party officials and voters characterized it as in need of protection and claimed that it had become restricted and increasingly attacked by both political actors and society, often with reference to unspecified political opponents.

When it comes to the media, both groups denounced it for what they perceived as a lack of objectivity and independence from political elites. Such accusations are typical populist argument regarding mainstream media. Both groups accused media institutions and actors of inaccurate reporting and perpetuating hoaxes: "In the past I have trusted the public service broadcasters ARD and ZDF, but not anymore. Not since all they are doing is government propaganda" (Interview 014).

European Union/Euro

As mentioned before, political issues concerning the EU or the Euro seemed to be of less importance to voters than to the party. This could be due to a then starting transformation of the AfD's voters from Eurosceptic positions towards more ideologically right orientated stands as the literature suggests.[49] Despite this disparity in importance, an enemy construction of the EU and European Central Bank can be found consistently across both groups, in all speeches and in half of all interviews. Most arguments related to European issues referred

48 *AfD Rheinland-Pfalz* (2016, February 22). Rede von Dr. Alice Weidel (AfD) in Ludwigshafen. [Video file]. https://youtu.be/m9wz0fgm_so (06/04/2020).

49 *Arzheimer/Bernin* 2019 (fn. 7); *Bieber et al.* 2018 (fn. 7).

to the EU as a financial burden for Germany or criticized perceived centralization attempts as interfering too heavily into national sovereignty and the personal lives of citizens. Populist claims of both party officials and voters also tended to link the EU and the European Central Bank to unpopular national politicians:

"And then they principally want a kind of European central state or something, I am not sure if that is the right word. In other words, the CDU and Merkel they want/ Basically that there is no more proper government but instead just a central European thing where just one person is in charge, then there will be no more German politicians or others, but everything will be managed from just one thing, from Brussels and/" (Interview 095).

5 Discussion

This comparison of AfD party officials and voters provides an important first step towards a broader understanding of populism, especially its manifestation and reproduction in political discourse. It contributes by analyzing what voters of populist parties have to say about politics, rather than just labeling them as discontent or classifying them according to sociodemographics and isolated attitudes.

The results show strong similarities between the political communication of AfD officials and rhetoric used by voters when discussing specific political issues. Populist anti-elitism against political personnel, and exclusionary enemy constructions, for example against refugees and migrants; are reproduced on the individual level of voters and political claims of both analyzed groups are often based on a vague notion of the interests of 'the people'. AfD officials and their voters paint a picture of politics today as a moment of profound political dissatisfaction. Common points of reference for the AfD party officials and its voters are the perceived dysfunction of democracy and politics in general as well as issues of migration and integration, often in connection with questions of national and personal security. The analysis does also highlight some differences between the party and its voters, especially the stronger focus regarding European issues by party officials as well the salience of patriotism and national identity for the AfD.

Some limitations have to be kept in mind concerning the analysis of this article. The relatively small number of analyzed documents and the focus on one party allows for a first exploration but limits the generalizability of the results. Future research should include more representative material, also of party officials and voters of other populist parties, thus broadening the scope of analysis. Regarding the interview material, in-depth analysis of the coded segments points towards specific interview and context effects, given that the interviews used for this analysis were originally conducted with a different research goal.[50] Nonetheless, this research may provide a model for future studies on the relationship between populist parties' and their voters' political communication.

As mentioned in the introduction, these findings are also of importance from the perspective of these voters' subjective wellbeing, as a strong albeit diffuse discontent with the democratic process impairs their ability to experience self-efficacy in political life and to meaningfully participate in the democratic society.

---

50 For further critical discussion see *Sinner* 2019 (fn. 2).

PART 4: CIVIL SOCIETY, GOVERNANCE AND CREATION OF WELLBEING

NGOs Social Projects in the Development of the Urban Social Space

Elena Chernenkova

Summary

The focus of modern city development strategies on creating a comfortable and creative urban environment through the development of social partnership and intersectoral interaction has become a generally accepted response to the challenges of our time. The role of civic activism and social design in achieving a new quality of life for urban populations is manifested both in the European and Russian official agendas and occupies a significant place in public and research discourse of various countries. In general, the contours of municipal policy are determined by the construction of ergonomic infrastructure and the production of an innovative environment. Social projects of non-governmental organizations have an essential place in this process. These projects can transform into drivers of social innovation theory by consolidating the work of many actors toward the implementation of urban development strategies. This article presents results of project activities of socially oriented organization in Petrozavodsk urban district. It focuses on projects supported by the Presidential Grants Foundation in the Petrozavodsk urban district. The Presidential Grants Foundation provides the largest support, by scale and volume, for innovative social projects, which in turn foster the development of NGO activities

Keywords: creative social space, social innovation theory, socially oriented organizations, Petrozavodsk urban district

The contours of modern urban policy refer to the Istanbul Declaration on Human Settlements and the Habitat Agenda, adopted by the United Nations conference on human settlements (Habitat II) in 1996, and calls for "the universal goals of ensuring adequate shelter for all and making human settlements safer, healthier, and more livable, equitable, sustainable, and productive."[1] The main tools for achieving set goals are determined by the principles of partnership and public participation on the one hand, and transparency, accountability and responsiveness of local government bodies to the needs of people on the other. In accordance with these guidelines, the human dimension is declared as the primary basis for updating the principles of urban planning and the construction of the modern social space of cities at the supranational, national and local levels.

At the same time the renewal of urban life involves the transformation of the "hard" and "soft" infrastructure of urban spaces. In Russian studies this classification is presented by N.A. Ivanova.[2]

1 *The United Nations* 1996: Istanbul Declaration on Human Settlements and the Habitat Agenda, (1996) Report of the United Nations conference on human settlements (Habitat II) (Istanbul, 3–14 June 1996). https://www.un.org/ruleoflaw/wp-content/uploads/2015/10/istanbul-declaration.pdf (30/03/2020).

2 *Ivanova, N.* 2014: Regional infrastructure objects' classification. In: Modern High Technologies. Regional Application, 1, pp. 38–43 (in Russian).

It is generally accepted, that "hard infrastructure" is understood as a set of physical components of interconnected urban systems necessary for maintaining and improving the living conditions of the population.

The key task in terms of "hard infrastructure" is the renovation of space and the construction of an ergonomic urban environment as a place of living for the urban community. In modern Russia the principles of sustainable development of the environment are defined by state and municipal acts of strategic and territorial planning. Social wellbeing and harmony, the development of human potential, balanced space development, and the creation of a comfortable and safe environment are defined as objectives at the "Concept of long-term socio-economic development of the Russian Federation until 2020"[3].

Within the North-West Federal District, improvement of the living environment is identified among the key goals of state policy in the social sphere in the strategy for socio-economic development of the North-West Federal District for the period until 2020[4], while in the Republic of Karelia the goal of creating a humanistic urban environment is specified in the strategy for socio-economic development of the Republic of Karelia for the period until 2030.[5] At the level of municipalities the principles of strategic planning are also aimed at the implementation of these tasks, for example, in the Petrozavodsk urban district a qualitative change of the urban environment and the creation of conditions for comfortable living are identified among the top priorities of the strategy of socio-economic development of the Petrozavodsk urban district for the period until 2025.[6]

Since 2016 the priority project "Formation of a comfortable urban environment"[7] has been implemented on a national scale, at all levels of state and municipal government. This project suggests the creation of universal mechanisms for involvement of interested citizens and organizations into the implementation of measures to improve municipality territories. The provisions of the programs at the regional and municipal levels of public administration correspond to the provisions of the federal program. With regard to the Republic of Karelia the elaboration and approval of regional and municipal programs refers to 2017, when the state program of the Republic of Karelia, "Formation of the modern urban environment for 2018–2020", was approved. The task of increasing the level of involvement of interested

3 *The Russian Government* 2008: Concept of long-term socio-economic development of the Russian Federation until 2020, approved by Government Directive of November 17, 2008. No. 1662-r. http://www.consultant.ru/document/cons_doc_LAW_82134/79d98ab0c15af433ffc39eee86f1c76b48dced89/ (30/03/2020) (in Russian).

4 *The Russian Government* 2011: The strategy of socio-economic development of the North-West Federal District for the period until 2020, approved by the decree of the Government of the Russian Federation of November 18, 2011. No. 2074-r. https://docs.google.com/viewer?url=http://www.economy.gov.ru/wps/wcm/connect/6de4fa79-0549-46ed-9d1f-89bd5325f24c (30/03/2020) (in Russian).

5 *The Government of the Republic of Karelia* 2018: The strategy of socio-economic development of the Republic of Karelia for the period until 2030, approved by Decree of the Government of the Republic of Karelia on December 29, 2018. No. 899r-P. http://economy.karelia.ru/action/4868/ (30/03/2020) (in Russian).

6 *The Petrozavodsk City Council* 2015: The strategy of socio-economic development of the Petrozavodsk urban district for the period until 2025, approved by the decision of the Petrozavodsk City Council of February 18, 2015. No. 27, pp. 31-489. http://docs.cntd.ru/document/465407025 (30/03/2020) (in Russian).

7 *The Presidential Council on Strategic Development and Priority Projects* 2016: The priority project "Formation of a comfortable urban environment", approved by the Presidium of the Presidential Council on Strategic Development and Priority Projects of November 21, 2016. Minutes No. 10. http://government.ru/projects/selection/649/25517/ (30/03/2020) (in Russian).

citizens and organizations into the implementation of measures to improve municipal territories is among the top priorities of the republican program.[8] The municipal program of the Petrozavodsk urban district, "Formation of the modern urban environment"[9], envisaging the participation of Petrozavodsk city residents in public discussions for choosing activities related to the improvement of yard and public territories, was adopted in the same year.

Similar programs were adopted and are being implemented in all municipalities of the Republic of Karelia. In total, 52 settlements in Karelia are participants in the priority project. Annually up to 100 thousand residents of the republic take part polls on projects on transforming public spaces in municipalities.[10] Public commissions are created to ensure the implementation of the priority project in municipal entities. In 2018 the regional forum "Formation of a comfortable urban environment: current issues of project implementation in 2018," was held for the first time in the Republic of Karelia. Starting from the same year, municipal projects are presented at the annual All-Russian contest of the best projects for creating a comfortable urban environment in small towns and historical settlements. Thus, over the past few years, a whole system of norms, organizational and financial instruments have been formed in the country at all levels of public administration to ensure the renovation of urban spaces. It should be emphasized, that in this case, public participation is considered as a tool for updating the "rigid" infrastructure of urban spaces.

Thus, in recent years a comprehensive system of norms, as well as organizational and financial tools, aimed at the renovation of urban spaces, has been elaborated in the country at all levels of public administration authority organization. It should be noted, that in this case public participation is considered as a tool for updating "hard infrastructure" of urban spaces.

Along with the term "hard infrastructure" used to describe the city as a living environment, the social purpose of a modern city is described by the term "soft infrastructure", the essence of which is transmitted into the Russian field of urban studies by a number of authors conducting interdisciplinary studies of the phenomenon.[11]

---

8 *The Government of the Republic of Karelia* 2017: The state program of the Republic of Karelia "Formation of the modern urban environment for 2018–2020", approved by the Decree of the Government of the Republic of Karelia of August 31, 2017. No. 301-P. http://docs.cntd.ru/document/465414512 (30/03/2020) (in Russian).

9 *The Administration of the Petrozavodsk urban district* 2017: The municipal program of the Petrozavodsk urban district "Formation of the modern urban environment", approved by the resolution of the Administration of the Petrozavodsk urban district of November 30, 2017. No. 3964. http://docs.cntd.ru/document/465416434 (30/03/2020) (in Russian).

10 *The Ministry of Construction, Housing and Public Utilities and Energy of the Republic of Karelia* 2019: Press Center. Ministry news. http://минстройрк.рф/press-centr/novosti_ministerstva/podvedeny_itogi_rejtingovogo_golosovaniya_v_rajonah_karelii/ (30/03/2020) (in Russian).

11 *Fedulov, S.* 2000: Social infrastructure of a modern Russian city. In: Sociological studies, 1, pp. 122–125 (in Russian); *Nefedyev, A.* 2011: Innovative infrastructure. In: Creative Economy, 5. https://en.creativeconomy.ru/lib/457 (23/07/2019) (in Russian); *Ivanova* 2014 (fn. 2); *Rusakova, O./Rusakov, V.* 2012: Discourses and concepts of soft impacts in contemporary humanities. In: Vestnik Novosibirsk state university. Series: Philosophy, vol. 10, is. 3, pp. 161–167 (in Russian).

In urban studies, "soft infrastructure" is defined as the combination of all institutions necessary to maintain the living standards of an urban community. Among its key components, there are not only organizational structure, which includes municipal authorities, municipal organizations and institutions, primarily education, culture, healthcare, the business community and civil society institutions, but also the rules that govern the operation of these systems, as well as financial and informational systems that ensure the functioning of urban life in general.

At the same time, the concept of "soft infrastructure" is practically combined with the concept of social infrastructure, developed as part of the constructivist approach, according to which the social space of a city is considered primarily as the space of interactions of norms, actors, and practices. It is the practices of social interaction that construct and transforms the social space of cities.

This peculiarity of the urban system in its economic, political, administrative, and communitarian aspects was first introduced by Max Weber[12] and Georg Zimmel[13]. This approach was taken up by Robert Park[14] and other researchers of urban lifestyles. In this perspective, urban lifestyles can be considered as a set of various socio-cultural life worlds of numerous urban communities that differ by the specifics of standards, norms, cultural and value attitudes, and at the same time interact with each others within urban space.

The role of social dialogue (i.e. exchange and discourse among citizens and authorities) in the life of modern cities is noted by both Western and Russian researchers.[15] In this case, public participation is no longer considered a tool of implementation in the goal of updating the "space of places", but as a means of generating discourse about the urban way of life.

In modern conditions, the policy of a new urbanism involves, along with recognition of the importance of updating the urban facilities, identifying as a priority the optimization of its exploration and use in the interests of the entire urban community. Moreover, the solution to the problem is considered via the use of soft "flexible creative social, cultural, and communicative technologies,"[16]. In relation to "soft infrastructure", the key goal is the development of the social space of a city as creative and innovative.

The formation of a creative social space is the essential trend of urban policy. Despite the fact that this trend is relatively new for Russia, many Russian cities (including medium and small ones) are involved in the elaboration of fundamentally new urban development strategies, using and modifying the existing potential of the dialogue practices of urban institutions and communities.

12 *Weber, M.* 2017: The City, Moscow (in Russian).

13 *Zimmel, G.* 2002: Large cities and spiritual life. In: Logos, 3 (34). http://magazines.russ.ru/logos/2002/3/zim.html (23/07/2019) (in Russian).

14 *Park, R. E.* 2002: The City as a Social Laboratory. In: The Russian Sociological Review, vol. 2, no. 3, pp. 3–12 (in Russian).

15 *Goheen, P. G.* 1998: Public space and the geography of the modern city. In: Progress in Human Geography, 22, 4, pp. 479–496; *Akalelova, T.* 2014: The social space of the modern city. In: Theory and Practice of Social Development, 9, pp. 23–25 (in Russian).

16 *Rusakova/Rusakov* 2012 (fn. 11).

Certainly, in this case each city appears to be in a special situation. However, in modern conditions the possibility of development is directly connected with building attractiveness and comfortable living conditions, the possibility of self-realization for all groups of the urban population, not so much by adapting cities to existing conditions, but by updating municipal practices in the context of the principles of a creative city.

These principles were first formulated by Charles Landry and Franco Bianchini[17] and subsequently became the basis for the modern policy of cities aimed at updating and building up their competitive advantages. In this case, the primary basis for creative decisions is the principle of public participation: "It is necessary in some way to involve into solving problems those whom they directly concern. Solving problems by external means leads to the formation of unstable solutions [...]. Only work from within the community, including training and mutual assistance mechanisms, can bring sustainable results,"[18]. In Landry's perception, a creative city is a collection of urban communities whose members are able to critically evaluate and build up their creative capital, which is the basis for applying innovative approaches to transforming urban social space.

Thus, in the discourse of "soft infrastructure", a city is considered a socially constructed space that is in the process of constant development, and a knot of social and cultural interactions of different level actors. At the same time, in modern research, creativity is verified, with certain variations, as an environment which is favorable for the use of available resources and innovative approaches in order to create social innovations necessary for urban development. In the field of Russian studies of modern urban policy, the principle of public participation as a key feature of the discourse of a creative city is especially emphasized by O.F. Rusakova.[19] Rusakova shows the importance of civic activism and the presence of networked communicative urban structures in pursuing the development goals of urban communities.

Two paths can be distinguished in the construction of these communicative structures in modern Russian cities. The first path is the development of festival and forum platforms, emerging spaces of teamwork, and an evolving system of interest clubs. The second path is that of non-governmental organizations which articulate public needs and solve problems of local communities based on the principles of social design. The institutionalized formalization of this communication structure building, its scale and social effectiveness, determines the potential of SO NGOs as drivers in the pursuit of innovative solutions to urban community social problems. At the same time, the development of urban communication structures, especially in the area of non-governmental organizations, is subject of to legally defined norms.

Beginning with the ratification of the federal law "On amendments to curtail legislative acts of the Russian Federation on socially oriented non-profit organizations support"[20] in

17 *Landry, C./Bianchini, F.* 1995: The creative city, London.

18 *Landry, C.* 2011: The creative city, Moscow (in Russian).

19 *Rusakova, O.* 2013: The Concept and the Strategy of the Creative City. In: Discourse-P, no. 13, pp. 78–81 (in Russian).

20 *Russian Federation* 2010: On amendments to certain legislative acts of the Russian Federation on socially oriented non-profit organizations support. Federal law dated 5 April 2010 no. 40-FZ, Consultant Plus Database. http://www.consultant.ru/cons/cgi/online.cgi?req=doc&base=LAW&n=163542&fld=134&dst=100 0000001,0&rnd=0.3041035777206901 (30/03/2020) (in Russian).

2011 Russian federal law changed and thus created the modern system of legal norms which governs interactions between state and non-profit organizations.

This normative act legally fixed the status of socially oriented organizations as organizations that carry out socially significant types of activities. It also defined the types and directions of their activities and provided with various forms of state stimulation.

As a result of these legal changes, the number of SO NGOs that can apply for state support has increased. Currently there are 18 legislatively approved directions for activities of socially oriented organizations (hereinafter – SO NGOs) provided with state support. These can range from environmental protection and animal welfare, to perpetuating the memory of victims of political repressions.

The representation of these areas in organizational documents makes groups eligible to receive state subsidies on a competitive basis, and receive other forms of organizational, informational, and methodological state support.

The process of creating a normative framework for SO NGOs to receive state support is done through federal legislation. At the same time, regional legislatures also take into account the existing participation of republican SO NGOs in the implementation of social policy. In the regional law "On support of socially oriented non-profit organizations in the Republic of Karelia"[21], adopted in 2011, the federal list of activities SO NGOs could receive state support for was supplemented with additional activities which the legislature determined had fundamental value for the republic.

In particular, the regional law envisaged assistance in the implementation of measures for the revival, preservation, and free development of the national culture of Karelians, Vepsians and Finns living in the territory of Karelia; as well as the perpetuation of the memory of the citizens of the Russian Federation, whose life, labor, and creative and social activities were connected with the republic.

Since 2014, support for socially oriented non-profit organizations in the republic has been implemented based on the state program "Development of civil society institutions and the development of local self-government, protection of human and civil rights, and freedoms for 2014-2020"[22]. The Ministry of national and regional policy of the republic acts as the responsible executor of the Program. Regional ministries and departments of the social groups are associate contractors. In addition to the normative activity, essential work has been carried out over the years in the republic aimed at forming a system of organizational, informational, and methodological support for the projects implemented by SO NGOs.

21 *Republic of Karelia* 2011: On support of socially oriented non-profit organizations in the Republic of Karelia. Law of the Republic of Karelia of December 5, 2011 No. 1562-RKZ. http://www.karelia-zs.ru/zakonodatelstvo_rk/prav_akty/1562-zrk/ (30/03/2020) (in Russian).

22 *The Government of the Republic of Karelia* 2013: On approval of the state program of the Republic of Karelia "Development of civil society institutions and the development of local self-government, protection of human and civil rights and freedoms" for 2014–2020 (with amendments and additions), approved by the resolution of the Government of the Republic of Karelia of December 19, 2013 no. 365-R. http://base.garant.ru/23177899/#ixzz4HrPH1aWH. (30/03/2020) (in Russian).

Thus, in the period from 2010 to 2014, the status of socially oriented organizations was formalized, and the types and directions of permitted activities were identified and ensured of various forms of state support, including a significant increase in funds allocated by the state to support non-profit sectors.

However, the mechanisms and tools for the distribution of resources became the focus of criticism, from SO NGOs themselves[23] as well as researchers.[24] In their analysis, organizations and researchers found that the distribution of public funds was insufficiently transparent which increased the risk of biased distribution, conflicts of interests, misuse, and suboptimal use of funds.[25]

Since 2015, the Civil Chamber of the Russian Federation has become the main dialogue platform that determines the nature of discussions about the state of the non-profit sector and the peculiarities of its interaction with government institutions. It was the Civil Chamber that initiated the organization of the forum "Community", which takes place annually in all federal districts of the Russian Federation. Within the framework of the forums in 2015, key proposals on how to optimize the activities of state institutions in their interaction with the "third sector", including the sphere of increasing openness and transparency in the system of state subsidies and grant support for SO NGOs, were developed. As a result, the authorities have significantly modified the procedures of the so-called competitions which allocate state funds.

Since 2017 the Presidential Grants Foundation has become the most important institution providing support to NGOs and the most ambitious in funding allocations. Competitions for these grants are organized on the basis of orders of the President of the Russian Federation, adopted annually, and the regulations of the competitions are adopted on the eve of each new round of competitions.

The effect of the updated system for state support for NGOs is the development of the social design system in "third sector" institutions through competitions. Based on the majority of recent studies, the activities of the "third sector" are actually turning into the most important instrument of social policy today. An examination of the typical projects implemented by the SO NGOs of the Petrozavodsk urban district exemplifies these findings.

The first peak of activity designed by SO NGOs in the region occurred in the mid-90s. According to the opinion of the one of the first researchers of SO NGOs in the Republic of Karelia A. Demidov[26], this process was largely connected with the activation of Western funds, which strengthened organizational, methodological and fiscal support for social pro-

---

23 *Transparency International-R* 2013: Research of information openness of the state support distribution system for NGOs: 2012–2013//Autonomous non-profit organization "Center for anti-corruption research and initiatives", "Transparency International-R". https://transparency.org.ru/images/docs/research/2015_Transparency_NGO_Public_Support_2012-2013.pdf (30/03/2020) (in Russian).

24 *Smirnov, V.* 2016: Project activity of Russian non-profit organizations: key problems and contradictions. In: Sociological Studies. no. 2, pp. 62–69 (in Russian).

25 *Nikovskaya, L./Yakimets, V.* 2016: Institutional Development of Cross-sectoral Partnership in Russia. In: Polis. Political Studies. no. 5, pp. 37–48.

26 *Demidov, A.* 2008: Non-profit organizations in public policy and administration: participation in the development and implementation of social policy (The case of the Republic of Karelia), Dissertation in Political Sciences, St. Petersburg, p. 193 (in Russian).

jects by SO NGOs in the border region during this period. Moreover, in the case of the Republic of Karelia, the support of Western funds was provided specifically for social projects. The political effects were not obvious.

A. Demidov uses this to explain the features of the development of the "third sector" of this period. The main features were: focus on participation in social policy, willingness to engage in a dialogue with the authorities on the implementation of specific social projects, self-identification of SO NGOs as providers of social services, focus on solving significant social problems.

These activities received full support from the regional and municipal authorities and led to the construction of trusting relations between SO NGOs and government institutions.

Demidov also argues that the process for the dispersion of Western funds created a competition between groups for resources. This limited the possibilities of consolidating NGOs and formulating a coherent regional public agenda. NGOs focused on projects for which institutions provided funding rather than building projects around specific problems facing the public.

Through the use of social design policies, SO NGOs were able to develop and inherit positive relations with institutions of authority and overcome the fragmentation which had typified the early period of Western funding.

In many respects, this was due to the state's renewed interest in maximizing the involvement of SO NGOs in addressing social problems.

The positive effect of the state's renewed interest in the "third sector" is reflected in the number of newly registered NGOs in the region as seen in figure 1.

Figure 1: Number of NGOs newly registered in Petrozavodsk

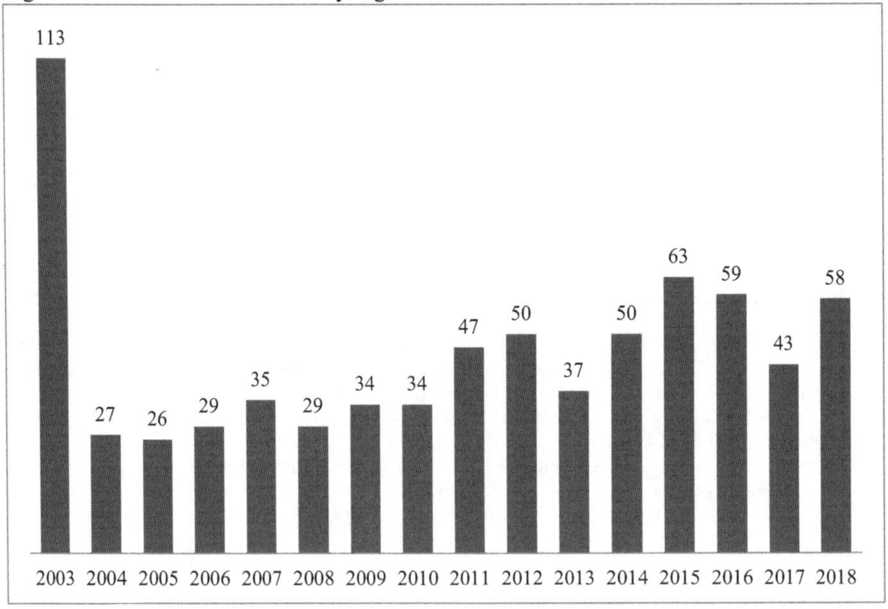

Source: own calculation based on Data of *The Presidential Funds Foundation.*

Starting from an overall number of 116 NGOs registered in the unified register if the Ministry of Justice of the Russian Federation in 2002, the overall number of NGOs raised in the following years, but there are clear differences in terms of new registrations by year. The highest numbers of newly registered NGOs per year coincide with the renewal of support for NGO activity by the state through programs such as the Presidential Grants Foundation, especially in 2010–11 and 2014–15. By May 2019, the register of the Ministry of Justice of the Russian Federation included 891 NGOs registered in the Petrozavodsk urban district from 1362 registered in the Republic of Karelia as a whole (65.4 percent). Currently 45.3 percent of the population of the republic lives in Petrozavodsk.

Another way to view the development of NGOs is to estimate it through the data of NGOs per capita. In the whole Northwestern Federal District (where the Republic of Karelia is a part of), there are on the average 1.7 NGOs per 1,000 people, and in the Republic of Karelia 2.2 NGOs per 1,000 people. At the same time, Petrozavodsk urban district has 3 NGOs per 1,000 people, while all other municipalities have an average of only 1.3 NGOs per 1,000 people. Given the relatively dense distribution of NGOs in Petrozavodsk urban district, it is important to consider their potential influence and capabilities in solving urgent issues of urban life and constructing a creative social space in Petrozavodsk.

In order to assess the intensity, direction and potentials of SO NGO activities in the Republic of Karelia and the city of Petrozavodsk and the character of cooperation between government and civil society that initially was seen as positive[27], several studies were carried out. The Ministry of national and Regional Policy as well as the Civil Chamber of the Republic of Karelia both are monitoring the participation of SO NGOs in terms of effectiveness of providing public welfare. As a result, since 2015, a Petrozavodsk State University research group (PetrSU RG) led by Elena Chernenkova carried out continuous monitoring of SO NGO performance and success in grant contests. They used the following indicators:

- the number of submitted applications / grants won;
- the ratio of submitted applications / grants won from Petrozavodsk and municipal regions;
- the ratio of submitted applications / grants won in grant directions (i.e. specific areas of funding);
- the number of applications conforming / non-conforming to formal requirements
- targeted groups of projects supported by grants;
- informational support for the activities of grant applicants and grant recipients in the Internet;
- availability of public reports provided by grant recipients.

The success of NGOs in the Republic competing in grant contests were analyzed by [group who did it] to measure [what?].The data analyzed and presented in the following sections stems from the monitoring conducted by the PetrGU RG and was compiled by the author. Comparing the results of participation of NGOs in the competitive selection of 2017 and 2018 with previous years, we can see a significant jump in the number of grants won by republican

27 *Gorny, M. B.* 2011: Interaction of the nongovernmental organizations and authorities: the comparative analysis of the legislation. In: The Journal of Social Policy Studies. vol. 9, no. 2, pp. 219–232 (in Russian).

NGOs. In the period from 2013 to 2016, twelve competitions were held. In 2017 and 2018, four competitions were held. The success of republican NGOs is shown in figure 2.

Figure 2: Number of grants received by republican organizations

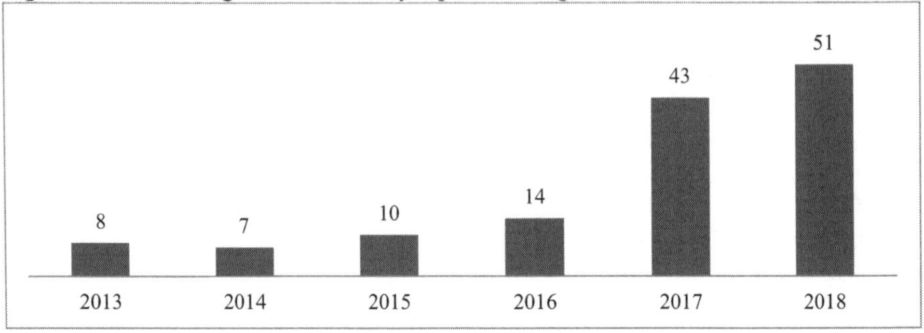

Source: own calculation based on Data of the Presidential Funds Foundation.

In 12 competitions held during the period 2013–2016, 39 projects were supported, in four competitions 2017–2018 – 94 projects. The results of the previous period were increased in three times. The average values of the allocated grants within the framework of one competitive selection also differ significantly. If in the period 2013–2016 in the framework of one competition, on average about 3 projects were supported, then in the period 2017–2018 the average number exceeded the indicator of 23 projects. In other words, a seven-fold excess of average values in competitions of the last period can be witnessed.

The same trend can be observed in the analysis of funds allocated for the implementation of projects.

Table 1: Petrozavodsk NGOs results in terms of the number of grants and the amount of financial support

Year	Number of grants	Grant amount in RR
2013	8	8876516
2014	7	6130369
2015	10	7513678
2016	14	19900948
2017	43	56996153
2018	51	85 055 004

Source: own calculation based on Data of the Presidential Funds Foundation.

If we compare the amounts of grant funds allocated for the implementation of the supported projects of SO NGOs of the republic, the results are as follows: from 2013 to 2016 the amount of allocated funds accounted for about 42.5 million rubles, in 2017–2018 – more than 142 million rubles.

The scale of activity of organizations of the Petrozavodsk urban district is revealed in comparison with the results achieved by organizations of municipal regions of the republic.

A comparison of the data on the number of organizations participating in the competitions and the results of this participation is presented in the following diagram (see figure 3).

Figure 3: The overall results of the Karelian NGOs participation in presidential contest grants 2013–2018

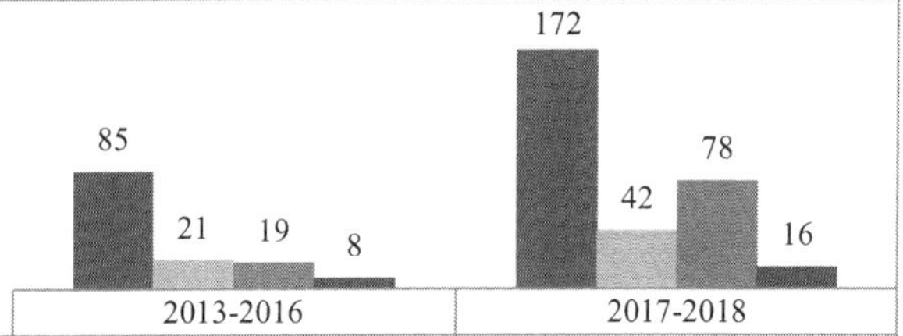

	2013-2016	2017-2018
Number of Petrozavodsk NGOs involved in filing	85	172
Number of NGOs municipal districts involved in filing	21	42
Number of Petrozavodsk NGOs that received grants	19	78
Number of NGOs of municipalities that received grants	8	16

Source: own calculation.

The data presented in the diagram show that with a twofold increase in the number of Petrozavodsk organizations participating in competitive selections, the number of grants received in 2017–2018 increased by 4 times.

In addition to increase in the number of grants received, the amount allocated for the implementation of projects increased in 2017–2018 significantly.

So, in 2017 the total amount of funds allocated by the grant operator for the implementation of 34 projects to organizations of Petrozavodsk amounted to 43,217,554 rubles (≈ 726,102 Euro at the December 2017 exchange rate). In 2018, this amount increased to 73,650,525 rubles (≈ 976,668 Euro at the exchange rate of December 2018) allocated for the implementation of 40 projects.

Thus, during this period the increase in received funds amounted to about 70 percent with an increase in the number of supported projects by 17 percent. It means that organizations submit to the competition increasingly ambitious and large-scale projects that find support from the grantor.

At the same time, nowadays the organizations of the Petrozavodsk urban district manage to achieve equally stable results hardly in all areas of grant support. As follows from the data presented in the diagram "Ranking of projects by fields of activity in accordance with the number of grants" (see figure 4), a significant part of the allocated grants was distributed in the following areas: social services, social support and protection of citizens, preservation of historical memory, youth projects, protecting the health of citizens, promoting healthy lifestyles, projects in the field of culture and art, projects in the field of science, education.

The results are much smaller in the following direction: development of public diplomacy, strengthening inter-ethnic and inter-religious harmony, support for family, motherhood, fatherhood and childhood, protection of animals and environment, protection of human (citizens) rights and freedoms.

Figure 4: Ranking of projects by fields of activity in accordance with the number of grants

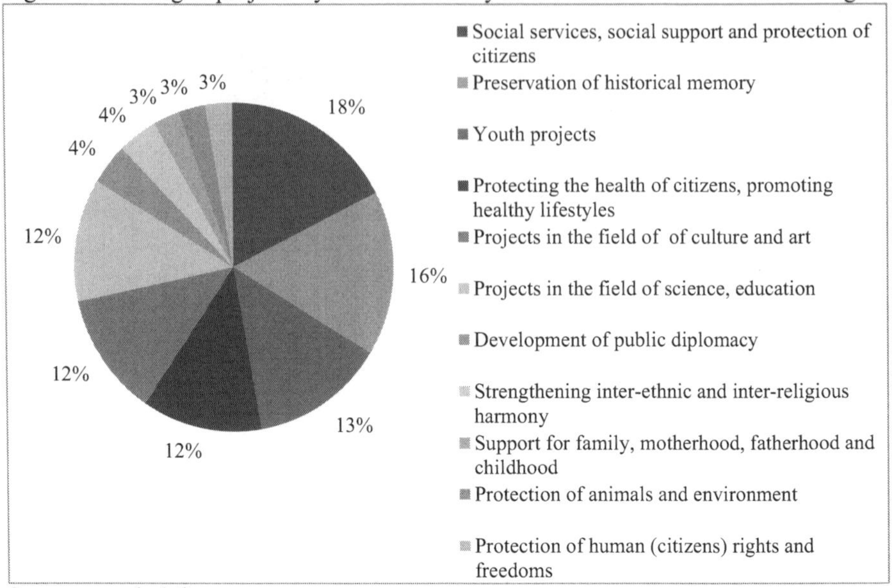

Source: own calculation.

Such a distortion is also characteristic in the case when the ranking of projects by areas of activity is determined in accordance with the allocated funds (see figure 5).

Figure 5: Ranking of projects by fields of activity in accordance with the amount of allocated funds

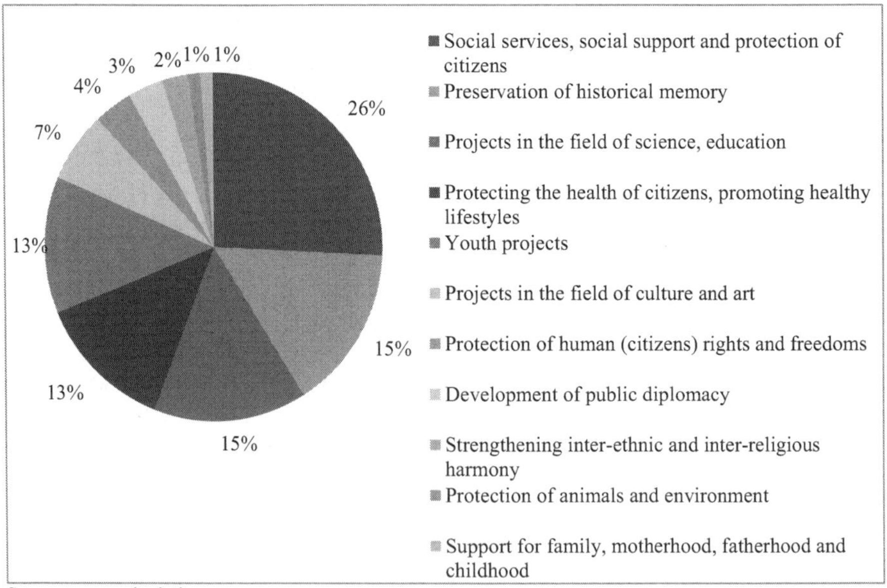

Source: own calculation.

As shown by the presented data, more than a quarter of the allocated funds were provided for the implementation of projects in the field of social services, social support and protection of citizens.

It should be noted that these indicators quite clearly indicate the interest in participation and the potential of SO NGO of Petrozavodsk in the implementation of the main directions of social policy articulated at the state level.

The available potential is also evidenced by the volume of own funds invested by organizations in project implementation. The principle of co-financing is not a prerequisite for obtaining grants; however, the willingness of organizations to invest their own funds demonstrates their capabilities and appears to be an indirect confirmation of their ability to effectively manage the allocated grants.

The volumes of co-financing itself show that a pool of self-sufficient organizations has developed in the republic and these organizations can accumulate funds received from various sources for the implementation of the proposed projects. The information on the volumes of co-financing of projects of SO NGO of Petrozavodsk in relation to the directions of grant support in 2017–2018 is presented in the following table (see table 2).

Table 2: Volumes of NPGOs' own funds spent on project implementation

Direction of grant support	Own funds (rubles)	Allocated funds (rubles)
Social services, social support and protection of citizens	7,306,660	30,103,969
Preservation of historical memory	7,095,826	17,970,910
Youth projects	6,660,727	14,825,984
Protecting the health of citizens, promoting healthy	6,471,052	15,157,216
Projects in the field of science, education	3,743,834	17,211,014
Projects in the field of culture and art	2,431,450	7,651,622
Protection of human (citizens) rights and freedoms	654,280.00	4,312,126
Protection of animals and environment	490,700.00	1,382,377
Development of public diplomacy	376,489.00	4,005,331
Strengthening inter-ethnic and inter-religious harmony	338,788.00	2,881,627
Support for family, motherhood, fatherhood and childhood	211,425.00	1,365,901
The overall result	35,781,232	116,868,079

Source: own calculation.

Thus, it can be noted that in the total amount of funds spent on projects, 77 percent are funds of the Presidential Grants Foundation, 23 percent are own funds of organizations.

Taking into account the own funds of SO NGOs, the total amount of funds spent on the implementation of 74 projects in 2017–2018 amounted to 152,649,312 rubles (≈ 2,150,000 Euro).

It should be borne in mind that funds shall be spent, and projects shall be implemented within 1 year, upon the expiry of which organizations must submit a public report on the completed project and the achieved social effects.

The most ambitious projects implemented by the organizations of Petrozavodsk are presented according to the results of competitive selection of 2018 (see table 3).

Table 3: projects with the highest funding in 2018

Contest	Direction:	Organization	Project	Grant
1 contest 2018	Social services, social support and protection of citizens	Center for social and educational rehabilitation of children with disabilities – “Blagodat” (“Grace”)	Inclusive center of psychological rehabilitation and social adaptation “Your World”	9,929,476 rub. (≈ 140,000 Euro)
	Support for projects in the field of science and education	„Budget Monitoring Center“	“Start your labor biography from the Arctic and the Far East!”	4,402,075 rub. (≈ 62,000 Euro)
2 contest 2018	Social services, social support and protection of citizens	NGO for the protection of animals “First shelter”	„The Road of Good [...]“	6,785,673 rub. (≈ 95,500 Euro)

Source: own calculation.

In general, starting from 2017 the number of projects that are provided with quite impressive funds has been steadily increasing. If in the fund competitions of 2013–2016, grants of more than 1 million rubles were allocated for the implementation of 9 projects, then over the past 2 years 20 projects received grant support of more than 1 million rubles and 18 projects – over 2 million rubles in size.

At the same time showing the interest in supporting projects from the regions, the Presidential Grants Foundation presents clearly defined requirements for the quality of submitted applications. The list of criteria for evaluating applications (there are 10 in total) by the experts of the fund includes such positions as the relevance and social significance of the project, innovativeness, uniqueness of the project, the scale of the project, and informational openness of the organization[28].

Regarding the projects submitted by organizations of the Petrozavodsk urban district, it should be noted that 78 out of 172 projects submitted for competitions during this period (45.3 percent) met the requirements, including the indicator of innovativeness and uniqueness of the project.

28 *Presidential Grants Fund* 2017: Regulations on the competition for the provision of grants of the President of the Russian Federation on the development of civil society. https://президентскиегранты.рф/public/home/contest-documentation (30/03/2020) (in Russian).

Among organizations successfully participating in competitive selections there are:

3 organizations received grants 3 times:

- NGO for the protection of animals "First shelter"
- "Center for the Development of Volunteering"
- Charitable Foundation named after Arina Tubis.

14 organizations became grantees twice, 38 organizations implemented one project each.

At the same time along with organizations that are experienced and have been represented in the public space of the republic for long time, recently formed, but effective and creatively developing NGOs are participating in the competitions quite successfully.

- 3 organizations operate for 1–2 years
- 9 organizations have been operating for less than 5 years
- 20 organizations – from 5 to 10 years
- 6 organizations – 10–15 years
- 17 organizations – more than 15 years

The content analysis of applications released to the public on the Foundation's website makes it possible to summarize information on the territorial aspect of projects implemented by Petrozavodsk organizations, which to a large extent go beyond the boundaries of the urban district and cover events with local communities not only in the Republic of Karelia, but also beyond (see figure 6).

Figure 6: Geography of implemented projects

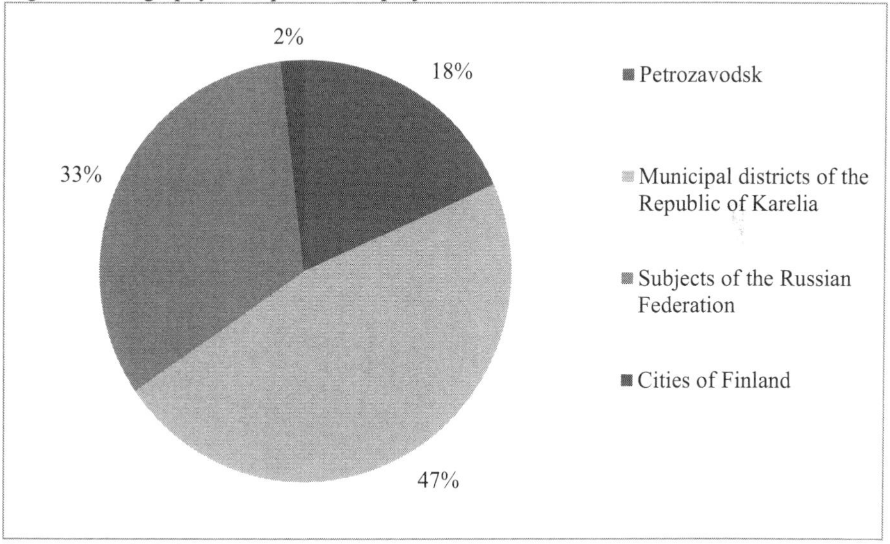

Source: own calculation.

An analysis of the presented data shows that almost half of the project activities (47 percent) were aimed at communities of the municipal regions of the republic, a third of the events were held in the territorial subject of the Russian Federation, in addition, project activities aimed at developing of public diplomacy and supporting compatriots were held in three cities of Finland. The expansion of the territory of ongoing projects is also evidence of the growing influence of SO NGO of Petrozavodsk, their ability to coordinate the interaction of interested groups of various local communities at the municipal as well as regional and international levels.

Changes are taking place in the definition of the address groups that the projects are aimed at, organizations – grant applicants are increasingly declaring professional and local communities, as well as civic activists (see figure 7). Previously there were no such communities in the list of target groups, for example, in 2016 children and adolescents, youth and students and pensioners and veterans were in the first positions in the list of address groups, and the projects themselves were primarily aimed not so much at development, but at solving the existing problems of these social groups. The ability of SO NGO of Petrozavodsk to involve new groups in the activities of ongoing projects is one of the evidences of growing professionalism in the field of social design, updating the nature of ongoing projects, building up the innovative component and, as a result, the growing of social significance of this activity. SO NGOs of Petrozavodsk are more and more confidently playing the role of drivers of social innovation, and offering to professional and territorial communities new approaches to solving developmental issues relevant to loci.

Figure 7: Reference groups of ongoing projects (percent)

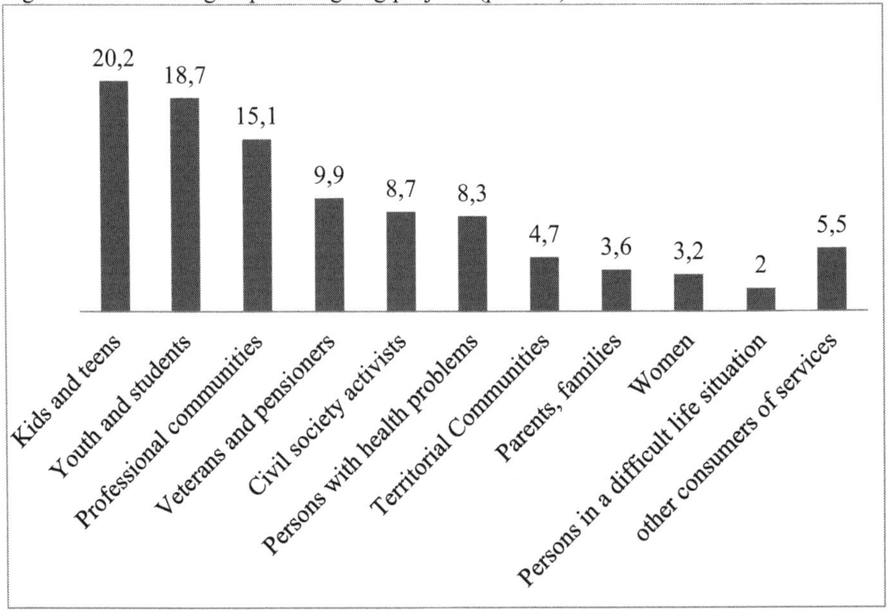

Source: own calculation.

Updating the nature of project activities is accompanied by changes in the information policy of socially oriented organizations.

According to studies of the state of civil society, organized with the support of the Ministry of national and regional policy in accordance with the provisions of the state program of the Republic of Karelia "Development of Civil Society Institutions and Local Self-governance, Protection of Human and Civil Rights and Freedoms for 2014–2020", in recent years there have been significant changes in the sources of information and the degree of public awareness of the activities of SO NGOs. So, in 2015[29] only 7 percent of the population of the republic had detailed information about the activities of NGOs, and its main source was either NGOs' employees themselves or those who received their services, it means that information was transmitted orally primarily. According to the study of 2018, more than half of the respondents confirmed full (17.8 percent) or partial (47.9 percent) information awareness. At the same time, the respondents noted that the main source of information is Internet resources, webpages of official regional and municipal authorities, social networks and webpages of SO NGOs themselves.

Concerning the development of the principle of publicity, transparency and the information support of ongoing projects, the most significant changes have occurred in the use of the capabilities of social networks (see figure 8).

Figure 8: Information openness of organizations-grantees (comparison with 2016 data)

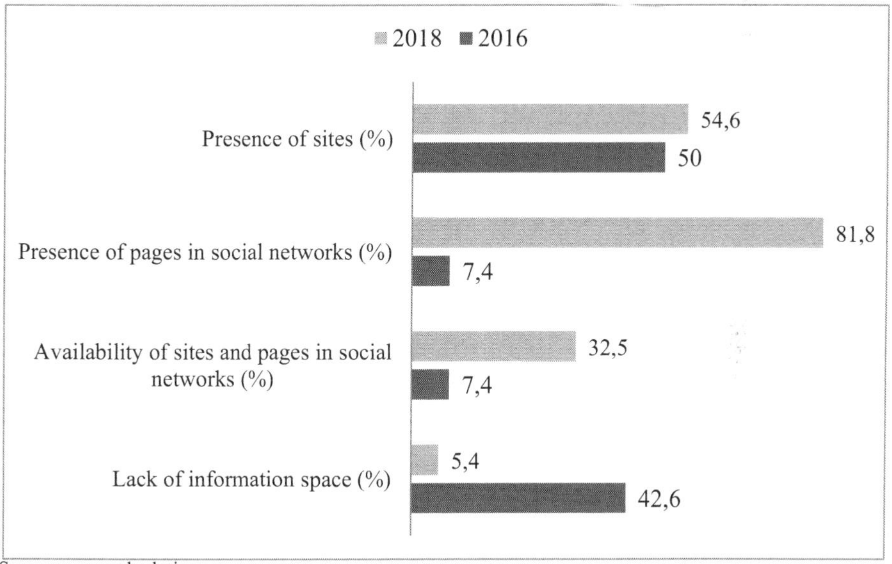

Source: own calculation.

In this case this indicator is considered in relation to those projects that were supported by presidential grants.

29 *Non-profit organizations of the Republic of Karelia "Civil Society of a Multinational Region"* 2017: The results of sociological research of socially oriented non-profit organizations of the Republic of Karelia. http://nko-karelia.ru/projects/523 (30/03/2020) (in Russian).

Active work in social networks increases the recognition of organizations. The main tasks that NGOs solve in social networks are informing, mobilizing supporters and attracting volunteers. For grant recipient organizations social networks have become an effective platform for promoting ongoing projects.

Organizations use various social networks, but the most common in Karelia is the social network Vkontakte. The following table (see table 4) presents information about organizations whose activity on social networks has caused the greatest reaction from the audience.

Table 4. Organizations with the largest number of subscribers in social networks

Organization	year of registration	number of projects	informational resources	number of subscribers in social networks
Karelian Republican Public Organization for the Protection of Animals "First Shelter"	1993	3	website and social networks page	24,894
Charitable Foundation named after Arina Tubis	2014	3		17,567
Karelian regional charitable foundation "Maternal Heart"	2009	1		6,555
Karelian regional public youth organization "Center for the Development of Volunteering"	2009	3		4,370
Non-governmental public institution "Academy of Photography Petrozavodsk"	2011	1		3,502
Karelian Republican Public Organization Marine Club "Polar Odyssey"	2013	1		3,055

Source: own calculation.

Regardless of key areas of activity of SO NGOs, if they manage to offer not so much a grantor as a society relevant, high-demand projects that meet public needs, accumulating the creative potential of local communities, this activity receives unconditional understanding and support from the population. This applies also to the projects directly aimed at constructing creative spaces, developing creative industries, and projects related to the tasks of preserving the traditional way of life and filling it with new meanings, and projects to ensure the quality of life of all categories of citizens, including people with disabilities.

The ability of organizations to promote new ideas and the plasticity of society in their perception determine the growing role of SO NGOs in the system of modern social interaction.

As a concrete example of how rather traditional activity of social services, social support and protection of citizens can become significant in the construction of a creative space for social interaction and the development of social innovation, it is possible to mention the projects of the Karelian regional public organization for the protection of animals "First Shelter". For the period 2017–2018 this organization has become the recipient of presidential grants three times, grants were allocated for the implementation of the projects related in one way or another to the development of the canister therapy system and the organization of rehabilitation, education and enlightenment events on the basis of a public animal shelter. In the second competition round of 2017, the project named "Give a paw, friend" received support in the amount of 2,080,463 rubles, in the first competition round of 2018 the sum of 2,605,585 rubles was allocated for the implementation of the "Open Hearts" project, in the second competition of 2018, the fund transferred the sum of 3,977,780 to organizations for the implementation of the project "By the road of good". The last two projects are the consequential realization and development of the ideas proposed by the first project, and today these ideas are in progress. However, according to the results of the first project, we can mention unique experience not only for the republic, but also for the country.

In the course of this project, the organization "First Shelter", a fairly well-known, respected, stable functioning for many years primarily due to charitable assistance from citizens, has managed to convincingly demonstrate that the specific structure created to help homeless animals can be an effective driver of social innovation. Based on the idea that communication with animals has a powerful emotional and therapeutic effect, the organization developed and implemented with the assistance of presidential grants a series of projects aimed at creating a canister therapy system for the rehabilitation of sick children in a children's city hospital, as well as special children studying in correctional boarding school. This activity culminated in the creation of the unique Center for Social Work and Canistherapy "Open Hearts".

In addition to this direction, it is possible to distinguish educational and training events among the implemented tasks, namely "Lessons of Kindness" on the formation of a socially responsible attitude to animals in educational institutions of the republic. Another area of activity was to increase the competence of animal advocates, volunteers who were involved in preparing dogs from the shelter for working with children.

In the framework of the first project, more than 3.5 thousand people already participated in the organization's activities, among them were recipients of services, sick and special children, their parents, pupils of educational institutions, as well as employees of medical institutions, educators, teachers, specialists and volunteers, working with animals. The obvious effects of using the methods developed by the organization have caused the need to replicate the accumulated experience among other official and public institutions involved in rehabilitation and educational activities. Specialists of the Children's Hospital and the Ministry of Health have begun to create a regional standard for the use of dogs in rehabilitation activities. The organization has managed to unite a wide range of volunteers; another result was the expansion of the circle of philanthropists and sponsors. The result of informational support of project activities was also significant. Twenty-one materials were posted; including six television reports, in the press, on the pages of republican newspapers, in television programs, in social networks, one of the reports was shown on a federal channel. As emphasized in the organization's report on the results of the project, "the success of the project is largely ensured by the novelty of the ideas in the basis. Firstly, the rehabilitation direction of canistherapy was completely new and, until recently, practically unknown in our region [...] Secondly, an approach that uses the potential of animal protection organizations and animal shelters to work in the social sphere has turned out to be completely new and extremely promising: in upbringing, education, leisure activities, and rehabilitation of children with disabilities. The novelty and creative potential in these areas made it possible to interest the general public, to attract volunteers [...] From the narrow sphere of rescue and animal welfare in the shelter we went into a wide area of social practice".[30]

The given example clearly demonstrates the importance of dialogue practices, the results of which depend on the emerging norms of interaction between authority and public institutions, as well as on the qualities of specific actors interacting in the constructed public space of a modern city.

The own logic of the development of urban communities, the presence of social, creative, innovative capital in relation to the unique, historically formed urban environment determines the parameters of modern urban space.

Summarizing main research findings, it can be noted that the focus of the development strategies of modern cities on the formation of a comfortable and creative urban environment through the development of social partnership and intersectoral interaction has become a generally accepted answer to the challenges of our time. The role of dialogue practices in achieving a new quality of life for the urban population is manifested both in the European and Russian official agendas, occupies a significant place in the public and research discourse of various countries. The construction of ergonomic infrastructure and the production of an innovative environment determine the contours of municipal policy generally. A significant place in its implementation is taken by social projects of SO NGOs, turning into authoritative and recognized drivers of social innovation, oriented towards consolidating of the efforts of all actors involved in the implementation of urban development strategies.

30 *Presidential Grants Fund* 2019: Project "Give a paw, a friend: a system for organizing leisure, education, rehabilitation and the formation of a socially responsible attitude to animals in children on the basis of a public animal shelter." The main results. https://оценка.гранты.рф/award/about/9f2bf1d3-fd60-4423-8a76-c038acfaaf10 (30/03/2020) (in Russian).

New Approaches to Cooperation between NGOs and Local Government Bodies for Civil Society Development

Ksenia Chumak

Abstract: This article considers the conditions of the Republic of Karelia for the development of civil society and interaction between Karelian NGOs and governmental authorities at the regional and municipal levels. Using a case study of one Karelian NGO, this article examines the various forms of cooperation between NGOs and authorities. These forms of cooperation are analyzed in an attempt to define what problems may exist, and how these can be best addressed.

Keywords: civil society, social projects, NGO, the Republic of Karelia, model of interaction between authority and NGOs

In the modern world in the context of the active development and the formation of civil society, great attention is paid to non-governmental organizations (NGOs) and their orientation "to solve the most urgent problems in all spheres of life, to prevent possible threats, to ensure an adequate response to any challenges that society faces"[1]. Within this field, one area of great importance is the study of the model of interaction between the state and the third sector (the economic sector consisting of non-governmental organizations and other non-profit organizations).

In the example of Russia, one sees an improvement in the interaction between state and NGOs. At the Community forum in Moscow in November 2017, Russian President Putin V. stated "Russia needs thousands of socially oriented non-profit organizations that will become a reliable partner of the state"[2].

In recent years, non-profit organizations have received substantial support for the implementation of socially significant projects through the Presidential Grants Foundation. Funding is allocated in a competitive process, for which NGOs can apply several times per year. For example, in 2019 the amount of funding for three fund competition rounds totaled 8007.9 million rubles[3].

Additionally, great attention is paid to the activities of NGOs at the international arena at the highest levels of government. At the meeting with representatives of Russian non-profit organizations in Moscow in 2018, the Minister of Foreign Affairs of the Russian Federation Lavrov S. stated that the Ministry was interested in the active participation of Russian NGOs in international multilateral platforms, such as the UN, OSCE, Council of Europe and others. Lavrov S. noted that the Ministry of Foreign Affairs considers public organizations

1 *Tselnicker G.F./Nemov A.A.* 2018: The interaction of civil society and public authorities in the Russian Federation. In: Bulletin of the Volga University, pp. 51–58.

2 Putin: NGOs should become a reliable partner of the state. In: TVC, Moscow, 03.11.2017. https://www.tvc.ru/news/show/id/126865 (31/03/2020).

3 Federal Law of November 29, 2018 No. 459-ФЗ "The Federal Budget for 2019 and for the Planning Period 2020 and 2021". http://www.consultant.ru/document/cons_doc_LAW_312362/ (31/03/2020).

as "partners in promoting our aspirations at the international arena, where we want to see a positive, non-confrontational agenda that allows us to find compromises and overcome the temptation towards dictatorship and ultimatums, which, unfortunately, some of our partners exhibit"[4].

Thus, it is emphasized at the highest level that the authorities are ready for dialogue and cooperation with public organizations and hope that they help in solving important social issues.

In contrast to the minister's positive rhetoric, conditions in the Russian Federation offer a challenging environment for many NGOs associated with foreign funds. For example, the law of "foreign agents" significantly complicated the work of many NGOs. The law was adopted in 2012 and obliges non-governmental organizations to register as a foreign agent, if they receive funding from abroad and are engaged in "political activity". This law started to be applied actively in 2014, when the president signed the law, which gives the Ministry of Justice of Russia the right to include non-profit organizations in the register of "foreign agents." According to experts, these laws "launched the process of deinstitutionalization of the public sphere – some organizations are liquidated, others are engaged in endless reporting instead of substantive work, new activists (because of excessive bureaucratic costs) refuse to create officially registered structures. As a result, the non-profit sector is slowly being pushed into the shadows, the effectiveness of public work is declining"[5]. Additionally, the status of a "foreign agent" is perceived by the public as "an enemy of the people – according to sociological studies"[6].

Thus, the interaction of authorities and NGOs remains a controversial and complex issue. Because of this, the interaction of civil society and the state is "often a zone of acute tension"[7], where there are clashes and conflicts regarding the most pressing issues of society in a particular region. However, this is not universally negative, and some argue that such conflicts "are inevitable and are an important channel of communication".

Because the interactions between authorities and NGOs have far reaching effects on programs addressing social issues, they have been the subject of a great deal of research. There are a number of works devoted to the topic of the interaction of the authorities and NGOs: Chernyshov A.N. "Interaction Between the State and NGOs: Opportunities, Mechanisms, Problems and Ways to Solve Them"[8], Alyabyeva, S. A. "Relations Between NGOs and the

---

4 Speech by Russian Minister of Foreign Affairs Sergey Lavrov at the meeting with representatives of Russian non-profit organizations, Moscow, June 15, 2018. Ministry of Foreign Affairs of the Russian Federation. Official site. http://www.mid.ru/press_service/minister_speeches/-/asset_publisher/7OvQR5KJW VmR/content/id/3260122 (31/03/2020).

5 *Volkov, D./Gontscharov, S.* 2014: Potential of civic participation in solving social problems Consolidated analytical report. https://komitetgi.ru/upload/uploaded_files/potencial_grazhdanskogo_uchastiya.pdf.

6 *Barkovskaja, E.* 2017: The law on "foreign agents" – 5 years. How the life of non-profit organizations and the entire public field of Russia has changed. In: Novaya Gazeta. https://www.novayagazeta.ru/articles/2017/11/20/74607-5-let-odinochestva (31/03/2020).

7 *Public Chamber of the Russian Federation* 2018: Report on the State of Civil Society in the Russian Federation. https://www.oprf.ru/files/ 1_2019dok/Doklad_OPRF_2018.pdf. (31/03/2020).

8 *Chernyshov A.N.* 2018: Interaction between the state and NGOs: opportunities, mechanisms, problems and ways to solve them. In: Management Consulting, No. 10, 2018, pp. 89–98.

State - The Concept of "Civil Society" at the Regional Level"[9], Tselnicker G.F., Nemov A.A. "Interaction of Civil Society and Public Authorities in the Russian Federation"[10], Okatov, A. V., Okatov, V. N. "Regional Civil Society: Social Activity of Public Organizations and Dialogue with Authorities"[11], Suldina, G. A., Glebova, I. S. "Interests of Public Organizations and Municipal Authorities in the Regions of Russia: Contradictions and Forms of Interaction"[12], the monograph "Authority and Society in the Regions of Russia: Interaction Practices"[13], etc. Interaction Practices"[14], etc. While these studies provide valuable insight and analysis of the relationship between civil society and authorities in Russia, the constant development and transformation of these groups and their relationship to one another necessitates continued research.

While valuable and insightful, the aforementioned studies focus on the central regions of Russia while largely ignoring the role of border regions in the development of Russian civil society. This gap basically ignores regional factors and influences on state-civil society cooperation. This paper adds to fill this gap by focusing on an example from the Republic of Karelia, which is due to its border to Finland and intense cross-border cooperation quite unique.

Interaction Forms

According to Tselnicker and Nemov, interactions between governments and NGOs are a necessity because "the fundamental basis of a social state is a constant dialogue between society and bodies of state authorities"[15]. Because of this NGOs that work with authorities occupy a key place among civil society institutions as "a manifestation of civic activism and responsibility"[16]. It should be noted that "the significant part of the work on the interaction of government and NGOs is carried out locally: at the level of regions and municipalities"[17].

In modern studies of interaction between the authorities and NGOs public-state partnerships, initiative or participatory budgeting and participation in various consultative institutions, such as public chambers, public and advisory councils are commonly mentioned. According to the researchers on the development of public-state relations in Russia, "the most

9 *Alyabyeva, S.A.* 2011: Relations between NGOs and the State – the concept of "Civil Society" at the regional level. In: Bulletin of the Tambov University. Series: Humanities, pp. 336–342.

10 *Tselnicker, G.F./Nemov, A.A.* 2018: Interaction of civil society and public authorities in the Russian Federation. In: Bulletin of the Volga University, pp. 51–58.

11 *Okatov, A.V./Okatov, V.N.* 2009: Regional civil society: social activity of public organizations and dialogue with authorities. In: Bulletin of the Tambov University. Series: Humanities, pp. 9–16.

12 *Suldina, G.A./Glebova, I.S.* 2009: Interests of public organizations and municipal authorities in the regions of Russia: contradictions and forms of interaction. In: Scientific notes of Kazan University. Humanities Series, pp. 261–274.

13 *Khaliy, C.A./Aksenova, O.V./Biyanova, E.K./Levchenko, N.V./Oreshkina, T.A./Podjachev,K.V.* 2015: Authority and society in the regions of Russia: interaction practices [monograph], Institute of Sociology RAS. https://www.civisbook.ru/files/File/Vlast_i_obshestvo_2015.pdf.

14 Ibid.

15 *Tselnicker, G.F./Nemov A.A.* 2018: Interaction of civil society and public authorities in the Russian Federation. In: Bulletin of the Volga University, pp. 51–58.

16 Ibid.

17 *Chernyshov, A.N.* 2018: Interaction between the state and NGOs: opportunities, mechanisms, problems and ways to solve them. In: Management Consulting, pp. 89–98.

effective method of [improving] relations between local governments and the population [has been the] creation of public councils and the creation of civil chambers at the regional level of the Russian Federation"[18].Two examples of this are the Presidential Council for the Promotion of the Development of Civil Society Institutions and the Public Chamber of the Russian Federation which have been operating since 2004 and 2006 respectively. The Civil Chambers of the subjects of the Russian Federation and municipalities are created gradually. The main aim of the Chambers is to ensure interaction of citizens and NGOs with state authorities and local governments in order to take into account the needs and interests of residents, protect their rights and freedoms in the formation and implementation of state policy, as well as to implement public control over the activities of authorities.

As there are many forms and ways of cooperation between NGOs and governmental structures, researchers offer different classifications of models of interaction between authority and NGOs. For example, Tselnicker G.F. and Nemov A.A. emphasize three models of interaction - asymmetric (aimed at meeting the needs of state bodies and creating a positive image in any way), bilaterally asymmetric (public reaction is taken into account because it can be beneficial for the authorities) and bilaterally symmetric (taking into account the needs and expectations of the public, its interest, successful interaction). Chernyshov suggests dividing interaction models into those that is based on direct administrative regulation of NGO activity by the authorities and those that is based on equal partnership. In this article, we will consider forms of interaction between the authorities and NGOs where the latter are seen as independent and equal partners.

The Situation in the Republic of Karelia

In June 2019, 1362 non-profit organizations were registered in the Republic of Karelia. Among them there were 6 legal organizations, 61 charitable foundations, 48 youth organizations, 224 religious organizations and 15 national associations. This number is relatively high in comparison to other regions of the country and suggests a high level of civil society development.

According to the article by I.V. Mersiyanova "Differentiation of Russian regions in the context of the prerequisites of creation of a civil society"[19], there are six categories of preparedness for the formation of civil society in the Russian Federation, with each region qualifying for a specific category. The author assigned the Republic of Karelia to the fifth category along with the Irkutsk, Kemerovo, Kirov and Orenburg regions as well as the Komi Republic. According to the study, in these regions the prerequisites for the formation of civil society are defined as "favorable, but the value of only one indicator is strongly expressed – the level of participation. The values of all other indicators are medium, with the exception of the indicator of predisposition to social solidarity and collective action, which is low"[20].

18 *Tselnicker, G.F./Nemov, A.A.* 2018: Interaction of civil society and public authorities in the Russian Federation. In: Bulletin of the Volga University, pp. 51–58.

19 *Mersiyanova, V.I.* 2008: Differentiation of Russian regions in the context of the prerequisites for the formation of civil society. In: Journal "Authority", no. 8 (2008), pp. 9–18.

20 Ibid.

As a border region, Karelia and Karelian NGOs benefit from the opportunity to participate in development financing programs of foreign countries. This opportunity is very important for the development of civil society in the region. The Republic of Karelia actively participates in the ENI CBC KARELIA program, funded by the Russian Federation, the Republic of Finland and the European Union. Since 2017 the active participation of Karelian NGOs in the program of the Nordic Council of Ministers has been resumed, after suspending because of the recognition of the NCM representative office in Russia as a "foreign agent". In addition, there are opportunities for participation in the programs of the European Commission, the Norwegian Barents Secretariat, and other development programs funded by various consulates and embassies.

Because Karelian NGOs deal so heavily in international funds, the application of the law on "foreign agents" is especially relevant in the region. Non-governmental organizations receiving foreign funding must act very carefully in cooperation with authorities so that their actions do not fall under the concept of political activity.

In 2018 the third calling of the Civil Chamber of the Republic of Karelia took place. According to the legal provisions, "The Civil Chamber of the Republic of Karelia provides interaction between citizens of the Russian Federation living in the territory of the Republic of Karelia and non-profit organizations created to represent and protect the rights and legitimate interests of professional and social groups operating in the territory of the Republic of Karelia with territorial authorities of federal executive bodies, bodies of state authority of the Republic of Karelia, bodies of local self-government in order to take into account the needs and interests of citizens, protect the rights and freedoms of citizens, the rights and legitimate interests of non-profit organizations "[21].

Thus, there are special conditions for the development of civil society, which have the impact on the model of interaction with authorities at the regional and municipal levels in the Republic of Karelia.

Forms of interaction between the authorities and NGOs, which are applied in Karelia to various extents, can be divided into economic and non-economic. The following forms belong to economic forms of interaction:

- the provision of grants and subsidies by authorities to NGOs;
- the provision of tax and other benefits;
- the provision of other benefits to NGOs, including full or partial exemption from fees for the use of state and municipal property.
- Non-economic forms of interaction include:
- carrying out joint activities;
- community expert councils;
- participation of NGOs in the legislative process (article 42 of the Constitution of the Republic of Karelia provides NGOs with such a right but, unfortunately, NGO uses this right quite rarely);
- mutual consultations, training, information exchange, etc.

21 Official webpage of The Civil Chamber of the Republic of Karelia: https://opkarelia.ru/ (date of retrieval).

Activities of the Association "Karelian Resource Center of Public Organizations"

The Association "Karelian Resource Center of NGOs" (hereinafter – KRC NGOs) was established in 2001. The Center is a socially oriented non-profit organization aimed at consolidation of the efforts of its members for the development of public structures in the Republic of Karelia. The main goal of the Center is to increase the effectiveness of the activities of associations of citizens and public organizations and to strengthen their role in interacting with government bodies to solve public problems and to promote the values and practice of civil policy in Russia. By creating resource opportunities, KRC NGOs contributes to the development of the non-profit sector, the formation of civil society in Russia, the establishment of a constructive dialogue between the public, the government and business in order to improve the quality of human life, and the socio-economic development of the Republic of Karelia.

KRC NGOs operates in 2 main directions – as a resource center and as a public organization implementing social projects. As a resource center, the center's employees provide legal and accounting consultations, as well as consultations on project management free of charge. Everyone can sign up and receive consultations on how to develop an organization's charter, how to register an organization, how to write a project application, where to find partners and what project grant competitions it can be applied for. In addition, KRC NGOs offers training opportunities in seminars and in the development and editing of methodological manuals

As a public organization implementing social projects, the KRC NGOs implements projects in various fields. Over 18 years of its existence, the Center has implemented more than 50 major projects dealing with a variety of social concerns, including: working with the elderly, accessible environment, adaptation of migrants, combating youth unemployment, the development of creative industries, gastronomy, the development of tourism, military-patriotic education, and so on. Thus, the staff of the KRC NGOs have practical experience on a breadth of issues which aids them in their consultation work.

The center's experience in cooperating with authorities can also be divided into two areas. As a resource center for NGOs of the republic, firstly, the KRC NGOs helps authorities to respond to citizens' requests. Representatives of active groups and NGOs often address to ministries with questions about solving specific problems, and if government officials see that this problem can be solved within the framework of the project activity, they advise the representative to contact KRC NGOs. The KRC NGOs then provides a consultation for the group or representative in question on the specific issue. The result is that applications received by ministries after this process are easier for the ministries to process and have a high chance of success. This lowers the amount of work for the ministries and enables greater development of Karelian civil society. In addition, together with the ministries, the Center conducts training events for existing NGOs, for people who plan to create NGOs, as well as for active youth. Finally, at events organized by authorities, representatives of the Center often act as experts, and consulting participants at educational seminars and conferences.

In the process of implementing a social project, there are many opportunities for interactions between NGOs and the authorities. When writing a project application, ministry specialists from the relevant field can provide consultation in order to ensure that the proposal is relevant to the needs of society. For example, the Ministry of national and regional policy of the Republic of Karelia is consulting on writing applications for the Presidential Grants Foundation competition, as well as for regional grant competitions. During the implementation of projects, officials from the government also give recommendations to ensure that a project's activities are consistent with the related state programs, complement the work of relevant ministries and departments, draw attention to burning issues, and do not duplicate the work and activities of government bodies. In this spirit, a large number of projects implemented by KRC NGOs are dedicated to the exchange of experience and enhancing the competencies of specialists representing authorities in various fields. These events serve as forums for the exchange of ideas between regions, and countries as well as an opportunity to showcase the work done in Karelia.

It is worth mentioning that in 2018–2019 KRC NGOs had three projects dedicated specifically to the issues of interaction between authorities and civil society, KRC NGOs began these projects to highlight the municipal opportunities available to NGOs throughout the republic, and to improve communication between civil organizations and authorities. The fact that multiple funds contributed to these projects speaks to the faith many have in their potential to positively impact the relationship between civil society and authorities. The projects in question are:

1. The project "From Interaction to Mutual Respect – a Model of Cooperation of the Center for Interethnic Cooperation with Local Government Bodies of the Republic of Karelia", funded by the Ministry of National and Regional policy of the Republic of Karelia. The aim of the project is to create a model of effective interaction between the Centers for Interethnic Cooperation in the regions of the Republic of Karelia and municipal authorities with the goal to achieve international peace and harmony. The project activities were primarily aimed at providing a platform for communication and discussion of possible forms of cooperation for target groups. It is worth mentioning, that the Centers for Interethnic Cooperation can be considered as an informal institution of civil society. The experience of creating such a Center is a good example of the interaction between authorities and NGOs. Currently in the Republic of Karelia there are 13 Centers for Interethnic Cooperation operating in 11 municipal districts and 2 urban districts of Karelia. The centers operate at local libraries or ethno-cultural centers but unite active citizens who conduct friendship lessons for children and talk about the culture of different peoples living in Karelia.

2. The project "Civil Dialogue", funded by Nordic Council of Ministers. The aim of the project is to promote the development of local democracy and the exchange of best practices and experiences between the Nordic countries and the Russian regions involved. The project focuses on the collaboration with citizens in local communities, using the full potential of municipalities and making community centers, including libraries as centers of local public life and exchange.

3. The project "Dialogue with Citizens", financed by the Ministry of National and Regional policy of the Republic of Karelia. The aim of the project is to create conditions for improving the quality and level of openness, accessibility and transparency of information on the activities of non-profit organizations and the implementation of public initiatives in the Republic of Karelia.

The single most important characteristic of the aforementioned projects is that each provides a platform for communication on equal terms between representatives of civil society and governmental bodies to discuss current issues and seek solutions.

In addition, KRC NGOs participates in five public councils at various ministries and departments of Karelia, where it has the opportunity to express its opinion on various issues of the development in the republic, share its experience involving development practices, and stay up to date on current issues.

Thus, the Association "KRC NGOs" has extensive experience in interacting with authorities, both in the framework of dialogue platforms and in the process of implementing specific projects.

Besides projects and participation in ministry forums, KRC NGOs makes use of various forms of print and digital media to maximize visibility and promote transparency. KRC NGOs maintains a website and a group on the popular Russian social media network Vkontakte, where they post important information about upcoming and ongoing events, information from authorities on the results of work, upcoming events, training and financing opportunities. KRC NGOS also produces manuals on project management, papers on how to best interact with government bodies and business, as well as the newspaper "Vestnik of Karelian NGOs".

In sum, the equal partner cooperation model, as applied by KRC NGOs, has proven effective and beneficial to both the government and civil society. By engaging one another as equals, citizens' voices have been allowed to play a larger role in shaping the priorities and goals of government projects to reflect their lived in needs and desires. Likewise, government has been able to better communicate their goals, achievements, challenges, and opportunities back to citizens leading to a more harmonious an equitable process of development between the two parties.

Despite these successes, there remain significant hurdles for the development of the equal partner model in Karelia. Many NGOs still lack the necessary technical and administrative skills to navigate the strict budgeting and reporting rules imposed by the Foreign Agent law. Additionally, competition between NGOs prevent efficient funding and action on individual issues as multiple organizations attempt to solve a single problem. Finally, the lack of good relations between many NGO and government representatives creates and environment that resists compromise and limits the willingness of both sides to work with the other in good faith.

We believe that the interaction between the authority and NGOs should be based on the model of equal partner cooperation. NGOs should not require financial support but offer innovative and relevant ways to solve existing problems, while authorities should seriously take initiative citizens and public organizations and their potential for influence. The basic principle of joint work should be the complementarity of activities within the framework of one area of work, which can only be achieved through dialogue and coordination of joint activities. The desire to solve relevant problems of the community using the most effective and innovative forms should be in the basis of the activities of both authorities and NGOs.

Additional References

Russian Federation 2012: Federal Law of the Russian Federation "On Amending Certain Legislative Acts of the Russian Federation Regarding the Regulation of the Activities of Non-Profit Organizations Performing the Functions of a Foreign Agent". http://www.consultant.ru/document/cons_doc_LAW_132900/ (31/03/2020).

Gorny, M.B. 2011: The interaction of non-profit organizations and government: a comparative analysis of the law. In: Journal of Social Policy Studies, 9 (2), pp. 219–232.

Kolesnikova, N.A. 2013: Civil society institutions in the Tula region, their interaction with regional authorities. In: Bulletin of Tula State University. Humanities, pp. 291–301.

Kulkova, V.Y. 2018: Organizational mechanism of interaction between the state and non-profit organizations in the provision of palliative care. https://cyberleninka.ru/article/n/organizatsionnyy-mehanizm-vzaimodeystviya-gosudarstva-i-nekommercheskih-organizatsiy-v-okazanii-palliativnoy-pomoschi (31/03/2020).

Kutergina, G.V./Pazdnikova N.P. 2018: On the development of forms of organizational support for initiative budgeting in the region. In: Bulletin of Perm National Research Polytechnic University, Socio-economic sciences, (1), pp. 171–185.

Zabbarov, A.G. 2009: Models of interaction between authorities and public associations of the "Third Sector". In: Bulletin of the Volga Institute of Management, (4), pp. 78–82.

Local Initiatives: Awakening of Rural Communities

Anatoly Tsygankov

Abstract: This article takes stock of the development of local initiatives in the rural areas if the Republic of Karelia. Local self-government is a core principle implemented in Russian and Karelian law. But as local government bodies face multiple problems and budgetary limitations, they often are not able to solve these problems. Dissatisfaction rises and People start initiatives. In 2014 the Republic of Karelia implemented a local initiatives support program (LISP) based on the Ideas developed by the World Bank This article presents an overview and analysis of local initiatives in the Republic of Karelia with a special focus on rural areas. This includes initiatives of territorial public self-government (TPSG) as well projects on public budgeting, and Comfortable urban environment. Successful initiatives enhance responsibility, independence and mutual trust among citizens and thus contribute to wellbeing in the, often neglected, rural areas.

Keywords: Local government, local initiatives LISP, TPSG

1 Characteristics of Karelia: General Information

To understand the development of the local government in the Republic of Karelia, one must have at least a general idea about the organizational structure of local power in the republic. Let us begin by comparing. We shall do it using examples, which are understandable for the German seminar participants. Karelia, which occupies an area of 180,500 km^2, can accommodate five federal lands of Baden-Württemberg an area of 35,700 km^2. At the same time, the population density of Baden-Württemberg is 306 people per km^2, but in Karelia – only 3.4 people per km^2. Therefore, the population density of the German land Baden-Württemberg is nearly one hundred times higher than Russian Karelia. The south of Karelia, where 73 percent of the population resides, is better inhabited than other districts of the republic. Here the population density is 8.7 people per kilometer^2. Northern territories, however, are sparsely populated and contain only 14 percent of the Karelian population, with a population density of just 1,5 people per square kilometer. According to data from 2019, 618,100 people reside in Karelia[1], of whom more than 280 000 live in the capital of the republic – Petrozavodsk. The most populous districts of Karelia are Kondopozhsky (35,900 people) and Segezhsky (35800). The smallest is Kalevalsky (6,600). The total population distribution of Karelia is 78 percent urban and 22 percent rural. For many years the migration process of rural dwellers to towns has been under way, primarily to Petrozavodsk, where over 45 percent of the republican population resides today. As a result, there is continuing reduction of the population in almost all municipalities of Karelia, the only exception being the district

1 For official data on the Republic of Karelia referenced in the antecendent paragraphs*: Federation Council of the Federal Assembly of the Russian Federation* 2019: Republic of Karelia. http://council.gov.ru/en/structure/regions/KR/ (31/03/2020). Additionally, see https://en.wikipedia.org/wiki/Republic_of_Karelia (31/03/2020).

of Prionezhsky, which is the suburb of Petrozavodsk. A slight reduction of the population has been happening during the last five years in three municipalities: Kostomuksha, Segezhsky and Pryazhinsky districts. There has also been a steady reduction of the total population in the Republic recently. Since 2015, the population has decreased by 14,500 people. We can say that in five years the population of an average municipality will have all but disappeared. The average annual population loss in Karelia is between 1,300–1,900 people.

2 Local Government: Structure

Let us look now at the local government system in the Republic of Karelia. There are two urban districts (Petrozavodsk and Kostomuksha) made up of 16 municipalities and 107 settlements, 85 of which are classified as rural settlements despite the fact that they belong to an urban district. Overall, there are 845 settlements in Karelia, of which 13 are cities. For a territory of this size, this is a low number of settlements: The territory runs 660 km from north to south and 424 km from east to west. By the way, the western border is the border with the European Union; the common border with Finland is 798 km long. At present, there is a *two-level model* of the local government structure, where –

the first level – settlements,

the second level – municipal districts including several settlements each.

On the first level, the local government bodies are formed through the popular election of heads of urban and rural settlements (executive power) and deputies of the communities (representative power). *On the second level,* municipal, the representative power is made up of deputies and community heads delegated by communities to the district deputy councils. The chairman of the deputy council, by virtue of position, is the head of the district. Regional council members select heads of district administrations from the persons preliminary selected on a contest basis (a contest committee is created for this purpose).

Local government is an independent power institution (local self-government is a constitutional norm) from government power bodies. Legally local government is independent[2], but actually it depends on regional and federal government financially. Budgets of nearly all urban and rural communities are deficient; therefore, issues of local government cannot be resolved without federal and regional subsidies. Some authority of the local government is delegated to the regional level (health care, social services, school and pre-school education), while some is executed by local government bodies at the expense of federal or regional budgetary funds. As a result, local government is often subordinated to regional power bodies despite its formal independence.[3] On the level of settlements and municipalities, admin-

2 Constitution of the Russian Federation. http://www.constitution.ru/en/10003000-09.htm (30/03/2020). In Chapter 8 on "The local self-government", the role of the municipalities is specified in Art. 130–133. E.g. Article 130,1 says, that "[l]ocal self-government in the Russian Federation shall ensure the inde-pendent solution by the population of the issues of local importance, of possession, use and disposal of municipal property."

3 Cf. *Frankenberger, R.* 2017: Does the systemic environment matter? In: *Frankenberger, R./Chernenkova, E. (eds.)*: Local politics in a comparative perspective. The cases of Petrozavodsk and Tübingen, Baden-Baden, pp. 21–33.

istrations have more authority than the deputy corps (even though the latter adopt budgets and determine the normative basis for operation of rural and urban territories). From the legal point of view, deputy corps are independent and self-sufficient, but frequently become dependent on the executive power bodies (local administration). The success of local deputies' work and their independence depend on two conditions: (1) professional preparedness of deputies to work as representatives of the local population, and (2) party affiliation (deputy fractions, if any, are bound by party discipline).

Institutes of public local government are weak in Karelia. But the process of involving citizens into public administration of the territory is under way and supported by regional powers.

3 Local Initiatives Support Program[4]

Local government bodies are often incapable of acting on local community issues due to the budgetary weaknesses of some villages, a multitude of urgent local problems requiring immediate action. These issues, as a rule, concern communal and social infrastructure such as: repairs of yards, lighting of streets, the water supply and improvement of settlements, building children's playgrounds and sports grounds, etc. The list is long. As a result, problems stay unresolved for years. This has led to increased dissatisfaction among the population with the entire system of power and increasing social tension. One possible solution to this crisis is to change the process and provide the means and opportunities for the population to address their problems directly. Such programs have already been tested in parts of Karelia. The regional government formed a monetary fund dedicated to *support local initiatives*. The pre-condition for funding is compulsory co-funding on the part of the local community. One could attract sponsor's funds, but inhabitants of villages wishing to get budget money for their projects must invest their own funds into the project's realization. It is not the amount that matters, but the fact of financial participation. People giving money for the project begin treating it as their own. This creates a different psychological atmosphere of social relations within the community.

The local initiative support program has been implemented in Karelia since 2014. It provides for the provision of funds:

(1) on the *contest basis*,
(2) on the *terms of co-financing*,
(3) *supported by the population at general meetings* and
(4) aimed at the *development of social infrastructure*.

To receive financial support, one must win the contest collecting a certain number of points depending on the contest.

4 For general Information on the Program: *Shulga, I./Vagin, V./ Sukhova, A./Khachatryan, G./ Gavrilova, N./ Shapovalova, N./Shilov, L.* 2017: Initiative Budgeting. Russian Experience of Citizens' Participation in Addressing Local Issues, Moscow. https://www.buergerhaushalt.org/sites/default/files/WB_ini_budget_A5_eng.pdf (31/03/2020).

Terms of Project Financing

The LISP monetary fund consists of *three parts* (percentage is calculated from the total project amount):

Republican budget funds:

- Urban 70 percent and rural 80 percent.

Municipal budget funds:

- urban settlements – 20 percent,
- rural settlements – 15 percent.

Funds of the inhabitants:

- urban –10 percent,
- rural – 5 percent.

The total amount of money invested by the population can include sponsorship funds, for instance support from a local business. Special terms of project financing are established for Petrozavodsk and Kostomuksha, where the municipal share must be at least 30 percent of the project amount.

Who Wins the Contest?

The maximum number of points participants can earn is 100. The selection committee members take into account:

- the levels of project co-financing,
- the social significance of the project,
- the social effect of the project realization,
- the number of project participants (how many people supported it with their money),
- the number of beneficiaries,
- the level of awareness generated among the population.

Additional points can be earned if a previous project of that community was implemented without violations and completed before September 1st. Points can also be deducted from applications if previous projects were not implemented successfully or violations of policy occurred.

Table 1: The number of participants in LISP meetings

Year	Number of participants (persons)
2014	3,815
2015	5,901
2016	10,484
2017	10,986
2018	9,889
2019	Up to 10,000

Source: own compilation.

How the Terms of the Contest Changed

Since their establishment, the terms of participation for local initiative support programs have changed. In 2014, only rural and urban settlements could take part in the LISP, but in 2015 the rules were changed to allow urban districts to participate as well. This trend of inclusion continued and since 2016 municipal districts have also taken part, meaning that today all 125 municipal formations in Karelia are eligible to participate in contests.

Amounts of Budgetary Subsidies by Year

In 2014 – 8 million rubles were allocated for the program from the budget (17 projects were implemented);

2015 – 26.2 million rubles (40 implemented projects);
2016 – 37.5 million rubles (52 implemented projects);
2017 – 50 million rubles (61 implemented projects);
2018 – 50 million rubles (70 implemented projects);
2019 г. – 60 million rubles (80 projects).

In five years, the number of subsidies from the republican budget increased more than sevenfold. The maximum amount allocated for the implementation of a single project increased as well: in 2014 and 2015, it could not exceed 500,000 rubles, in 2016 this was increased to 800,000, and in 2017, this was increased to 1 million rubles. In five years, the number of project applications submitted for the contest *more than doubled*: from 36 in 2014 to 95 in 2019. The number of participants also multiplied: from 3815 people in 2014 to more than 10 000 in 2019. Over five years *241 projects were implemented.*

Specifics of Project Financing

Funds from the republican budget are only distributed after completion of the LISP. The contracting organization performs the work at its own expense and is then reimbursed for the completed work after the object acceptance. Advance payment under contract is allowed but may not exceed 30 percent of the total cost.

Algorithm of Actions for Accepting and Implementing LISP

Selection of programs for the following year happens during meetings from September-November of the current year, for example in the autumn of 2018 general meetings for selecting LISP projects for 2019. Before December 10, administrations of municipal formations send the projects selected by the inhabitants to the regional contest committee. After this, the government checks the documents and makes the decision to admit or deny the project into the contest. Once the contest is decided, the government of Karelia makes a decision for the distribution of budget funds (subsidies) among the winners. As soon as the contest results are announced, regional administrations conclude agreements with the winning settlements and the project realization begins. Communities receive the money via local budgets. Communities themselves then pay contractors for the completed work. Selection of contractors is done on the tender basis within the framework of federal legislation. If the municipality has leftover funds after completing its project goals, it can direct these funds to additional operations within the project with approval from the government. All project work must be completed by November 15. The first five years of LISP implementation data show a clear trend across the region. Cities are more active than villages, and the south is more active than the north. If we view the implemented projects on a map of Karelia, it becomes obvious that application campaigns from the northern districts of Karelia lose out to projects submitted to the contest from southern Karelia. This problem, in the opinion of the Ministry for National and Regional Policy, can only be solved through additional financial stimulation for the inhabitants of northern communities, or the introduction of special nominations for northern districts.

4 Territorial Public Self Government[5]

The abbreviation "TPSG" speaks for itself. It is when inhabitants of a certain settlement take up management of the territory, they reside on themselves. There are two types of TPSGs. *The first one is* similar to a non-commercial, non-government organization, which is *registered* at the justice department and obtains the rights and obligations of an NGO. *The second type is an informal community* of citizens (countrymen), united for the sake of solving communal, economic, sociocultural, and other problems existing on their common territory of residence.

In both cases, people unite into a village commune for arrangement of their lives. Everyone residing in this territory can be considered a member of the TPG. At the same time, there is no formal membership into the TPSG, and the relationship remains an informal one for most citizens. Still, the initiative group of citizens must be *legally organized* holding a meeting and making a decision on the creation of a territorial public government. The minutes of the meeting must be submitted to the local government body, and the administration must legally register the TPG thereby *designating the territory of their operations*. Once a TPSG is established, any actions on subjects of management and administration of the territory must be approved by the local community (TPSG). TPSGs and the communities are free to decide between a formal or informal organization. In Karelia, there is a strong preference for the informal type of organization which is reflected in the TPSG population of the region. Of the 113 TPSGs operating in Karelia today, only two are formally registered using the NGO form with the Ministry of Justice Republic of Karelia. The other 111 TPSGs all act as informal local communities with their own charters and are registered only with local administrations. As a result, these 111 are spared the excessive reporting obligations which burden the formal TPGs.

This model of a territorial public government is most suitable for rural communities even though the history of Russian TPSGs started in capital cities. The first TPSG "Perevalka" was founded in Petrozavodsk in 1995. By the early 2000s there were 11 TPGs in Petrozavodsk, but their work could hardly have been called efficient. In most cases, they stopped working right after their establishment. A federal legal basis for the functioning of TPG existed, but territorial communities did not develop in the republic. The expansion of TPSGs

5 For general Information on the program: *Shulga et al.* 2017 (fn. 4).

has also been uneven even in regions neighboring each other. Archangelsk, which border Karelia, established its first TPSG in 1998 but has seen explosive growth and the region now boasts 1,100 TPSGs. In contrast Karelia boasts only 113 TPGs today and the expansion of TPSGs occurred largely after 2017. In Karelia they decided to first develop TPSGs in rural communities. The most active participants were TPSGs from southern districts of Karelia.

Table 2: Number of TPSGs in Karelia

Year	Number of TPSGs
1995	1
before 2000	11
August 2017	16 registered, of them 11 were inactive
January 2018	55
January 2019	88
April 2019	110
June 2019	113

Source: own compilation.

Although TPSGs were established in only 51 out of 109 municipal formations, provisions for TPSGs to operate were adopted in all 109 formations meaning, in theory, communities can initiate new TPSGs at any time.

Financial Support for TPSG

The government of Karelia provides TPSGs with grant and subsidy support in order to stimulate civil activity.

The specific forms of support available for TPSGs include:

- subsidies for ensuring activities of newly formed TPSGs,
- grants based on contest results,
- bonus payments to the best TPSGs (the contest “Best TPSG of Karelia” was announced in 2019; prize fund is 400,000 rubles).

To provide TPSG initiators with some funds for their activities (first of all, for project launching), the republican budget allocates funds for stationary and organizational events. Each TPSG receives approximately seven thousand rubles. In 2018, 34 TPSGs received this support, and in 2019 that number rose to 50. TPSGs decide how to spend the money at their general meetings. While the amount of funding is miniscule, the allocation on the part of the government demonstrates official support for TPSGs and provides moral support to TPSG organizers. Since 2018, contests have been held in territorial communities with money awards aimed at supporting small projects. Winners received 300 000 each from the republic budget. As with the local initiatives support Program, the benefits were conditional on compulsory co-financing on the part of TPSGs. The minimum contribution was 10 percent of the total funding received. In 2018, 43 projects were presented by TPSGs for the republican contest, 16 of them became winners receiving about three million rubles from the total budget for their projects. Up to 90 percent of the projects’ costs were funded by the republican budget. The remainder was covered by members of the TPSGs, sponsors, or local budget allocations.

In 2019, the budget of Karelia allocated 18.3 million rubles for the support of TPSGs. From this amount, about 96 percent is for financing TPSG projects, two percent for operational support of newly established TPSGs for statutory work, and two percent for monetary awards for the best TPSG contest. The contest will be held for the first time in 2019 and provides for five winners. In February 2019, the government of Karelia increased funding for the socially significant projects of TPSG contest to 17.5 million rubles. As a result, all 72 applications to the contest were supported. By comparison, 1,100 TPSGs in the Archangelsk region were allocated 32 million rubles from the regional budget for project activities in 2019, of which 25 million rubles were for projects in rural areas.

Besides local funding, TPSGs can also enter LISP contests, apply for grants, and participate in both presidential and republican grant programs. However, to do so, TPSGs must be registered as legal entities. An exception to this rule is that TPSGs may participate in LISP contests represented by initiative groups of citizens who apply on behalf of local populations. In the case of non-registered TPSGs, money allocated for project realization is sent to municipal budgets (to special accounts), since these TPSGs have no legal entity and consequently no bank account. TPSGs and municipal administrations look for contractors to do the work (tender is not compulsory; the amounts are small, so direct procurement of services is allowed). If a TPSG is registered as a legal entity, it bears the cntire organizational and material-financial responsibility for grants and contracts. This has not yet occurred in Karelia. TPSGs solving problems of their territories take part in supporting initiative groups seeking for LISP money. Participants of TPSGs assist in holding community meetings for determining priorities for project applications within the framework of LISP, and take part directly, as the inhabitants of the village, in voting on project selection.

Inhabitants' Contribution in TPSG Projects

By including community members in the project activity, psychological patterns shift over time. Participants begin to buy into the idea that combining means and efforts are the key to producing positive effects in the work and as a result, they become more invested in projects. In the territories where local communities actually form, local inhabitants willingly invest their own money into common projects. Dependency disappears. Let us show a few examples of this (analyzing the data of 2019).

Megrega Village of Olonets District (5 TPSGs operate in this territory)

The total amount of five projects attracted to solve the village issues is 2.14 million rubles This amount includes the funds from the republican, local budgets and private persons with sponsor funds. The budget of Megrega for 01.06.2019 was 2.31 million rubles. These are own taxable and non-taxable funds excluding gratuitous revenues. We can make a conclusion that activity of the TPSG movement participants actually *doubled the village budget.* If we take the common revenue budget together with gratuitous revenues (5.03 million rubles), its share will amount to 42.5 percent.

Padany Village of Medvezhegorsk District (12 TPSGs)

The total cost of 12 projects is 3,440,103 rubles (this is common contribution from all the sources – region, municipality, inhabitants). The budget of Padany on 01.06.2019 (own income without gratuitous revenue) – 3.87 million rubles. Share – 88 percent. If we take the common revenue budget together with gratuitous revenues (8.03 million), the share will be 42.8 percent. Even in this case it is almost half of the village budget.

Kotkozero, Olonets District (3 TPSGs)

The total cost of three projects is 871,651 rubles (common investment). The budget of Kotkozero on 01.06.2019 (own income without gratuitous revenue) was 2.94 million rubles, which constitutes a share – 29.6 percent. If we take the common revenue budget together with gratuitous revenues (7.40 million rubles), the share will be 11.8 percent.

Hiitola, Lahdenpohja District (2 TPSG)

The total cost of two projects is 684,228 rubles (common investment from all sources). The budget of Hiitola on 01.06.2019 г. (own income without gratuitous revenue) – 4.89 million rubles, a share of14 percent. If we take the common revenue budget together with gratuitous revenues (5.86 million rubles), the share will be 11.7 percent. This data shows how communities buying into TPSGs can significantly affect local budgets. The result of such support leads to significantly higher budgets that provide the resources for action on local concerns which will have a positive effect on inhabitants' quality of life.

Examples of TPSG Activities

Almost all TPSGs deal with issues of territorial development such as the construction of playgrounds and sports grounds, water supply, street lighting, and repairs of yards, but they also sponsor many original projects. Such projects include:

- The creation of the School of *Quadro Cross* in Olonets. 60 percent of the project was self-financed (206,300 rubles collected by TPSG and sponsors), the state allocated 300,000 rubles for the project.
- *The restoration of a church* in Megrega, Olonets district. Five TPSGs in the territory of the village united forces and funds for the restoration of the church.
- *Song festivals* in Rybreka, Prionezhsky district.
- *A car park* in the yard of a building in Yanishpole, Kondopoga district.
- Master classes for *restoration of folk traditions* and sewing of national costumes in Reboly, Muezersky district.

How many People are Involved in TPSG Work in Karelia?

Although TPSGs in Karelia are of the informal variety and therefore do not keep official membership rolls, it would be fair to say that around 3,500 people are involved in TPSG activities in Karelia. There are places in Karelia where several TPSGs have been created. For instance, in the Padany, Medevezhegorsk region, 12 TPSGs have been created although the total population of the region is only a little over 1,000 people. The reason for this is that the settlement is comprised of 12 communities and each one has its own TPSG. The local administration felt this best benefited the inhabitants because every TPSG could then participate separately in grant contests. The Megrega, Olonets district includes eight communities with a total population of about 970 people and boasts five TPSGs.

Informational Activity of TPSG

Some TPSGs in Karelia have their own pages on social media networks. There is also a group in the social media network "VKontakte" called "TPSG Association of the Republic of Karelia" which has been active since July 2018.

Advantages and Disadvantages of TPSG Activities

Let us begin with advantages. TPSGs form civil solidarity, mutual support between neighbors, and an environment of collective responsibility for the common property of the community. It also develops the economy of the community, thus preserving it. By participating in grant contests, TPSGs supplement community budgets, and provide additional funding for programs addressing housing, communal, and social problems. Thanks to TPSGs people get involved in the socially beneficial activity. For young people it is a great form of socialization. *But there are also disadvantages.* The creation and activities of TPSGs can initially provoke some backlash and resentment from members of a community. These challenges are typical in situations where direct democracy is used and must be addressed early on. A strong TPSG representing a rural community can complicate the work of local power bodies by forcing them to take notice and action on issues they may have previously ignored. This shift in power can lead to a slowdown of action by local administrations and prevent action on other issues. This slowdown due to a change in the administrative power dynamic is expected and is a necessary cost of bringing a wider range of issues to the forefront of administrative concerns. Finally, excessive administration on behalf of the local power bodies in relation to TPSGs can kill them. To avoid this threat, TPSGs must form networks of regional and interregional TPSG communities. These associations of TPSGs could then represent their networks in order to resolve conflicts with existing power structures. In conclusion, the potential advantages of well-run TPSGs for development and community engagement far outweigh the few disadvantages and complications which can occur.

5 Village Headman

The institution of village headmen is not yet fully developed in Karelia. The Law "On Headmen of Rural Communities in the Republic of Karelia" was adopted on July 22, 2019. In other parts of Russia this institution of local government has been successfully operating for a long time. The legal basis for it is Federal Law "On General Principles of Organization of Local Government in Russian Federation" in the Article "Headman of a Rural Community"

(Article 27.1). The republican law on village headmen, which came into effect, included them in the system of territorial self-government.

The law provides for elections of headmen by community deputies upon the recommendation of the local inhabitants, who will decide at a general meeting, who they wish to entrust with representing their interests. Afterwards the deputies must legally confirm the decision of the meeting. The right to choose remains with the people. The law stipulates that the headman is neither a public nor municipal servant and cannot be employed by the local government bodies. This means that the headman cannot be influenced like the head of the community who is the head of the executive power and is paid by the municipal budget. The local budget is not required to pay the headman for their work, but at the discretion of the local administration, he may receive a certain allowance. Besides this allowance, the headman is compensated for costs related to business trips and clerical expenses. The law also stipulates that a headman can only be a local resident who enjoys trust and respect among the local population. According to the law only a person permanently residing in the community may be elected headman.

The law vests the headman with the right to represent the community in agreements with outside authorities such as municipal or state power bodies. They gather the problems and concerns of local people and, acting on their behalf, informs the municipal administration of them, and later takes part in resolving the issues formulated by the community. The headman acts on behalf of local people, and it means that the forms of direct democracy will have to develop more actively, when all the significant questions get resolved at public meetings and by way of local referendums. In this model, the institute of territorial public self-government will be in great demand. The public office of the headman fits very well into this scheme.

The question then arises about the feasibility of further preserving the office of heads of community elected by popular vote since the work of the heads of community is paid for from the local budget but duplicates that of the headman, who works free of charge. Rural budgets are rather small almost everywhere, but a large part of them is spent on support of the local administration and head of the village. As a result, many communities face questions over the structure of their local administration and public discussion on this topic is long running.

The village power structure is such that the elected head constantly finds themselves living in the administrative center of the settlement few opportunities to visit the communities included within the settlement. The settlement of Padany is an extreme example where the distance between the various communities is almost 80 kilometers. For such cases, the presence of a headman as a public representative of a village can play a vital role. The headman's placement within a rural community allows them to better represent the interests of the community and to respond to problems as soon as they arise.

At present, almost all districts in the Republic of Karelia are experiencing administrative mergers between the district and district city administrations. According to government representatives, the merging of two administrations into one makes the management system more easily understood by the people because they are no longer confused about which power body is responsible for what functions. In addition, a single administration produces savings for the overall community budget. At the same time, there are two different budgets

– district and district center; bodies of representative power of each level also preserve their independence. The formation of the institution of headman in Karelia has just started, but the experience of adjacent regions shows that the attitude of local population to the headmen is positive. In Vologda region there are already about fifteen hundred headmen, in Komi there are 199.

6 Project "People's Budget"[6]

The essence of the project proposed by the Ministry of Finance of Karelia is to involve people in the budget distribution process. The overwhelming majority of people have no idea how the budget is formed, what it consists of, and what the priorities of the expenditure are. By including citizens in the process of drafting budgets, officials hope that citizens through municipalities and villages will gain a fuller understanding and appreciation for budget management. In this way, the "People's Budget" project is a mechanism of developing civil society in Karelia.

The core feature of the project asks citizens to distribute a part of the local budget themselves. A people's budget committee is formed from local citizens, who then determine the priorities of the budget policy and decide how to spend the money allocated to the people's budget committee.

In 2019, three pilot urban communities will be selected to participate in the "People's Budget" project. The budget committee in each community will be formed through a random drawing of names from applications submitted by local people.

It is presumed that the size of the budget will be at least 2.5 million rubles per community. Two million come from the regional budget and half a million from the local budget. The framework of the budgeting process is such that budget decisions made during the current year will be realized the following year.

It would be appropriate to call the "People's Budget" project an educational program. It teaches citizens to distribute budget money responsibly. How is the budget formed? What is a subsidy? Why is it important to pay taxes in good faith? The project supplements people's participation in the work of TPSGs and teaches them to spend the funds received for support of local initiatives rationally.

7 The Program "Comfortable Urban Environment"[7]

The federal program "Comfortable Environment" is financed from the federal, regional, and municipal budgets. If we compare three relatively similar programs – 1) federal "Comfortable Urban Environment", 2) republican Local Initiative Support Program, and 3) TPSG, the volumes of financing strike you in the eye. In the first case, the money is allocated by the federal center for large-scale projects (10–20 million rubles each), in the second – for projects with average financial support (up to 1 million rubles) and for the third group we can

6 For general information on the program: *Shulga et al.* 2017 (fn. 4).
7 For general information on the program: *Shulga et al.* 2017 (fn. 4).

use the definition of micro-financing (300–500 thousand rubles). The cash fund of the second and third group of projects is financed from regional, municipal budget and personal funds of people. But what is important – synchronization is possible between the projects, when they supplement each other creating a synergy effect and allowing for solution of larger problems than those initially set by the project authors.

In Karelia in 2017, using the funds of the "Comfortable Urban Environment" program, more than 200 yards and public areas in 30 municipalities were repaired. The total volume of funds for the program realization in 2017 was over 165 million rubles. The total volume of funds for the realization of the "Comfortable Urban Environment" program in 2018 was the same as in 2017, but in 2019 bigger – 191 million 890 thousand rubles, of which Petrozavodsk got 84,305,000 rubles(more than 44 percent of the total sum).

Public territories and land improvement facilities are determined by preferential voting. The more active is the outreach campaign of the concerned citizens (public lobbyists), the more chances they have to see their project among the winners. Public discussions, maximal involvement in the selection process to apply forces and means, form the state of collective participation of the population in managing the territory of their residence. A public organism is formed in the form of a neighborhood whose participants learn to articulate their collective interest and defend it. Discussions of the "Comfortable Urban Environment" program in 2019 attracted almost one hundred thousand people of the Republic, i.e. practically every third person in Karelia over 15 years of age (there are 311,600 such people) took part in the voting. It is a very high index of civil participation in solving public problems.

8 Conclusion

The beginnings of collective independence of citizens are developing in communities. People become aware of common responsibility for everything happening in their communities. Trust between people is becoming stronger in the society as well as the aspiration for joint resolution of problems, improving the quality of life as a result. Communities become convinced in the good perspectives for their places, social stability and economic sustainability. A new economic environment is formed. There are possibilities for the development of local economy. People of different ages take part in project implementation, there is socialization of children and adolescents. Dependency disappears from public life people understand that the quality of their personal lives depends on the common efforts of their countrymen.

Wellbeing and Trade Unions: A Review at Local Level

Stewart Gold and Carmen Thamm

Abstract: The purpose of the study is to examine the significance of public services or wellbeing concept for trade union actors. What kind of participation and social opportunities at local level are offered to trade union actors in the field of public services and how are they used? With the help of an online survey and interviews with local trade union actors, significant knowledge and communication deficits were identified. Both limit the power to act. The survey also reveals a different picture of trade unions regarding the importance of and responsibility for this policy field. Here, the trade union self-perception and the trade union self-image are essentially affected and reveal a conflictual tension within union structures.

Keywords: trade unions, local trade union representation, wellbeing, public services, privatization, Germany

To improve working and pay conditions for employees is at least historically the core activity of trade unions. However, workers' overall wellbeing depends on requirements that are not covered by this approach; those include health, education, quality of political rights and social relations, mobility and communication terms, environmental conditions as well as energy and water supply or waste disposal. In Germany, the welfare state principle in article 20, German Basic Law, obliges the state to establish a "social state". After World War II, a cross-party consensus on an active role of the state in providing public services and equal opportunities developed. Moreover, a specific distribution of competences between the federal government, federal states and municipalities shapes the structure of public service provision in Germany. To enforce the interest of employees of a high-quality level of wellbeing, trade unions in Germany can influence public decision-makers within the framework of corporatist participation. In addition, they can affect the public discourse.

However, for several decades, liberalization and privatization processes have triggered a reorganization in the German structure of public services provision. They have led to a dissolution of the state monopoly and replaced individual needs with economic and budgetary objectives. These dynamics increased the demand of trade union commitment in public services dramatically. At the same time, the structural change in Eastern and Western Germany, but also more recent developments like the strengthening of new right-wing populist parties, processes of political emancipation and the growing explosiveness of climate and environmental problems have established new potential areas of activity for a trade union policy that keeps an eye on a holistic wellbeing of employees.

At federal level, German trade unions have largely integrated such a holistic view into their political demands. The European Trade Union Confederation (ETUC) and its ten European trade union federations have also prioritized public services and wellbeing in their political agenda. Especially the attempt of the European Union to subordinate national agreements of public services provision to its paradigm of fair competition. But the clear trade union demands formulated on national and supranational level need to be combined with a stronger engagement on local level to create enough political pressure; particularly in Germany, where local authorities are responsible for most public services.

But how do local unionists perceive the urgency of those rising problems in public services? Do they identify public services policies as a trade union field of action at all? To answer these questions, we asked local trade unionists for their understandings of public services and their assessment of the trade unions' role in this field. The survey shows that, on the one hand, local trade unions perceive public services as a valuable and defensible good. On the other hand, it reveals that the level of knowledge regarding public services is comparatively low.

In order to pursue these questions, we start with an overview of the historical developments in Germany and the theoretical embedding of public services (chapter 1). Chapter 2 is dedicated to the liberalization processes and its impacts on public services provision. The following chapter provides our research design (chapter 3). Chapter 4 presents our observations and first findings. Thereupon, we tried to figure out the meaning of trade union's action within social services is reflected within the trade union's identity. Finally, we contextualize our findings with current researches in political science and make some recommendations for a better performance of local trade unions within the field of public services.

1 Historical Contextualization and Theoretical Foundations

By the time, industrial capitalism became the leading economic characteristic in 19th century Europe, trade unions emerged as coalitions of employees to struggle for higher wages and better working conditions. By the end of the 19th century, trade unions in Germany became mass organizations and working-class parties gained increasing support for their political demands at national elections. Altogether, the German labor movement developed into a critical social force, whose claims for the abolition of the monarchy and the transition to socialism could no longer be ignored by the ruling class. Therefore, the state as well as the capitalist class recognized that they had to change their strategies of domination to prevent themselves of a loss of power. Consequently, the Wilhelmine state started to assume duties in regulation of wage conditions by creating various institutions that still exist within the German welfare state – insurances such as public health (1883), accident (1884), pension and invalidity (both 1990). Meanwhile, employers began to accept trade unions gradually as negotiating partners (finalized in Stinnes-Legien-Agreement 1918) and the number of wage agreements grew.[1] During this process, two important structural changes in Germany took place: first, by political interference the target group for trade union demands has broadened. Second, trade unions developed from illegal, usually small and segmented organizations to socially accepted and integrated actors.

Moreover, the economic reorganization process of the 19th century accelerated the formation of public services. The initially privately organized public services like water, energy and power supply as well as local transport had been progressively municipalized since 1850. Meanwhile, the German Länder focused on railway expansion and the state organized postal services and telecommunications by founding the Deutsche Reichspost in 1871.

1 *Schneider, M.* 2000: Kleine Geschichte der Gewerkschaften – Ihre Entwicklung in Deutschland von den Anfängen bis heute, 2nd revised edition, Bonn.

Finally, the Weimar Republic assumed responsibility for a national education sector by introducing nationwide school law in 1919. Following a large number of setbacks during both World Wars, these progressions have been revitalized and strengthened by the establishment of the "Modell Deutschland". Its main characteristics in public sector trace back to its specific historical formation: first, state industry sector was less important than in other European countries (e.g. Austria). That is why, second, we can identify a significant concentration on infrastructure. Third, as mentioned above, a specific but not mutually exclusive division of competences between the three federal levels in Germany exists.[2] The federal government in Germany remained responsible for railway, post, telecommunications, air and shipping traffic as well as road construction, whereas the Länder received competences for the education and science system, broadcasting and regional banks. Lastly, a large part of competences in public services stayed on a local level: water and energy supply, waste disposal, public transport, saving banks, kindergartens and many leisure and cultural facilities. Besides its huge value for a nationwide provision, the public services sector was a crucial factor to establish a broad class compromise, because it made it possible to distribute the wealth that has been generated in German export industries.

Based on a progressive integration into decision-making after World War II, trade unions in Germany evolved into intermediary organizations[3] that pursued the target to reconcile capital and worker's interests. In the meantime, the demand for a socialist reorganization almost entirely disappeared from union's programs in Germany, because post war prosperity permitted extensive concessions to the German workforce. In this context, German unions set new objectives – (participation in) growing prosperity and social cohesion for its consolidation – and criteria for action (cooperation and compromise). Thereby, a new trade union's identity has become consolidated, as Hyman[4] argued. An important precondition for an internalization of "integrated unionism" was the decision to reorganize trade unionism according to the principle of trade union unity (Einheitsgewerkschaft) by overcoming former ideological divisions. So, the trade unions' function as a regulative factor instead of a countervailing power came to the fore.[5] Two crucial pillars mainly carried this post war trade union identity. First, the collective bargaining autonomy (Tarifautonomie), guaranteed by German Constitution, gave an assurance to the unions (and employers) that they have the right to bargain on wages and working conditions without state intervention. While other policy fields remained within state competence, unions invested most of their resources in tariff policy. Especially single unions[6] that organize employees in specific economic areas decided to concentrate on bilateral negotiations with corresponding employers' associations.

---

2 *Bieling, H.-J.* 2008: Liberalisierung und Privatisierung in Deutschland: Versuch einer Zwischenbilanz. In: WSI-Mitteilungen 10/2008, pp. 541–547 (541 f).

3 *Müller-Jentsch, W.* 1982: Gewerkschaften als intermediäre Organisationen. In: Kölner Zeitschrift für Soziologie und Sozialpsychologie, special issue 24, pp. 408–433.

4 *Hyman, R.* 2001: Understanding European Trade Unionism – Between Market, Class & Society, London/ Thousand Oaks, CA.

5 *Schmidt, E.* 1971: Ordnungsfaktor oder Gegenmacht – Die politische Rolle der Gewerkschaften, Frankfurt a. M.

6 The DGB has a de facto monopoly in German trade unionism. Under its umbrella 8 single unions that cover every branch and economic sector in Germany are organized. Depending on the number of members: IG Metall, ver.di, IG BCE (IG Bergbau, Chemie, Energie), GEW (Gewerkschaft Erziehung und Wissenschaft), IG BAU (IG Bauen-Agrar-Umwelt), NGG (Gewerkschaft Nahrung-Genuss-Gaststätten), GdP

However, the second pillar – the corporatist involvement in political decision-making process – is more important, although not solely, for the German Trade Union Confederation (DGB) that coordinates the interests of its member unions and represents them vis-à-vis policymakers at all federal levels. If we exclude the wage and working conditions of employees in this sector, public services – namely, its organizational structure and the quality of services provided – were not considered a priority by the single unions in Germany. However, it is an important field of action for the DGB that, by its financial dependency on its member unions, does not have enough action enabling resources at its disposal. The lack of resources has primarily an impact on local level where policy competences lie in many areas of public services. Furthermore, there is a difference in unions' engagement concerning public services between the levels of trade unions' organization. As already mentioned, policy competences lay on local level in many areas of public services. But although, on national level DGB and its member unions – like the two largest ones ver.di (service sector union) and IG Metall (metal, textile and wood industrial union) – draft far-reaching demands, their implementation has to be pushed through by local trade unionists. Therefore, there is a need for a local reference or urgency and of course enough resources to transform national demands – like a more ambitious regulation of private companies or even a return to common property[7] – into local demands and action.

2 The Liberalization Process in Public Services

Until the 1980s, trade unions could be certain that the cross-party interpretation of the constitutional guideline of the welfare state principle guaranteed a relatively high quality and appropriate costs of public services. When the "Modell Deutschland" entered a state of crises during the 1980s and 1990s, framework conditions of public services system changed fundamentally.[8] The gradual extension of social and public services grinded to a halt as a general political paradigm shift took place. Due to the end of a period of continuous prosperity and a subsequent rise of public debt, fiscal consolidation and streamlining of state's responsibilities in favor of market forces moved up the agenda to overcome economic stagnation. In the public services sector these changes translated into some (partial) privatizations of state-owned companies on federal level (e.g. reforms of Bundespost and Bundesbahn) in the late 1980s. The German reunification or, rather its political handling, contributed significantly to a consolidation of the new economic approach, as thousands of state-owned enterprises were privatized. When the debt of the German state increased despite this extensive privatization during the reunification process, the economic disengagement of the state was deepened and extended to other areas and levels of public services. European integration even

(Gewerkschaft der Polizei), EVG (Eisenbahn- und Verkehrsgewerkschaft). For more information see *Fulton, L.* 2019: National Relations, an update. Labour Research Department and ETUI (online publication). http://www.worker-participation.eu/National-Industrial-Relations (14/04/2020).

7 *DGB* 1996: Grundsatzprogramm des Deutschen Gewerkschaftsbundes. Beschlossen auf dem 5. Außerordentlichen Bundeskongreß am 13.–16. November 1996 in Dresden, p. 22; *Ver.di* 2010: Grundsatzerklärung der ver.di. Beschlossen vom Gewerkschaftsrat am 18. März 2010, p. 4; *IG Metall* 2019: Beschlüsse. Miteinander für Morgen. Solidarisch und gerecht, p. 167 f, pp. 215–218.

8 *Bieling* 2008 (fn. 3), pp. 542–546.

intensified this process, for example by several sectoral liberalization directives that should ensure a fair access to the national energy markets for private market participants.[9] The wave of privatization also entered the municipal level, as many municipalities saw an opportunity to relieve their strained budgets by outsourcing public services. In the first place, they (just) reconstructed publicly owned companies under commercial considerations, but later they completely left them to private investors. Also, so called Public Private Partnerships emerged as a third phenomenon of the local privatization process: temporarily limited outsourcing of subtasks in public services.[10] These dynamics took place in nearly every area of public services located on local level, e.g. public transport, energy supply, hospitals and leisure facilities.

The comprehensive privatization process increased the pressure on trade unions to invest more effort to influence public services policies for two reasons. First, from the perspective of trade unions, privatization always threatens existing employment relationships because it is often accompanied by a rationalization strategy; weather by job cuts or by raising the workload, extending the work duration or by cutting wages and additional services. To fight these changes is part of the trade unions' core business and accordingly, unions that are active in these companies accept these new challenges. Especially, on the local level where single municipalities decide to relinquish responsibility in public services to the market unions devote increasing resources to prevent privatization or at least to safeguard jobs and working conditions.[11] Second, trade unions should be also interested in a high quality, low cost and an easy accessibility of public services to provide a high degree of wellbeing, of course for all employees but also for each citizen. This claim is not only compatible with their internalized identity as a socially responsible actor. A stronger commitment in ameliorate wellbeing could also improve trade unions' position in the general public discourse. A strategy that may strengthen trade union demands in several fields.

3 Research Design

That is why this article is interested in figuring out what meaning public services contributing to a higher standard of wellbeing have for trade union policies. As most public services are provided on the local level, the study also focuses on the local level. To get first impressions of unions' sensitivity for this topic, we conducted a short online survey of full-time and honorary unionists throughout Germany. The questionnaire comprised six questions in total: one open question and five questions using a Likert scale and giving the option of adding open answers. 75 out of 320 trade unionists[12] took part in the survey. The answers revealed misunderstandings, new aspects as well as not noted issues and first insights into trade unions' perception of wellbeing in the range of public services. Therefore, we conducted CATI in-

9 *Hermann, C./Flecker, J. (eds.)* 2012: Privatization of Public Services, Abington/Oxford.

10 *Röber, M.* 2018: Public Private Partnerships (PPP). In: *Voigt, Rüdiger (ed.)*: Handbuch Staat, Wiesbaden, pp. 1127–1139.

11 *Brandt, T./Schulten, T.* 2008: Liberalisierung und Privatisierung öffentlicher Dienstleistungen und die Erosion des Flächentarifvertrages. In: WSI-Mitteilungen, 61 (10), 2008, pp. 570–576.

12 We wrote to 320 members of following trade unions: IG Metall (143), ver.di (78), GEW (37), DGB (31), IG BCE (5), NGG (1); additional staff council in institution of public service (25); full-time officer (254), honorary office (66).

terviews[13] with six local trade unionists from the country chapters of Tübingen and Reutlingen (IG Metall, ver.di, DGB) to audit and deepen the initial findings. Compared to the first survey, these interviews focused on the situation, problems and unions' policies in this region.

4 Findings: Frequently only Low or Medium Importance for Public Service Provision

At first, it is crucial to know, which importance public services have for trade unionists. For this purpose, it is essential to distinguish between personal opinion and the perception in the function of a trade unionist. In this way, we could unambiguously assign the answers to the specific roles of the interviewees. Actually, the respondents assigned a different degree of significance: more than 81 percent attributed a high or very high importance as a private person, whereas just about 56 percent made this estimation for trade union action (see table 1). Consequently, almost 40 percent of the respondents, ascribe secondary or no significance of public services to trade unions (see figure 1). This group splits into two parts: 18.75 percent gave medium importance, whereas 20.32 percent assigned "no significance" (4.69 percent) or "little importance" (15.63 percent) to public services provision (see table 1).

Fig. 1: Importance of public services as private person and trade unionist

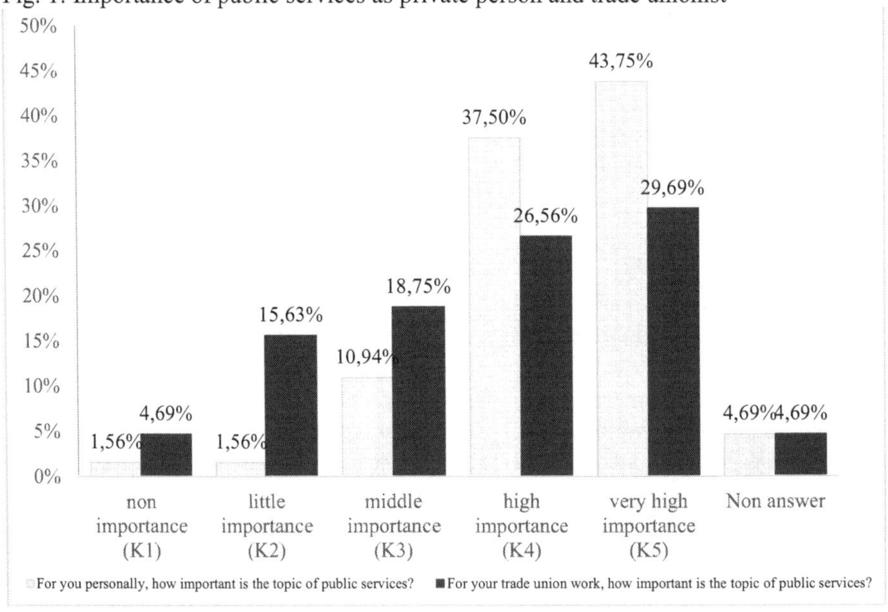

Source: own compilation.

The reasons for this outcome are various, but also complementary and interdependent. Analyses of the online survey and the interviews identify two dimensions: level of knowledge (1) as well as trade union priorities / sense of responsibility (2).

13 In the following analysis (chapter 4 and 5) the interviews will be numbered with romans from I to VI.

Table 1: Different significance of public services as private person and trade unionist

	For trade union activities	For them as a private person
High and very high importance	56,25%	81,25%
Little and no meaning	20,32%	3,12%

Source: own compilation.

4.1 Level of Knowledge

In general, a high-quality level of public services is crucial for both, the respondents who participated in the online survey and the separately interviewed trade unionists: "Good and comprehensive public services is existential for a well-functioning society" (70).[14] [15] Nevertheless, results of the online survey and the interviews show that knowledge of the field of public services is limited. However, the functional definition came easy to them: in particular, most interviewed unionists agreed that public services are commonly used goods. The state should guarantee an equal and low-threshold access to public service goods (II; III; IV; V). Nonetheless, the classification of public services and the distinction from other policy fields was more difficult for many surveyed local unionists. Also, the results of the online survey show that the knowledge about the meaning of public services at the German multilevel governance system vary strongly.

On the one hand, respondents failed listing a complete set of public service divisions: just one interviewee enumerated a complete list (communication, education, energy, electricity and water supply, financial supply, health care, leisure and culture facilities, public childcare, public transport, waste disposal) (IV). This fact may relate to his/her leadership position. Overall, the most frequently identified areas were health care, education, public transport. Only one person mentioned leisure and culture facilities as well as financial supply as a field of public services. On the other hand, the unionists mistook parts of the social security system (i.e. pension system) as a public services provision.[16]

These findings are also reflected in respondents' statements about past local trade unions' activities in the field of public services. Moreover, measures like attempts at privatizing local waste disposal and parts of the health care sector were rightly named.

Most of the unionists did not remember more than one or two only activities ranked among public services. Instead, they reported on union's work targeting an improvement of social security, fair rent or even the introduction of minimum wage (63; 76; II; III; IV; V; VI).

In this regard, it is interesting to note that the interviewed unionists mostly estimate themselves as well informed when it comes to public services. However, in contrast, one trade unionist stated that more help was needed from the higher union level unless his union improved in this area: "Now, we get more information [from higher union level], but in my opinion too little" (VI). Nevertheless, regarding both members and citizens and grassroots

14 The authors translated all German to English translations on their own.

15 The respondents of the online survey are numbered from 1 to 75.

16 However, social security benefits are individually purchased benefits because social security system in Germany is organized in accordance to the insurance principle. Therefore, social security must be distinguished from public services.

officials, the interlocutors agreed that increasing knowledge through awareness-raising and/or better dissemination of information is a task for trade unions. “There should be an organized force that raises awareness of connections in public services” (III; similar: IV).

In the same way as their general professional competence in the public service, the trade unionists interviewed assessed their level of knowledge in dealing with the federal distribution of competences in the public service (I; II; III; IV; VI). Nevertheless, when we evaluate the interviews and the results of the online survey, we see major gaps in knowledge. In particular, the trade unionists interviewed evaded the demand to assign specific areas of the public service to a certain federal level of responsibility. In addition to several statements by the trade unionists interviewed, the open answers in the survey to the question of the different meanings of the federal level showed that the trade unionists interviewed do not know exhaustively at which level policy-making takes place in the specific area. Despite this disclosed gap in knowledge, respondents of the online survey gave greater importance to the local and the national level (68 respectively 70 percent) than to the federal state or EU-level (56 respectively 44 percent). Even though the knowledge about fields and competences in public services is incomplete, a vague picture about the need for action at the local level exists.

In sum, we face a lack of knowledge when it comes to public services provision, especially on local level. This result is to some extent in line with the treatment of this issue at central trade union level. Although union programs include demands for high quality of public services, a clear demarcation between public services provision and employment in public services or the social security system could not be found.[17] Together with a flawed system of sharing information, this circumstance gives first impressions of the reasons for the limited knowledge of public services system at the unions’ grass roots.

The lack of knowledge, of course, affects the unions’ capacity to act when deteriorations in public services for example through privatization or rationalization at local level are imminent. If this is the case, local union organizations must react quite quickly: “At that moment, you cannot attend an educational seminar” (I). Then, the lack of knowledge makes it difficult or even prevents to draw up a comprehensive campaign.

4.2 Priorities and Responsibilities

We argued that the level of knowledge in the field of public services needs be improved. However, also organizations’ own priorities play a crucial role explaining why significantly more than one third of respondents do not give high importance to public services for trade unions’ activities.

First, many answers refer to the limited personal and financial resources: “With regard to working hours of union secretaries, I do not see room for engagement in bodies of public services” (77). Especially the statements from the online survey show that trade unions’ activities mainly concentrate on their core businesses: “Employment security and wage increase have priority” (12). Although respondents assigned high personal importance to public services, they did not identify this field as an important area for their own work as a unionist: „To support, to represent and to acquire members has top priority for my work“ (41). Instead,

17 *DGB* 1996 (fn. 7); *ver.di* 2010 (fn. 7); *IGM* 2019 (fn. 7).

union work is still focused on employment in their specific industries or sectors: "As a union we primarily stand up for collective agreements. Therefore, the company is our place to be" (23).

Furthermore, respondents often equate public services with public sector employment and therefore, especially trade unionists from industrial unions, assign this field to the responsibility of the German United Services Trade Union (ver.di) (58). In a mirror image, ver.di trade unionists also assess the relevance of the public sector for trade unions other than ver.di as even more secondary. (IV). Following up on this, they label ver.di as "driving force" (II; similar: IV) for a higher quality in public services. The underlying assumption often is that poor or worsening working conditions lead to poorly provided circumstances in public services and wellbeing (39; II). Two frequently mentioned examples for trade union activities in healthcare reflect this interrelation: for the first time since 2014, unions and staff councils of the University Hospital of Tübingen demand a revised staff allocation. They argue that too heavy workloads reduce the quality of care and this connection is relevant for every citizen (II). A second example is the attempt to privatize the District Clinics of Reutlingen in 2019, where unionists used a very similar argumentation.

But whenever there is no link between the increasing risk of a decline in quality in the public service and working conditions in the sector, trade unionists refer to the remit of the DGB (66): "DGB is the citizen's mouthpiece" (V). At the same time, respondents are aware that the lack of organizational power on this level makes it difficult to enforce these political interests, e.g. due to the prohibition of political strike (II).

In general, we got the impression that the respondents and interviewees do not always see the provision of public services as concrete living conditions and thus as the interests of the employees.

5 Trade Union Identity: Attitudes towards Unions' Engagement in Public Services

Based on empirical evidences, we were able to identify initial clues for an understanding of the limited significance of public services for trade union work. At the same time, these reflected a specific self-image regarding public services. The core issue is conflict between the role model of an actor in collective bargaining at company or sectoral level and an actor with a socio-political mandate.

The first position sees the (core) task of trade unions in collective bargaining. This interrelation – that the trade unionists focused on the so-called core task of trade unions – was confirmed by numerous statements made by the trade unionists surveyed (see 4.2). It is important to consider that not all responds share this point of view and locate the tasks of trade unions solely in collective bargaining. Some of them mention pragmatic reasons, like scarce resources: "The priority in trade union work is the company. There is a lack of personnel (especially voluntary) resources for more" (60).

Representatives of this position of trade union performance refer to the competence of the sectoral trade union ver.di with regard to working conditions and collective bargaining policy. "For an industrial trade union, the topic is 'only' indirectly important in that we are not responsible for the sectors of public services, e.g. ver.di" (58).

Furthermore, we refer to the responsibility of the DGB as 'political arm' of the trade unions. The individual trade unions – beyond ver.di – do not see themselves first and foremost as having a duty there: "The IG-Metall belongs to the DGB, for which reason the political fields/topics are anchored there" (76).

The second, opposite position sees the trade unions guiding principle as an actor with a social political mandate. This is based on a holistic view as an agent of all interests, particularly relating to issues of the civil society, of trade union members or, going further, the total labor force: "As a trade union, our original goal is to maintain and improve the living and working conditions of the members we represent [...]" (54). Or more precise:

"Public services of general interest must ensure that people do not feel or actually are excluded. Everyone must have the chance to live a satisfying life. Trade unions must work for this. This is an essential foundation of our democracy, which is challenged by right-wing politicians and the AfD" (61).

This is even more clearly expressed by 12 percent of the respondents in the online survey. They take the point of view that trade union responsibility for public services or the importance for trade union work is bigger than the personal relevance they place on the importance of public services.

A lot of respondents from both the interviews and the online survey attribute equal opportunities, participation, co-determination, appreciation, solidarity and the possibility of combining work and family of public services of general interest.

"'Public services of general interest' is a central point for trade unionists both as citizens and as employees: a good public infrastructure (day-care centers, schools, ...) shape the working and living conditions outside the workplace. The appreciation of public services of general interest must also be reflected in the appreciation of the employees" (20).

The cohesion of society and distributive justice are also general political topics that can be found in statements about the importance of public services:

"A good and comprehensive public service is essential for a functioning society. It is necessary - in addition to good working conditions, for example – in order to stop the division of society. Conversely, the dismantling of services of general interest means that people with low to average incomes are more affected than those with higher incomes. The former are for example dependent on free education and cannot switch to privately financed schools. Reducing this inequality of opportunities, resources etc. and therefore using it as a means to advocate for stronger and more comprehensive public services is an important task for the DGB" (70).

Liberalization and privatization of public services and services of general interest, including PPP (public private partnership) models, promoted by neo-liberalism, have been recurring issues in the financing of public institutions for about 20 years. In Tübingen and Reutlingen this has been a regular topic in the discourse on public services. Concerns about this political issue are also expressed in the responses in the online survey: "For example, I have a dramatic experience of the economization of health care" (15).

In Chapter 4.2., we mentioned two campaigns reflecting the conflict between and ensuring a high quality in the healthcare sector. The first case related to the staffing respectively capacity calculation and therefore the quality of care at the university hospital in Tübingen and the second one related to the attempt at privatizing the public hospital in Reutlingen. In addition, there are actions initiated and carried out in 2014 by local DGB members and in particular by the ver.di district Fils-Neckar-Alb (responsible for Tübingen and Reutlingen). In this respect again, trade unions had to fight the public withdrawal from a service of general interest, namely the Tübingen waste collection service (see Chapter 4.1). Through various actions and cooperation with other NGOs[18] in Tübingen, this could be prevented, according to local trade unionists.

These three examples show that general political issues such as privatizations and the economization of public services are a major political issue for trade union actors, not only on the federal political stage but also at a local level. This is about much more than just a labor dispute or a collective bargaining. This is about the quality of care and health care, ecology, municipal participation, tax burden and so on – the quality of public services in general and their governance by citizens.

There is a field of high tension – based on both statements from the online survey and interviews – between the different groups of actors in the trade union.

6 Conclusion, Needs for Research, Action and Outlook

There is hardly any research focusing on trade unions' activities in the field of public services. In a nutshell, we were able to show that explicit deficits and obstacles exist regarding the local trade unions' participatory skills in this field. We identified a notable lack of knowledge as a main problem.

Most of the trade unionists not only had problems in assigning policy areas to the public sector; they also had difficulties in placing them at the responsible political decision-making level in Germany's multi-level governance structure. During the interviews, there was evidence of insufficient and inadequate communication between the national and local levels regarding public services. We believe that lack of knowledge and insufficient communication have a direct impact on the responsiveness of local trade unions and their ability to act when changes in public services are planned. A second set of problems included trade union prioritization and the question of who was responsible for the policy field of public services. It apparent that the trade unions' focus on the local level is on their traditional core business: the improvement of employees' working conditions. Even when in some cases others underlined that external constraints like limited financial and personal resources are responsible for this perspective. The prioritization is closely linked to an ambiguous perception of organizational responsibilities within the field of public service provision, because unionists usually regard the field as an employment sector instead of giving it significance for employees' needs in general: on the one hand industrial unions like IG Metall do not see public services provision as their authentic remit. On the other unionists of ver.di give higher importance to the public services, but just because ver.di members are employed in public services. If employment does not play a role at all, unionists classified the DGB as responsible actor. Consequently, unions do not exploit their full potential while countering political attempts that might cause a decreased quality of public services provision.

We argue that these findings indicate a more general conflict within trade union organizations: an increasingly obvious controversy between a trade unions' identity as an exclusively

18 Cf. Flyer of "Attac Tübingen, DGB-AK Tübingen und ver.di Ortsverein Neckar-Alb laden ein: Unsere Müllabfuhr: Privat oder kommunal? Ein Informations- und Diskussionsabend zur fortschreitenden Privatisierung unserer kommunalen Daseinsvorsorge", 27. April 2010, Tübingen.

economic player (business unionism) or an actor with a wider scope of interests (integrated unionism).

Due to the relatively low number of cases, the current survey does not make a claim to be representative or exhaustive. Still, we believe that a more intensive follow-up study will be able to strengthen their validity. In the context of such a study, interviews could focus on examining the initial results to better understand the inner mechanisms of action. Furthermore, to increase significance, unionists from more regions should be questioned. This is even more important in the light of von Meise's[19] findings that local structural differences and their local organizational and cultural strategies influence local trade union work and the concrete practice of trade union representativeness.

However, based on the initial findings, the first needs for local trade union action in the field of public services provision are emerging. In order to enable trade unionists at a local level to represent the interests of trade union members in the fields of public services in an improved way, the following points should be considered as options for action and could be useful here:

- open internal trade union debate on the tasks of trade unions: specification of objectives and tasks of trade unions in the field of public services within the programs;
- greater transparency of actions towards citizens and society;
- better networking with other civil society actors (local alliances, stronger public relations work);
- better dissemination of information to the grassroots (both generally on the field of public services to improve knowledge and on actions/campaigns at district/board level);
- increased use of institutionalized participation possibilities on EU-level (e.g. European Citizens' Initiative).

It must be considered that employees are also citizens and thus the interests of employees represent the interests of citizens as users of services of general interest.

If we extend our considerations beyond the acute local recommendations for action, further aspects of future trade union development, as already mentioned by various other authors, are reflected in our findings. Meise[20] shows a tension between the different logics[21] – "logic of membership" and "logic of influence" (collective bargaining system) – within trade union structures. This tension can be supplemented by a third logic, the logic of citizenship. This considers the existing power structures and rules of the game within the respective fields of action and the balance of power between the heterogeneous groups of actors and interests within the trade unions. The existing power relations, consisting of the complex demands of politics, the economy and the everyday cultures of the social milieus, have an

---

19 Cf. *Meise, S.* 2015: Gewerkschaften als "intermediäre" Akteure in der lokalen Demokratie. In: Intermediäre in der Stadtentwicklung, Forum Wohnen und Stadtentwicklung, Zeitschrift des vhw – Bundesverband für Wohnen und Stadtentwicklung e.V., issue 5/2015, pp. 243.

20 Ibidem.

21 This concept relies on *Streeck, W.* 2017: Vielfalt und Interdependenz: Überlegungen zur Rolle von intermediären Organisationen in sich ändernden Umwelten. In: Kölner Zeitschrift für Soziologie und Sozialpsychologie, special issue 56, pp. 525–548.

impact on the fields of action, which in turn leads to a multi-layered structure of relationships within the fields of action.[22]

New alliances and networks – accompanied by coordinated policy approaches for the pursuit of trade union interests in public services – could lead to the strengthening of societal discursive power resources.[23] On the one hand, in this way, they could contribute to increasing trade union organizational power and assertiveness and create social majorities for the interests of wage-earning employees. On the other hand, the capacity to act and the organizational power thus gained could counteract the erosion of the sectoral collective agreement and the weakening of the dual system of interest representation.

22 Ibidem.

23 Cf. *Dörre, K.* 2019: Die Gewerkschaften – progressive Akteure einer Nachhaltigkeitsrevolution? In: Bewegte Zeiten: Linke Bewegungen, Proteste und gewerkschaftliche Kämpfe Zeitschrift für sozialistische Politik und Wirtschaft (spw), issue 233.

PART 5: SISTER CITY RELATIONS AND WELLBEING

Public Participation in Sister-Cities Relations: The Case of Petrozavodsk

Natalya Lavrushina and Ekaterina Shlapeko

Abstract: The article is devoted to practical and theoretical aspects of public participation in sister-cities relations. The sister-city phenomenon appeared after World War II and is typically defined by the establishment of social, cultural, and political ties between municipalities in separate nation-state. Based on concepts of public participation, we put forward and test the hypothesis that the role of public participation in sister-cities relations has grown significantly in modern realities. The practical materials for analyses are based on the history of Petrozavodsk sister-cities' relations. Currently Petrozavodsk has sister-cities and cooperation agreements with 12 cities of Europe, Asia and North America. To prove the hypothesis, an analysis of the formation and development of the contacts between cities is made. The methodology is descriptive, i.e., the plotting of partnerships by date and drawing certain conclusions from the resulting trends of cooperation. The described trends in international municipal relations are important in our aim to understand phases of city-to-city cooperation. The increase of international projects initiated by third sector has been revealed. It is concluded that public participation in sister-cities relations has a positive effect on the development of good neighborly relations and stimulates local communities for solving urban-related problems.

Keywords: public participation, sister-cities, civil diplomacy, city-to-city cooperation, NGO, Petrozavodsk

Concepts of Public Participation, Sister-cities Relations and Civil Diplomacy

In recent decades, there has been an increase in the involvement of individual citizens and public groups in solving social problems in various spheres of public relations. The most active processes happen at the local level and are characterized by a multi-vector focus: from top to bottom, governments stimulate social activity by funding and expanding mechanisms of citizens' engagement in local issues; from the bottom up, populations strengthen cooperative processes and more often use protest or support rallies to draw attention to urgent problems.

The concepts of civic and social participation appear in American sociological research in the areas of urban studies, theories of civil society, and applied research and community practices in local communities. In the late 1930s and 40s, empirical and theoretical studies of social participation had become systematic in American sociology.[1] The focus of the research concentrated on the participation in the life of the local community, in particular, the influence of the family type, social status, and gender on the nature of participation. Further research continued to study the correlation between demographic factors, economic well-

1 *Anderson, W.A./Arnold, C.* 1939: The pattern of Social Activities in a High Participation Group In: Rural Sociology 4, pp. 463–464; *Skalaban, I. A.* 2011: Social, Public and Civil Participation – the Problem of Conceptual Understanding and Misunderstanding. In: Herald Tomsk State University Vol. 1 (13), pp.130–139.

being and types of public and social participation in urban and rural areas. In their 2008 publication, Kenneth Newton and Heiko Giebler[2] analyzed the nature of public and civic participation in 22 countries and noted that participation is a key condition and component of the contemporary human life along with human happiness, democracy, and economic wellbeing.

The sister city model of civic cooperation can be seen as international form of social participation, operating at personal and community levels for the establishment of social, cultural, and political ties between municipalities in separate nation-states. Wilbur Zelinsky, an American cultural geographer, calculated that since 1950, more than 11,000 pairs of sister-cities in some 159 countries have entered into twinning agreements.[3] He also suggested that the links, originating from the 1950s onwards are predominantly cultural and involve primarily the countries of the developed world.

Forms of urban diplomacy, such as twinning, have been known since ancient times[4], but the twentieth century opened the doors for truly wide public participation in the field of International Relations.

For all those who studied and worked in the Soviet Union, there are still vivid memories of many activities related to the sister-cities friendship: workers of factories as well as sports and cultural delegations visited sister-cities, cities exchanged gifts, pen-friends exchanged letters, and "corners of friendship" telling about the sister-cities' history and traditions were arranged at schools.

Nowadays it might seem that with the opening of borders, internet access and the ability to study or travel abroad, the practice of "friendship" with other countries has disappeared. In fact, this is not entirely true: collaboration has simply changed its forms.

Cities today operate and compete in a different world than they did 70 years ago. By 2030, it is projected that the global urban population will reach 75 percent, and over 90 percent of global GDP will result from urban activity.[5] However, a sustainable partnership between cities needs to go beyond the commercial and geopolitical interests of their respective governments and requires a strengthening of civil society exchanges and collaborative people-to-people relations. Thus, motivations for developing these relationships have continued to be rooted in idealism, solidarity, politics, economic development, and an interest in knowledge transfer, all underpinned by the desire to showcase and share local culture.

The choice of partner country and the specific community within said country is not a random process. In Europe, agreements between cities tend to occur from the top down when the mayors of two cities meet and agree to become partners. In the US, however, they are more likely to be developed at the grass roots level when individuals get together to form a sister-city committee and request that their local government forms an official partnership.

---

2 *Newton, K/Giebler, H.* 2008: Patterns of Participation: Political and Social Participation in 22 Nations. In: Discussion Paper SP IV, p. 201. https://www.econstor.eu/bitstream/10419/49726/1/587500093.pdf.

3 *Zelinsky, W.* 1991: The Twinning of the World: Sister Cities in Geographic and Historical Perspective. In: Annals of the Association of American Geographers. vol. 81, no.1, pp. 1–31.

4 *Sayamov, Yu.* 2008: Cities' Diplomacy. In: The International Affairs, no. 8. https://interaffairs.ru/jauthor/material/1574 (30/03/2020).

5 *Ballantine, J.* 2014: How sister city partnerships can play a new role in a global economy. Cities Today, April 2014, pp. 28–31. https://www.academia.edu/9635691/How_sister_city_partnerships_can_play_a_new_role_in_a_global_economy (30/03/2020).

Historically, sister-city partnerships are those that begin between two cities that have something in common. Certainly, historical connections, shared economic, cultural, recreational, ideological concerns, and even the distance play meaningful roles. External organizations such as Sister Cities International in the USA or The Council of European Municipalities and Regions in Europe act as facilitators for developing partnerships between municipalities.[6]

James Marshall, a law professional after the Second World War, argued that diplomacy needed to open up to the public domain to regain democratic legitimacy: "Not until there is broader participation in the planning, the development, and the execution of foreign policy can it be said that the people take part in their own foreign relations."[7]

Katharine Graham and Susan Phillips analyzed the municipal international policy activity of the Vancouver region starting from the 1940s up until the 1990s. They identified four policy phases with different characteristics of civil participation: the ad hoc police phase (1940s–1970s); the rational policy phase (1980–1986); the strategic policy phase (1987–1990); and the global policy phase (1990s).[8] Later in the article, we will make an attempt to identify phases and patterns of Petrozavodsk sister-city model of civic cooperation. The ad hoc phase was oriented primarily towards cultural and educational exchanges and worked best where it had a clear community base and ongoing community support. The change of mayor in 1980 shifted the city's international focus to a more economic rationale. This was reflected in the organization and funding of international initiatives including the promotion of Vancouver as Canada's "Pacific Gateway". Municipal constituent diplomacy in the strategic phase established informal linkages with cities that were identified as "gateways" to significant regional and national economies. Each sister-city committee included a strong ethno-cultural community and business component. This resulted in institutions such as the Asia Pacific Foundation, which encompassed business, cultural, academic, and governmental areas for cooperation and provided community input in developing long-term relations to contribute to economic development in the Vancouver region.[9]

Linking local economic development and sustainability, more generally, a variety of interests have placed issues like ecology back on municipal and metropolitan agendas. Promoters of the globalist phase have increasingly suggested that local communities and their municipal governments are no longer prepared to passively wait for senior governments to take action on pressing global matters.[10] Pushed by their citizen movements, municipalities are becoming directly involved in a variety of issues to counter threats to humanity and improve the quality of life for individuals locally and beyond. The joint project work (preparation of applications for funding) goes beyond cultural and symbolic partnerships; it promotes modernized partnership serving as a tool for municipalities and towns to face mutual issues:

6 *Popov, E.S./Prikhodko, V.A.* 2015: Institute of twin cities in international relations of the Altai Republic on the example of the city of Vladivostok. In: International Journal of Applied and Fundamental Research, vol. 8, no. 2, p. 391.

7 *Marshall, J.* 1945: International affairs: citizen diplomacy. In: American Political Science Review, 43 (1), pp. 83–90.

8 *Graham, K.A./Phillips, S.D.* 1998: Citizen Engagement: Lessons in Participation from Local Government, Institute of Public Administration of Canada, p. 242.

9 Ibid., p. 69.

10 Ibid., p. 70.

economic development, water management, waste recycling, and the improvement of social services or language exchanges.

International Activity of Petrozavodsk City

Petrozavodsk established its first sister city relation in 1965 with the Finnish town of Varkaus. Foreign relations between Finland and the Soviet Union were based on the Treaty of Friendship, Cooperation and Mutual Assistance (1948) and were supported by the activities of the "Finland – Soviet Union Friendship Society". In 1962, the Karelian branch of the USSR – Finland Society was formed and began to circulate Finnish magazines and newspapers, staged performances in the Finnish language, and exchanged cultural delegations. Later, the Association for Relations between Soviet and Foreign Cities (1964) was created to expand contact with foreign cities "through partnership of hundreds of cities of the Soviet Union with foreign cities, the main direction of foreign policy was implemented – strengthening peace, mutual understanding and friendship between people."[11]

In 1965, an agreement was adopted on the twinning of 50 Soviet and Finnish cities at the proposal of the Soviet government during an unofficial visit of the President of Finland, Urho Kekkonen, to the USSR. The Chairman of the Executive Committee of the City Council of Petrozavodsk Ivan Grishkin sent a proposal to the mayor of Varkaus Eino Salmi, which was "unanimously adopted at the Council of city commissioners of Varkaus."[12] During the 1960s and 1970s, activists of the Finnish Communist Party visited Petrozavodsk and the districts of Karelian Autonomous Soviet Socialist Republic, showing great interest in the development of the "forest industry, youth camps, and concert performances by artists from different cities of Finland." During this period, the Karelian branch of the Soviet Union - Finland Society engaged in the systematic exchange of tourists, held film screenings, and involved city organizations to further develop closer relations. Among the organizations participating were: Petrozavodsk State University, The Institute of Language, Literature and History of the Karelian branch of the Russian Academy of Sciences, labor unions, and The Finnish Drama Theater. All of this was done with the idea that personal interactions between citizens of different states could change opinions and perceptions both within countries and beyond and become "an example of [a] beneficial and positive neighborhood."[13]

Ten years later in 1975, the Sweden – Soviet Union society started an initiative to establish twinning relations between Petrozavodsk and the capital of the province of Västerbotten – the city of Umeå. The letter sent to the Umeå municipal council emphasized the commonalities of the cities, namely, similar climate conditions and presence of the large universities as scientific centers[14]. In 1976, the Treaty of Friendly Relations between Umeå and Petrozavodsk was signed. Its content coincided with the text of the treaty with Varkaus signed in

---

11 *Gromov, B.V.* 2007: International movement of twin cities and people's diplomacy. In: Twin-cities, April, p. 5.

12 *Itkonen, H./Koivula, J./Lavrushina, N.V./Meshko, V.A./Shlapeko, E.A.* 2005: Petrozavodsk – Varkaus – twin cities, Petrozavodsk, p. 11.

13 *Council of Foreign and Defense Policy* 2001: Russia's interests in the North of Europe: what are they? http://www.svop.ru/ files/meetings/m023613379348922.pdf.

14 *Isaksson, A./Lavrushina, N.V./Meshko, V.A./Sevander, S.* 2006: Umeå – Petrozavodsk. 30 år av vänska, Petrozavodsk, p. 10.

1975. Both agreements noted "the desire to develop and deepen friendly and cultural ties between cities [...] through the exchange of delegations and information between cities."[15] It is noteworthy that a twinning fund for the support of exchange programs, cultural and sports events was established in Umeå. In 1978, representatives of the Blue Highway International Association visited Petrozavodsk and offered the city membership to the association. The proposal was accepted, and for a long time afterward, Petrozavodsk was the final destination of the international tourist route connecting Norway, Sweden, Finland and Russia.

The Blue Highway Association was formed in the early 1960s to establish closer relations between the province of Västerbotten (Sweden), which included the city of Umeå and the town of Mo i Rana (Norway) through the reconstruction of a road that ran through the mountains. Subsequently, the project made a significant contribution to the organization of transport links between the cities of Umeå and Vasa (Finland). The Blue Highway project was one of the first transport and tourism cross-border projects that combined the cities of Northern Europe and the Republic of Karelia.

Besides the contact with the cities in the neighboring Nordic countries during 1970s, active contact had been developing with Neubrandenburg in the DDR since 1969 (but the first agreement between the cities was signed only in 1983). Moreover, because Neubrandenburg was the only partner city from a socialist country, more citizens from both cities could visit each other. As a result, there were many exchanges between authorities, enterprises, schools, and cultural institutions. In 1973 sister-relations with La Rochelle (France) were established. Contact between Petrozavodsk and La Rochelle supported the teaching of French in Petrozavodsk and Russian in La Rochelle and let to the establishment in 1986 of the long-term and ongoing educational exchange between Karelian State Pedagogical Institute (now Petrozavodsk State University) and Lyceum J. Dautet.

All these relations were supported and controlled by the central authorities in Moscow. Nevertheless, the sister-relations enjoyed the active support of the citizens of Petrozavodsk as well, who had an opportunity for communication with external world. This tradition continues today. The period from 1960 until the mid-1980s can be considered as time of exchange enthusiasm, characterized by a strong desire to establish contact and learn from each other.

The socio-economic transformations that began in 1985 in the USSR caused, on the one hand, an increased interest in "perestroika" among residents of foreign cities, and on the other, spurred the Soviet government to expand, deepen, and diversify its international relations[16]. In particular, in 1986 Petrozavodsk was chosen as the venue for the first meeting of the twin-cities of Sweden and the USSR. During the negotiations, the basis for the development of trade exchange between countries was discussed. Then, in March 1989, for the first time, city enterprises brought their products to an exhibition in Varkaus, where it was also decided to participate in the town's upcoming youth exhibition Savon-Sampo-91 in Varkaus as well as the Nolia Trade and Industrial Fair in Umeå. In the wake of perestroika and "new

15 For the common aim: *Vitukhnovsky, A L. (ed.)* 1980: International relations of Karelia. 1917–1977. Documents and materials, Petrozavodsk, p. 206, 228, 269.

16 *Mezhevich, N.M./ Radvilavicius, S.* 2010: The role of cross-border cooperation between the European Union and the Russian Federation in bilateral and regional economic development programs. https://docplayer.ru/296125-Rol-prigranichnogo-sotrudnichestva-mezhdu-evropeyskim-soyuzom-i-rossiyskoy-federaciey-v-dvustoronnih-i-regionalnyh-programmah-ekonomicheskogo-razvitiya.html (30/03/2020).

thinking", a project called Varkaus Friendship House (later Finland's Friendship House) was discussed. The idea of a "House of Finland" has been repeatedly returned, but for financial reasons it has never been realized.

In 1987 and 1989 respectively, new sister-city relations were established with Duluth, USA and Tübingen, West Germany. It was very new experience for both sides and significant as both Duluth and Tübingen residents had been discussing and searching for a partner city in the Soviet Union for some years.

The case of Duluth's relationship with Petrozavodsk, opened a very interesting page in the history of both cities. Many American Finns moved to Soviet Karelia between the late 1920s and mid1930s and many of them were from Minnesota and neighboring Wisconsin. However, their presence was not widely publicized or known even within the USA. In Karelia, the topic of American Canadian Finns was closed for decades. When the first group of Dulutians arrived in 1986 to Petrozavodsk, they were surprised when one of the locals who met them at the station spoke beautiful American English. It was Mayme Sevander, dean of the Foreign languages department of the Karelian State Pedagogical Institute, who had been only a child when she came with her parents to the USSR. This meeting helped start an academic exchange program between higher educational institutions in Duluth and Petrozavodsk that continues today. Today Petrozavodsk University and the College of St. Scholastic in Duluth continue to host student language camps aimed at learning Russian and English languages and getting to know the culture and traditions of both countries.[17]

In the case of Tübingen, several important initiatives have created and sustained the close relations between Petrozavodsk and Tübingen since they first came into contact. Humanitarian help from Tübingen in the 1990s, joint cultural and informational "friendship ships" from the late 1990s until the mid-2000s, a unique case of cooperation between the Petrozavodsk Jewish community and Tübingen's Dietrich Bonhoeffer Evangelical community, and active cultural exchanges over the past 30 years all served to create a deep bond between the cities. Many joint activities and projects were developed and realized by the Tübingen "West-Ost" society and its leader Dr. Jorg Bohse. All of this has contributed to a particular understanding and the destruction of many stereotypes.[18]

After the collapse of the Soviet Union, the countries of Northern Europe and Russia revised their approaches to foreign policy. In 1992, an agreement was adopted to regulate cooperation of the Russian Federation with the neighboring territories of Finland (a new version of this agreement from 2012 is currently in force). For its time, the agreement was rather progressive and fixed the right of the regions to conduct foreign economic activity, which was later included in the Constitution of the Russian Federation and a number of other federal laws. According to Article 2, the main areas of cross-border cooperation were social, cultural, economic, environmental, and communication among others. In the same year, the Ministry of External Relations of the Republic of Karelia established (it closed in 2002) and a branch of the Consulate General of Finland in St. Petersburg was opened in Petrozavodsk. In 1992, a twinning agreement was signed between Petrozavodsk and Mo i Rana (Province of Norland), and in 1993 the Republic of Karelia and the provinces of Norland, Finnmark,

17 *Benson, J./Lavrushina, N./Meshko, V.* 2007: Duluth – Petrozavodsk. 20 Years as Sister Cities, Petrozavodsk, p. 57.
18 *Lavrushina, N. et al.* 2012: Tübingen – Petrosawodsk: Städtepartnerschaft, Petrozavodsk, p. 6.

and Troms (Norway) joined the Barents Regional Council. In 1994, a cooperation agreement was signed between the Republic of Karelia and Västerbotten Province with the aim of developing friendly and mutually beneficial relations between the two regions in all areas of common interest. With the assistance of Karelia, Västerbotten was later admitted to the Barents Regional Council, despite opposition from Norrbotten.

In 1994, Petrozavodsk signed a partner agreement with the city of Joensuu, which was the closest regional center on the Finnish side of Northern Karelia. This event was preceded by almost two decades of contact between regional universities and scientific institutions. The cooperation agreement with Joensuu was updated in 1998, 2002, 2007 and covered areas such as trade, tourism, education, healthcare, social protection of the population. A very successful instrument of cooperation between Joensuu, Finnish Northern Karelia, and Petrozavodsk since the mid-2000s has been the joint Karelia cross-border cooperation programs of the European Neighborhood Partnership Instrument (ENPI) and the European Neighborhood Instrument (ENI) financed by the EU, Finland and Russia.

The next round of sister-relations' initiatives took place in the 21st century[19]. Contact established in 2002 with Brest (Belarus) and Nikolayev (Ukraine, terminated at the initiative of the Ukrainian side in 2017), in 2003 – with Alytus in Lithuania and Echmiadzin in Armenia, and Narva in Estonia in 2005–2006. Some of these sister-agreements were signed the same year and some later – after "getting to know each other" and confirming already established relations. All the cities used to be part of the former Soviet Union which helped establish mutual understanding even if not all relationships became very active and diverse.

The cooperation of twin cities has created unique opportunities for a direct exchange of experience in areas such as urban economy, sustainable development, and the application of advanced management technologies. The development of diverse social contacts helps to familiarize the population of foreign countries with life in Russia and has a significant impact on the formation of a "positive attitude of the world community to the state's foreign and domestic policy"[20].

Interested regional parties involved into public diplomacy take part in the implementation of the agreements. Among them are local and regional institutions like schools, universities, cultural groups, industrial and municipal enterprises, and of course, NGOs. First and foremost, the friendship societies deserve consideration. Since the 1960s and 1970s, such associations, most commonly at that time branches of the all-Union organizations, were created in cities that demonstrated their interest in international contact and had established sister-relations with foreign cities. The common goals of friendship societies are promoting the development of trust and cooperation between residents of countries, regions, and cities, as well as familiarizing the population of another country with the history, culture, and way of life of peoples from the partner country such as, their language, crafts, and folklore.

Societies like the USSR – DDR, the USSR – Finland, the USSR – Sweden, Petrozavodsk's Friends of France had both individual and institutional members such as schools and enterprises and cooperated with similar partner institutions in their sister-cities. For example,

19 Also, at the turn of 1990–2000, contacts with Portomaggiore in Italy and Ohara in Japan developed for a short time.

20 *Gromov, B.V.* 2007: International movement of twin cities and people's diplomacy. In: Twin-cities, April, p. 5.

created in 1990s the Karelian "Friends of Norway" society has played an active role throughout the cooperation between Petrozavodsk and Mo i Rana. These associations used to organize national holidays of "their" countries, meet their partners. Their partner organizations like Suomi – Venäjä Seura in Finland with local branches in different municipalities and regions, "Druzhba" in La Rochelle, Tübingen's "West-Ost Society" united local citizens interested in cooperation with the Russian friends. The agreement on cooperation between the Norwegian Province of Troms and the Republic of Karelia (1996) was signed thanks to the establishment of contact with the town of Salangen (in Troms). In addition, for the first time in Norway, an organization of friendship with Russia was created – "Friends of Karelia", at the proposal of the former mayor of Salangen Haakon Bendiksten.

Another example of public diplomacy is the Swedish organization Foreningen Vänortsbarn (Children of the Twin City) which has provided assistance to the Ladvinsky orphanage and other social institutions in Petrozavodsk since the 1990s. The founder for this organization was Umeå resident Anna Christensen, who attracted attention of the Swedes to Russia's social problems via newspapers. The work of this NGO shows the potential benefits of extensive transnational networks achieved through urban diplomacy such as sister-city initiatives. These initiatives include fundraising for projects, facilitating the exchange of people and information, for instance, by means of organizing exhibitions and festivals.

In 2005, two important events aimed at developing cooperation between Russian and foreign NGOs, as well as developing forms of communication between authorities and civil society were held in Petrozavodsk and Kondopoga town. The first was a conference on the contribution of NGOs to the development of cross-border cooperation of northwestern Russia. The Russian Foreign Minister Sergey Lavrov took part and welcomed participants. It was the first conference of its kind in Russia.

The second was the international forum "NGOs co-operation Development in the European North: Current Situation and Perspectives." It was organized by the Council of NGOs under the Chairperson of the Legislative Assembly of the Republic of Karelia and the Council of NGOs under the Interparliamentary Group of the Russian Federation. The forum was supported by the Russian Foreign Ministry, the Russian Chamber of Commerce and Industry, the Head of the Republic of Karelia, and the Council of Europe. More than 400 representatives of both state authorities and NGOs from the Nordic and Baltic countries and Russia took part in the event. "The main objective of the Forum was to analyze the existing experience and search for new forms and models between Russian and Foreign NGOs the model of interaction between Russian and foreign NGOs in the development of international (cross-border) cooperation as the major component in strengthening the international relations according to the fundamental principles established by the UN and the Council of Europe".[21]

The forum focused on several topics and included a number of workshops: "Child's rights. Protection of Childhood", "Civil education", "Business and Civil Society", "Education and Science", "Ecology: Role of NGOs in Solving Water Quality Problems in the European

21 *International Forum* 2005: International Forum Materials "NGOs co-operation Development in the European North: Current Situation and Perspectives" (September 15–16, 2005), Petrozavodsk, p. 75.

North" and a round table "Discussion of proposals on amending the Russian federal law on cross-border cooperation"[22].

Both events boosted activities of the third sector and promoted the involvement of different non-governmental organizations in international cooperation.

Today in the Republic of Karelia, much attention is paid to the development of civil society institutions. There are 107 national public organizations, friendship societies, and branches of regional national public organizations in the 16 municipal districts and two urban districts of the republic. Eighty-three organizations (77.6 percent) have official registration with the Office of the Ministry of Justice of the Russian Federation for the Republic of Karelia, while eighteen organizations work without official registration. Six of these have suspended activities.[23] Sixty-two organizations (57.9 percent) carry out work at the republican level and the majority is located in Petrozavodsk.

Participants of civil diplomacy are not only NGOs, but also municipalities, social institutions, the business community, and the public at large. Twin-cities and cross-border cooperation provide maximum opportunities for potential civil diplomacy in the region and in localities. But today a lot of initiatives in the field of public diplomacy are realized by NGOs which get support of state organizations and regional authorities through different programs. The Ministries of Culture, Social Protection, Healthcare, National and Regional Policy of the Republic of Karelia, and Petrozavodsk city all allocate funds to support of socially oriented non-profit organizations[24] in the region and among them are working in the field of public diplomacy as well. In addition, NGOs attracted more than 85 million rubles within the presidential grants to the republic in 2018. Fifty-one Karelian NGOs received grants in 2018.[25] In 2019, 24 organizations received grants totaling 42 million rubles in the first round of the Presidential Grants Program for NGO.[26] And 30 projects more were approved in the second round 2019 for almost 41 million rubles.[27] Since 2018, a dimension for the development of civil diplomacy and the support of compatriots was added to the presidential grants priorities. As a result, many civil diplomacy groups have been able to expand their activities. For instance, the friendship society "Karelia – Finland" in 2018, with the support of the presidential grants program, held the "Solar Circle" International Puppet Theater Festival in Sortavala

22 Ibid., p. 58.

23 *The Republic of Karelia* 2018: Information on the results of monitoring of local authorities of municipalities and urban districts in the Republic of Karelia. http://nationalkom.karelia.ru/assets/Dokumenty/MonitoringOMSUpervyjkv.2018.pdf.

24 In accordance with article 2, paragraph 2.1, of Federal Law No. 7-FZ of 12 January 1996 on socially oriented non-commercial organizations are defined as non-commercial organizations established in the forms envisaged by this Federal Law (with the exception of State corporations, State companies, public associations that are political parties) and carrying out activities aimed at solving social problems and developing civil society in the Russian Federation. Types of activities of socially oriented NGOs are listed in the Law. https://minjust.ru/ru/node/286923 (30/03/2020).

25 *Republic of Karelia* 2019: 27 Karelian NGOs became winners of the second contest of Presidential Grants Program for NGOs. http://www.gov.karelia.ru/gov/News/2018/11/1101_18.html (30/03/2020).

26 24 projects from Karelia will receive presidential grants. http://rk.karelia.ru/social/24-proekta-iz-karelii-poluchat-prezidentskie-granty/ Respublika Karelia Online 01/06/2018. (30/03/2020).

27 *Government of the Republic of Karelia* 2019: 20 Karelian NGOs became winners of the Presidential Grants Fund competition. http://gov.karelia.ru/news/15-10-2019-20-karelskikh-nko-stali-pobeditelyami-konkursa-fonda-prezidentskikh-grantov/ (30/03/2020).

town in Karelia. The Petrozavodsk city public organization "Friends of France" realized the Russian-French youth exchange "Winter Camp of the Russian language" project. Another example is the project "The School Museum is a Meeting Place and a Platform for Twin-City Cooperation" implemented by the Karelian Resource center of NGOs in Petrozavodsk.

Conclusions

The conducted empirical study reveals three main phases in the development of Petrozavodsk sister-cities relations:

1) from mid-1960s to 1989 *ideological phase.* In the Soviet years the idea to establish twinning relations was initiated by the central authorities in order to strengthen contacts between the countries of the communist camp. Thus, the sister-city partnerships of the phase focused mainly on ideological goals, were organized top-down and controlled by representatives of the central government. In the 1970s, the "policy of openness" provided opportunities for limited networking with towns in the "capitalist" countries of Western Europe;
2) from 1989 to early 2000 *phase of expansion of participation and introduction of new areas of cooperation.* After the political transformations in 1989/1990 municipalities became self-determining legal units. From then, international contacts could have been developed freely in an official way with the active participation of citizens, and as a result the number of city-to-city agreements has grown. At these phase local authorities shared experience and innovation in the field of town and municipal management techniques and encouraged people to break down perceptual gaps. Additionally, they generated flows of goods and people as part of exchange programs initiated by local governments and organized with their assistance. Since this time civil society and NGOs had been more involved into development of sister-relations and international cooperation in general;
3) from early 2000 to the present-day *civil diplomacy phase.* The contemporary phase is characterized by voluntarily nature of the partnerships and strong local activism. Local institutions helping to maintain international contacts are schools, universities, non-governmental organizations like friendship societies, public institutions, culture centers and others. Taking into account the needs and preferences of local people, they successfully initiate projects and search financial resources using various fundraising tools: national governments, sub-regional international organizations or through cross-border programs.

The case of the city of Petrozavodsk suggests that grass roots participation in sister-cities relations has grown significantly in modern realities. The best and most likely platforms for local participation are cultural, social and recreational activities. Therefore, most of the projects are carried out in the fields of culture, social protection, ecology and education. The public participation in sister-cities relations has a positive effect on the development of good neighborly relations and stimulates local communities for solving common challenges. The NGOs very often are the initiators and the link between different stakeholders to address socially important issues. In this way, public participation contributes to the public welfare.

Sister-City Connections as a Tool for the Development of Social Creativity (on the Example of Petrozavodsk)

Ekaterina Shestakova

Abstract: This article focuses on the concept of creativity which can push a city to a qualitatively new level of development. In this article creative social space is defined as an urban environment (a combination of places and social interactions) favorable for the use of cultural resources and innovative approaches in order to create social innovations which are necessary for urban development. The aim of the research reported in the article is to determine the sister-city relations potential in the formation of Petrozavodsk's creative sociocultural environment and to demonstrate that sister-city cooperation can be an efficient instrument for fostering wellbeing. The phenomenon of sister-cities is analyzed though the example of international interaction between Petrozavodsk and its sister-cities from Northern Europe because of geographical proximity, similar climatic features, and similar challenges to urban development as well as a long history of cultural contacts. In order to achieve the aim, various forms of international communication at different stages are compared: the period of establishing friendly relations (1965–1991), the post-soviet period (1991–2013), and the present period of international collaboration (2014–2019). Based on the content analysis of joint project activities, interviews with local specialists responsible for cultural policy and international relations, and a resident questionnaire survey, it can be concluded that accumulated positive experience of international sociocultural partnership requires further intensification taking into account the specifics of civic activism in Petrozavodsk. Although the potential of sister-city connections aiding development is not fully utilized at this time, the untapped potential of such connections is widely discussed and the activity of the local community including NGOs confirms the existing understanding that combinations of cultural and scientific, as well as standard and non-standard approaches to urban problem solving can be a driving force for territorial development.

Keywords: sister-cities cooperation, urban development, creativity, wellbeing, creative social space, sociocultural resources, people's diplomacy

In the modern world states are no longer the only players in the international arena. In the 1950s G. Almond raised the issue of "actors pluralism".[1] Subsequently, these ideas were supported by neoliberals J. Rosenau and C. Deutsch, who stated that in each state there are certain groups capable of maintaining direct ties with similar groups in other countries without direct involvement of government structures.[2] In 1971 after the release of the book "Transnational Relations and World Politics" written by R. Keohane and J. Nye, the idea that universal, regional, specialized, intergovernmental and non-governmental organizations

1 *Almond, G.A.* 1960: The American People and Foreign Policy, Michigan.

2 *Rosenau, J.* 1984: Pre-Theory Revised: World Politics in an Era of Cascading Interdependence. In: International Studies Quarterly, 1, pp. 3–29.

as well as regions should be perceived as new actors in international relations was firmly established. Alongside these other players, cities too became active participants in international cooperation.

The growing activity of cities is largely explained by the lack of internal resources necessary for the development of their territories. Resources for self-development are often located in external environments which is why cities began to seek external partners. Although globalization increasingly puts cities in competition with one another for resources, greater interaction has also exposed opportunities for cooperation which can prove to be a catalyst for modernization. One consequence of this has been the establishment of sister-cities in border regions between countries in order to promote the exchange of experience.

Sister-cities are cities located in different states, which officially established friendly relations in order to strengthen mutual understanding between peoples and to develop comprehensive cooperation to solve similar urban problems.[3] From the theoretical point, cross-border cooperation is explained by *paradiplomacy* and *social constructivism*. Paradiplomacy defines the main forms of international interaction: internationalization, transnationalization, cross-border cooperation[4] while social constructivism indicates the main methods of forming actors and subagents of international relations: socialization, internalization, "cultural selection", "Foucault effect".[5] The potential positive influence of the external sociocultural environment often encourages cities to join international organizations such as the Association of European Border Regions (AEBR), World Federation of Twin Cities (WFTC), International Association of Related Cities or to unite in regional groups such as the Euroregions Karelia, Baltic, or Neman in order to more successfully promote shared municipal interests.

In Russia international cooperation of regions and cities is controlled by the Ministry of Foreign Affairs of the Russian Federation and is regulated by international laws, the Constitution of the Russian Federation, federal law, decrees of the President, legal acts of the Government, constituent entities, and municipalities. According to Federal Law No.179-FL "On the Basics of Cross-Border Cooperation", the key objectives of cross-border collaboration are: "improving the quality of life in border areas, providing assistance for social and economic development of cross-border territories, and developing and strengthening mutually beneficial and friendly ties in order to create an atmosphere of trust, mutual understanding, and good neighborliness"[6]. The history of establishing twinning relations between Petrozavodsk and its sister-cities from Northern Europe (Varkaus, Joensuu from Finland, Umeå from Sweden, and Mo i Rana from Norway) goes back to the soviet period and since then these contacts have become an effective tool for fostering wellbeing and prosperity. Coop-

3 *International Association "Twin Cities"* 2015: Twin Cities. http://goroda-pobratimy.ru/porodnennye-goroda (02/04/2020).

4 *Yarovoy, G.O.* 2013: Paradiplomatic activity as an instrument of regional development: to the formulation of the question. In: Studia Humanitatis Borealis, 1, pp. 28–41 (32).

5 *Makarychev, A.S.* 2010: Regionalism through the eyes of constructivism: agents, structures, identities. In: Neprikosnovennyj zapas: a debate about politics and culture, 3, pp. 137–150 (149); *Wendt, A.* 1999: Social theory of international politics, Cambridge; *Onuf, N.* 1998: International Relations in a Constructed World, New York, pp. 58–78.

6 Federal Law No. 179 "On the basics of cross-border cooperation", approved by The Council of the Federation on July 19, 2017. http://pravo.gov.ru/proxy/ips/?docbody=&nd=102439324&intelsearch=%EE%F2+26+%E8%FE%EB%FF+2017+%E3. (09/08/2019).

eration occurs in cultural, economic, environmental, and social spheres through regularly held conferences, seminars, and exchange programs.

In the scientific literature, the phenomenon of twinning is largely analyzed as an economic activity or as a dialogue between municipal authorities. However, few authors pay attention to the influence of external factors on the sociocultural development of a city or the influence that sister-city institutions have on the formation of creative urban environments.

In the era of globalization, the formation of creative environments is more important than ever in successful urban policy. As the concept of city becomes more and more complex, it is necessary to use unconventional and creative approaches to regulate and create sociocultural spaces of interaction for citizens. That is why the problem of insufficient innovative activity is becoming more and more important issue for cities both large and small. Many cities around the world have already begun to develop fundamentally new strategies of urban planning. These strategies adopt provisions of the creative city concept since creative solutions enable the city to improve its image, increase tourism and investment attractiveness, strengthen competitiveness, actualize historical and cultural heritage, raise standards of living, and retain young people among many other benefits. In addition, development of sociocultural space in the cities can positively affect the standards of living of the entire region.

In the 1970s, the British urban planner Charles Landry developed the concept of a creative city, which combined concepts of socio-economic geography, sociology, and economics. Since then, the theory's popularity has increased with its successful application. According to Landry, modern cities face an urban crisis as they make transition from an industrial economy to an innovative one, which has largely abandoned material values. In such circumstances, creativity can help the towns and cities to overcome negative consequences of plants and factories closing.

In his books "The Creative City"[7], and "The Art of Regeneration: Urban Renewal Through Cultural Activity"[8], Charles Landry argues that today it is necessary to perceive culture as an efficient resource for fostering wellbeing. Creativity is the process of identifying the hidden possibilities of a city; it is a method of exploiting cultural resources – skills and abilities of people who form a creative class[9]. In other words, its implementation is the practice of a new idea, which is obtained through the creative thinking of a creative class. So, creativity is not just about generating ideas, it includes various stages such as finding resources for implementation, introducing indicators to evaluate the results, disseminating the final product, working with mass media and post-project monitoring.[10] It is important to keep in mind that the entirety of the process is important to achieve success. Creative ideas by themselves are not enough and failure to use all aspects of the process can lead to failure of even the most promising projects. For instance, a grandiose modernization plan for Petrozavodsk's embankment designed in 2013 during a joint international project was not

7 *Landry, C.* 2011: Creative City, Moscow.

8 *Landry, C. et al.* 1996: The Art of regeneration. Urban renewal through cultural activity, Stroud.

9 *Landry* 2011 (fn. 7).

10 *Davidenko, L./Butenko, L.* 2016: Cognitivist concepts as basis of proficiency on the highroad to success and professional creativity. In: International Journal of Applied and Fundamental Research 2, p. 52. http://www.science-sd.com/pdf/2016/2/25093.pdf (02/04/2020).

implemented because it remained in the development stage of generating ideas. It was too ambitious and didn't take into account financial opportunities.

In addition to the points above, it should be emphasized that creativity is not limited solely to the activity of artists or scientific or technological innovations. In this context, "innovation" should be considered a holistic process covering different areas – politics, culture, ecology, social sphere, etc. Based on these criteria, there are but a few cities that can be called creative. Among these are New York, Vienna, Paris, Amsterdam, London and Moscow.[11] However, what is important is that any settlement has an opportunity to become more creative than it is at the present stage. Any city can start to solve its problems with greater innovation and turn its weaknesses into strengths.

A creative city is a complex, constantly changing living organism, the fundamental characteristics of which are: adaptability, flexibility, reflexivity, ability to find innovative solutions. One of the elements of a creative city is perception of the "world around us as a resource, containing hidden opportunities"[12] as well as careful attitude to existing traditions. The obvious competitive advantage of Petrozavodsk is a long tradition of cooperation with its sister-cities. A creative city is a city, which develops due to the continuous exchange of ideas between of all kinds of actors. Indeed, modern cities are able to solve urban development problems by building dialogues within urban communities. As a result, innovations arising from the accumulation of creative efforts of different populations within a given city begin to shape their environments. The main principles of a creative city are: the formation of a cooperation network – citizens, businesses, NGOs, local authorities, etc. – for solving urban planning problems, an integrated approach to urban development issues, the use of cultural resources to create innovations, the use of the cultural heritages' potential or non-standard application of yesterday's innovations, the formation of a clear identity of a city, a sufficient number and variety of urban organizations and platforms for interaction, and the application of non-standard approaches to solve urban problems.

On July 18, 2018 during the International Urban Forum held in Moscow the Russian President Vladimir Putin emphasized that renovations were the key factor for the development of modern cities. For Putin renovations entailed a combination of measures aimed at preserving originality of settlements through the use of advanced technologies, new innovative management decisions, innovations in environmental protection, attracting youth as well as specialists in the field of urban studies, and using IT-technologies to improve urban planning. According to Putin, a modern city is a city of opportunities for all categories of citizens; it is a comfortable social space for "uniting and implementing creative cultural, scientific, and social projects"[13]. There are many examples of organizations and projects which promote the exchange of creative development experiences. For example, the European Commission Scientific Center conducts an annual study of creative cities; while NGOs such as Creative Practices in Russia provide assistance to cities trying to form creative spaces.

11 *Landry* 2011 (fn. 7).

12 *Saponov, D.I.* 2012: Creative action in a creative city. In: Sociologicheskoe obozrenie, No. 3, pp. 169–177 (172).

13 *Melnikov, V.* 2018: Putin announced a large-scale program to transform Russian cities, July 18, 2018. https://ria.ru/20180718/1524853764.html (02/0472020).

Turning to the sociocultural development of cities involved in cross-border cooperation, special attention should be paid to the role of people's diplomacy. This term was introduced by E. Gullion in is defined as a method of disseminating a country's values to the international community through participation in various public associations, foundations, NGOs, and interactions between individuals. This kind of diplomacy is aimed at increasing international understanding, getting rid of existing stereotypes, easing distrust and tensions between countries, creating a positive image of a city or a region and establishing long-term neighborly contact at the municipal level. People's diplomacy is especially typical for border areas where international contact is common, and people have an opportunity to visit each other and to initiate joint projects. In the Foreign Policy Concept 2008 it was mentioned that one of the tasks of Russia was to "develop international cultural cooperation to ensure mutual understanding between peoples, using the resources of civil society in the field of peoples' diplomacy"[14]. The main forms of people's diplomacy are tourism, activities of Friendship Societies, exchange programs, and the implementation of projects in fields such as culture, ecology, education, healthcare, etc.[15] For example, in 1965 representatives of the Friendship's Society Finland-Soviet Union Department in Varkaus established sister-city relations between Petrozavodsk and Varkaus.[16]

Many NGOs in the north-west Russian territories have already had positive project experiences with partners internationally, which is why "foreign partners are not afraid to continue cooperation with Russian organizations"[17]. Projects in the north-western Russian territory of Karelia provide a prime example of international cooperation and partnership in development. Karelian NGOs sociocultural projects are most often implemented within EU cross-border cooperation programs such as "Southeast Finland – Russia", "Kolarctic", "Karelia". As a result of the high concentration of international projects, local communities consolidate efforts to solve national and transnational territorial problems and managerial change is encouraged.[18]

International cooperation is not just limited to cooperation between local authorities. NGOs also play an important role in this field. The activities of NGOs reflect the interests of civil society and are a powerful resource for effective regional development. NGOs projects unite representatives of different professions, which helps create a strong link between formal and informal institutions. Such projects deal with issues affecting almost every social category of citizens imaginable, including the most vulnerable ones. As a result of NGO

14 The Foreign Policy Concept of the Russian Federation, approved by the President of the Russian Federation on November 30, 2016. http://www.mid.ru/foreign_policy/news//asset_publisher/cKNonkJE02Bw/content/id/2542248 (09/08/2019).

15 *Medvedeva, T.I.* 2007: The main methods and forms of people's diplomacy in the modern political process. Vlast, 4, pp. 71–74 (72).

16 *Vavulinskaya, L.I.* 2008: Sister-city relations of the USSR and Finland in 1960–1980s. as an example of the formation of new forms of cooperation at the regional level on the example of Petrozavodsk and Varkaus. In: Humanitarian research, 1, pp. 65–76 (67).

17 *Shlapeko, E.A.* 2017: Institute of Public Diplomacy and its Place in Cross-Border Social and Cultural Space. Oikumena. In: Regional Studies, 1 (40), pp. 152–162 (157).

18 *Shlapeko, E.A.* 2013: International project activities of the Republic of Karelia as a resource for regional development. In: Scientific notes of Petrozavodsk State University. Series "Social and Human Sciences", 3(132), pp. 42–45 (44).

projects, for example, “NGOs for better life of aged people in Baltic Sea region” launched in 2017 disabled and elderly people from the Republic of Karelia (Russia), the North Karelia (Finland), the Latgale region (Latvia), the Glubokoye district (Belarus), the Pomeranian voivodeship and the city of Gdansk (Poland) now have equal access to education, the labor market, and the cultural sector. For example, in 2017 the Norwegian public organization “Friends of Karelia” partnered with the German community of St. Martin’s church to build a playground for wheelchair users in one of the centers for disabled children in Petrozavodsk.

Such cases show that substantive changes which can be brought about through peoples’ diplomacy. Peoples’ diplomacy leads to the consolidation of different communities (horizontal network of cooperation or multi-channel participation) around the city’s problems, and contributes not only to the exchange of experience, but also to the development of fundamentally new and mutually beneficial approaches to problem solving. It acts as a platform for creative interaction and for finding new inventive solutions.

In order to evaluate the influence of twinning on the development of Petrozavodsk’s creative social space, information about international sociocultural events and projects, which are prerequisites for the formation of creative environment, was collected. Based on the analysis of cooperation during the soviet period (1965–1991), it can be stated that from the beginning cooperation was not limited to the provision of humanitarian assistance, as it was in many other cities, but multidimensional and encompassing of the social sphere as well as the fields of culture, science, education, and sport. For example, in 1978 Petrozavodsk accepted the offer to join the Blue Road International Association and as a result, it became the final destination of an international tourist route travelling through Norway, Sweden, Finland and terminating in Russia.

The post-soviet period (1991–2013) saw the expansion of cooperation in the fields of ecology, information technology, investment, municipal governing, development of democracy and human rights. The most visible result of the cooperation between sister-cities is the embankment of Petrozavodsk. The sculpture “Tree of Wishes” (a gift from Umeå) was installed in 1996 and in 1997 the “Wave of Friendship” appeared on the city's embankment, symbolizing friendly relations with Varkaus. In 2001 Norwegian sculptors from Mo i Rana presented Petrozavodsk with the art-object “Meeting Place”, and in 2003 the Finnish city of Joensuu presented the sculpture “Unity (Spark of Friendship)”. In addition, during this period the first attempts to implement large-scale projects were made. They were characterized by complex approaches to solving urban problems. Some of the successful programs of that time included “W.A.S.T.E.”, “Restoration of transboundary salmon rivers”, and “Contemporary Old City: Enhancing Cultural Tourism Across the Border”. The international conference “Cities by the Water: New Appearance and New Opportunities” held in February 14–15, 2013 deserves special attention. The conference stands out because not only were local stakeholders invited, but participants from sister-cities were also included and explicitly asked for input on development strategies and planning. During the conference, proposals were made which included calls for increased exchange among international partners on the topic of territorial planning.[19] The results of this cooperation were seen in Petrozavodsk's social and economic development strategy.

This trend of increasing cooperation has continued into the current period as well. Based on recent interactions, we can hypothesize that comparing to the previous periods the process of constructing a creative environment at the present is achieved through more active participation of NGOs in the city's life. Earlier the main participants of international cooperation were local authorities, but now NGOs have become one of the leading actors. At the present stage, it is exactly NGOs who initiate most international projects. NGOs, in its turn, attract many other groups of population to cooperation: the expert community, business, etc. As a result, an extensive network of participants is formed. According to Landry, it is this type of horizontal network which is effective and can contribute to the sociocultural development of the city. Additionally, comparing to the previous periods, a gradual increase in joint projects between Petrozavodsk and its sister-cities from Northern Europe seeking new innovative approaches to urban development can be stated. Now the goal of formation of a creative environment has become a priority. It is prescribed in projects descriptions that creative development is their goal. It is important, because previously there was absolutely no emphasis on this. Among the events which contributed to formation of a creative environment of Petrozavodsk one can name projects on sustainable water management education, on new sustainable inclusive cultural services for disabled people, on baby-theater, eco-festivals, conferences on sustainable urban development and wooden architecture, on the development of creative industries and green economy. All these projects raised topics that were not previously discussed and proposed innovative approaches to existing problems. Moreover, nowadays a much more diverse set of international initiatives than it was before can be emphasized. It also affects positively the formation of creative environment since different event formats are suitable for different problem-solving tasks. Between 2014 and 2019, 70 international events were held in Petrozavodsk. During this period at least 14 international projects, nine working meetings, six roundtables, nine cultural celebrations, nine festivals, six concerts, five seminars, three international conferences, three forums, three study-tours, three international youth camps, and three exhibitions were organized. Despite a brief decline in international activity during 2015 (2014 –13 events per year; 2015 – 7 events; 2016 – 12 events: 2017 – 13 events; 2018 – 17 events), the overall trend for international cooperation measured by the number of events is positive in the region.

During this period, the majority of events (46) could be described as focused on cultural contact and exchange. Events focused on cultural contact accounted for 65.71 percent of all international events during this period. In addition to cultural exchange, events focused on encouraging young people to participate in international cooperation and strengthening their civic engagement (13) were also common. For instance, in 2017–2018 with the financial support of the Nordic Council of Ministers, the Karelian resource Centre of non-governmental organizations realized a projected called "Youth Trio – Socialization, Culture, Creativity". The main purpose was to establish cooperation between the countries of Northern Europe to develop programs aimed at socializing young people to participate in art projects and

19 *Conference "Cities by the Water* 2013: New Appearance and New Opportunities" 2013. http://www.petrozavodsk-mo.ru/petrozavodsk_new/city/relations/info.htm?id=10523991@cmsArticle (02/04/2020).

cultural festivals. The prominence of these two types of events may be explained by growing understanding of the importance of socio-cultural exchange and attempt to encourage the most active and initiative groups of population to take part in international cooperation which can positively affect the development of the city. Other events were aimed at: modernization in the social sphere (9), tourism (5), marketing and business (4) and ecology (4).

Necessity to support sociocultural initiatives is enshrined in the Social and Economic Development Strategy of Petrozavodsk. It is noted that "formation of the most important strategic direction of the city's development will be based on cultural potential"[20]. Potential for sociocultural exchange with sister-cities from Northern Europe is mentioned in the section "Competitive Advantages of the City" (sister-cities from other countries are not mentioned in the Strategy for some reason which emphasizes the prospect of developing cooperation in this direction). It is emphasized that it is necessary to cooperate with sister-cities for "enriching urban cultural practices, creative exchanges".

In order to find out if the influence of sister-city relations on urban development is noticeable for Petrozavodsk citizens, exploratory research was conducted in the form of a public opinion poll. The poll was conducted orally standing downtown. Using spontaneous sampling, 200 people answered the questionnaire. The questionnaire included nine questions: Have you ever heard expression "creative city"? (agree or disagree). Can you say that Petrozavodsk is a creative, innovative city? (agree or disagree). What can contribute to the successful development of the city? Choose no more than 3 variants (multiple choice). Do you know that Petrozavodsk has sister-cities in Finland, Sweden, Norway? (agree or disagree). Does this international cooperation influence the development of Petrozavodsk? (agree or disagree). Which areas of urban life has international cooperation the greatest influence on? Choose no more than 3 variants (multiple choice). What international events within the framework of sister-city relations have you heard about or participated in? (open response). What spheres of the city life do you consider prior for the development of Petrozavodsk? Choose no more than 3 variants (multiple choice). Is it necessary to attract sister-cities representatives to elaboration of Petrozavodsk's spatial development strategy? (agree or disagree). Explain why? (open response).

The results showed that 78 respondents (39 percent) heard the expression creative social space and creative city for the first time, but for 61 percent it was familiar. Only three respondents consider Petrozavodsk a creative and innovative city; 71 chose a less definite positive answer ("More likely yes"); 22 residents were sure that "it is not creative" and the majority of respondents 52 percent (104 people) believe that Petrozavodsk "probably does not match this description". According to the same poll, the main factors respondents believed could contribute to successful development of the city were: inclusion of citizens in the design and implementation of city development solutions (91 percent), openness of local authorities to suggestions from the local community (81.5 percent), formation of a network of cooperation (including businessmen, experts, NGOs, etc.) for solving urban planning problems (49.5 percent), and an integrated approach to the problems of urban modernization (47.5 percent).

20 The Social and Economic Development Strategy of Petrozavodsk for the period up to 2025, approved by Petrozavodsk City Council on February 18, 2015. http://www.petrozavodskmo.ru/petrozavodsk_new/activity/economyka/strategy/info.htm?id=10546027@cmsArticle. (09/08/2019).

On the topic of sister-cities, the majority of respondents knew that Petrozavodsk has sister-cities in Northern Europe (73 percent) while the remaining respondents (27 percent) answered that they "know, but not about all of them". The majority of the respondents (57 percent) are sure that cooperation with these cities has an impact on the development of Petrozavodsk. Of those who believed that sister-cities have an impact on development in Petrozavodsk, (75 percent out of the total number of respondents) felt there was an impact in the cultural sphere, (60 percent) felt there was an impact on tourism, and (40 percent) felt there was an impact on youth socialization. It should be stressed that respondents could choose up to three variants from the list (economy, social sphere, culture, ecology, tourism, science and education, infrastructure and other) at the same time.

At the same time, the results of the survey revealed the prevalence of "industrial thinking" because of historical industrial memory (respondents answered that "it is necessary to reopen plants, to start production", concentrating on the experience of the past) and a weak perception of the city's development prospects through the prism of culture. The priority areas for urban development according to respondents were: the economy (63 percent out of the total number of respondents), the social sphere (56 percent out of 200 respondents), and infrastructure (45 percent out of 200 respondents). Answering this question, the respondents had a multiple choice (economy, social sphere, culture, ecology, tourism, science and education, infrastructure and other) and could choose three variants at the same time. This indicates a gap of understanding between the public and creative city proponents on the potential benefits of adopting creative city solutions. Additionally, it was difficult for respondents to name events conducted in cooperation with sister-cities in which they took part or heard about. Only 40 respondents gave an answer to this question. They named general examples (Days of Umeå, Varkaus, etc., school exchanges, photo exhibitions) instead of concrete ones. No large-scale international projects were named. It implies that there may be problems with project information support and the promotion of projects' final results among the general public. Nevertheless, 46 percent of the respondents agreed with the statement that sister-cities' specialists should be involved in the composing of spatial development strategies of Petrozavodsk. The respondents noted that "brainstorming is always helpful" and "outside perspective can be useful". However, 33 percent replied that while cooperation could be done, it was not necessary, and 22 percent rejected any cooperation. They justified their answer by saying that "cities themselves and their levels of development are different" and "it should not be done because of security concerns."

In general, it can be stated that Petrozavodsk residents recognize the influence of international sister-city connections on urban development, but they are poorly aware of new non-standard approaches to spatial development based on cultural resources.

On the basis of the interviews conducted with specialists responsible for the cultural policy and international relations of Petrozavodsk, factors that hinder effective development of international creative practices include: international tensions at the federal level, differences in countries' legislation (different degrees of authority of countries' regions), a lack of flexibility at border crossings, the absence of concrete tools necessary for implementation of international projects under the law, a lack of strategic planning for international cooperation on the municipal level, the abolition of the department responsible for international cooperation, financing problems, the problem of not systematic character of international projects, the lack of a post-project monitoring phase, insufficient diversity of project participants, poor promotion of events to the public.

However, all the experts interviewed agreed that it was necessary to move in the direction of creative development and certain steps are already being taken. For instance, a non-governmental art-venue Art Residence (AiR Karelia) is functioning in Petrozavodsk which aims to showcase the creative potential of different cultures. During the period 2015–2018 approximately 50 domestic and foreign artists including specialists from Finland, Sweden and Norway took part in the work of the Residence. Or, for example, in April 2019 Petrozavodsk became a member of the smart-city urbanization digitalization project.

The specialists stress that interactions with sister-cities from Northern Europe are a significant asset for the city's development, especially in such areas as ecology, infrastructure and urban upgrading in which foreign partners are more competent. In addition, international cooperation contributes to the formation of Petrozavodsk's image as a city being open for constructive communication and receptive to new trends.

In conclusion, "a city" should be considered not only as a territorial-administrative unit, but also as a socially constructed space that is in constant development and as a knot of sociocultural interaction between actors of different levels. All cities (including settlements which do not have material resources for their development) are unique in their nature and, therefore, are able to become more creative. Creativity should be considered an opportunity and a goal for cities' strategic development. It is a process of identifying and applying hidden resources and skills of the creative class in order to move to a higher stage of development. In accordance with the theory, cities' most important socio-economic problems can be solved with cultural strategies. Since creativity is a key to the long-term spatial development of cities, reassessment of urban planning strategies using the principles of a creative city has substantial potential for application in domestic urban spaces. Meanwhile, international cooperation in the framework of twinning (exchange of experience) can bring significantly closer "to become more creative". International events organized together with sister-cities from Northern Europe undoubtedly affect the sociocultural life of the city. Although, cooperation in the field of innovative development is relatively new, local communities like Petrozavodsk have expressed a readiness and willingness to explore new kinds of interactions and the preliminary results indicate that creative solutions such as twinning are worth continued study.

Authors

Dr. Daniel Buhr is Adjunct Professor for Political Science at the Institute of Political Science, Eberhard Karls University Tübingen and Head of the Steinbeis Transfer Center Social and Technological Innovation.

Elena Chernenkova, PhD is Associate Professor at the Department of World History, Political Science and International Relations, Institute of History, Political and Social Sciences, Petrozavodsk State University.

Ksenia Chumak is Deputy Director General of the Karelian Resource Center of NGOs, Petrozavodsk.

Dr. Rolf Frankenberger is senior lecturer and researcher at the Institute of Political Science, Eberhard Karls University Tübingen.

Kirill Fitisov is a student at the Department of Sociology and Social Work Institute of History, Political and Social Sciences, Petrozavodsk State University.

Dr. Christopher Gohl is a researcher and teacher at the Weltethos Institute at the University of Tübingen.

Stewart Gold, M.A. is a research officer at the Institute of Political Science, Eberhard Karls University Tübingen.

Polina Kopteva is a student at the Department of Social Science and Social Work, Institute of History, Political and Social Sciences, Petrozavodsk State University.

Alisa Kruglova is a student of Political Science at the Department of World History, Political Science and International Relations, Institute of History, Political and Social Sciences, Petrozavodsk State University.

Natalya Lavrushina is Development manager at the Karelian Resource Center of NGOs, Petrozavodsk.

Irina Miljukova, PhD, is Associate Professor at the Department of Social Science and Social Work, Institute of History, Political and Social Sciences, Petrozavodsk State University.

Yuliya A. Petrovskaya, PhD, is Associate Professor at the Department of Sociology and Social work Petrozavodsk State University.

Dr. Maria Pitukhina is a senior researcher at the Karelian Research Center of the Russian Academy of Sciences, Petrozavodsk.

Denis I. Sachuk is senior lecturer at the Department of Social Science and Social Work, Institute of History, Political and Social Sciences, Petrozavodsk State University.

Anni Schlumberger, M.A. is Director of the Human IT Service GmbH, Tübingen and Counsellor at the Integrata Foundation for Humanistic use of Information Technology.

Dr. Martin Seeleib-Kaiser is Professor for Comparative Public Policy at the Institute of Political Science, Eberhard Karls University Tübingen.

Ekaterina Shestakova is a student of International Relations at the Department of World History, Political Science and International Relations, Institute of History, Political and Social Sciences, Petrozavodsk State University.

Ekaterina Shlapeko, PhD is a researcher at the Institute of Economics, Karelian Research Center of the Russian Academy of Sciences.

Anna Simakova is a research officer at the Budget Monitoring Center, Petrozavodsk State University.

Isabel Sinner holds a B.A. in Political Science from the University of Tübingen and currently is enrolled in the M.A. Democracy and Governance in Europe at Eberhard Karls University Tübingen.

Elisa Söll holds a B.A. in Political Science and Middle East Studies from Eberhard Karls University Tübingen and works at the Human IT Service GmbH, Tübingen.

Irina Stepus is a researcher and Head of Department at the Budget Monitoring Center, Petrozavodsk State University.

Dr. Carmen Thamm is a research officer and managing staff at the European Center for Research on Federalism at Eberhard Karls University Tübingen.

Anatoly Tsygankov is Head of the Karelian regional public office "Center Of Political And Social Researches Of The Republic Of Karelia 'Civil Society'".